Export Handbook

SUBSCRIPTION NOTICE

This Wiley product is updated on a periodic basis with supplements to reflect important changes in the subject matter. If you purchased this product directly from John Wiley & Sons, Inc., we have already recorded your subscription for this update service.

If, however, you purchased this product from a bookstore and wish to receive (1) the current update at no additional charge, and (2) future updates and revised or related volumes billed separately with a 30-day examination review, please send your name, company name (if applicable), address, and the title of the product to:

> Supplement Department
> John Wiley & Sons, Inc.
> One Wiley Drive
> Somerset, NJ 08875
> 1-800-225-5945

For customers outside the United States, please contact the Wiley office nearest you:

Professional & Reference Division
John Wiley & Sons Canada, Ltd.
22 Worcester Road
Rexdale, Ontario M9W 1L1
CANADA
(416) 675-3580
1-800-567-4797
FAX (416) 675-6599

John Wiley & Sons, Ltd.
Baffins Lane
Chichester
West Sussex, PO19 1UD
UNITED KINGDOM
(44) (243) 779777

Jacaranda Wiley Ltd.
PRT Division
P.O. Box 174
North Ryde, NSW 2113
AUSTRALIA
(02) 805-1100
FAX (02) 805-1597

John Wiley & Sons (SEA) Pte. Ltd.
37 Jalan Pemimpin
Block B # 05-04
Union Industrial Building
SINGAPORE 2057
(65) 258-1157

Export Handbook
Accounting, Finance, and Tax Guide

Edited by

Robert Feinschreiber

JOHN WILEY & SONS, INC.

New York • Chichester • Brisbane • Toronto • Singapore • Weinheim

This text is printed on acid-free paper.

Robert Feinschreiber
Export Handbook: Accounting, Finance, and Tax Guide
ISBN 0471-13323-X

Printed in the United States of America

10 9 8 7 6 5 4 3 2 1

About the Editor

Robert Feinschreiber is a partner at Feinschreiber and Associates. His clients include exporters, foreign-owned U.S. businesses, and companies facing transfer pricing issues. He received a BA from Trinity College in Connecticut, an LLB from Yale, an MBA from Columbia Graduate School of Business, and an LLM in Taxation from New York University. Mr. Feinschreiber was a CPA in Florida.

He has written and edited many books on taxation, including *Foreign Sales Corporations, Fundamentals of International Taxation, Domestic International Sales Corporations, Tax Incentives for U.S. Exports, Tax Depreciation Under the Class Life ADR System, International Tax Planning Today, Subpart F, Earnings & Profits, Allocation and Apportionment of Deductions,* and *International Reorganizations.* Mr. Feinschreiber is also the author of *Tax Reporting for Foreign-Owned U.S. Corporations* and *Transfer Pricing Handbook* published by John Wiley & Sons. Mr. Feinschreiber has written many articles on tax and tax-related subjects, including international taxation. He has been quoted as an authority by the *Tax Court, Business Week,* and *Forbes.* He has also been a consultant to several foreign governments.

Mr. Feinschreiber is the editor of the *Interstate Tax Report.* He was the founding editor of the *International Tax Journal* and has been the editor of *Export Tax Report* and U.S. editor of *Tax Haven and Shelter Report.* He has been the U.S. correspondent for the *Tax News Service,* which is published by the International Bureau of Fiscal Documentation.

He has taught accounting at Yale and law at Wayne State University Law School. He was a director of the International Tax Institute. Mr. Feinschreiber has lectured at various tax conferences on such topics as foreign sales corporations, domestic international sales corporations, intercompany pricing, Subpart F, the foreign tax credit, research credit, and depreciation. He has lectured for the World Trade Institute, the American Management Association, International Business Seminars, the International Tax Institute, and other organizations.

About the Contributors

Richard D. Boltuck is a senior economist at Trade Resources Company, a former policy analyst at the Office of Management and Budget (OMB), and a former international economist at the U.S. International Trade Commission.

Kenneth C. Boyle, CPA, is a tax manager of Engelhard Corporation with more than 10 years of corporate tax experience. He is a member of the American Institute of Certified Public Accountants and the New Jersey Society of Certified Public Accountants.

Rafeal E. Brown, CPA, Macc, is an international tax manager for Arthur Anderson LLP in its San Francisco Office.

Charles L. Crowley is the Director of the Deloitte and Touche Global Customs and International Trade Practice. He is the former president of the Customs Lawyers Association and was formerly an attorney with the Office of Regulations and Rulings with U.S. Customs in Washington, D.C. He is a member of the Court of International Trade, U.S. Tax Court, the Court of Appeals for the Federal Circuit and the bars of New York, Massachusetts and Washington, D.C.

Robert J. Cunningham, JD, LLM (Taxation), is a tax partner in the Chicago office of Baker & McKenzie.

Roland Ryan Davis, JD, is an international tax manager in KPMG's Metro-New York office.

Robert C. DeGaudenzi, JD, CPA, is an international tax manager in the New York office of Coopers & Lybrand LLP, specializing in international taxation. He is also a member of the firm's FSC Team, a national discussion group focusing on new developments and planning strategies relating to FSCs.

Lisa T. Fair, CPA, is an international tax manager in the Atlanta office of Arthur Andersen LLP. She is the international training coordinator for AA's Southeast Region.

James A. Geraghty is a member of the Customs and International Trade Practice Group at Deloitte and Touche. Previously, he engaged in the private practice of law, specializing in Customs. He is a former member of the Board of Directors of the Customs and International Trade Bar Association, a lecturer on import documentation for the American Management Association and a past president of the World Trade Association of New Jersey.

Seth T. Kaplan, Ph.D., is Director of Economic Research at Trade Resources Company, Professorial Lecturer in Economics at George Washington University, and a former international economist at the U.S. International Trade Commission.

Jeffrey A. Levenstam, CPA, is the Director of International Tax Competence for the Northern California and Salt Lake City offices of Arthur Andersen LLP. He is also a member of the FSC Specialist Group.

Glenn S. Miller is an associate with the Washington, D.C. law firm of Swindler & Berlin, Chartered. He graduated summa cum laude from Louisiana State with a B.S. in economics, and received his J.D., cum laude, from Harvard Law School. Mr. Miller specializes in the income taxation of U.S. persons investigating and operating abroad and of foreign persons investigating and operating in the United States.

Robert G. Rinninsland, JD, is Director of Taxes for Engelhard Corporation, a $2.5 billion chemical and catalyst company. He has worked in the corporate tax area for more than 17 years. He is on the Board of Directors of the International Tax Institute and on the faculty of the World Trade Institute and is a member of the Manufacturer's Alliance Tax Council II.

Michael N. Schwartz, CPA, is the partner in charge of KPMG's Metro-New York International Tax Practice.

Stanley G. Sherwood, CPA, is an international tax partner at Coopers & Lybrand in New York. He is responsible for providing international tax and business accounting services to multinational companies (outbound and inbound) on cross-border transactions. He is the author of numerous articles and chapters on a variety of international tax topics and a frequent speaker in the area.

Edward Tanenbaum, JD, LLM, is an international tax partner at Walter, Conston, Alexander & Green. He is a frequent lecturer at the World Trade Institute, American Tax Institute in Europe, and Executive Enterprises Ltd. He is president of the International Tax Institute and the NYU Tax Society.

Mark C. Thompson, CPA, is a tax principal in the Minneapolis office of Arthur Andersen, LLP. He is head of AA's Foreign Sales Corporation specialty team and a member of the Advisory Board of Directors for the FSC/DISC Association.

Stephanie M. Wilshusen, is a junior economist at Trade Resources Company.

Preface

Tax incentives for U.S. Exports have had a checkered history. In earliest times, there were no tax incentives for exports per se. Instead, tax-favored international programs could be used by exporters and others, but exporting itself was not a prerequisite for obtaining these benefits. Most important of these programs was the Western Hemisphere Trading Corporation, or WHTC, which reduced the tax rate for eligible activities in Central and South America.

The first tax-specific export program was Subpart G, enacted in 1962. This provision was a rudimentary attempt to encourage exports, and was supposed to serve as a counterpart to Subpart F. Almost all companies declined to participate in Subpart G as the benefits were small and the rules were exceedingly complex.

The Domestic International Sales Corporations (DISC) provide a tax deferral to companies that set up a specific entity for that purpose. These provisions were first suggested late in 1969, too late to be included in the Tax Reform Act of 1969. The DISC provisions were included in the 1970 Trade Act, but these provisions were not enacted at that time. However, DISC was enacted in 1971.

During the early 1970s, taxpayers could choose between a DISC or a WHTC. Oceana Publishers asked me to prepare an analysis that compared the two incentives. As a result, the book *Tax Incentives for U.S. Exports* was published in 1973. A large number of exporters preferred the WHTC program because of its simplicity. However, the 1976 act eliminated the WHTC program over a four year period beginning in 1975. At that time, DISC became the only tax incentive for U.S. exports.

The Practicing Law Institute asked me to prepare a comprehensive analysis of the DISC program, and this book *Domestic International Sales Corporations* was published in 1978. The DISC program became successful, as more than 10,000 DISCs were incorporated. But this success led to challenge on the part of America's trading partners. DISC was accused of violating the Tokyo-round General Agreement on Tariff and Trade (GATT) accords. In response, the United States limited DISC benefits and instituted the Foreign Sales Corporation (FSC) provisions in 1984. Corporate Tax Press published my *FSC—The Foreign Sales Corporation* in the same year.

The FSC program was minor in scope compared with the DISC program, as only a few thousand FSCs were established and often used only infrequently. Coupled with the initiation of the FSC program, Congress instituted new source rules

that forced many taxpayers to choose between foreign tax credits and FSC benefits. The reduction in foreign tax rates, coupled with the increase in the tax base to
vitiate the tax reduction, caused U.S. tax rates to be below taxes imposed by other
countries. American companies seeking the foreign tax credit were now faced with
excess tax credits and unable to earn FSC benefits.

Now the FSC program is growing, caused by an unlikely and unintended
source. Many of America's trading partners have reduced their tax rates, often
eliminating excess foreign tax credits for American companies. Faced with this
diminution of excess credits, American companies became free to explore FSC
benefits. Accordingly, John Wiley & Sons, Inc. requested me to edit and contribute
to the *Export Handbook*.

Robert G. Rinninsland and Kenneth C. Boyle provide the first chapter to *Export
Handbook,* "Practicalities Operating a Foreign Sales Corporation." As experienced
tax practitioners and administrators, Mr. Rinninsland and Mr. Boyle provide insight into the management of the FSC program. Their company, Engelhard, made
use of DISC and FSC.

One essential ingredient in establishing a DISC or FSC is to make an affirmative election for the export entity. Disqualification of the DISC or FSC election can
have serious consequences to the exporter. In the second chapter of *Export Handbook*, Glenn S. Miller indicates the techniques and pitfalls in "Election Requirements for Foreign Sales Corporations and Domestic International Sales Corporations."

Gross receipts are an essential ingredient in determining intercompany pricing
between the DISC or FSC and the manufacturer. In addition, gross receipts provide
one of the two tests to continue a DISC. In the third chapter, Stanley G. Sherwood
and Robert C. DeGaudenzi explore "Foreign Trading Gross Receipts."

Export property is the property that is sold or leased outside the United States,
but these provisions are subject to numerous technical requirements for DISC and
FSC, including an origin test, a destination test, and timing constraints. In the
fourth chapter, Michael N. Schwartz and Roland Ryan Davis examine the myriad
export property issues.

Services, in addition to export property, are the primary sources of export income for DISCs and FSCs. In the fifth chapter of *Export Handbook*, related and
subsidiary income as well as other services income are discussed by Lisa T. Fair
and Mark C. Thompson.

A FSC must meet detailed and complex foreign economic process requirements
to maintain FSC status. These topics are discussed by Jeffrey A. Levenstam and
Rafael E. Brown in the sixth chapter of *Export Handbook*.

In addition to meeting the foreign economic process requirements, a FSC must
meet foreign management requirement to maintain FSC status. In the seventh
chapter, Edward Tanenbaum explores the role of the foreign management requirements.

DISC and FSC have special transfer pricing rules that transcend the normal
arm's length pricing. In addition, taxpayers can get additional benefits from group-

ing or segregating export transactions. In the eighth chapter, I explain the pricing provisions.

The early FSC years saw a plethora of FSC providers; most of which have since fallen by the wayside. Some providers had ulterior motives, such as a hotel seeking FSC business solely to create occupancy or a major west coast bank keen on using certain FSC provisions to facilitate transfers of currency between tax haven-bank secrecy jurisdictions and the United States. In the ninth chapter of *Export Handbook,* "Foreign Sales Corporations and Their Service Providers" are explored.

The preparation of the DISC or FSC return has many complexities, especially as to the interrelationship of one section to another in the form. Rafeal E. Brown and Jeffrey A. Levenstam explore these issues in the tenth chapter of this book.

The taxpayer and the IRS can dispute tax issues, whether under audit or on litigation. In the eleventh chapter, Robert J. Cunningham explores litigation issues.

Exporting is much more than taxes, as customs issues are often paramount. In the twelfth chapter, Charles L. Crowley and James Geraghty explore the "Customs Aspects of Exporting."

Antitrust issues and tax considerations should be considered when exporting and are examined in chapter thirteen of *Export Handbook.*

In the fourteenth chapter of *Export Handbook*, Richard D. Boltuck, Seth T. Kaplan, and Stephanie M. Wilshusen explore "Export and Antidumping Practice."

Readers are encouraged to contact me at Suite F-301, 1121 Crandon Boulevard, Key Biscayne, Florida 33149, telephone 305-361-5800, fax 305-361-7722 to let me know of FSC or DISC audits, strategies on the part of the government or the taxpayer, or potential litigation or legislation. A supplement to the Export Pricing Handbook is planned; taxpayers and tax officials are welcome to provide comments or suggestions.

Robert Feinschreiber
Miami, Florida
January 1996

Export Handbook

Contents

CHAPTER 1

Practicalities of Operating a Foreign Sales Corporation

Robert G. Rinninsland
Kenneth C. Boyle

1.1 Introduction

Foreign sales corporations (FSCs) and domestic international sales corporations (DISCs) play an important role for U.S. multinational corporations as they focus on their corporate visions of achieving world-class status through customer satisfaction and global efficiencies. Success or failure is, in turn, measured by reference to internal strategic goals, which are generally financial in nature. Examples of these goals include earnings per share, returns on investments, internal rates of return, and shareholder value. Each goal entails consideration of the tax consequences of corporate actions since it depends on a net-income-after-tax figure as a basis of computation.

(a) Strategic Goals

Within the context of the corporate vision, the merit of any undertaking must be seen in the context of achieving a strategic goal. Tax savings attributable to a FSC in particular must be seen by the corporate organization as something that contributes to a strategic goal. Tax saving is a condition precedent to an involvement and willingness to commit time and effort needed outside a company's tax department for FSC analysis. Fulfilling this condition precedent is the responsibility of the tax department. This is the "enrollment" process, which represents the first step in the operation of a FSC within the corporation.

(b) Interacting with Other Departments and Business Groups

The first step is to encourage other departments and business groups to participate. The "enrollment" process both represents a necessary first step in the FSC process and provides an opportunity for a positive interaction with the rest of the corporate organization. The basis from which to begin this enrollment process is a knowledge of the various business operations and their overall business strategies. Second, an appreciation of the flow of relevant business data through the business group to the reporting/analytical functions within the corporate organization is needed.

The level of knowledge required for a particular business varies, depending on the nature of the business. Generally, however, one should understand the functions employed in a given business in order to bring a product "from concept to customer." In effect, the functional analysis performed for purposes of intercompany pricing forms the basis for FSC analysis. The aim of the analysis is to develop insight into the activities that contribute to the profitability of a given product line. This insight will be instrumental in the ultimate determination of the FSC pricing strategy.[1]

A sufficient level of business acumen will be needed to deal with the detailed FSC transfer pricing rules contained in Temp. Treas. Reg. 1.925(a)-1T. These rules are designed to ensure that the FSC operation reflects the realities of the underlying business economics and is not just a mechanical tax calculation.

Knowledge of the business must be supplemented by knowledge about the flow of financial data used to quantify and analyze business results. The veracity of the

---

[1] For a comprehensive technical analysis, see two books on tax incentives: Robert Feinschreiber, *Domestic International Sales Corporations* (1978); and Robert Feinschreiber, *FSC: The Foreign Sales Corporation* (Corporate Tax Press, 1984).

FSC calculation will be dependent on both the quality and understanding of the financial data available. One must initially be aware of what non-tax purpose the financial data is meant to serve. If the non-tax purpose is sufficiently similar to the FSC area, it is likely that the data can be taken at face value. However, if the purposes are not similar, adjustments will have to be made to either the format or the content of the data. In the latter case, it is most important to document any adjustments to the data so that one can always reconcile it when necessary, as, for instance, in an audit.

(c)   Interface with the Tax Department

The business knowledge and appreciation of the informational flows discussed earlier require tax department interface with business people and with other financial people. Input received by the tax department from these individuals will have to be matched by input from the tax department. Tax department input should emphasize the overall benefits to the corporate organization from the FSC operation.

Discussions should emphasize both tax benefits themselves and the benefits from additional insights into the dynamics of the businesses resulting from the tax analyses.

(d)   Assigning Responsibility

Proper enrollment of the corporate organization and constructive interface outside the tax department will allow the commencement of the FSC operation itself. A team approach should be employed, where possible, to ensure an adequate level of information flow and analysis on an ongoing basis. Resorting to the corporate culture and its application of modern team-building techniques is advisable.

The team should be formed to set up the FSC operation for the corporate organization. Like any other team, the FSC team should be cross-functional, drawing on expertise in the areas relevant to the FSC calculation. The team, therefore, should have members from the business group, business accounting, and corporate accounting, in addition to the tax department.

The respective roles of the FSC team members should be clearly defined. The tax department should take the lead in the actual day-to-day operation of the team, emphasizing the timely flow of data and input and ensuring that all members are clear as to the requests they must meet. Finally, and most important, the operation of the team should be as transparent as possible as to the other job functions of the non-tax members. This operation of the FSC team is accomplished to the extent that technical tax analysis can be performed from existing business data, as opposed to creating additional data bases. The FSC analyses represents in effect another business planning exercise that is supported as is any other exercise.

1.2   FSC Benefit

The anticipated tax benefit from a successful FSC operation is an integral part of a U.S. corporation's net income which, in the case of a publicly held company, must be reported to its shareholders and the public at large pursuant to the relevant Securities and Exchange Commission (SEC) reporting requirements.

(a)   Forecasting the FSC Benefit

The FSC tax benefit must be estimated, on an annual basis, pursuant to the accounting rules embodied in APB 28. APB Opinion No. 28, ¶ 19, requires that the effective tax rate expected for the full taxable year should be applied to pretax profit for the interim reporting period (usually the quarter). The paragraph specifically states that the effective tax rate so projected include anticipated credits and tax planning alternatives. This effective tax rate analysis, by any reasonable interpretation, includes benefits from the FSC operation.

The SEC and accounting rules in effect require an ongoing analysis of potential FSC benefit during the course of the taxable year. The ongoing analysis commences with the full year forecast and continues, based on year-to-date figures coupled with updated or revised forecast figures.

Publicly held U.S. corporations are subject to various SEC reporting requirements, a discussion of which is beyond the scope of this chapter. A successful FSC operation has both favorable balance sheet and profit and loss effects for the corporation. The FSC results are reflected in reported operating income, earnings per share, and financial ratios contained in various SEC documents. The Annual Report and 10K information concerning the FSC and its shareholders represent the two principal sources of corporate data from which prospective investors make their decisions. This information also reflects important benchmarking, which affects internal corporate issues ranging from business strategy to executive compensation.

(b)   Business Planning

Forecasting the FSC benefit becomes an exercise in business planning that entails tax department contact with and understanding of the business planning and forecasting process within the corporate organization. It is impossible to set forth a generic set of "rules and regulations" to be followed because business planning and forecasting processes are specific to particular corporate organizations. However, it is both possible and valuable to appreciate the general goals and objectives that may be common to these processes from a holistic perspective.

The business planning and forecasting process should reflect the vision of the corporate organization (e.g., becoming a world-class competitor, being first or second in all product lines, or being customer focused). The process should also address the specifics of attaining strategic goals identified as integral to achieving the corporate vision. Strategic goals would in turn focus on such items as market share, margins, and diversification, all leading toward acceptable financial returns. The acceptable financial returns would be determined according to the measurement criteria (e.g., return on equity, shareholder value) seen as controlling by the corporate organization.

Forecasting the FSC benefit, therefore, is a matter of collecting and analyzing the relevant information generated through the business planning and forecasting process. This is the major role of the FSC operation team, and the reason that participation by non-tax personnel is crucial. The team personnel from the business group and from the accounting group provide the insight necessary to link the business and tax analyses through the proper informational flows from one to the other.

(c) Projecting FSC Gross Receipts

The first and most important step in assessing the potential benefit of a FSC is to develop a forecast of the business's qualified gross receipts. The technical tax concept should be redefined in a manner that relates to the planning and forecasting process described previously. This redefinition is in fact the first task the assembled team must address.

The tax department must engage in some preparatory analysis based on some fundamental input from other members of the team, so that the entire team can begin its work. The initial input from the team to the tax department should focus on the products or product groupings that may generate overseas revenue. Strategic business units (SBU) are very often the categories identified in this regard.

In a perfect tax world the categorization of FSC activities will equate to the lowest level in a given business for which a worldwide business strategy can be developed. The lower the level, the more flexibility the tax department will have to plan for advantageous product groupings, as are discussed in Section 1.5. From a technical tax perspective, the definition of gross receipts is broad. From a business perspective, the broad tax definition expands the activities that are attributable to the FSC operation.

For example, a particular SBU may be identified as one that generates overseas sales revenue. In addition, a characteristic of this particular SBU is the necessity of ongoing relations with customers after the initial sale of the product to furnish necessary technical services to the customer to ensure the continued performance of the product. The definition of gross receipts includes both revenue from the product sale and from the follow-up services. This relationship is crucial for product lines that are designed for customer specifications rather than being sold "off the shelf." Follow-up technical service is a key element to customer relations.

A complete understanding of the business SBU generating the qualifying gross receipts can also raise interesting opportunities to examine nonoperating income and expense items to the extent that these items are incurred in the generation of export receipts. A functional analysis should be performed in the FSC context as in any other intercompany pricing situation. Functional analyses are designed to identify value-added functions and the assumptions of risk in the commercial transaction. The more value-added functions and risk assumptions, the greater the amount of qualified gross receipts and exempt foreign trade income, and thus the more FSC tax benefits.

1.3 FSC Benefit as an Analytical Tool and Performance Measure

FSC benefits can become an analytical tool as well as a performance measure. An unstated but important role of the tax department within a corporate organization is to employ tax analyses that benefit the businesses themselves by providing some insight into current or forecasted business decisions and strategies. The FSC analysis is an excellent example of this principle because of its emphasis on product sourcing and direct product costing. The FSC's generation of foreign trading gross receipts focuses on outward-bound U.S. manufactured products with U.S. content. The computation of exempt foreign trading income highlights the immediate direct and indirect production costs of a particular product. From a business standpoint, analysis should result in utilization of manufacturing capacity and contribution margins.

(a) Analytical Technique

The broad commercial definition of foreign trading gross receipts discussed earlier raises the issue of the location of the business's economic assets and income-generating capabilities. Generally, decisions to locate these items are based primarily on considerations such as market presence, change in market share, customer relations, and how these items are reflected, positively or negatively, in the computation of operating income. Similarly, the definition of exempt foreign trade income focuses on the operating income generated from the foreign trading gross receipts. Operating income is defined as gross receipts less cost of sales and selling, general and administrative expenses.

A business may maintain a strategic goal addressing cash flow or an internal rate of return derived from operating income. Nevertheless, the analysis is incomplete unless some methodology of measuring after tax net income can be developed. The ability to attribute a FSC tax benefit to the U.S. manufacture of a given product line can add significant insight to the operating income analysis, bringing the FSC benefits more in line with the strategic goal at the overall corporate organization level.

(b) Example

An illustration of the factors that affect the location of an economic asset is the key business decisions that relate to the utilization of existing manufacturing capacity, potential additional manufacturing capacity, and the gross margin analysis for a given product line. Products generating foreign trading gross receipts could be sourced from the United States to take advantage of a FSC operation, while products requiring foreign content could be manufactured abroad.

Sourcing a manufacturing decision, as discussed previously, could have an added business benefit of reducing the raw material and shipping costs incurred in bringing the foreign-sourced product to market. Analyses of gross margin, on the other hand, focus primarily on the functions performed within the plant location by manufacturing personnel. The FSC operation isolates these costs by product grouping and computes a pure return on the gross receipts, particularly when marginal costing is being used. Such a calculation can be used to quantify and compare the respective product groups' contributions to the fixed costs of the business group. These, which costs are not identified with any particular production, reduce gross margin to arrive at operating income. Determinations of contribution margins constitute a key factor in decisions to expand or dispose of a given product line because of concern regarding the ability of the remaining product lines or businesses to "absorb" additional fixed costs (which do not disappear) and maintain profitability.

(c) Analytical Benefits

Analytical benefits of a FSC operation will not be apparent to the corporate organization unless the tax department can quantify and communicate these benefit. Thus, it is necessary for the tax department to develop sufficient business acumen to combine tax law and business strategy. To address this tax objective, a tax department must consider professional development and seminars.

The tax department must go beyond the classic technical tax orientation and address the business issues faced by the corporate organization as a whole. The upside potential for perparing the analysis is significant. The FSC operation will be an accurate reflection of the business activities, which is always a plus when taking the company's tax affairs through audit, and quantifiable business benefits may also be realized. The combination of these factors brings the tax department into the mainstream of the corporate organization, from where additional tax opportunities can be pursued.

1.4   Detailed Product Review

Company organizational support that results from the communication and analytical actions by the FSC team should include an integral part of the detailed review of products to determine those to be incorporated in the FSC operation. The starting point is the definition of export property in terms of the key business activities of manufacturing, including raw material purchasing, sale, and end use by the customer. The tax department can match the specific export property requirements with activities that lead to the ultimate sale of the product. This can be done through the functional analysis that can be accomplished with the help of the business group members of the FSC operational team.

(a) Functional Analysis

The functional analysis procedure is a useful tool in product identification because it focuses on the functions, risks, assets, and intangibles used within the corporate organization to effect the product sale.[2] Exhibit 1.1 is an example of a functional analysis matrix. Its purpose is to record, within the context of intercompany transfer pricing, the assumptions of the value-added functions integral to a product sale between a U.S. parent and its foreign subsidiary where both companies together provide such functions.

---

[2] Rinninsland, "Applying Functional Analysis" in *Transfer Pricing Handbook,* ed. Feinschreiber (New York: John Wiley & Sons, 1993).

Exhibit 1.1

FUNCTIONAL ANALYSIS MATRIX

Major Activity	Where Performed	
	U.S.	*Country*
R&D		
Product Design		
Manufacturing Process Design		
Purchase Material for Production		
Local Marketing/Sales		
Order Coordination		
Customizing/Assembly		
Quality Control Testing		
Shipping/Receiving		
Inventory Control		
Production Control		
Sales Forecasting		
Billing and Collection		
Credit Analysis		
General Administration/Treasury		
Technical Services		
Patents and Trademark Responsibility		
Distribution		
Warehousing		

The functions identified are delineated into broad general categories: research and development (R&D, product design); manufacturing (manufacturing process design, purchase material for production, customizing and assembly, quality control); factory administration (shipping/receiving, inventory and production control); sales and marketing (including distribution and warehousing); technical services; and general and administrative. Identifying a qualified product and sales under the applicable regulations entails, in effect, sourcing the activities identified by the functional analysis as either U.S. or foreign-related activities in a manner sufficient to prove or disprove inclusion in FSC operation.

A practical application of this identification concept could proceed somewhat as follows: In functional analysis terms, qualified property would most likely have been developed from R&D and product design work performed in the United States. Any manufacturing process design work would most likely relate to a U.S. facility, but it can include some foreign manufacturing activities under certain circumstances.[3] Factory administration activities are crucial to proper identification of qualified products and sales owing to the specific requirements of the FSC regulations.

---

[3] *See* Temp. Reg. 1.927(a)-1T(c).

Finally, any technical support and general and administrative activities provide a double analysis, one entailing attribution to a qualified product, and one quantifying consideration received for these activities, which may be included in qualified sales income. Based on these considerations, it is possible to restate the matrix as a FSC operation analysis of qualifying products and sales. A typical FSC fact pattern illustrating common issues for proper product identification is set forth in Exhibit 1.2.

As seen in Exhibit 1.2, this analysis of the business activities can tie FSC benefits with the qualification requirements of the FSC regulations. Furthermore, the location of some of the activities could be planned, with the goal of addressing any issues related to foreign management or presence, or to economic process tests.

1.5 Product Grouping Options

The functional analysis technique will allow for proper identification of the products to be included in the FSC operation. FSC benefits are realized through optimum grouping of the products that will constitute the export trade income ultimately earned by the FSC.[4]

Exhibit 1.2

FSC OPERATION FUNCTIONAL ANALYSIS

Major Activity	Economic Substance Domestic/Foreign	Qual. Prop. Crit.
R&D	Dom.	U.S. Manufacture
Product Design	Dom.	U.S. Manufacture
Manufacture Product Desgn.	Dom.	U.S. Manufacture
Purchase Material	Dom./For.	Foreign Content
Local Market/Sales	Dom./For.	Foreign Use/Consumption
Order Coordination	Dom./For.	Foreign Destination
Customizing/Assembly	Dom.	U.S. Manufacture
Quality Control Test	Dom.	U.S. Manufacture
Shipping/Receiving	Dom./For.	Foreign Destination
Inventory Control	Dom.	Foreign Use/Consumption
Production Control	Dom.	U.S. Manufacture
Sales Forecasting	Dom.	Foreign Use/Consumption
Billing and Collection	Dom./For.	Foreign Use/Consumption
Credit Analysis	Dom.	Foreign Use/Consumption
General Admin/Treas.	Dom.	Overall FSC Operation
Technical Services	Dom./For.	Foreign Use/Consumption
Patents/Trademarks	Dom.	U.S. Manufacture
Distribution	Dom./For.	Foreign Destination
Warehousing	Dom./For.	Foreign Destination

---

[4] *See* Feinschreiber, *Transfer Pricing Handbook* (New York: John Wiley & Sons, 1993), Chapter 13.

Business input from the non-tax members of the FSC operational team is the starting point for the analysis of FSC grouping options. This procedure applies where the related supplier to the FSC sells the qualified property to the FSC for resale or where the FSC acts as a commission agent on sales of the qualified products by the related supplier to third parties.

(a) Basic Grouping Provisions

Three intercompany pricing methods contemplated by the FSC regulations are the gross receipts method, the combined taxable income method, and the Section 482 method.[5] The first two are referred to as the "administrative pricing methods." While a complete analysis of these methods is beyond the scope of this book, certain points are basic to the practicalities of qualified product groupings.

No FSC income is generated under the administrative pricing rules if there is a combined loss on the qualified product transaction or grouping elected by the FSC. Thus, FSC income cannot be created at the expense of the related supplier by allowing the FSC to earn a profit when the related supplier has a loss.[6] If the FSC realizes income from the related supplier's loss under the Section 482 method, the administrative methods cannot be used for any product within the same three-digit Standard Industrial Classification (SIC) as the product sold in the subject transaction.[7] Thus, FSC income cannot be artificially increased for similar products (three-digit SIC are considered similar for this purpose) by applying administrative pricing methods selectively. Nevertheless, loss sales can be an advantage in some circumstances.

The practical result of these rules is to emphasize the relationship of the product grouping chosen to the underlying business economics. The underlying business economics should be defined as a function of the individual profitability of the specific qualified products. The three possible product groupings are the transactional, multiproduct, and SIC groupings. Each needs to be evaluated within the parameters discussed here.

(b) Evaluating Transactional Grouping

Individual transactions can be reported separately. In this case, FSC income is maximized by totaling the results from each individual sale. Proper application of transactional grouping requires sufficient costing detail. This method is not necessarily advantageous. Any significant cost allocations between product lines adversely affects the separateness of the income calculations; thus some sort of product grouping is required.

---

[5] Temp. Reg. 1.925(a)-1T(b)(2).

[6] Temp. Reg. 1.925(a)-1T(e)(1)(i).

[7] Temp. Reg. 1.925(a)-1T(e)(1)(iii).

(c) Evaluating Product Grouping

An alternative to reporting FSC income on a transaction-by-transaction basis is to organize the qualified product sales into an appropriate grouping or groupings. This process in fact complements the information flow provided by most corporate accounting systems, particularly where the U.S. manufacturing sites have responsibility for multiple product lines.

There are two significant advantages to product grouping. First, using product grouping can allow for advantageous allocations of fixed manufacturing costs from a qualified product line to costs of other product lines that are incurred within the plant itself. Second, if a given manufacturing plant having responsibility for qualified products is particularly profitable for any reason, product grouping at the overall plant level can take advantage of this situation.

The plant profitability is usually attributable to location savings. (The application of the intercompany pricing principle of location savings is quite relevant here.) These location savings can be derived from such items as lower direct and indirect labor costs, utilities savings, and shipping and handling savings. Product grouping, therefore, is essentially an opportunity to take advantage of economies of scale in the corporate organization's manufacturing operations as they may relate to the sale of the qualified products. Taxpayers have considerable flexibility in determining product group, but "wheeling and dealing" is prohibited.[8]

(d) Evaluating SIC Grouping

The third product grouping alternative employs the SIC prepared by the Office of Management and Budget. SIC codes are used in U.S. Customs Service product classifications. The SIC concept has also found its way into other areas of tax law, most notably the allocation and apportionment of research and experimental expenditures to U.S. and foreign source income for foreign tax credit purposes.[9]

In practice, this SIC grouping method provides less flexibility than standard product grouping to the extent that it assumes the grouping together of a predetermined category of qualified products. However, SIC grouping can be quite representative of the business economics where the corporate organization incurs substantial R&D expenditures. In this case, the allocation of the R&D expense throughout the entire SIC grouping, pursuant to the interplay between the foreign tax credit and FSC regulations, may ensure profitability in the grouping as a whole if the alternative is a transactional or more specific product grouping showing losses in certain qualified products.

(e) General Grouping Procedure

Product grouping elections must be made by the FSC for its taxable year. Issues and key assumptions will vary by corporate organization, but in any case the aim

---

[8] Robert Feinschreiber, *Transfer Pricing Handbook* (New York: John Wiley & Sons, 1993), Chapter 13 and Robert Feinschreiber, *Export Handbook*, Chapter 8.

[9] *See* Reg. 1.861-8(e)(3), *see* Robert Feinschreiber, *Allocation and Apportionment of Deductions*.

of the product grouping election is to allow for use of both the administrative pricing methods and the Section 482 pricing method in determining the transfer pricing between the FSC and its related supplier.

Identifying qualified products and determining proper product groupings are prerequisites to a successful FSC operation. These exercises represent the necessary coordination with the businesses that must occur for the tax law technicalities to be applied. It is also crucial that this coordination be developed into a process that can operate with a minimum of supervision and provide the relevant facts for tax analysis from the natural flow of the business data. Such a system will allow for efficient day-to-day management of the FSC operation, thus providing opportunities to combine and interrelate the FSC operation with the overall tax strategies of the corporate organization.

1.6 Day-to-Day Management

Under the FSC rules, taxpayers are entitled to a partial tax exemption of their qualified export income if certain statutory conditions are satisfied. In particular, the FSC must satisfy the foreign economic process requirement,[10] foreign presence requirement,[11] and foreign management requirement.[12] Consequently, an important aspect of the day-to-day management of a FSC involves planning and complying with these requirements.

(a) Safeguarding the FSC Benefits

The foreign economic process requirement must be satisfied to derive foreign trading gross receipts.[13] This requirement consists of two separate tests, the foreign sales participation test[14] and the foreign direct cost test.[15] To satisfy these tests, certain activities must be performed by the FSC or by a party under contract with the FSC. For many taxpayers, it is efficient to contractually assign some of these responsibilities to another party, particularly when that party is already performing these functions.

(b) Foreign Participation

The foreign sales participation test requires that the FSC participate outside the United States in the solicitation of an order, in the negotiation of an order, or in the preparation of a contract for an order. Performance of any one of these activities

---

[10] IRC § 924(b).
[11] IRC § 922(a).
[12] IRC § 924(c).
[13] IRC § 924(a).
[14] IRC § 923(d)(1)(A).
[15] IRC § 923(d)(1)(B).

will satisfy the test. However, taxpayers desiring to use the "safe haven" administrative pricing methods must perform all these activities, although only one must take place outside the United States.[16] Taxpayers often find it administratively efficient and cost effective to have another party, acting as an agent of the FSC, perform these functions. Assignment of these activities may be accomplished through an oral agreement or a written contract. It is preferable that the agreement be reduced to a writing, typically in the form of a formal service agreement.

At a minimum, the contract should specify that the service provider is performing the activities on behalf of the FSC. The activities must be carefully defined in the agreement to comply with the requirements in the code. The contract should also indicate that the services will be performed either directly by the contracting service provider or indirectly by one of its subagents. Finally, the agreement should state that it applies only to activities related to the sale of qualified export products.[17]

(c)   Direct Costs

The foreign direct cost test is satisfied when the foreign direct costs of a transaction (i.e., direct costs attributable to activities performed outside the United States) exceed 50 percent of the transaction's total direct costs. Alternatively, the test is also satisfied when the foreign direct costs in two of the direct cost categories exceed 85 percent of their respective total direct costs.[18] Taxpayers desiring to use the "safe haven" administrative pricing methods must satisfy the requirements for all of the direct costs.

Direct costs include advertising and sales promotion, processing of customer orders, and arranging for delivery, transportation, determination and transmittal of a final invoice, and the assumption of the credit risk.[19] To satisfy the test, taxpayers frequently select two direct cost activities that the FSC, or person under contract with the FSC, performs exclusively outside the United States. The costs associated with these activities will be incurred by the FSC and recorded in its books. The remaining three direct cost activities are then satisfied by entering into a contract with the person presently performing those activities.

The costs frequently identified as being most easily performed by the FSC outside the United States are the determination and transmittal of a final invoice, advertising and sales promotion, and assumption of credit risk. In most cases, these activities can easily be assumed by the FSC without disrupting the related suppliers' activities and processing.

(d)   Foreign Management

The foreign management requirement prescribes that all formally convened meetings of the board of directors and shareholders be conducted outside the United

---

[16] IRC § 925(e).

[17] IRC § 927(a)(1).

[18] IRC § 924(d)(2).

[19] IRC § 924(e).

States, that its principal bank account be maintained in a foreign country, and that disbursements of dividends, legal and accounting fees, and salaries of officers, and board of directors fees be made from an account outside the United States.[20]

There is no requirement under U.S. tax law that the FSC hold regular board of directors or shareholders meetings. Such meetings may be required under the local laws of the foreign jurisdiction where the FSC was established. When meetings are necessary, the participants with a majority of the voting power (including proxy rights) should be physically located abroad. The IRS deems a meeting to be held where the shareholders or directors with a majority of the voting power are physically located.[21] A meeting found to be held in the United States can result in the loss of all the FSC benefits in that year.

(e) Waivers and the Foreign Management Test

Ordinarily, taxpayers want to minimize the cost and inconvenience of conducting shareholder meetings abroad. A technique used by many taxpayers is to have the U.S. shareholder(s) prepare and execute a proxy statement that transfers its voting power to the nonresident director. The proxy transfer permits the meeting to be conducted outside the United States by the nonresident director. Taxpayers may also consider appointing an employee who frequently travels abroad as a director. He or she can then participate in meetings while outside the United States on routine business.

Board of directors meetings can be handled in a similar fashion. U.S. directors can prepare and execute "waivers." These documents serve to notify the nonresident board member that they will not be attending the meeting and authorize him to conduct all the corporation's business. This technique effectively transfers the U.S. board members' voting power to the nonresident director, who can then vote on specific corporate resolutions.

Teleconferencing is also a very popular tool for conducting meetings. This technology makes it possible to hold a meeting with individuals from around the world without physically congregating in one location. In the FSC context, however, the taxpayer must ensure that participants with a majority of the voting power are located outside the United States.

(f) Principal Bank Account

The foreign management requirement also imposes restrictions on the principal bank account of the FSC. Specifically, its principal bank account must be maintained in a qualified foreign jurisdiction, and certain specified payments are to be made from this account. The principal bank account rules are relaxed somewhat under the regulations.

---

[20] IRC § 924(c).

[21] Reg. 1.924(c)-(1) (b).

The statute indicates that dividend payments should be disbursed from the FSC's principal bank account. In many cases, these distributions require the parent to pay down an intercompany payable balance with the FSC to fund the dividend distribution back to the parent. The IRS apparently recognizes the administrative inconvenience and transactional expense associated with "round-tripping" cash and permits taxpayers to execute these dividend payments through bookkeeping entries.[22] The elimination of round-tripping is accomplished by netting the dividend distribution directly against the intercompany receivable balance with the parent.

There is also some flexibility with other types of payments between the FSC and its supplier. The regulations allow the related supplier to make the payments on behalf of the FSC, provided that they are reimbursed by the FSC within a reasonable time.[23] Unlike the payment of dividends, however, these payments may not be made by bookkeeping entries.

(g)   Maintaining Books and Records

Most of the FSC initial requirements are addressed when the corporation is organized. Ongoing requirements are that the FSC maintain a permanent set of books, including invoices, at its qualifying foreign office.[24] Responsibility for ongoing requirements is commonly delegated to the related supplier under a formal service agreement. Typically, the related supplier will prepare the financial reports and compile the invoices that are sent and maintained at the FSC's foreign office. At a minimum, the FSC must maintain quarterly income statements, a final year-end income statement and balance sheet, and all final invoices (or summary of invoices) or statements of account.

Preparing income statements based on income computed under the administrative pricing methods can be a formidable task. The FSC profit calculation requires a substantial amount of detailed financial data and many separate computations. The IRS recognizes the burden quarterly pricing calculations would place on taxpayers and allows "reasonable estimates" to be used in the quarterly income statements. Estimates, however, are not permitted in the preparation of either the year-end financial reports or the U.S. estimated tax payments.

The related supplier is also routinely responsible for the preparation of the FSC's sales invoices. In many cases "qualified export sales invoices" are processed along with the related supplier's invoices. This type of invoice processing often makes it difficult to segregate the FSC's export sales invoices from other sales invoices. If this type of invoice processing is being performed, the taxpayer may need to meet with the appropriate sales and accounting people to modify the database and reports to capture the needed information.

---

[22] Reg. 1.924(c)-1(d) (1).

[23] Reg. 1.924(c)-1(d) (2).

[24] IRC § 922(a) (1) (D) (2).

(h)   Tax Calendar

Failure to comply with the statutory filing and reporting requirements can result in a loss of some or all of the FSC benefits. To ensure that all of the requisite FSC activities are completed in a timely manner, it is a good idea to set up a "FSC tax calendar." This calendar should include tax filing deadlines, financial reporting dates, scheduled shareholder and board of directors meetings, and all other required activities that must be performed throughout the year.

The calendar can be as simple as a handwritten list or as sophisticated as a computer tax tickler program. No matter which format is selected, the most important attributes of a useful tax calendar are that it is accurate and comprehensive. The calendar must include all the compliance requirements of the FSC and their respective deadline dates. In addition, the calendar should be regularly reviewed and updated by the taxpayer.

(i)   Automation of Calculations

The computation of the FSC profit under the administrative pricing rules requires a substantial amount of financial data and many repetitive calculations. Taxpayers testing alternative pricing methods and product groupings exponentially increase the work required to determine the final FSC profit, but electronic spreadsheets are extremely efficient in sourcing the financial information and performing the required computations.

(i)   Using Electronic Spreadsheets.   Most electronic spreadsheet programs can import financial data directly from an electronic file. The importation of this data is generally performed in two steps. First, the raw data is downloaded from the corporate database into a separate file. This file is then converted and imported directly into a worksheet file by the spreadsheet program.

(ii)   Databases.   Typically, the download from a corporate database will be in the form of a print file (i.e., filename.prn). A print file is created when a predefined report is saved to a file rather than sent to a printer. A printout of this file should be maintained to support the figures used in the worksheets. Some spreadsheet programs convert the print file in two steps. The print file is first converted into an ASCII format and saved to a new file. The converted data is then imported directly into the spreadsheet. Most of the new spreadsheet programs do not require this intermediate step.

Most of the taxpayers' time will be spent learning about the corporate database and establishing the criteria used to extract the financial data. Taxpayers must carefully review the financial reporting programs and related database files to determine the systems' capabilities and limitations. In many cases the corporate database will be insufficient to permit a complete automation of the data-sourcing process. Taxpayers will frequently be asked to make a number of judgment decisions regarding the parameters used in the program.

For example, a program designed to extract qualified export sales has to identify the corporation's "qualified export products." This identification necessitates an analysis of the component parts of each product.[25] To qualify as "export property," less than 50 percent of the fair market value of the product can be attributable to component parts imported into the United States. Most corporate databases do not provide this level of product detail. Consequently, the taxpayer would have to independently identify the qualified export products and incorporate these determinations directly into the program.

(iii)   Worksheets.   Once the data has been extracted from the corporate database and downloaded into a worksheet file, the taxpayer must design the worksheets required to compute the FSC profit. The worksheets should be programmed to compute the FSC profit under the administrative pricing rules and test alternative pricing methods and assumptions. The specific design of the program will ultimately depend on the needs of the taxpayer and the quality of the financial data.

The administrative pricing calculations require a substantial amount of detailed financial data and many separate calculations. The designer, however, should resist the temptation to create a few large spreadsheets with many complicated formulas. It is preferable to create several smaller worksheets, each performing a subcalculation. This approach will require less sophisticated programming and make the worksheet easier for the reviewer to understand.

(iv)   Spreadsheets.   Spreadsheet programs have several advanced capabilities that are particularly useful in the FSC applications. In particular, most spreadsheet programs allow the user to create and cross-reference several separate worksheets in the same file. The program allows the designer to create several subworksheets, each performing a single calculation. The results from the separate calculations can then be referenced in other worksheets as needed.

Today's spreadsheet programs are capable of referencing figures from other spreadsheet files. In the Windows environment, spreadsheet designers will also be able to reference information from other application programs.

"Global data" refers to data used in several different calculations simultaneously. It is typically data relating to the organization's worldwide, affiliated group, or companywide operations. This type of data is most frequently used in the expense allocation calculations under Treas. Reg. 1.861-8.

A properly designed spreadsheet program should also minimize the amount of redundant data entry. "Global data" should be entered on a separate worksheet and referenced into specific calculations as needed. This program reduces potential keypunch errors and streamlines future data updates. This approach also makes it possible to perform sensitivity analysis on these global variables.

(j)   Using Software Programs

There are some software programs specifically designed to compute the FSC profit under the administrative pricing methods. Such programs are typically de-

---

[25] IRC § 927(a)(1)(C).

signed around a database file. This kind of software is typically written and compiled into machine-readable language. Consequently, it is usually not customizable to the needs of the individual taxpayer.

The advantage of this type of software is that it can quickly test multiple combinations of groupings and assumptions, which can be particularly advantageous to taxpayers with a large number of products and individual transactions. Taxpayers applying the administrative pricing methods on a transaction-by-transaction basis may achieve significant tax savings.

1.7 Relation of the FSC to the U.S. Consolidated Return

U.S. manufacturers that sell overseas may generally treat 50 percent of their export sales income as "foreign source income" for purposes of the foreign tax credit limitation.[26] This allocation of income can be extremely beneficial to taxpayers in an excess foreign tax credit position. These export sales constitute foreign source income, which increases the limitation, resulting in a larger foreign tax credit.

(a) Resourcing Rule

FSC taxpayers using the administrative pricing rules are subject to a resourcing rule[27] under which a portion of the related supplier's export sales are reclassified as U.S.-source income. The tax effect of this rule will depend on the particular circumstances of the taxpayer. Taxpayers currently subject to the foreign tax credit limitation should be particularly sensitive to this rule.

The reduction of U.S. corporate tax rates combined with the limitations placed on the foreign tax credit have left many companies with excess foreign tax credits. Consequently, this resourcing rule will have a significant impact on these companies. Any decision to operate a FSC must factor in this potential reduction in the foreign tax credit.

The tax impact of the resourcing rule should begin with a quantification of the additional foreign-source income generated by "turning-off" the FSC (i.e., so that no resourcing would be applied). This foreign-source income amount can be used to determine the incremental foreign tax credit and then compared with the projected FSC tax benefit. Taxpayers deciding to turn off the FSC should consider reactivating the FSC when the taxpayer's foreign tax credits are no longer limited.

(b) Alternative Minimum Tax Considerations

In general, FSC distributions to domestic corporate shareholders are not subject to tax because of the 100 percent dividends received deduction.[28] The Alternative

---

[26] IRC § 863(b).

[27] IRC § 927(e).

[28] IRC § 245(c)(1)(A).

Minimum Tax (AMT), however, limits this deduction to the portion of the distribution that was previously subject to U.S. taxation.[29] Consequently, a portion of the FSC's exempt foreign trade income must be included in the shareholder's Alternative Minimum Taxable Income (AMTI), thus, in effect, recapturing a portion of the FSC benefit.

As a result, taxpayers subject to the AMT get no current tax benefit from the FSC and, in fact, can incur a current tax cost (see Exhibit 1.3). The tax benefit derived from the FSC's income exclusion is more than offset by the FSC's higher tax rate (FSC's regular tax rate of 35 percent versus the related supplier's AMT rate of 20 percent) and the related supplier's reduced dividend-received deduction.

An issue related to the taxpayer's overall AMT position, illustrated in Exhibit 1.3, is the retention of the FSC while in AMT (reference the "With FSC" fact pattern in Exhibit 1.3). A strategy used by some AMT taxpayers is to operate the FSC and incur the AMT expense related to the FSC AMT adjustment (i.e., 20 percent of $107.50). In exchange for the additional AMT, the taxpayer obtains a deferred tax

Exhibit 1.3

ALTERNATIVE MINIMUM TAX

	With FSC		Without FSC	
	Parent	FSC	Parent	FSC
Book Income	1,000.00		1,000.00	
FSC Income	(250.00)	250.00		
FSC Exclusion (15/23 of Income)		(163.04)		
Dividend Paid by FSC*	219.57			
100% Dividend Received	(219.57)			
Regular Taxable Income	750.00	86.96	1,000.00	
AMT Adjustment—FSC**	107.40			
AMT Adjustment—Other	800.00		800.00	
AMTI	1657.40	86.96	1,800.00	
Regular Tax @35%		30.43		
AMT Tax @ 20%	331.48		360.00	
Total Tax Expense		361.91		360.00
Cost of Operating FSC				1.91

Dividend	219.57			
FSC Exclusion%	65.22%	FSC Income	250.00	
ACE Addback%	75.00%	FSC Tax	(30.43)	
**AMT Adjustment	107.40	*Dividend	219.57 (E&P)	

---

[29] IRC § 56(g)(4)(C)

benefit in the form of an AMT credit. This credit will then be available to offset the company's regular tax liability, albeit in a later year.

Proper tax planning to utilize the AMT credit against future regular tax liability ensures that the permanent FSC tax benefit (i.e., 35 percent times the FSC exclusion of $163.04, or $57.06) is realized over a period of time. This permanent tax benefit, coupled with the recapture of the $21.50 AMT credit in a timely fashion, provides a delayed but real (in net present value terms), FSC tax benefit.

(c)   Special Allocation Issues

To compute combined taxable income (CTI) under the administrative pricing rules, the taxpayer must allocate and apportion expenses of the affiliated group[30] to the FSC's foreign trading gross receipts (FTGR). Rules provide for allocating and apportioning expenses (other than interest) of an affiliated group. In general, the taxable income of each member of the affiliated group shall be determined by allocating and apportioning expenses to each member, including the FSC. The allocation and apportionment fractions are to be computed as if all members of the group were a single corporation.

This allocation and apportionment is accomplished by allocating "directly related" expenses to their respective classes of gross income.[31] These amounts are then apportioned to statutory and residual groups within each class. Expenses not related to any specific class are apportioned to all classes of gross income.

(d)   General Apportionment

The general allocation and apportionment rules[32] apply to all expenses other than research and development expenses, state and local income taxes, interest expense, and charitable contributions. These later deductions are subject to very specific and ridged allocation and apportionment rules.

The general allocation and apportionment rules permit the taxpayer to use any reasonable apportionment method that reflects a factual relationship between the deduction and gross income. Consequently, taxpayers can frequently identify alternate apportionment methods for many of their expenses. To maximize the FSC benefit, the taxpayer must select the method that yields the lowest FSC expense.

The process of selecting the optimal apportionment method starts by identifying all the reasonable apportionment methods. For example, it may be possible to apportion salary expense using a method based on gross sales, gross income, cost of sales, or time. After all the permissible methods have been identified, they should be tested to determine which apportions the least expense to the FSC gross income. Absent other tax considerations, this will ordinarily be the method selected.

---

[30] Reg. 1.861-14T.

[31] Reg. 1.861-8T.

[32] The allocation and apportionment regulations relating to FSCs are contained in Temp. Reg. 1.861-8T through 14T.

(e)   Review Procedures

It is important that the taxpayer review all the corporate expenses and their corresponding allocation and apportionment methods. This review should focus on ways to reduce the FSC expenses and increase the FSC benefit. Two of the taxpayer's primary objectives should be to ensure that all "non-FSC" directly related expenses are allocated specifically to their related classes of gross income (i.e., allocated directly to a non-FSC class of gross income) and to minimize the amount of nonallocable expenses. This latter objective is important, because all expenses not allocable to a specific class of gross income are apportioned to all classes of gross income. Consequently, a portion of the expense might be indirectly allocated back to the FSC.

Selling, general, and administrative expenses come under the category of supportive expenses,[33] which are subject to the general allocation and apportionment rules. These expenses relate to activities that augment or assist other activities of the taxpayer. In most cases they are not allocable to a particular class of gross income and would be apportioned to all classes of gross income, including FSC income.

(f)   Shifting Expenses

An opportunity may exist to reduce the amount of support expenses apportioned to the FSC. The taxpayer may be able to "load" a portion of these expenses into the allocation and apportionment of other expense classifications. The portion to be allocated to the other expense categories may be based on factors such as units sold, space utilized, time spent, and so forth.[34] The apportionment of these expenses to other expense classifications may be based on any one of several methods. This strategy is most effective when the activities corresponding to this "other expense" classification do not (directly or indirectly) assist in generating qualified export sales income. In other words, this technique works when the expense is "loaded" into another expense classification with more favorable allocation and apportionment ratios.

The expense technique is not without some practical implementation issues. The initial expense allocation may require information that is not currently available or is difficult to obtain. For example, an allocation of salary expense to another classification of expense may be based on a ratio of employee time spent in a corresponding activity. This may require that employees maintain time reports to support the allocation. Obviously, such a requirement would not appeal to many persons in the organization. It is important, therefore, that the taxpayer weigh the additional administrative expense and inconvenience to the organization against the potential tax benefit to be derived.

---

[33] Temp. Reg. 1.861-8T(b)(3).

[34] Temp. Reg. 1.861-8T(c)(1) enumerates several of the possible methods available to the taxpayer.

(g) Interest Expense

The interest expense allocation and apportionment rules are specifically defined and rather inflexible. They are based on the approach that "money is fungible and that interest expense is attributable to all activities and property regardless of any specific purpose for incurring an obligation on which interest is paid."[35] Accordingly, interest expense allocations must be made on the basis of assets of the affiliated group.

To minimize the interest expense allocation to FSC gross income, the taxpayer should review several important components of the allocation computations. In particular, a review of the affiliated group's assets should be performed to determine that the proper U.S. or foreign attribution has been attached to each asset. The U.S./foreign attribution of an asset is based on the source and type of income generated by the asset. The physical location of the asset is not determinative.

(h) Asset Valuation

Another area for review is asset valuation. The general rule is that the value of the assets used in the calculations is their average net tax value. The taxpayer may elect, however, to use the assets' fair market value. Where taxpayers have substantially appreciated U.S. assets, the FMV method has the effect of shifting more of the worldwide interest expense to a U.S. source. In many cases the fair market value of the group's assets is not immediately available. It may even be necessary for the company to perform a valuation of the company's assets for use in the apportionment formula. This can be costly and must be weighed against a projection of the FSC tax benefit to be derived.

(i) Supportive Costs

The Code, regulations, and accounting literature are neither precise nor consistent regarding the classification of supportive costs. It may, therefore, be advantageous for corporations to undertake a cost study to evaluate the nature and characteristics of their expenses. A cost study will ensure the proper classifications of costs, develop the appropriate apportionment and allocation methods that reflect a factual relationship between the expense deductions and the foreign- and U.S.-source income, and provide support under audit. It will also provide information needed to select the allocation and apportionment methods that produce the largest FSC benefit.

These studies may be performed by the FSC operational team discussed earlier or by outside consultants. In either case the development of the study plan and its objectives should be carefully defined, including the degree of documentation required.

---

[35] Reg. 1.861-8(e)(2).

Taxpayers must be prepared to support their expense allocations if the FSC tax return is selected for an IRS audit examination. It is quite possible that a taxpayer will be asked by an IRS agent to explain and support the FSC expenses several years after the return is filed. The IRS agent may want to know why a particular method was selected and how the expenses were determined. It is, therefore, essential that the taxpayer fully document the rationale for selecting each method and maintain detailed workpapers of the actual calculations.

1.8   Tax Compliance

FSCs generally file and pay taxes in the United States and in their foreign jurisdictions. Ordinarily, FSCs locate their offices in overseas locations having favorable tax conditions; specifically, low taxes and minimal filing requirements. Most of a FSC's tax liability and filing requirements will center on the U.S. federal income tax. This tax must be paid through quarterly estimated tax payments, and the corporation must file an annual federal income tax return.

(a)   Preparing the Federal Income Tax Return

Each year the FSC must file a U.S. Income Tax Return of a Foreign Sales Corporation, Form 1120FSC. The return is due on the 15th day of the third month following the end of the tax year. A six-month extension of time to file may be requested by filing an Application for Automatic Extension of Time to File Corporation Income Tax Return, Form 7004. This does not extend the time to pay the balance of any tax due. The request for extension must be filed on or before the original due date of the FSC tax return.

A substantial amount of time and effort may be required by the taxpayer to prepare an accurate and complete tax return. Taxpayers typically need to collect and analyze a great deal of financial data to prepare a FSC tax return, particularly when "safe harbor" administrative pricing methods are used to compute the FSC profit. Unfortunately, the financial reporting systems in many companies were never designed to capture the data needed to extract FSC financial information. Consequently, the taxpayer may often devote an inordinate amount of time manually compiling information.

Taxpayers manually compiling this financial data will frequently use tax reporting packages. These packages contain questionnaires and worksheets designed to capture the information needed to prepare the FSC tax return. They are usually completed by those people responsible for maintaining the relevant financial data. This method of gathering data is comprehensive and reduces data duplication. It is, however, very time-consuming, particularly when the same information must be reentered into the FSC electronic worksheets or software.

The knowledge and insights of the FSC operational team must be used to maximize the FSC benefit. Frequently, the person completing the tax package is intimately familiar with the financial data. With their combined expertise the team can analyze the information from a tax perspective and identify tax savings in the underlying data.

The analysis of the export sales data should include a review of the criteria used to identify (or extract) qualified export sales, as discussed earlier. Criteria used in a prior year may not be currently valid. The taxpayer should examine the component parts of the "qualified export products" to confirm that they still qualify under the code. The shipping and billing addresses of the sales should also be checked. The review should not be limited to only those products identified as qualified export products in prior years.

(b) Making Estimated Tax Payments

The FSC must make estimated income tax payments four times a year. Calendar year taxpayers must compute and pay quarterly estimated tax payments on March 15, June 15, September 15, and December 15. The amount due each quarter should amount to 25 percent of the annual liability or an amount computed under the Annualized Income Installment Method or Adjusted Seasonal Method. Unlike the amounts used in quarterly income statements, reasonable estimates are not permitted for estimated income tax purposes.

A substantial amount of time is required to compute the actual quarterly FSC profit and corresponding estimated tax payment. Consequently, taxpayers will not routinely perform full-blown calculations each quarter. The practical solution to this problem is to use a conservative estimate of the quarterly tax liability as the basis of the FSC's estimated payment. The estimate should be high enough to safely avoid the imposition of interest and penalty assessments.

Estimated income tax must be paid directly to the IRS when a FSC does not maintain an office in the United States. The payment, made by check or money order, should include the FSC's employer identification number, "Form 1120-FSC," and the tax year. The payment should be sent to the Internal Revenue Service Center, Philadelphia, PA 19255. a FSC with an office in the United States will be required to deposit these payments in an authorized commercial bank depository or Federal Reserve Bank, using Federal Tax Deposit Coupons (Form 8109).

1.9 FSC and Related Tax Regimes

When U.S. income tax rates are higher than those in foreign jurisdictions, taxpayers have an incentive to shift income from the United States. In the past, taxpayers were able to reduce their overall tax expense by contributing their cash and short-term investments to a controlled foreign corporation in a low-tax jurisdiction. The corresponding investment income was then subject to tax at the lower foreign rate; any remaining after-tax profit was retained and reinvested by the foreign corporation. The income was subject to U.S. taxation only when it was repatriated as a dividend to the U.S. shareholders.

Congress concluded that taxpayers should not be encouraged to use corporations, including foreign corporations, to avoid U.S. income tax. Consequently, tax laws were written to infer a tax avoidance purpose whenever U.S. shareholders owned corporations with excessive nonbusiness income or accumulated earnings in excess of their reasonable business needs. Where a tax avoidance purpose is found, the corporation may be subject to a penalty tax or the shareholders may be deemed to have a dividend distribution from the corporation. In either case, these tax avoidance provisions are designed to promote current distributions of corporate profits. The specific provisions addressed in this chapter are the accumulated earnings tax, personal holding company tax, and the foreign personal holding company tax.

These "tax avoidance" provisions were primarily aimed at the abusive practices of individual shareholders. In addition, the FSC tax provisions independently discourage earning and accumulating nonbusiness income (i.e., Non-FTI) in the FSC. Consequently, even though the taxpayer must be aware of their existence, a FSC will not normally become subject to these provisions.

(a)   Foreign Personal Holding Company Tax

The foreign personal holding company (FPHC) provisions are designed to remove the tax incentive to shift certain types of assets and income offshore into tax haven jurisdictions. These provisions apply to foreign corporations, including FSCs, that satisfy a "gross income test" and a "stock ownership test." Shareholders of a FPHC are currently taxed on their portion of the FSC's undistributed foreign personal holding company income (FPHCI).[36]

FPHC rules closely resemble those under Subpart F relating to deemed dividend distributions from controlled foreign corporations (CFCs). Under both sets of rules, the U.S. shareholder is deemed to receive a dividend distribution of the corporation's tainted income. The two provisions do not overlap with respect to FSCs, because they are specifically excluded from the Subpart F provisions.

Although shareholders of FSCs must currently report their portion of the FPHCI as a deemed dividend, the inclusion relating to interest or carrying charges has been largely eliminated by the Tax Reform Act of 1986. The Act provides an 85 percent dividends received deduction for this type of income.[37] Dividends received deduction is not available for distributions of FTI computed under the transfer price rules of Section 482.

As a practical matter, the most significant factor affecting the taxation of FPHCI (i.e., investment income) relates to its classification under the FSC rules. FPHCI is considered income effectively connected with a U.S. trade or business subject to current U.S. taxation. Nor is it included in the FSC's FTI, which is partially excluded from U.S. taxation. Consequently, it is not likely that investment assets will be transferred or maintained in the FSC.

---

[36] IRC § 551(a).

[37] IRC § 245(c)(2)(A).

(b) Personal Holding Company Tax

If a FSC qualifies as a FPHC, then the personal holding company (PHC) provisions will not apply. Conversely, the FSC may qualify as a PHC even though it fails as a FPHC. The taxpayer, therefore, should test the FSC under the FPHC provisions before considering the PHC provisions.

To qualify as a PHC, the FSC must again satisfy a "gross income" test and a "stock ownership" test. Foreign corporations treated as PHCs will be taxed on their personal holding company income (PHCI) undistributed at the end of the year. This tax is in addition to any regular tax liability incurred during the year.

(c) Accumulated Earnings Tax

If a FSC qualifies as a FPHC or a PHC, then the accumulated earnings tax (AET) provisions do not apply. Conversely, the FSC may be subject to the AET even though it fails as a FPHC or a PHC. The taxpayer, therefore, should test the FSC under the FPHC and PHC provisions before considering the AET.

The AET was designed to discourage corporations from sheltering their earnings from taxation at the shareholder level. The tax is imposed on the corporation and is paid in addition to any tax otherwise payable, and is based on the corporation's accumulated taxable income of the year.

The AET applies to any corporation used for the purpose of avoiding income tax at the shareholder level by accumulating its earnings (i.e., not distributing its earnings and profits to its shareholders). The pivotal factual issue under this provision is the principal purpose for retaining the profits in the corporation. Where the earnings are needed for the "reasonable needs of the business" or, alternately, no tax avoidance purpose can be shown, the AET will not apply.

FSC shareholders are entitled to a 100 percent dividends received deduction on distributions of FTI. Consequently, it will be very difficult to establish a tax avoidance motive when there is no tax cost associated with a distribution of the accumulated FSC earnings. However, if a related supplier is in an AMT position, as discussed earlier, the FSC operation must be sensitive to the AMT imposed on its distributions. Failure to distribute in this circumstance could be considered tax avoidance within the meaning of the AET, although this has not been specifically addressed. The fact that AMT is itself a nonexpiring tax credit against future regular tax may argue against such consideration. The question would be, in regard to the previous discussion, the ability of the corporation to utilize the credit and whether this would offset any presumption of tax avoidance. Consequently, it seems that the AET will not be imposed on a FSC where the related supplier is consistently a regular taxpayer and, arguably, where it can use its AMT credits consistently.

The FSC must, however, be sensitive to the portion of the accumulated earnings converted into investment assets. As previously discussed, investment income does not qualify for any preferential FSC treatment. In addition, when this income is distributed in the form of a dividend it is not eligible for the 100 percent dividend received deduction. As a practical matter, it is advisable for the FSC to retain only small amounts of income to service its operational needs.

Section 245 (c) (1) (A) provides a 100 percent dividends received deduction for distributions out of the FSC's foreign trade income (FTI). To the extent these distributions are from Non-FTI, this special provision does not apply. The general rule that distributions from foreign corporations are fully taxable to the U.S. shareholder would apply.

1.10   Validating the Effort

(a)   Quantifying Cash Savings

The tax benefit for a FSC will depend on the particular circumstances of the existing organization. The creation and utilization of FSC does not automatically assure an overall tax savings to the group. For this reason, tax departments must compute the actual and projected tax effect associated with a FSC.

The tax consequence of operating FSC is determined by a "with and without" calculation (see Exhibit 1.4). The corporation's overall tax expense is computed with the FSC in operation, then recomputed without the FSC. The net of these two amounts is the cash tax benefit (or cost) derived from the FSC. This amount must then be reduced by the incremental direct operating costs of the FSC to determine the overall economic effect.

Exhibit 1.4

"WITH AND WITHOUT" CALCULATION

	With		Without	
	Parent	FSC	Parent	FSC
Book Income	25,000,000		25,000,000	
Commission Expense	(5,000,000)	5,000,000		
Exempt FTI		(3,260,870)		
Dividend Received*	4,391,304			
Dividend Received Deduction	(4,391,304)			
Regular Taxable Income	20,000,000	1,739,130	25,000,000	
Tax @35%	7,000,000	608,696	8,750,000	N/A
Federal Tax Expense—Parent		7,000,000		8,750,000
Federal Tax Expense—FSC		608,696		N/A
Direct Expenses (After Tax)		25,000		N/A
Total Expense		7,633,696		8,750,000
Cash Tax Reduction		1,116,304		

FSC Income	5,000,000		FTI	5,000,000
Federal Income Tax	(608,696)		Exemption %	65.217%
*Earnings & Profits	4,391,304		Exempt FTI	3,260,870

(b)   Reduction of Domestic Parent's Federal/State Tax

The quantification of the cash tax savings begins by computing the parent's federal and state income tax liability without the FSC. This will require an adjustment to the parent's federal taxable income if intercompany FSC entries were made during the year. In theory, this adjustment represents a reversal of all the intercompany entries made on the parent's books during the year and reflected in its net income.

The parent's tax expense is then recomputed with the FSC in place. If all the intercompany entries were made in the parent's books during the year, no further adjustment is necessary. This tax calculation, however, must reflect any collateral tax consequences to the final liability. For example, the foreign tax credit calculation may have to be adjusted to reflect the resourcing of some of the parent's foreign sales.

(c)   Additional FSC Federal Income Tax

The federal income tax expense of the FSC is another cost needed to determine the overall net tax benefit. The specific amount needed is the cash tax expense relating to the FSC's nonexempt FTI. Any tax imposed on investment income is not factored into this analysis, because it is taxed no differently with or without the FSC.

(d)   Additional FSC Foreign Tax

In general, FSCs are organized in low-tax jurisdictions. There is, nevertheless, a small tax liability imposed in most countries. This amount must be factored into the analysis as a direct expense related to the operation of the FSC.

(e)   Additional Costs of Administration

Direct costs of operating the FSC must be included in the analysis. Some of the specific costs that must be factored into the analysis are the office lease expense, management fees paid to representatives in the foreign jurisdictions, and any other sundry office expenses.

1.11   Financial Reporting Benefit

(a)   Effective Tax Rate Reduction

The partial exclusion of FSC FTI is a permanent difference for purposes of the financial statement tax provision. The current year exclusion income will not be reversed back to taxable income in another period. Consequently, the taxpayer obtains a cash tax savings and a reduction in the effective tax rate during the year. This can be particularly important to publicly traded companies where audited financial statements are widely disseminated. Under FASB 109, permanent differences are created when the treatment of transactions for tax purposes is different from their corresponding book (i.e., GAAP) treatment and these difference will not reverse in subsequent periods. In the case of a FSC, the portion of the FTI exempted from U.S. federal income tax will not reverse in a later period. It is a permanent benefit to the taxpayer.

The company's effective tax rate is a particularly important factor in evaluating the company's performance. Exhibit 1.5 illustrates this as follows: Book reported pretax income is 25 million before the FSC operation; results are reflected. Pretax income to which the U.S. federal statutory rate of 35 percent is adjusted to reflect FSC activity between the parent company and the FSC. Income subject to the tax rate is restated as domestic taxable income. Tax is recomputed accordingly, resulting in a lower effective tax rate of 30.435 percent vis à vis the statutory 35 percent.

(b)   Tax Department Effectiveness

The FSC benefit and its favorable effect on cash and book tax expense of the corporate organization represents an accurate measurement of the tax department's ability to work effectively within the corporate organization. Cash and book savings reflect the success of the FSC operation, which, in turn, reflects the ability of the tax department to apply the technicalities of tax law to day-to-day product line operations, enrolling non-tax personnel in the process. Thus, a successful FSC operation, the benefits of which are quantifiable and understood by the corporate or-

Exhibit 1.5

EFFECTIVE TAX RATE RECONCILIATION

	Parent ($)	FSC ($)	Elimination ($)	Total ($)
Book Income (before FSC)	25,000,000			25,000,000
Commission Expense	(5,000,000)	5,000,000		0
Intercompany Dividend	3,260,870		(3,260,870)	0
Book Income	23,260,870	5,000,000	(3,260,870)	25,000,000
Exempt FTI		(3,260,870)		(3,260,870)
DRD	(3,260,870)			N/A
Taxable Income	20,000,000	1,739,130		21,739,130
Tax @35%	7,000,000	608,695		7,608,695
Effective Rate*				30.43%

*Tax over book income

FSC Income	5,000,000
Federal Income Tax	(1,739,130)
*Earnings & Profits	3,260,870

ganization, are key to the tax department's participation in meeting the corporate organization's strategic goals and vision.

1.12 Conclusion

The practicalities of operating a FSC require extensive collaboration between tax and non-tax departments to marshal the resources of the company. Although a FSC is a tax-oriented structure, it is not designed in its entirety to achieve tax goals. A successful FSC requires input from both tax and non-tax departments.

CHAPTER 2

Election Requirements for Foreign Sales Corporations and Domestic International Sales Corporations

Glenn S. Miller

2.1 Introduction

An existing corporation must make an election to be treated as a foreign sales corporation (FSC), a small FSC, or an interest-charge domestic international sales corporation (DISC). The election must be made during the 90-day period preceding the beginning of the taxable year for which the election is to be effective. This election can be revoked at any time after the first taxable year of the corporation for which the election is effective, provided the corporation terminates the election at any time within the first 90 days of such taxable year. From this simple concept arise numerous complexities that must be fully understood by both tax planners and executives seeking to minimize income taxes on export activities.[1]

2.2 FSC and DISC Elections: General Rules

A corporation must make an election to qualify as a FSC, small FSC, or interest-charge DISC, in addition to meeting a number of organizational requirements. FSC and DISC elections are effective only upon the unanimous consent of all persons who were shareholders of the prospective FSC/DISC as of the first day of the first taxable year for which such election is to be effective.[2] Once consented to, such election will be considered valid for the taxable year of the corporation for which the election is filed and for all succeeding taxable years.

An election may be revoked and FSC/DISC status terminated for any taxable year of the corporation after the first taxable year for which the election is effective. Thus, all FSC/DISC properly filed elections will be effective for at least one

---

[1] There are a number of articles worth reading that discuss the formational requirements of DISCs. The most complete of these is Robert Feinschreiber and Alan Granwell, "Forming a DISC Under the Proposed Regulations, *Business Lawyer.* For a discussion of elections for export benefits, see Robert Feinschreiber, *Domestic International Sales Corporations* (1978), Chapter 2; and *FSC: The Foreign Sales Corporation* (Corporate Tax Press, 1984), Chapter 3.

[2] IRC §§ 927(f)(1)(B) and 992(b)(1)(B).

year. If the election is revoked at any time during the first 90 days of a taxable year, the termination will be effective for that taxable year and for all succeeding taxable years of the corporation (provided, of course, that the election has been in effect for at least one taxable year). If the election is revoked after the close of the first 90 days, the termination will be effective for the next taxable year and for all succeeding taxable years of the corporation.[3]

If a corporation fails to qualify as a FSC, a small FSC, or an interest-charge DISC for five consecutive years as a result of its violating one of the organizational requirements, the corporation's FSC/DISC election will be considered terminated and will not be in effect for any taxable year of the corporation after the fifth taxable year. For example, if a FSC fails to maintain an office outside the United States for five consecutive years, its election will be considered terminated for the sixth taxable year and for all subsequent taxable years unless FSC status is re-elected.[4]

2.3   Electing FSC and DISC Status

(a)   Timing of the Election

The scope of the timing requirements for making FSC and DISC elections depends on whether the corporation making the election is a new corporation or an existing corporation. A corporation electing to be treated as a FSC, a small FSC, or an interest-charge DISC for its *first* taxable year must make an election within 90 days *after* the beginning of that first year by filing IRS Form 8279 (IRS Form 4876-A in the case of an interest-charge DISC). A corporation electing to be treated as a FSC, a small FSC, or an interest-charge DISC for any taxable year other than its first taxable year must make its election during the 90-day period *immediately preceding* the first day of the taxable year in which the election is to be effective.[5]

An exception applies to the 90-day rule for existing corporations that in a prior year elected to be treated as either a FSC or a small FSC and that have continued to be treated as such since that time. These corporations are permitted to elect FSC or small FSC status within the first 90 days of the taxable year to which the election is to apply, provided the corporation terminates the prior FSC or small FSC election within that same 90-day period.[6]

In the event a corporation that has elected FSC, small FSC, or interest-charge DISC status is acquired in a qualified stock purchase,[7] and if an election is effective for that corporation, the corporation must re-elect FSC, small FSC, or interest-charge DISC status (whichever is applicable) no later than the date of the qualified

---

[3] IRC §§ 927(f)(3)(A) and 922(b)(3)(A).

[4] IRC §§ 927(f)(3)(B) and 992(b)(3)(B).

[5] Temp. Reg. § 1.921-1T(b)(1) Q&A-1.

[6] Temp. Reg. § 1.921-1T(b)(1), Q&A-1. *See also* Rev. Rul. 90-108, 1990-2 C.B. 185.

[7] IRC §§ 338(d)(34) and 338(a).

stock purchase election,[8] because the qualified stock purchase election is deemed to terminate all existing elections.[9] The qualified stock purchase treats the corporation as having sold all its assets and treats the corporation as a new corporation that acquired all the assets sold as of the beginning of the day after the acquisition date. The effect of this election is, inter alia, to step up the basis in the corporation's assets.

(b) Obtaining Shareholder Consent

Shareholders must consent to the election for it to be effective. Each person who is a shareholder of the electing corporation as of the beginning of the taxable year in which the election is to be effective must consent to the election in writing. Consent can be given either by signing the statement of consent contained in IRS Form 8279 (FSCs) or 4876-A (interest-charge DISCs) or by drafting a separate statement of consent and attaching it to the form. A shareholder's consent is binding on that shareholder and all transferees of its shares and may not be withdrawn after a valid election is filed by the corporation.

Transfer of shares may require consent of the transferee. If, prior to the first day of the first taxable year for which an *existing* corporation has elected to become a FSC or a DISC, a shareholder of that corporation transfers some or all of its shares without first having consented to the FSC/DISC election, the necessary consent must be given by the recipient of such shares on or before the 90th day after the first day of such taxable year. If, on or before the 90th day after the first taxable year for which a *newly formed* corporation elects to become a FSC or a DISC, a shareholder of that corporation transfers some or all of the shares it held as of the first day of such taxable year (or if the shares are newly issued, at the time the shares were issued) without having consented to the FSC/DISC election, the necessary consent must be given by the recipient of such shares on or before the 90th day after the first day of such taxable year.[10]

(c) Binding Effect

Under most circumstances, a shareholder's consent to a corporation's FSC/DISC election is binding on all future recipients of that shareholder's stock once the corporation has made a valid election, and the recipient need not also consent.[11] However, if the consenting shareholder transfers some or all of its shares prior to the beginning of the first taxable year for which such election becomes effective, the recipient of such shares also must consent to such election on or before the 90th day after the first day of such first taxable year for the election to be ef-

---

[8] IRC § 338(g)(i) and Reg. § 1.338-1(d).

[9] IRC § 338(a)(2).

[10] Reg. § 1.992-2(c) (1) and Reg. § 1.927 (f)-1(a), Q&A-3.

[11] Reg. § 1.927(f)-1(a), Q&A-3; Reg. § 1.992-2(b)(1)(i).

fective.[12] This rule is necessitated by the requirement that consent be given by the shareholder holding the stock as of the first day of the corporation's first taxable year.

If the shares are transferred before the beginning of the taxable year, the consent requirement will not have been met unless the recipient also consents. Although not clear from the regulations, the election of the previously described recipient should be effective only if that recipient holds onto the shares through the first day of the electing corporation's first taxable year. If the first transferee also transfers the shares prior to the beginning of taxable year, the next transferee in line must also consent, and so on.

(d) Form of the Consent

Consent, other than by means of the statement of consent set forth in IRS Form 8279 or IRS Form 4876-A, must be in the form of a statement that is signed by the shareholder (or appropriate officer in the case of a corporate shareholder) and that sets forth:

1. The name and address of the corporation and of the shareholder, and
2. The number of shares held by each such shareholder as of the time consent is given and (if consent is given after the beginning of the corporation's taxable year for which the election is effective) as of the beginning of such year.

If consent is given by the recipient of transferred shares, the statement of consent also must include the names and addresses of the person or persons who held the shares as of the beginning of the taxable year, and the number of such shares.[13]

The deadline for obtaining shareholder consent is, by default, the same as the deadline for filing the FSC/DISC election. Such election will not be effective unless all shareholders sign either the statement of consent on IRS Form 8279/4876-A or a separate statement of consent and attach it to this form. Where some of the electing corporation's shares have been transferred prior to the beginning of the corporation's taxable year, however, the due date for shareholder consent is 90 days *after* the beginning of the corporation's taxable year, even where the due date for the election is the end of the 90-day period *prior* to the beginning of the corporation's taxable year.

(e) Consent

Extensions of time for obtaining shareholder consent are available in limited circumstances. An election for which there has been a failure to attach the consent

---

[12] Reg. § 1.927(f)-1, Q&A-4.

[13] Reg. § 1.992-2(b)(1)(ii).

of a shareholder, or to comply with the 90-day requirements reserved for transferred shares, will not be invalid provided:

1. The taxpayer can show to the satisfaction of the Service Center that there was reasonable cause for the failure to consent, and
2. The delinquent shareholder files the proper consent within the boundaries of any extension granted by the IRS.

In the event a notice of consent is filed late, a copy of the IRS form on which the election was made or a statement of election must be attached to the form of consent and filed with the same Service Center with which the election was filed.[14]

In addition to properly electing FSC/DISC status and obtaining shareholder consents, a corporation must also meet various organizational requirements for an election to be effective.

(f) FSC Requirements

To elect FSC status, a corporation must meet a number of organizational requirements. First, the corporation must be created or organized under the laws of either (1) a foreign country that has in effect certain bilateral or multilateral agreements with the United States or an income tax treaty with the United States meeting certain standards relating to exchange of information requirements, or (2) a possession of the United States.

In addition, the corporation must not have more than 25 shareholders at any time during the taxable year, and may not have preferred stock outstanding during the taxable year. The corporation must also maintain a set of the corporation's permanent books of account (including invoices) at an office located in any foreign country in which a FSC could properly be organized (such as a U.S. possession). It also must maintain, at a location within the United States, the records which such corporation is required to keep under IRC § 6001. Finally, at all times during the taxable year, it must have a board of directors that includes at least one individual who is not a resident of the United States, and it must never be a member of any controlled group of corporations of which a DISC is a member.

To qualify as a small FSC, in addition to satisfying the previously described FSC requirements, a corporation must not be a member, at any time during the taxable year, of a controlled group of corporations that includes a FSC (unless that FSC qualifies as a small FSC).

(g) Interest-Charge DISC Requirements

A corporation must meet a number of organizational requirements to qualify as an interest-charge DISC. Among these requirements is that 95 percent or more of

---

[14] Reg. § 1.992-2(c)(1)(ii).

the gross receipts[15] of the corporation must consist of qualified export receipts.[16] In addition, the adjusted basis of the qualified export assets[17] of the corporation at the close of the taxable year must equal or exceed 95 percent of the sum of the adjusted basis of all assets of the corporation at the close of the taxable year. Moreover, a corporation seeking to be treated as a DISC may not have more than one class of stock, and the par or stated value of its outstanding stock must be at least $2,500 on each day of the taxable year. Finally, the corporation may not be a member of any controlled group of which a FSC is a member.[18]

(h) Violations of Organizational Requirements

The election to be treated as a FSC, a small FSC, or an interest-charge DISC will not be effective if a corporation fails to meet any of the forgoing requirements. For example, if a controlled group of corporations includes a FSC, any election by another member of that group to be treated as a small FSC will not be effective unless the FSC revokes its election.[19] Similarly, if a controlled group of corporations includes a small FSC, any election by another member of the group to be treated as a FSC will not be effective unless the small FSC revokes its election.[20]

On the other hand, if a member of a controlled group has in effect an election to be treated as an interest-charge DISC and another member of the controlled group elects to be treated as a FSC or a small FSC, the interest-charge DISC election will be treated as revoked for all purposes as of the date the FSC/small FSC election is effective.[21] As long as the FSC election is effective, no member of that controlled group may elect to be treated as an interest-charge DISC.

2.4 IRC § 9100 Extensions

The Commissioner has discretion, upon good cause shown, to grant a reasonable extension of the time fixed by regulations or other administrative guidance for making an election under the IRC, provided

1. The time for making the election is not expressly provided by a statute;
2. The request for the extension is filed with the Commissioner before the time fixed for making the election, or within such time thereafter as the Commissioner may consider reasonable under the circumstances, and

---

[15] As defined in IRC § 993(f).

[16] As defined in IRC § 993(a).

[17] As defined in IRC § 993(b).

[18] IRC § 992(a)(1).

[19] Reg. § 1.927(f)-1(a), Q-8.

[20] Reg. § 1.927(f)-1(a), Q-9.

[21] Reg. § 1.927(f)-1(a), Q&A-7.

3. It is shown to the satisfaction of the Commissioner that granting the extension will not jeopardize the interests of the government.[22]

Because the time limits for making FSC and DISC elections are contained in the Treasury Regulations, the Commissioner has discretionary authority to grant time extensions to taxpayers upon a showing of good cause. Requests for an extension of time to make an election should be addressed to:

Associate Chief Counsel (International)
Internal Revenue Service
P.O. Box 7604
Ben Franklin Station
Washington, DC 20044

Although the statutes provide certain deadlines for making FSC and DISC elections, these sections enable the Secretary of the Treasury to give consent (through regulations) to making elections at such other times as the Secretary may designate.

(a) Factors Affecting an Extension

Rev. Proc. 92-85[23] sets forth the factors that the IRS will consider in determining, under the facts and circumstances of each situation, whether a taxpayer has shown good cause for the granting of an extension. Basically, the IRS will look at whether the taxpayer that failed to make an election took reasonable actions and demonstrated good faith, and whether granting relief will be prejudicial to the interests of the government. Under Rev. Proc. 92-85 a taxpayer will normally be deemed to have acted reasonably and in good faith if the taxpayer applies for relief under this section before the failure to make the election is discovered by the IRS.

Where a taxpayer's failure to make an election is first discovered by the IRS, the taxpayer still will be deemed to have acted reasonably and in good faith if:

1. The taxpayer inadvertently failed to make the election because of certain intervening events beyond the taxpayer's control or, because after exercising reasonable diligence (taking into account the taxpayer's experience and the complexity of the return or issue), the taxpayer was unaware of the necessity of the election,

2. The taxpayer reasonably relied on the written advice of the IRS, or

3. The taxpayer reasonably relied on a qualified tax professional, and the tax professional failed to make or advise the taxpayer to make the election.

---

[22] IRC § 9100 Treas. Reg. 302.9100.
[23] 1992-2 C.B. 490.

(b)   Reliance

A taxpayer will not be considered to have reasonably relied on a tax professional if:

1.   The taxpayer knew or should have known the tax professional was not competent to render advice on the election, or
2.   The taxpayer knew or should have known the tax professional was not aware of all relevant facts.

Notwithstanding this reliance standard, a taxpayer will *not* be considered to have acted reasonably and in good faith if:

1.   The taxpayer seeks to alter a return position for which an accuracy-related penalty has been or could have been imposed under IRC § 6662 and the new position requires or permits an election for which relief is requested, or
2.   The taxpayer was fully informed of the required election and related tax consequences and chose not to file the election.

In addition, a taxpayer will not be considered to have acted reasonably and in good faith if the taxpayer uses hindsight in requesting relief. If specific facts have changed since the original due date of the election that make an election disadvantageous to a taxpayer, the IRS will not ordinarily grant relief. In such a case, the IRS will grant relief only when the taxpayer provides strong proof that the taxpayer's decision to seek relief did not involve hindsight.

(c)   Requests for Extension

A taxpayer's request for an extension will normally be denied as having prejudiced the interests of government if granting relief would result in a taxpayer's having a lower tax liability in the aggregate for all years to which the election applies, than the taxpayer would have had if the election had been timely filed (taking into account the time value of money) under Rev. Proc. 92-85. Similarly, if the tax consequences of more than one taxpayer are affected by the election, the government's interests will be deemed prejudiced if extending the time for making the election may result in the affected taxpayers, in the aggregate, having a lower tax liability than if the election had been timely filed.

In addition, the IRS will not ordinarily grant relief when tax years that would have been affected by the election had it been timely made, are closed by the statute of limitations. The IRS may condition a grant of relief on the taxpayer's providing the IRS with a statement from an independent auditor certifying that the requirements are satisfied.

Requests for an extension to file an election must provide evidence that will allow the IRS to evaluate the Rev. Proc. 92-85 factors outlined earlier. In addition to stating when the election was required to be filed and when (if at all) it was actually filed, the taxpayer must submit the following:

1. Any documents relating to the election or application for relief.
2. Where requested, a copy of the taxpayer's income tax return for the taxable year for which the taxpayer requests an extension and any subsequent returns affected by the election.
3. Where applicable, a copy of the returns of other taxpayers affected by the election.

(d) Affidavits

The taxpayer (or the individual who acts on behalf of the taxpayer with respect to tax matters) must also provide a detailed affidavit describing the events that led to the failure to file a valid election and to the discovery of that failure. Included must be complete information on any professional advice relied on, the engagement and responsibilities of the professional, and a description of the extent to which the taxpayer relied on the professional. Finally, the taxpayer must provide detailed affidavits from individuals having knowledge or information about the events that led to the failure to make a valid election. These include individuals who made a substantial contribution to the preparation of the taxpayer's return and any other accountant or attorney, knowledgeable in tax matters, who advised the taxpayer with regard to the election.

(e) Extension Requests: Examples

The following are representative examples of situations where the Commissioner has granted an extension for filing a FSC/DISC election:

1. Where the chief financial officer of a parent corporation (later terminated) failed to file an election to treat a subsidiary corporation as a FSC, and application for relief was made before such failure to file was discovered by the IRS.[24]
2. Where a taxpayer that was a validly elected FSC was moved from Country A to Country B, the assistant treasurer of the taxpayer misunderstood a letter from an advisor to mean that the move was by way of an "F" reorganization and failed to re-elect FSC status on that understanding, and where relief was requested before the failure to file was discovered.[25]
3. Where an advisor (who was responsible for making a FSC election for a taxpayer) drafted a letter to the IRS that he erroneously believed served as a valid substitute for IRS Form 8279 (a copy of which he could not find), and

---

[24] LTR 9537023 (June 20, 1995).
[25] LTR 9537022 (June 20, 1995).

an application for relief was filed before the IRS discovered that the letter did not constitute a valid election.[26]

4. Where a parent corporation engaged another corporation, Corporation X, to assist it in the incorporation of a FSC in the Virgin Islands for the taxable year ending December 31, 1992, the IRS informed the taxpayer (the purported FSC) that it had no record of IRS Form 8279 being filed, and Corporation X found the signed (but mistakenly never mailed) form in its files.[27]

5. Where a CPA of a small FSC desiring to convert to large FSC status revoked the small FSC election but failed to file a FSC election, under the erroneous assumption that FSC status was automatically elected upon termination, and relief was requested before the failure to file was discovered.[28]

(f) Extension Requests: Prior Law

The following are representative examples of situations before the publication of Rev. Proc. 92-85, where the Commissioner granted an extension for filing a FSC/DISC election. Their continuing validity is questionable where the holding of the ruling conflicts with Rev. Proc. 92-85:

1. Where a CPA erroneously advised a taxpayer that it should elect to be treated as a small FSC and the CPA took responsibility for the mistake, the taxpayer was granted an additional 30 days to file the large FSC election.[29]

2. Where an associate in a law firm failed to file Form 4876 when required to properly make a DISC election and the parent of the DISC discovered the omission 14 months after the election was supposed to have been filed, the taxpayer was granted an additional 30 days to file the election.[30]

3. Where an individual associated with a small FSC that desired to switch to large FSC status terminated the small FSC but failed to file a FSC election under the erroneous assumption that FSC status was automatically elected upon termination, the FSC was granted an additional 30 days to make the election.[31]

4. A taxpayer instructed a CPA 1 to prepare a FSC election that would ensure the maximum benefit to the taxpayer. The CPA 1 advised the taxpayer to elect small FSC status. The election was supposed to take effect for Year X. It was filed late, however, and first took effect for Year Y. The taxpayer

---

[26] LTR 9506042 (Nov. 16, 1994).

[27] LTR 9443037 (Aug. 1, 1994).

[28] LTR 9325020 (March 24, 1993). For other examples of rulings whereby extensions were granted, *see* LTR 9537021 (June 20, 1995); LTR 9506045 (Nov. 17, 1994); LTR 9506043 (Nov. 16, 1994); LTR 9506041 (Nov. 16, 1994); LTR 9506026 (Nov. 8, 1994); LTR 9450011 (Sept. 14, 1994); and LTR 9423011 (March 8, 1994).

[29] LTR 9051040 (Sept. 26, 1990).

[30] LTR 8251103 (Sept. 22, 1982).

[31] LTR 9103029 (Oct. 23, 1990).

discovered that CPA 1 was not qualified and retained CPA 2. CPA 2 advised the taxpayer that large FSC status, rather than small FSC status, should have been elected. CPA 1 took full responsibility for the erroneous small FSC election. The taxpayer was granted an additional 30 days to make a large FSC election for Year Y.[32]

2.5   Terminating FSC and DISC Elections

(a)   Voluntary Terminations

An election to be treated as a FSC, small FSC, or interest-charge DISC may be terminated by the voluntary revocation of the election for any taxable year of the corporation after the first taxable year for which the election is effective.[33] To terminate the election for a given taxable year and all future taxable years, the termination must be made on or before the first 90 days of such year. If the termination is made after the close of the first 90 days of a taxable year, the election will be effective for the succeeding taxable year and all future taxable years.

Terminating the election is achieved by filing a statement that the corporation revokes its election to be treated as a FSC, small FSC, or interest-charge DISC. Such a revocation statement must contain the corporation's name, address, employer identification number, and the first taxable year for which the revocation is to be effective. The statement must be signed by an authorized person and filed with the Service Center with which the corporation filed its return. However, if a DISC filed an annual information return under IRC § 6601(e)(2), the revocation should be filed with the Service Center where its last return was filed.[34] All revocations of FSC/DISC elections are effective for the entire taxable year.[35]

(b)   Automatic Terminations

A corporation's election to be treated as a FSC, small FSC, or interest-charge DISC will be terminated automatically by the corporation's failure to meet the requirements of FSC, small FSC, or interest-charge DISC status for five consecutive years.[36] In this event, the election will not be in effect for any taxable year after the fifth taxable year.

(c)   Acquisitions

In addition, there are a number of automatic terminations that result from transactions involving FSCs, small FSCs, and interest-charge DISCs. A FSC and a small

---

[32] LTR 9051040 (Sept. 26, 1990). *See also* LTR 8126049 (March 31, 1981); LTR 8147067 (Aug. 26, 1981); LTR 8302070 (Oct. 12, 1982); and LTR 8729026 (April 19, 1987).

[33] Reg. § 1.927(f)-1(b), Q&A-11.

[34] Reg. § 1.927 (f)-1(b), Q&A-14; Reg. § 1.992-2 (e)(2). The Service Center will normally be Philadelphia.

[35] Reg. § 1.927(f)-1(b), Q&A-13.

[36] IRC §§ 927(f)(3)(B) and 992(b)(3)(B).

FSC may not be members of the same controlled group. Termination is automatic when a small FSC ("target") is acquired by another corporation ("acquirer") and either the acquirer or a member of its controlled group is a FSC, unless the corporations in the controlled group elect to terminate the FSC elections contained within the controlled group.

Similarly, if a FSC target is acquired by an acquirer, and either the acquirer or a member of its controlled group is a small FSC, unless the small FSC elections contained within the controlled group are terminated prior to the acquisition, the target's FSC election will automatically terminate as of the day prior to the date the target and the acquirer become members of the same controlled group. If the target was a small FSC and terminated the election, the target would receive FSC benefits for the period prior to termination. The $5 million small FSC limitation would be reduced proportionately by the number of days remaining in the taxable year at the time of the termination. For example, if one fourth of the taxable year had elapsed prior to the termination, the $5 million limit would be reduced by three fourths to $1.25 million.

(d) Interest-Charge DISCs

A FSC or a small FSC cannot be a member, at any time during the taxable year, of any controlled group of corporations of which an interest-charge DISC is a member. Therefore, if any controlled group of corporations of which an interest-charge DISC is a member establishes a FSC or a small FSC, the interest-charge DISC will be treated as having terminated its status as an interest-charge DISC as of the date the FSC or small FSC election is effective.[37] This treatment is to be contrasted with the treatment of FSCs (or small FSCs) where a member of the same controlled group attempts to elect small FSC (or FSC) status. In this situation, rather than the existing elections being terminated (as in the case of existing interest-charge DISC elections), the new election will be deemed ineffective unless the existing FSCs (or small FSCs) first terminate their elections.[38]

In the event an interest-charge DISC election is terminated, the $10 million qualified export receipts limitation of the DISC will be reduced proportionately by the number of days remaining in the taxable year at the time of the termination.[39] For example, if one fourth of the taxable year had elapsed prior to the termination, the $10 million limit would be reduced by three-fourths to $2.5 million.

(e) Qualified Stock Purchases

The election is terminated if a corporation that has elected FSC, small FSC, or interest-charge DISC status, or a shareholder of that corporation, is acquired in a qualified stock purchase under IRC § 338(d)(3), and if an election is made under

---

[37] Reg. § 1.927(f)-1(a), Q&A-7.

[38] Reg. § 1.927(f)-1(a), Q&A-8, Q&A-9.

[39] Prop. Reg. § 1.995-8(a).

IRC § 338(a). As a result, the corporation would have to re-elect FSC, small FSC, or interest-charge DISC status (whichever is applicable) not later than the date of the election under IRC § 338(a). Otherwise, a new election would have to be filed within the 90-day period prior to the start of the next taxable year of the FSC/DISC. FSC/DISC status could be interrupted for up to a year, depending on the taxable year of the FSC/DISC.[40]

(f)   Alternative to Terminating FSC/DISC Election

Taxpayers preparing to terminate a FSC election should consider whether an alternative is possible. A taxpayer may wish to terminate the FSC election to minimize the amount of export income attributable to the FSC, for example, to improve its foreign tax credit position, as discussed in Section 2.7. Instead, the taxpayer should consider whether amending its franchise agreement with the FSC/DISC to minimize the amount of export income run through the FSC/DISC can achieve the same effect of terminating the FSC election. This technique would leave the FSC/DISC election intact and allow the taxpayer to use the FSC/DISC again if the need arises, without meeting the various requirements for reelecting FSC/DISC status.

2.6   Taxable Year Issues

The decision to elect or terminate FSC, small FSC, or interest-charge DISC status may raise taxable-year issues. Of initial concern, the accounting period of a FSC, small FSC, or interest-charge DISC must be the same as that of its "principal shareholder."[41] A principal shareholder is the shareholder with the largest percentage of voting power of the FSC, small FSC, or interest-charge DISC. If two or more shareholders could be the principal shareholder (i.e., they have equal voting power and no other shareholder has more voting power), the FSC/DISC may use the fiscal year of either shareholder.[42] If the principal shareholder changes its accounting period, the FSC/DISC must change its accounting period to conform to the change. The FSC/DISC does not need to obtain IRS consent to conform its accounting period to that of its principal shareholder.[43]

(a)   Reduction in Shareholding

If the voting power of the principal shareholder is reduced by an amount equal to at least 10 percent of the total shares entitled to vote, and such shareholder is no longer the principal shareholder, the FSC/DISC must conform its accounting pe-

---

[40] Temp. Reg. § 1.921-1T(b), Q&A-1.

[41] IRC § 441(h)(1); Temp. Reg. 1.921-1T(b)(4), Q-4.

[42] IRC § 441(h)(2).

[43] Temp. Reg. § 1.921-1T(b)(4), Q&A-4.

riod to that of the new principal shareholder. However, in determining whether a shareholder is a principal shareholder, the voting power of the shareholders is determined as of the beginning of the FSC's taxable year.

For example, assume that for Year 1 a FSC adopts a calendar year period as its annual accounting period to conform to that of its principal shareholder. If in March of Year 1, there is a 10 percent change in voting control and a shareholder whose annual accounting period begins on July 1 becomes the new principal shareholder, the FSC would not be required to adopt the annual accounting period of the new principal shareholder until July 1 of Year 2. The FSC will have a short period for the period January 1 to June 30 of Year 2.

(b) Short Periods

If the termination of a small FSC or interest-charge DISC election is effective at any time other than the end of the corporation's taxable year, a short period will result if the small FSC or interest-charge DISC must change its fiscal year, either as a consequence of the initial FSC/DISC election or upon a change in the taxable year of its principal shareholder.[44] Short periods can produce some unusual tax consequences for FSCs and DISCs.

For example, assume that a corporation is organized on January 1 and mistakenly indicates on its IRS Form SS-4 that its taxable year will end December 31. The principal shareholder of this corporation has a taxable year that ends on January 31. If the corporation decides to elect FSC status, it would have 90 days to make the election and obtain shareholder consent—a time well after the corporation's first taxable year would have closed, that is, on January 31, assuming the corporation's taxable year conformed to that of its principal shareholder as required under the IRC.

Although this result is unusual, it should not cause the corporation any real problems. The date on which the FSC's first income tax return is due, and the point at which a corporation's taxable year normally is established, would not occur until the 15th day of the third month following the close of its taxable year (April 15).[45] This date will occur after the deadline for the FSC election. When the corporation files its return (assuming a FSC election was made within 90 days of January 1), it would state that it adopted the taxable year of its principal shareholder, and that the period from January 1 to January 31 is a short period. The FSC election would relate back to January 1 and be in full force and effect for future years.

(c) Binding Effect

A DISC/FSC will not be bound by the statement of taxable year required on Form SS-4 (application for taxpayer identification number), Form 8279 (FSC election), or Form 4876-A (interest-charge DISC election) under the reasoning of Rev.

---

[44] A "short period" is defined generally in IRC § 443 as a return covering a period of less than 12 months.

[45] IRC § 6072(b).

Rul. 73-81, 1973-1 C.B. 357. In Rev. Rul. 73-81, a taxpayer elected on Form 4876 to be treated as a DISC and indicated it would use a taxable year ending December 31 for filing its annual returns. The management of the DISC later decided that it wished to employ a taxable year ending March 31. The IRS ruled that the taxable year of a corporation is established by the filing of an annual return and that the DISC was free to adopt any taxable year consistent with the principles of IRC § 441, and that the DISC election was valid despite the erroneous tax year listed on Form 4876. The same principles contained in Rev. Rul. 73-81 as to Form 4876 are equally applicable to the statement of taxable year required to be made on Form SS-4, 8279 and 4876-A.

(d) Proration for Small FSCs and DISCs

If either a small FSC or an interest-charge DISC files its return for a short period, it will be necessary to prorate the $5 million foreign trading gross receipts limitation of the small FSC and the $10 million qualified export receipts limitation of the interest-charge DISC according to the number of days the small FSC or interest-charge DISC was in existence during the short period. For example, if a corporation was a small FSC for 87 days at the time its small FSC election was deemed terminated as a result of its acquisition by a FSC, the $5 million foreign trading gross receipts limitation for the time it was a small FSC would be reduced to 87/365 of $5 million, or $1,191,780.

A number of complexities arise if a short-period small FSC or interest-charge DISC is a member of a controlled group containing other small FSCs/interest-charge DISCs. All small FSCs in a controlled group as of December 31 are limited to one $5 million limitation amount for each of their taxable years that include December 31. The amount of the $5 million limitation must be apportioned equally among the various small FSCs unless all the member small FSCs consent to an "apportionment plan" providing for an unequal apportionment of the $5 million limitation.[46]

(e) Apportionment of the $5 Million FSC Amount

Where the taxable year including December 31 of any member small FSC is a short period, the portion of the $5 million allocated to that member is reduced in the manner described earlier. This would suggest that any controlled group including one or more small FSCs with a short period should adopt an apportionment plan (rather than allow an equal allocation of the $5 million limitation) and should structure the apportionment plan so as to allocate as little of the $5 million as possible to the small FSCs with short periods. This would tend to minimize the amount disallowed.

---

[46] Temp. Reg. § 1.924(a)-1T(j)(2). This apportionment plan must satisfy the requirements of and be filed in the manner specified in Reg. § 1.1561-3(b).

If a small FSC has a short taxable year that does not include a December 31, and that small FSC is a member of a controlled group of corporations that includes one or more other small FSCs as to that short taxable year, the available limitation for the short year of that small FSC is determined by:

1.   Dividing $5 million by the number of FSCs that are members of that group on the last day of the short taxable year, and

2.   Prorating the remaining amount according to the amount of days in the short taxable year.[47]

For example, if the last day of a short taxable year is November 30 and on that date there are five small FSCs in the group of corporations, then $1 million of the limitation will be available to the particular small FSC and prorated according to the number of days in its short taxable year.

(f)   Apportionment of the $10 Million DISC Amount

All interest-charge DISCs in a controlled group as of December 31 are limited to one $10 million limitation amount for their taxable years that include December 31.[48] As in the case of small FSCs in a controlled group, the IRS has proposed that the $10 million limitation be apportioned equally among the member DISCs in the controlled group for their taxable years including December 31, unless all member DISCs consent to an apportionment plan providing for an unequal allocation of the $10 million limitation. If any of the member DISCs' taxable years is a short period, the portion of the $10 million allocated to that DISC will be reduced in the same manner as for short-period small FSCs in a controlled group.

In keeping with the parallel treatment of small FSCs and interest-charge DISCs, if an interest-charge DISC has a short taxable year that does not include a December 31, and that DISC is a member of a controlled group of corporations that includes one or more other DISCs for that short taxable year, the available limitation for the short year of that interest-charge DISC is determined by:

1.   Dividing $10 million by the number of interest-charge DISCs that are members of that group on the last day of the short taxable year, and

2.   Prorating the remaining amount according to the number of days in the short taxable year.[49]

The planning technique described in the preceding paragraphs would also apply to interest-charge DISCs.

---

[47] Temp. Reg. § 1.924(a)-1T(j)(2)(iii).

[48] Prop. Reg. § 1.995-8(f).

[49] Prop. Reg. § 1.995-8(f)(3).

2.7   Effect of Foreign Tax Credit Considerations

An exporter is frequently faced with the question of whether the FSC provisions will be more beneficial to that exporter than the foreign tax credit provisions, given the exporter's tax position. Since the Tax Reform Act of 1986, multinational corporations have been burdened with increasing amounts of excess foreign tax credits. This, in turn, has encouraged multinationals to seek ways to increase foreign source income to increase their foreign tax credit limitation.

Additional foreign source income increases the amount of the taxpayer's foreign tax credit limitation, thereby freeing up excess foreign tax credits which can be used to offset federal income taxes that otherwise would have been imposed on the additional income. The basic formula for determining a taxpayer's foreign tax credit limitation is as follows:

$$\frac{\text{Taxable income from foreign sources}}{\text{Worldwide taxable income}} \times \text{U.S. taxes imposed}$$

As can be seen from this formula, increasing the amount of foreign source income increases the numerator and denominator of the fraction, thereby increasing the amount of the foreign tax credit limitation and freeing up excess tax credits.

For example, assume a taxpayer has $100 in foreign source taxable income and $1,000 in worldwide taxable income. If a total of $350 in U.S. taxes was imposed (assuming a 35 percent marginal tax rate), the foreign tax credit limitation would be $35. If the taxpayer earned an additional $100 in foreign source income, the foreign tax credit limitation would increase to $70 (200/1100 × (350 + 35)). Therefore, the $35 in federal income taxes imposed on the $100 in foreign source income would be offset by the additional $35 in foreign tax credits that would now be useable.

Because the foreign tax credit limitation acts to reduce the creditability of foreign taxes paid, multinationals may well find that the tax benefits offered by a FSC outweigh the foreign tax credit benefits of exporting through a foreign subsidiary, paying foreign taxes, and seeking a foreign tax credit in the United States.

The tension between the FSC and foreign tax credit provisions can create a timing problem for the multinational, however. For example, although a multinational can delay making an election to terminate an existing FSC (or to elect FSC status for a newly formed corporation) until up to 90 days after the beginning of a FSC's taxable year, this may not give the multinational adequate time to determine whether FSC status is desirable. Past IRS rulings have suggested that multinationals have some leeway to change some or all of their elections after the normal election deadline—in effect, to increase or decrease the amount of income run through the FSC—once the multinational has a better idea of which structure would produce the most favorable tax results.[50]

---

[50] *See, for example,* LTR 9029068 (April 27, 1990) and LTR 9051040 (Sept. 26, 1990), in which taxpayers were permitted to reverse certain prior elections even though it would improve their tax position.

Rev. Proc. 92-85 will probably curtail substantially the practice of corporations waiting to make an election until the tax consequences of that election are clear. Section 5.02(1) of Rev. Proc. 92-83 could treat delaying the election as prejudicial to the interests of the government, and section 5.01(4)(B), which pertain to whether the taxpayer learned of the need for the election but chose not to make it, and 5.01(5), which pertain to whether the taxpayer used hindsight in requesting relief, could cause the corporation's action to be treated as being made in bad faith. There would now appear to be a significant risk that a corporation that adopted a "wait and see" approach in failing to file the FSC/DISC election on time would not be granted an extension.

2.8 Conclusion

The election requirements for a DISC or FSC can become complex in situations in which shareholding is other than with a single corporate shareholder; or where trusts, estates, partnerships, or other noncorporate forms are the owners of the DISC or FSC. The time periods are limited, and the IRS is unable to provide the taxpayer with leniency except for IRC 9100 relief.

CHAPTER 3

Foreign Trading Gross Receipts

Stanley G. Sherwood
Robert C. DeGaudenzi

3.1   Introduction

A foreign sales corporation (FSC) is required to have "foreign trading gross receipts" (FTGR), which are gross receipts from its qualifying export activities.[1] The "receipts" requirement is particularly important since its application has a direct impact on the maximization of the potential tax benefit.[2] The FTGR rules seem quite burdensome on the surface, but on closer examination it becomes apparent that U.S. exporters can qualify their normal export sales as FTGR with little additional work, provided they properly plan for and document the satisfaction of certain requirements.

FTGR are receipts from one of the following five activities:

1. The sale, exchange, or other disposition of export property,
2. The lease or rental of export property for use outside the United States,
3. Services related and subsidiary to the sale, exchange, or other disposition of export property, or lease or rental of export property,
4. Engineering or architectural services for construction projects located outside the United States, or

---

[1] Robert Feinschreiber, *FSC: The Foreign Sales Corporation* (Corporate Tax Press, 1984).

[2] Robert Feinschreiber, *Transfer Pricing Handbook* (New York: John Wiley & Sons, 1993), Chapter 13.

5. Under certain circumstances, managerial services performed for an unrelated FSC or interest-charge domestic international sales corporation (DISC).

This chapter focuses primarily on the FTGR requirement under the FSC rules. However, the legal authorities cited and discussed are generally applicable to both the FSC and the DISC regimes (both current and former DISCs). Under DISC rules, the analogous concept to FTGR is "qualified export receipts."[3] Certain elements that comprise the FTGR requirement are the same under both the FSC and DISC rules, because FSC rules were essentially patterned after DISC rules, with modifications to satisfy certain objections raised as to the original DISC regime by members of the General Agreement on Tariffs and Trade (GATT).[4] In fact, the legislative history of the FSC FTGR requirement cites the Internal Revenue Code provisions relating to DISC in describing the categories of qualifying activities. Because of their unified origin, both sets of rules frequently use the same terminology, such as "export property"; export property is essentially the same for FSC and DISC purposes.

3.2 Foreign Trading Gross Receipts

An FSC seeking FTGR must earn gross receipts relating to qualifying export activities, such as the sale or exchange, or the lease or rental, of export property. The concept of "export property" is discussed in detail in Section 3.3. The term *gross receipts* broadly encompasses all gross income "from whatever source derived."[5] Thus, gross receipts includes both income derived in the ordinary course of the FSC's business and other types of income, such as, passive-type income (e.g., dividends, interest, gains derived on the sale of property, etc.).[6] The method of accounting used to compute taxable income by the FSC or a related party of the FSC, as applicable, should be used in determining when any amounts received or accrued from income should be treated as gross receipts.[7]

The calculation of *gross* receipts, as the term denotes, does not include any reductions for items such as cost of goods sold or any other expenses or deductible items. In addition, gross receipts should not include proceeds received from the repayment of a loan or in connection with contributions to capital or exchanges of property for stock.[8] However, gross receipts should be reduced for any returns and allowances from the sale of export property.[9]

---

[3] *See* IRC § 993(a)(1).

[4] *See* Robert Feinschreiber, *Domestic International Sales Corporations* (New York: Practicing Law Institute, 1978).

[5] Temp. Treas. Reg. § 1.927(b)-1T(b); Treas. Reg. § 1.993-6(b).

[6] Temp. Treas. Reg. § 1.927(b)-1T(a); Treas. Reg. § 1.993-6(a).

[7] Temp. Treas. Reg. § 1.927(b)-1T(d); Treas. Reg. § 1.993-6(d).

[8] Temp. Treas. Reg. § 1.927(b)-1T(b); Treas. Reg. § 1.993-6(b).

[9] Temp. Treas. Reg. § 1.927(b)-1T(c); Treas. Reg. § 1.993-6(c).

A FSC will be considered to have FTGR if it satisfies the foreign presence test, foreign management test, or the foreign economic processes tests. The foreign management and foreign economic processes tests appear to be quite complex. A foreign corporation that elects to be treated as a small FSC is not required to satisfy the foreign management and foreign economic processes tests to earn FTGR. Rather, a small FSC need only satisfy the foreign presence test. The following subsection provides a discussion and analysis of the relevant requirements relating to the different categories of FTGR.

(a)   Sale or Exchange of Export Property

The sale or exchange of export property is the most common type of FTGR, and this category includes gross receipts derived from the sale, exchange, or other disposition of export property.[10] The definition of "export property" is the subject of Section 3.3.

A FSC may function as either a "buy/sell" FSC or, alternatively, as a "commission FSC." A buy/sell FSC functions as a trading company, buying products from either its U.S. parent corporation or other affiliate (in either case, commonly referred to under the FSC rules as the "related supplier") and selling to foreign customers. A FSC can function as an agent, earning a commission for services rendered in connection with the principal's export sales (a so-called commission FSC), which is much more common. Unlike a buy/sell FSC, which does take title, a commission FSC never takes title to the goods.[11] Certain foreign countries have an antideferral tax regime, and FSCs may be within its ambit, especially if the FSC operates on a commission basis.

(i)   Commission FSC.   A commission FSC will obtain FSC benefits only if its activities relate to arranging for the sale of export property to foreign customers for goods manufactured or purchased by its related supplier. The export sale to which the FSC's commission relates will be considered FTGR, provided the other requirements are satisfied. In contrast, any commissions paid to a FSC by a foreign customer in compensation for arranging for the purchase (as opposed to arranging for the sale) of goods manufactured in the United States will not qualify for FSC benefits. Thus, for example, a FSC cannot function as a buying agent for foreign purchasers of goods manufactured by unrelated parties in the United States.

In Revenue Ruling 73-338,[12] a DISC entered into a commission agreement with a related foreign corporation whereby such foreign corporation paid the DISC a commission for arranging for the purchase of goods manufactured by third-party

---

[10] IRC § 924(a)(1); IRC § 993(a)(1)(A).

[11] Unless otherwise noted, the FSC rules discussed in this chapter do not distinguish between commission and buy/sell FSCs.

[12] 1976-2 C.B. 233.

U.S. manufacturers. The IRS concluded that the income did not constitute qualified export receipts since it arose in connection with the *purchase* of property rather than from the *sale* of property in the ordinary course of trade or business.[13] A ruling held that commission paid to a DISC in connection with the DISC's arranging for the *purchase* of property by a foreign party did not give rise to qualified export receipts. Where, in substance, a DISC earns a commission for arranging for the *purchase* of property for a foreign party, no qualified export receipts are earned.

(ii) Title Considerations. Most FSCs are structured as commission FSCs rather than buy/sell FSCs. A primary reason for this practice is that a commission FSC can be virtually transparent from a business and operational perspective. In the case of a commission FSC, title to the exported products passes directly from the related supplier to the foreign purchaser. A commission FSC's FTGR is generated by reference to the sales of the related supplier to the foreign purchaser, which can include a related party subsidiary. If a buy/sell FSC is used, however, title is transferred to the FSC and then from the FSC to the foreign purchaser. Because a buy/sell FSC's FTGR are determined by reference to the FSC's sales to foreign purchasers, an additional issue raised in the context of buy/sell FSCs is whether the FSC's sales will be respected as such or, alternatively, recharacterized for tax purposes as, for example, a financing transaction.

A 1987 IRS private letter held that a buy/sell FSC did not have FTGR notwithstanding its ostensibly qualifying export sales.[14] The FSC did not bear the benefits and burdens of ownership regarding the property purchased and then sold to foreign customers. The "sales" made by the FSC were not sufficiently bona fide to constitute actual sales. Rather, the FSC's role under the facts of the ruling was that of a secured lender. Accordingly, because the FSC functioned as a lender, it did not generate any FTGR. However, the IRS carefully noted that the holding did not apply to FSCs structured as commission FSCs.

(iii) Related and Unrelated Foreign Parties. A FSC can derive FTGR from export sales made to both unrelated and related foreign parties. Since there are no specific prohibitions under the DISC rules regarding related party sales, such sales can generate qualified export receipts.[15] For example, products sold through a FSC to a foreign operating subsidiary (e.g., a distribution or marketing company) of a U.S. parent can generate FTGR. When goods are sold to related foreign customers, the price charged to such foreign affiliates will be subject to the IRC § 482 transfer pricing rules. In general, these rules require that goods sold between related parties be on "arm's-length" terms. Absent a special pricing election (which almost all companies make),[16] the IRC § 482 transfer pricing rules also apply to

---

[13] *Id.; see also* Rev. Rul. 73-228, 1973-1 C.B. 362; Priv. Let. Rul. 83-25-020 (Mar. 15, 1983).

[14] Priv. Let. Rul. 88-03-052 (Oct. 23, 1987).

[15] *See* Tech. Adv. Mem. 81-12-001 (Nov. 13, 1980).

[16] *See* Chapter 8, for a discussion of administrative pricing rules.

the sale or lease of property to a buy/sell FSC, or to the commission earned by a commission FSC. In these cases as well, the sales terms or commissions paid must be on arm's-length terms. To the extent the FSC does not have substantial operations (which generally might well be the case), little profit can be allocated to the FSC under IRC § 482. As noted earlier, however, FSCs can, and in most cases do, elect to apply certain administrative pricing rules that essentially provide "safe harbor" pricing terms. The election to use these rules generally prevents the IRS from challenging the FSC pricing methodology and, in addition, ensures that the FSC earns a sufficient profit to make the FSC tax benefit meaningful.[17]

(iv) Related Supplies. The products sold through a FSC can originate from either the related supplier's own manufacturing operations or, alternatively, from an unrelated U.S. manufacturer. When an exporting company purchases products from a manufacturer, the FSC tax benefit can be effectively split between the U.S. exporter and the manufacturer. The U.S. exporter can obtain FSC tax benefits from the income earned on its export sales through a FSC. Similarly, the U.S. manufacturer can obtain FSC tax benefits on its profits from selling its goods to such U.S. exporter through a FSC, provided certain requirements are satisfied, including that the U.S. exporter sells the goods to a foreign purchaser within one year.

Whether or not such products are purchased or manufactured by the related supplier, the products sold must satisfy a series of tests in order to meet the "export property" requirement. Therefore, if the goods are purchased from an unrelated party, it is generally more difficult to establish compliance with these tests. For example, one of these tests, the "foreign content test," requires that no more than 50 percent of the value of the exported goods relate to imported components. It may be difficult to obtain the necessary proof from the unrelated seller that this test is satisfied, since disclosure of such information may provide insight into the seller's pricing structure and, consequently, its profit margin.

(b) Lease or Rental of Export Property

The lease or rental of export property used predominantly outside the United States provides FSC benefits.[18] In recent years, the leasing of property, such as aircraft or equipment, through a FSC has increased dramatically. Depending on how the deal is structured, the economic benefits that can be achieved through a FSC leasing structure can enure to both the lessees and the investors in the FSC leasing entities. However, because of the complicated rules and requirements applicable to FSCs, the structuring of FSC leasing arrangements requires extremely careful planning.

The FSC, or its principal if the FSC is functioning as a commission agent, must hold the property, either as an owner or a lessee at the beginning of the lease term,

---

[17] *See* Chapter 8 for a discussion of administrative pricing rules.

[18] *See infra* Section 3.3(b) (discussing the foreign use test to qualify as export property).

to generate FTGR. In addition, the FSC must be qualified as such for the year in which the lease begins.[19] An ownership FSC is analogous to a buy/sell FSC, with the difference that an ownership FSC actually takes and maintains title to the leased property as owner, rather than functioning as a trading company. In the context of cross-border aircraft or equipment leases, both commission FSCs as well as so-called ownership FSCs can be used. As discussed in the following paragraphs, the decision as to which structure should be used (commission FSC vs. ownership FSC) can depend on several factors, including the tax posture of the lessor and whether the lessee is a U.S. or foreign person.[20]

(i) Commission FSC. If a FSC is functioning as a commission agent in a leveraged lease transaction, the structure usually involves a U.S. equity investor or U.S. company ("FSC owner/lessor") leasing to either a U.S. or foreign person. The tax consequences and structure are very similar to a standard leverage lease arrangement whereby the lessor finances the acquisition of business property, such as equipment with debt, and then leases such property to another party. Under a standard leverage lease arrangement (without a FSC), the deal would be structured so that the lessor would have, in the initial years, interest expense and accelerated depreciation deductions that would more than offset the lease income, thereby generating a net deductible taxable loss. In later years, when the accelerated depreciation deductions "turn around," the lessor would recognize net taxable income.

If a commission FSC is introduced, the arrangement is generally modified, in that the FSC owner/lessor must now pay a commission to the FSC for services rendered in connection with the lease. Thus, as in standard leveraged leases, the FSC owner/lessor will borrow a substantial portion of the funds needed to purchase business property, which is then leased to an unrelated lessee, with the FSC never taking title to the property. An example of this type of structure is illustrated in Exhibit 3.1.

Under the commission FSC structure, the FSC owner/lessor can claim depreciation deductions on the leased property. The FSC owner/lessor can claim accelerated depreciation deductions if the lessee is a U.S. person.[21] In addition, the FSC owner/lessor will have deductible interest expense on its borrowings to finance the purchase of such property. In fact, as with most leveraged leases, the FSC owner/lessor will likely have a net tax operating loss with respect to the leasing arrangement in the initial years of the lease. To the extent there is no taxable income in the early years of the lease, there can be no FSC tax benefits achieved. It is only when the lease "turns around" and begins to generate positive taxable income that FSC benefits are earned.

If the lessee is a foreign person with no U.S.-related activities, it is likely that only straight-line depreciation will be available to the lessor.[22] Therefore, in these

---

[19] Temp. Treas. Reg. § 1.924(a)-1T(c)(1)(ii); Treas. Reg. § 1.993-1(c)(1)(ii).

[20] *See* Chapter 8 for a discussion of administrative pricing rules and taxable income calculations applicable to commission FSCs vs. ownership FSCs.

[21] *See* IRC § 168(g)(3).

[22] *See* IRC § 168(g)(1)(A).

Exhibit 3.1

EXAMPLE OF COMMISSION FSC LEVERAGED LEASING STRUCTURE

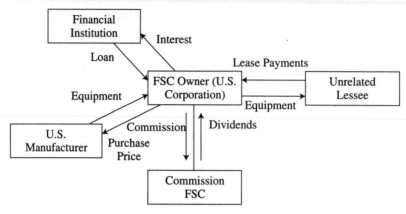

cases, an ownership FSC (discussed in the following paragraph) may prove more tax efficient. Similarly, if the lessor cannot use the additional tax deductions from accelerated depreciation and interest deductions, an ownership FSC may be preferable to a commission FSC.

   (ii)   Ownership FSC.   Unlike a commission FSC, an ownership FSC takes title to the leased property. A typical leveraged leasing structure using an ownership FSC usually involves an equity investor forming a new U.S. special purpose company (SPC). The SPC is financed with capital by the equity investor and funds borrowed from an unrelated financial institution. In practice, although no safe-harbor guidelines exist, it may be possible to capitalize the SPC using a debt-to-equity ratio in the range of 5-to-1. The SPC then forms a FSC and contributes such funds to the FSC. The FSC uses the funds to purchase equipment or aircraft and leases the property to an unrelated lessee. This structure is illustrated in Exhibit 3.2.
   Under the ownership FSC structure described previously, the interest expense on the debt used to purchase the leased property is incurred at the SPC level, while the rental stream is earned at the FSC/lessor level. As under the commission FSC structure, this structure provides the benefit of enabling the SPC to utilize the interest deductions. Presumably, this structure creates a federal tax benefit of 35 percent of such interest payments. At the same time, the associated lease income of the FSC will be subject to federal tax at a rate of approximately 24 percent, provided the IRC § 482 method is used. This 24 percent rate is achieved because, under the IRC § 482 method, 30 percent of the FSC's profit is exempt from federal tax and the remaining 70 percent is subject to the 34 or 35 percent federal rate.

   (iii)   Lease Prepayments.   Lease prepayments may qualify as FTGR payments if it is "reasonably expected" that throughout the term of the lease the leas-

Exhibit 3.2

EXAMPLE OF OWNERSHIP FSC LEVERAGED LEASING STRUCTURE

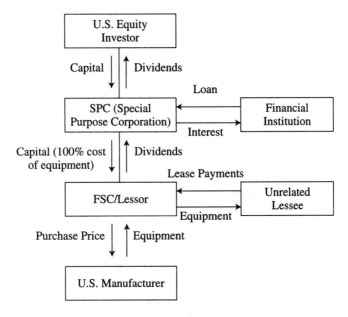

ing structure will qualify for FSC benefits; for example, the leased property will be characterized as export property for the entire lease term, receipts will qualify as FTGR for the entire lease term, and so forth. Thus, for example, if under the terms of a lease, the lessee makes a payment that covers the current year as well as the next year, the entire payment relating to the second year will be FTGR if it is expected that the leasing structure will qualify for FSC benefits for the entire lease period. To the extent it is expected that a particular leasing structure will not qualify for FSC benefits for the entire lease term, then only the portion of any prepayment that relates to the expected qualifying period will qualify for FSC benefits. In the example given, if it was expected at the time of the lease payment that the lease would qualify for FSC benefits only in the current year but not for the next year, then only the portion of the lease payment relating to the first year would be considered FTGR.

(c) Related and Subsidiary Services

A FSC can also generate FTGR by providing services that are considered both "related and subsidiary" to the sale or lease of export property, provided the sale or lease itself generates FTGR.[23] Such services could include, for example, product

---

[23] Temp. Treas. Reg. § 1.924(a)-1T(d); Treas. Reg. § 1.993-1(d).

warranty or repair services. Software maintenance services provided in connection with the export of software can potentially qualify as related and subsidiary services.[24] The regulations permit related and subsidiary services to be performed either within or outside the United States.[25] In addition, the regulations are liberal in their characterization of what services are deemed to be provided by the FSC. Under these rules, a FSC is regarded as providing such services if any of the following persons perform the services:

1. The person who sold or leased the property (e.g., such as the related supplier), provided that the FSC functions as a commission agent for both the sale or lease of the property and for the services

2. Another member of the controlled group to which the FSC belongs, provided the FSC functions as principal or commission agent for the sale or lease of the property and as commission agent for the services, or

3. The FSC as principal, or any other person pursuant to a contract with the FSC, provided the FSC acted as principal or commission agent for the sale or lease of the property.[26]

(i)   Related Supplier.   These guidelines for services are quite broad, but taxpayers must ensure that if the related and subsidiary services are provided by a person other than the FSC, the arrangement clearly falls within the regulatory language provided in the preceding paragraph. Thus, for example, if the person providing such services were to do so pursuant to a contract with only the FSC's *related supplier,* rather than pursuant to a contract with the FSC, such services will likely *not* generate FTGR. This was the result in a DISC Revenue Ruling,[27] in which the IRS held that service engineers acting under contract with a DISC's related supplier did not generate "qualified export receipts." In the ruling, the IRS held that since such engineers were not agents or employees of the DISC, their actions could not be attributed to the DISC for purposes of generating qualified export receipts.

Related and subsidiary services must also be provided by FSC in connection with its own sale or lease of export property or, alternatively, for a commission relating to its related supplier's sale or lease of such property. The mere provision of services "related" to another party's export sales or leasing activities will not qualify as FTGR. For example, in Revenue Ruling 72-580,[28] the IRS held that a freight forwarder's services could not qualify as related services under the DISC rules, since such services were performed for the benefit of unrelated U.S. exporters and did not relate to any sale or lease of export property by the freight forwarder.

---

[24] *See* Cullen A. Duke and Joseph Roth, *Maximizing FSC Benefits for Software Companies.*

[25] Temp. Treas. Reg. § 1.924(a)-1T(d)(1); Treas. Reg. § 1.993-1(d)(1).

[26] Temp. Treas. Reg. § 1.924(a)-1T(d)(2)(i)-(iii); Treas. Reg. § 1.993-1(d)(2)(i)-(iii).

[27] Rev. Rul. 75-332, 1975-2 C.B. 310.

[28] 1972-2 C.B. 459.

(ii) U.S. and Foreign Services. Qualifying related and subsidiary services may be performed either within or outside the United States. If such services are performed in a foreign country, attention must also be given to local country tax considerations. Depending on the circumstances, such services could create a taxable presence (or "permanent establishment" under an applicable treaty) for the FSC or other related person responsible for providing the services. In this case, the FSC or the other related person could be subject to tax in the foreign country where such services are performed for the income attributable to the services. If a local (taxable) presence is found, the FSC tax benefits associated with the provision of related and subsidiary services could be severely eroded by an offsetting foreign tax cost. Given the restrictions on the creditability of foreign income taxes associated with income earned by a FSC, any foreign income tax cost incurred in this regard could represent an incremental cost.[29] Therefore, in structuring a services arrangement to qualify for FSC benefits, taxpayers should carefully regulate the amount of local country services provided with a view toward reducing the exposure to local country taxation. Ideally, professional advice should be sought from both U.S. and foreign tax advisers in order to assess the likelihood and consequences of the proposed services arrangement.

(iii) Related Services. Services are "related" to the sale or lease of export property if they are considered of the type "customarily and usually furnished with the type of transaction in the trade or business in which the sale or lease arose."[30] In addition, to qualify as related services, the contract under which such services are to be rendered must be provided for, either expressly or implied, under the original sale or lease contract.[31] Alternatively, if such provision is not made, the services may nevertheless qualify as related services if the services contract is entered into within two years after the original sale or lease contract is entered into, provided certain other conditions are satisfied.[32]

Related services generally include warranty services, maintenance or repair services, and installation services. Financing services, however, are not considered a related service.

(iv) Subsidiary Services. In addition to being related to the sale or lease of export property, such services in the aggregate must be "subsidiary" to the gross receipts derived from the sale or lease of export property. Related services are subsidiary to the sale or lease of property if it is reasonably expected that, at the time of the original sale or lease, the gross receipts to be derived from all related services provided by the FSC will not exceed 50 percent of the sum of the gross receipts from the sale or lease of the property and the gross receipts from related services.[33]

---

[29] *See* Chapter 1 for a discussion of foreign tax credit analysis in context of FSCs.

[30] Temp. Treas. Reg. § 1.924(a)-1T(d)(3)(i); Treas. Reg. § 1.993-1(d)(3)(i).

[31] Temp. Treas. Reg. § 1.924(a)-1T(d)(3)(ii)(A); Treas. Reg. § 1.993-1(d)(3)(ii)(a).

[32] Temp. Treas. Reg. § 1.924(a)-1T(d)(3)(ii)(B); Treas. Reg. § 1.993-1(d)(3)(ii)(b).

[33] Temp. Treas. Reg. § 1.924-1T(d)(4)(i); Treas. Reg. § 1.993-1(d)(4)(i).

For purposes of applying this test, gross receipts are generally grouped by product line, as determined under the grouping rules applicable to the combined taxable income calculation.[34] In applying this test to the sale of export property, gross receipts from related services for the 10-year period following the sale are considered to be reasonably expected. If the property is leased, reasonable expectations would require that all related services performed up to the end of the lease term (without regard to lease renewals) be considered. In applying this 50 percent test, any amounts stated in a separate services contract or in the original sale or lease contract may not be respected; instead, the determination may be made based on the facts and circumstances.[35]

(d)   Engineering or Architectural Services

Engineering and architectural services provided by a FSC for construction projects located outside the United States provide gross receipts and FTGR.[36] The services may be rendered either within or without the United States. For example, gross receipts relating to engineering services performed by employees of a DISC's related supplier who were not U.S. citizens and who lived outside the United States could still qualify as "qualified export receipts."[37]

Further, the services need not relate to an actual or planned construction project. Thus, even if the services relate to feasibility studies, preliminary analyses, or other anticipatory work, and no project is ultimately commenced, FTGR may still be generated.[38] To qualify as FTGR under this category, the construction project must relate to the erection, expansion, or repair (not including minor remodeling or repairs) of new or existing buildings or other physical facilities, including roads, dams, canals, bridges, and other similar items.[39] In addition, receipts relating to the installation of equipment necessary to perform such activities can qualify as FTGR.

If the equipment is leased, such leasing income will not qualify as FTGR under this category; rather, provided the equipment qualifies as export property, the leasing income may still qualify under the lease or rental category of FTGR.[40] Engineering or architectural services provided by a person other than the FSC are treated as services provided by the FSC if that other person performs the services pursuant to a contract in which the FSC functions either as principal or commission agent.[41]

---

[34] Temp. Treas. Reg. § 1.924(a)-1T(d)(4)(iii); Treas. Reg. § 1.993-1(d)(4)(iii); Temp. Treas. Reg. § 1.925(a)-1T(c)(8); Treas. Reg. § 1.994-1(c)(7) (grouping rules).

[35] Temp. Treas. Reg. § 1.924(a)-1T(d)(4)(ii); Treas. Reg. 1.993-1(d)(4)(ii).

[36] IRC § 924(a)(4); Temp. Treas. Reg. § 1.924(a)-1T(e); IRC § 993(a)(1)(G); Treas. Reg. § 1.993-1(h).

[37] Temp. Treas. Reg. § 1.924(a)-1T(e)(1); Treas. Reg. § 1.993-1(h)(1); *see* Rev. Rul. 75-69, 1975-1 C.B. 253.

[38] Temp. Treas. Reg. § 1.924(a)-1T(e)(2); Treas. Reg. § 1.993-1(h)(2).

[39] Temp. Treas. Reg. § 1.924(a)-1T(e)(8); Treas. Reg. § 1.993-1(h)(8).

[40] *See supra* Section 3.2(b) for discussion of the lease or rental of export property.

[41] Temp. Treas. Reg. § 1.924(a)-1T(e)(7); Treas. Reg. § 1.993-1(h)(7).

(i) **Engineering Services.** Engineering services that qualify to create FTGR include a wide range of activities, which may be performed either within or outside the United States. Examples of such services include the supervision of construction projects to ensure compliance with plans and specifications or investigatory and planning services related to a proposed construction project. Services qualify as engineering services if the services require education, training, and experience in engineering and involve the application of special knowledge involving mathematics, physics, or engineering sciences.[42] Thus, under this standard, engineering-related activities may generate gross receipts that qualify as FTGR.

(ii) **Architectural Services.** Architectural services include many kinds of services.[43] In general, services that may generate FTGR include activities relating to the offering or furnishing of services involving aesthetic or structural design and the supervision of construction projects to ensure compliance with plans, drawings, or specifications.

(iii) **Excluded Services.** Certain services are specifically excluded from qualifying under this category of FTGR: (1) services relating to the exploration of oil or gas and (2) technical assistance or know-how, including activities or programs designed to enable business, commerce, industrial establishments, and government organizations to acquire or use scientific, architectural, or engineering information.[44]

(e) Managerial Services

FTGR also include gross receipts derived by a FSC from managerial services rendered to an unrelated FSC or DISC. Such services may be rendered by the FSC itself or by another person under contract with the service-providing FSC in which that FSC is functioning as either principal or commission agent. "Managerial services" in this context generally include staffing and operational services necessary to operate the unrelated FSC or DISC, not including legal, accounting, scientific, or technical services.[45] The types of services specifically envisioned include the activities required, for example, under the foreign economic process tests (e.g., sending product lists to customers, conducting export market studies, making shipping arrangements, and contacting potential foreign purchasers).[46]

FTGR can be generated by a FSC from managerial services only if at least 50 percent of its total FTGR is derived from the sale or exchange of export property, the lease or rental of export property, or related and subsidiary services relating to

---

[42] Temp. Treas. Reg. § 1.924(a)-1T(e)(5); § 1.993-1(h)(5).

[43] Temp. Treas. Reg. § 1.924(a)-1T(e)(6); § 1.993-1(h)(6).

[44] Temp. Treas. Reg. § 1.924(a)-1T(e)(3); Treas. Reg. § 1.993-1(h)(3).

[45] Temp. Treas. Reg. § 1.924(a)-1T(f)(2); Treas. Reg. § 1.993-1(i)(2).

[46] Temp. Treas. Reg. § 1.924(a)-1T(f)(2); Treas. Reg. § 1.993-1(i)(2).

these two categories. This 50 percent requirement is essentially aimed at ensuring that FSCs do not obtain tax benefits without actually engaging in a significant amount of activities that directly relate to export or export-related activities. The purpose for permitting managerial services to qualify at all as FTGR is probably one of equity and administrative convenience. For a FSC performing such managerial services to obtain FTGR, it must obtain a copy of the unrelated FSC's election to be treated as a FSC together with a sworn statement that the election has been timely filed.[47]

(f) Excluded Receipts

To effectuate certain policy objectives, Congress specifically carved out six categories of activities that cannot generate receipts qualifying as FTGR. Thus, gross receipts derived in connection with these activities are not eligible for any benefits under the FSC regime. Such receipts relate to the following:

1. The sale or lease of property for ultimate use in the United States.[48]
2. The sale or lease of export property, and furnishing of services, accomplished by subsidy.[49]
3. The sale or lease of export property, and furnishing of architectural and engineering services, for use by the United States;[50]
4. Related and subsidiary services performed in connection with excluded activities.[51]
5. Receipts from another FSC that is a member of the same controlled group.[52] For this purpose, "controlled group" has the same meaning as that used in IRC § 1563(a), except that the 80 percent ownership standard is substituted with 50 percent.
6. Factoring of receivables by a related supplier.[53]

3.3 Export Property

The property sold or leased must be "export property." To generate FTGR, export property must be "manufactured" (discussed in the next paragraph) in the United States and sold outside the United States in the ordinary course of business. Consistent with most other FSC requirements, the provisions describing the defi-

---

[47] Temp. Treas. Reg. § 1.924(a)-1T(f)(3); Treas. Reg. § 1.993-1(i)(3)(ii).

[48] Temp. Treas. Reg. § 1.924(a)-1T(g)(2); Treas. Reg. § 1.993-1(j)(2).

[49] Temp. Treas. Reg. § 1.924(a)-1T(g)(3); Treas. Reg. § 1.993-1(j)(3) (sale only).

[50] Temp. Treas. Reg. § 1.924(a)-1T(g)(4); Treas. Reg. § 1.993-1(j)(4).

[51] Temp. Treas. Reg. § 1.924(a)-1T(g)(5); Treas. Reg. § 1.993-1(j)(5).

[52] Temp. Treas. Reg. § 1.924(a)-1T(g)(6); Treas. Reg. § 1.993-1(j)(6).

[53] Temp. Treas. Reg. § 1.924(a)-1T(g)(7). There is no equivalent DISC provision.

nition of export property are quite detailed and require the satisfaction of various tests and subtests. In the case of most U.S. exporters, however, these tests can be met without significant additional action. Of equal importance, documentation that the tests are indeed satisfied is essential, particularly if it is necessary to establish these requirements upon an audit by the IRS.

Property will generally constitute export property if it meets the following three tests:

1. The manufacturing test,
2. The foreign use test, and
3. The foreign content test.

(a) Manufacturing Test

The primary motivating factor behind the original DISC (and FSC) regime was to encourage the export of U.S.-made goods.[54] This regime was intended not only to improve the U.S. trade deficit but also to stimulate the U.S. industrial sector to effectively compete in a global economy.[55] To carry out this policy, a necessary element of the DISC/FSC incentives was, and is, that only goods manufactured in the United States be eligible to create U.S. tax benefits. This is the rationale for the manufacturing test. In general, property will satisfy this test if it is "manufactured, produced, grown or extracted in the United States by any person other than a FSC."[56] Each of the elements of this test is discussed in the following paragraphs.

(i) Manufactured, Produced, Grown, or Extracted Within the United States.   Because manufacturers and other commercial producers often manufacture or produce products in stages at different locations both within and without the United States, it is first necessary to ascertain the meaning of the phrase "manufacture, produce, grow or extract." Depending on the stage (and corresponding location—U.S. or foreign) in which such activity occurs, a particular product may not be considered U.S.-made despite significant processes taking place within the United States. In general terms, a person will be considered to have "manufactured or produced" property if the property sold is not in effect the same property that the person purchased.[57]

In defining the phrase "manufactured or produced," FSC Regulations refer to the framework provided under Temp. Treas. Reg. § 1.954-3(a)(4)(ii), which addresses such terminology in the context of the antideferral regime under Subpart F.

---

[54] *See Brown-Forman Corp. v. Commissioner,* 94 T.C. 919, 924-925 (1990), *aff'd,* 995 F.2d 1037 (6th Cir. 1992); *CWT Farms, Inc. v. Commissioner,* 79 T.C. 1054, 1065.

[55] *See LeCroy Research Systems Corp. v. Commissioner,* 751 F.2d 123, 124 (2d Cir. 1984), *rev'g,* T.C. Memo 1984-145; S. Rept. 92-437 (1971), 1972-1 C.B. at 559. (1982), *aff'd,* 755 F.2d 790 (11th Cir. 1985); H. Rept. 92-533 (1971), 1972-1 C.B. 498, 529; S. Rept. 92-437 (1971), 1972-1 C.B. 559, 609.

[56] IRC § 927(a)(1)(A); Temp. Treas. Reg. § 1.927(a)-1T(c); IRC § 993(c)(1)(A); Treas. Reg. 1.993-3(a)(1).

[57] *Cf.* Treas. Reg. § 1.954-3(a)(4).

In general, Subpart F rules provide an exception to the general rule of U.S. taxation which provides that income earned by a "controlled foreign corporation" (CFC) (*see* IRC § 957) is taxable to its U.S. parent only upon distribution. Under Subpart F rules, the profit earned by CFCs attributable to certain sales of goods to, or on behalf of, related parties (i.e., "foreign base company sales income") is currently includible by the U.S. parent corporation in its U.S. tax return. However, under the so-called manufacturing exception, such income will not generally be subject to current inclusion if the CFC is considered to have manufactured or produced the goods sold.

Drawing on the "manufacturing exception" framework provided under Subpart F rules, FSC Regulations provide the following specific standards to determine whether certain commercial activities constitute manufacturing or production. So long as these activities are deemed to occur within the United States, the manufacturing test is satisfied.

(ii)   Substantial Transformation.   *The property has undergone "substantial transformation."*[58] Examples of this concept include the conversion of wood pulp into paper or the production of screws and bolts from steel rods.[59] Similarly, the processing and canning of fish would be considered the substantial transformation of property. Manufacturing took place where ore concentrate was converted into ferroalloy through chemical processing. The testing, assembly, and connection of peripherals to a product did not constitute manufacturing outside the United States so as to disqualify the product as export property.[60] The concept of substantial transformation even includes such activities as the production of scrap metal from old railroad rails.[61]

(iii)   Generally Considered Manufacturing.   *The property has undergone operations that are generally considered to constitute manufacturing.*[62] This standard is generally aimed at determining whether property that incorporates purchased component parts may be considered "manufactured." The application of this standard is based on analysis of all the relevant facts and circumstances. In *Webb Export Corp.,*[63] the Tax Court found that the taxpayer's harvesting, cleaning, and cutting of timber into veneer logs was both substantial in nature and generally considered to constitute production for purposes of the DISC rules.[64] The Tax Court, however, held that the veneer logs produced by the taxpayer were not export

---

[58] Temp. Treas. Reg. § 1.927(a)-1T(c)(2); Treas. Reg. § 1.954-3(a)(4)(ii); Treas. Reg. § 1.993-3(c)(2)(ii).

[59] *See* Treas. Reg. § 1.954-3(a)(4)(ii), examples 1 and 2.

[60] *See* Treas. Reg. § 1.954-3(a)(4)(ii), example 3; *see also* Rev. Rul. 75-7, 1975-1 C.B. 244 (ruling in context of IRC § 954 Subpart F). *But see* Priv. Ltr. Rul. 86-23-024.

[61] Rev. Rul. 73-279, 1973-1 C.B. 363.

[62] *See* Treas. Reg. § 1.954-3(a)(4)(iii); *cf.* Treas. Reg. § 1.993-3(c)(2)(iii).

[63] 91 T.C. 131 (1988).

[64] *See infra* for discussion of FSC rule prohibiting manufacture or production export property by a FSC.

property since the taxpayer, as a DISC, was ineligible to produce export property. In its rationale, the Tax Court placed emphasis on the time-consuming nature of the taxpayer's production process and the need for skilled labor and specialized equipment.

(iv) Conversion Costs. The regulations provide a safe harbor test under which property will be deemed to be manufactured if the "conversion costs" incurred in the production process account for 20 percent or more of the total cost of goods sold.[65] Conversion costs generally include the costs associated with the direct labor, factory burden, assembly and packaging costs, and similar items relating to the manufacturing or production process.[66] In the case of leased goods, the 20 percent test is applied to the adjusted tax basis of the export property.[67] Products can undergo significant processing and still not be considered manufactured for purposes of qualifying as export property. In *Garnac Grain Co.,*[68] a grain merchant that purchased, processed, and sold grain to customers around the world was found not to have been engaged in the production or growing of export property. This conclusion was reached even though it was shown that the grain processing required several distinct steps including cleaning, drying, aerating, fumigating, and blending of the grain.[69] The IRS, in Revenue Ruling 75-429,[70] held on facts similar to *Garnac* that grain purchasing and processing did not constitute production.

(v) Location. For purposes of determining whether manufacture or production occurred in the United States, the term "United States" also includes the Commonwealth of Puerto Rico.[71] Further, property manufactured by a domestic corporation in a U.S. foreign trade zone is considered manufactured within the United States.[72]

The manufacture of a product is often carried out in stages, some within the United States and some without. Property that is manufactured, produced, grown, or extracted in the United States may undergo additional production or processing outside the United States and still qualify as export property, but only if such property is reimported into the United States for further manufacturing, production, or processing prior to its final export sale.[73] For example, in Revenue Ruling 78-228,

---

[65] *See* Treas. Reg. § 1.954-3(a)(4)(iii); Treas. Reg. § 1.993-3(c)(2)(iv).

[66] *See* Tech. Adv. Mem. 78-15-004 (Dec. 1, 1977).

[67] Temp. Treas. Reg. 1.927(a)-1T(c)(2).

[68] 95 T.C. 7 (1990).

[69] *Id.*

[70] 1975-2 C.B. 312.

[71] IRC § 927(d)(3) and § IRC 993(g).

[72] Rev. Rul. 82-115, 1982-1 C.B. 108.

[73] Temp. Treas. Reg. § 1.927(a)-1T(c)(1); *see* Priv. Ltr. Rul. 78-15-004. The equivalent DISC provision is silent as to this possibility.

it was held that electronic devices produced in the United States, then shipped to a foreign country for further processing at a fee equal to 20 percent of their total cost of goods sold and then returned to the United States prior to their final export sale for additional processing, at a cost in excess of 20 percent of their total cost of goods sold, qualified as export property for DISC purposes.[74] The facts of this ruling as applied in the context of export property sold through a FSC are illustrated in Exhibit 3.3.

(vi)   Manufacturing by a Person Other Than a FSC.   The manufacturer or producer of the property must not be a FSC. Moreover, if products held by a FSC were manufactured by the FSC at a time when it was not a FSC, the products will not qualify as export property.[75] Similarly, where property has been grown by one party and processed by a FSC, the property will not qualify as export property. For example, timber cut, cleaned, and transported by a FSC would be considered "produced" by that FSC, so the resulting logs would not qualify as export property.[76] It should be noted that this restriction is perhaps more problematic in a DISC, rather than a FSC, context since most FSCs are incorporated in tax haven jurisdictions.

Exhibit 3.3

EXPORT PROPERTY PROCESSED WITHIN AND WITHOUT THE UNITED STATES (BASED ON FACTS SIMILAR TO REVENUE RULING 78-228)

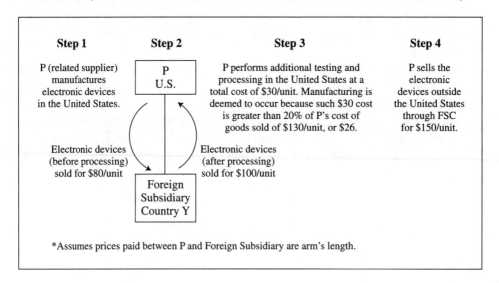

Step 1	Step 2	Step 3	Step 4
P (related supplier) manufactures electronic devices in the United States.	P U.S.	P performs additional testing and processing in the United States at a total cost of $30/unit. Manufacturing is deemed to occur because such $30 cost is greater than 20% of P's cost of goods sold of $130/unit, or $26.	P sells the electronic devices outside the United States through FSC for $150/unit.
Electronic devices (before processing) sold for $80/unit	Foreign Subsidiary Country Y	Electronic devices (after processing) sold for $100/unit	

*Assumes prices paid between P and Foreign Subsidiary are arm's length.

---

[74] 1978-1 C.B. 252.

[75] Temp. Treas. Reg. § 1.927(a)-1T(c)(1); Treas. Reg. § 1.993-3(c)(1).

[76] *See Webb Export Corp. v. Commissioner,* 91 T.C. 131 (1988).

A DISC, however, as a U.S. corporation, is more likely to have access to production capabilities.

(b) Foreign Use Test

The foreign use test requires that export property be held primarily for sale or lease in the ordinary course of a trade or business for direct use, consumption, or disposition outside the United States.[77] This test does not focus on whether the person using the property is a foreign or U.S. person, but rather on the location where such property is actually "used." Thus, for example, the export sale of paint to foreign-registered vessels would not qualify as a foreign use if such paint were applied in a U.S. port.[78] Similarly, paint applied to oil derricks located within the territorial waters of the United States would not be considered "used" outside the United States.[79] In contrast, if the paint was sold to U.S.-registered vessels but was applied on the high seas or in foreign ports, such use would constitute a foreign use.[80] However, FSCs or DISCs holding property in inventory, or for lease, prior to the property's sale or lease outside the United States will not disqualify the property from being export property.[81]

Fungible export property, such as grain and other commodities, must be physically segregated from nonexport property at all times after purchase or rental by FSC. Similarly, in the case of a commission FSC, such segregation must be made after the start of the FSC's commission relationship with its related suppliers as to that export property.[82] Although the DISC regulations do not have this segregation requirement, the IRS, through a Revenue Ruling, effectively imposed this requirement on DISCs.[83] In the ruling, the IRS held that grain sold to a cooperative did not satisfy the destination test because it was commingled with grain sold within the United States. In contrast, under both the FSC and DISC regimes, nonfungible export property does not need to be physically segregated.[84]

To establish that property is sold or leased for use, consumption, or disposition outside the United States, the regulations require that three subtests be met:

1. The destination test,
2. The proof of compliance test, and
3. The use outside the United States test.[85]

---

[77] Temp. Treas. Reg. § 1.927(a)-1T(a)(2); Treas. Reg. § 1.993-3(d)(1)(i).

[78] *See* Rev. Rul. 72-581, 1982-2 C.B. 461.

[79] *Id.*

[80] *Id.*

[81] Temp. Treas. Reg. § 1.927(a)-1T(d)(1)(ii); Treas. Reg. § 1.993-3(d)(1)(ii).

[81] Temp. Treas. Reg. § 1.927(a)-1T(d)(1)(ii); Treas. Reg. § 1.993-3(d)(1)(ii).

[82] Temp. Treas. Reg. § 1.927(a)-1T(d)(1)(ii).

[83] Rev. Rul. 77-484, 1977-2 C.B. 289.

[84] *Id.*

[85] Temp. Treas. Reg. § 1.927(a)-1T(d)(1)(i); Treas. Reg. § 1.993-3(d)(1)(i).

(i) Destination Test.   The destination test states that export property must be delivered by the seller or lessor, or agent of the seller or lessor, to one of the following:[86]

1. Within the United States, to a carrier or freight forwarder for ultimate delivery outside the United States to a purchaser or lessee;[87]

2. Within the United States, to a purchaser or lessee if the property is ultimately delivered outside the United States by the purchaser or lessee within one year of the sale or lease. The Tax Court upheld the validity of DISC requirement that export property sold to a U.S. purchaser be transferred outside the United States within one year;[88]

3. Within or outside the United States, to a purchaser or lessee that is a FSC or an interest-charge DISC and that is not a member of the same controlled group as the seller or lessor. The destination test is satisfied when sales by a DISC are made to an unrelated DISC which, in turn, sells the same property to another unrelated DISC;[89]

4. From the United States, to a purchaser or lessee at a point outside the United States by means of the seller's or lessor's own ship, aircraft, or other delivery vehicle;[90]

5. Outside the United States, to a purchaser or lessee by way of a warehouse, storage facility, or assembly site also located outside the United States, if the property was previously shipped by the seller or lessor from the United States;[91] or

6. Outside the United States, to a purchaser or lessee, if the property was previously shipped by the seller or lessor from the United States and if the property is located outside the United States pursuant to a prior lease by the seller or lessor, and either:

    a. The prior lease terminated at the expiration of its terms or by action of the prior lessee acting alone,

    b. The sale occurred or the term of the subsequent lease began after the time at which the term of the prior lease would have expired, or

    c. The lessee under the subsequent lease is not related to the lessor and the prior lease was terminated by action of the lessor, acting alone or with the lessee.[92]

---

[86] *See* Priv. Ltr. Rul. 82-12-043 (Dec. 23, 1981) (The destination test was not satisfied when equipment sold to foreign government was not delivered because seller could not obtain export license).

[87] Temp. Treas. Reg. § 1.927(a)-1T(d)(2)(i)(A); Treas. Reg. § 1.993-3(d)(2)(i)(A).

[88] Temp. Treas. Reg. § 1.927(a)-1T(d)(2)(i)(B); Treas. Reg. § 1.993-3(d)(2)(i)(B); *see Sim-Air, USA, Ltd. v. Commissioner,* 98 T.C. 187 (1992).

[89] Temp. Treas. Reg. § 1.927(a)-1T(d)(2)(i)(C); Treas. Reg. § 1.993-3(d)(2)(i)(C); *see, e.g.,* Rev. Rul. 73-229, 1973-1 C.B. 362.

[90] Temp. Treas. Reg. § 1.927(a)-1T(d)(2)(i)(D); Treas. Reg. § 1.993-3(d)(2)(i)(D).

[91] Temp. Treas. Reg. § 1.927(a)-1T(d)(2)(i)(E); Treas. Reg. § 1.993-3(d)(2)(i)(E).

[92] Temp. Treas. Reg. § 1.927(a)-1T(d)(2)(i)(F); Treas. Reg. § 1.993-3(d)(2)(i)(F).

(ii)   Applying the Destination Test.   For purposes of satisfying this test, the FOB point, as well as the time and place at which title or risk of loss passes, are disregarded. Purchase and lease of property occurred within the United States for purposes of the destination test even though title passed outside the United States since all actions required to effect the transaction occurred within the United States.[93] Moreover, it does not matter whether the property is to be used by the purchaser or, alternately, resold.[94] However, property will not qualify as export property if it has been the subject of "use (other than for purposes of resale or sublease), manufacture, assembly or other processing" by any person between the time of the sale or lease by the seller or lessor and delivery outside the United States.[95]

In *General Electric Co.*[96] the Tax Court invoked the analogous DISC provision to disqualify as export property aircraft engines and thrust reversers that were sold through a DISC to unrelated U.S. airframe manufacturers, which in turn sold the items to foreign purchasers. The Tax Court found that the airframe manufacturer's "building up" of the aircraft engines[97] and attachment of such engines and reversers to the airframes constituted a prohibited "assembly" before delivery outside the United States. Citing the legislative history behind the export property requirement, the Tax Court noted that the engines and reversers were not export property because, in order for such items to perform their "intended use," they had to be installed on the airframe.

Example

USCo. manufactures sheet metal that is sold through a FSC to a wholly owned foreign subsidiary, FS. FS converts the sheet metal into chain links that are then sold to unrelated foreign parties. The sheet metal sold by USCo. to FS will constitute export property. The sheet metal has undergone additional processing by a related party prior to resale by FS and such processing has occurred outside the United States.

Property may qualify as export property if the property is located outside the United States at the time it is purchased or leased and then imported into the United States prior to its further sale or lease or sublease outside the United States. Installation of a product by a manufacturer after sale but prior to delivery does not constitute "use" that would disqualify the property under the destination test, partly because "operational use" would not take place until the product was delivered outside the United States.[98] An election may be made to determine the

---

[93] Temp. Treas. Reg. § 1.927(a)-1T(d)(2)(i); Treas. Reg. § 1.993-3(d)(2)(i); *see, e.g.,* Priv. Ltr. Rul. 86-49-024 (Sept. 8, 1986).

[94] Temp. Treas. Reg. § 1.927(a)-1T(d)(2)(i), (ii); Treas. Reg. § 1.993-3(d)(2) (i), (ii).

[95] Temp. Treas. Reg. § 1.927(a)-1T(d)(2)(iii); Treas. Reg. § 1.993-3(d)(2)(iii).

[96] T.C. Memo. 1995-306 (1995).

[97] The procedure of "building up" the engines, which involved the attachment of more than 2,000 additional parts, was necessary to enable installation into the airframe. *Id.*

[98] Temp. Treas. Reg. § 1.927(a)-1T(d)(2)(iv); Treas. Reg. § 1.993-3(d)(2)(iv); *see, e.g.,* Priv. Ltr. Rul. 84-36-028 (June 5, 1984).

foreign content of the property imported into the United States, which was originally manufactured in the United States, if the property is subjected to further
manufacture or production after its importation.[99]

(iii) Proof of Compliance Test.   The seller or lessor must establish ultimate
delivery, use, or consumption of property outside the United States by providing
one of the following:[100]

1. A facsimile or carbon copy of the export bill of lading issued by the car-
    rier;[101]

2. A certificate of an agent or representative of the carrier disclosing delivery
    outside the United States;[102]

3. A facsimile or carbon copy of the certificate of lading executed by a cus-
    toms officer of the country to which the property was delivered;[103]

4. If the country has no customs administration, a written statement by the per-
    son to whom delivery outside the United States was made;[104]

5. A facsimile or carbon copy of the Shipper's Export Declaration, a monthly
    shipper's summary declaration filed with the Bureau of Customs, or a mag-
    netic tape filed in lieu of the Shippers Export Declaration, covering the
    property;[105] or

6. Any other proof that establishes to the satisfaction of the Commissioner that
    the property was ultimately delivered, or directly sold, or directly consumed
    outside the United States within one year after the sale or lease.[106]

The proof of compliance test is considered to be satisfied even if the documentation does not disclose the name of the ultimate consignee or the price paid for the
goods, provided the country in which delivery is made is still disclosed or the document still indicates that the property was delivered outside the United States. The
proof of compliance test under DISC rules does not require that the identity of the
buyer or the price of goods be disclosed.[107] A statement from a broker/consolida-
tor, acknowledging receipt of the goods within the United States and providing that
the goods will be shipped outside the United States within one year of the date of
sale, will satisfy the proof of compliance test.[108]

---

[99] Temp. Treas. Reg. § 1.927(a)-1T(e)(4)(i)(B). No such election is provided for in the DISC rules.

[100] Temp. Treas. Reg. § 1.927(a)-1T(d)(3)(i); Treas. Reg. § 1.993-3(d)(3)(i).

[101] Temp. Treas. Reg. § 1.927(a)-1T(d)(3)(i)(A); Treas. Reg. § 1.993-3(d)(3)(i)(A).

[102] Temp. Treas. Reg. § 1.927(a)-1T(d)(3)(i)(B); Treas. Reg. § 1.993-3(d)(3)(i)(B).

[103] Temp. Treas. Reg. § 1.927(a)-1T(d)(3)(i)(C); Treas. Reg. § 1.993-3(d)(3)(i)(C).

[104] Temp. Treas. Reg. § 1.927(a)-1T(d)(3)(i)(D); Treas. Reg. § 1.993-3(d)(3)(i)(D).

[105] Temp. Treas. Reg. § 1.927(a)-1T(d)(3)(i)(E); Treas. Reg. § 1.993-3(d)(3)(i)(E).

[106] Temp. Treas. Reg. § 1.927(a)-1T(d)(3)(i)(F); Treas. Reg. § 1.993-3(d)(3)(i)(F).

[107] Temp. Treas. Reg. § 1.927(a)-1T(d)(3)(ii); Treas. Reg. § 1.993-3(d)(3)(ii); *see* Rev. Rul. 73-70, 1973-1 C.B. 361.

[108] Rev. Rul. 77-249, 1977-2 C.B. 265.

(iv)   Use Outside the United States Test.   Export property must *not* be sold or leased for ultimate use within the United States. The property will be deemed to be for ultimate use within the United States and thus will not qualify as export property if any of the following conditions are satisfied:[109]

1. The purchaser is a related party in respect to the seller and the purchaser ultimately uses the property, or a second product into which the property is incorporated as a component, in the United States;[110]

2. At the time of the sale, there is an *agreement or understanding* that the property, or a second product into which the property is incorporated as a component, will be ultimately used by the purchaser in the United States. Knowledge disseminated by trade associations to the U.S. public did not constitute an agreement or understanding that property would be incorporated as a component of other property within the United States. "An agreement or understanding" will not be found solely by virtue of the fact that the property in question is sold in substantial quantities in the United States;[111]

3. At the time of the sale, a reasonable person would have believed that the property (or second product that incorporates such property) would be ultimately used by the purchaser in the United States, unless in the case of the sale of components the fair market value of the components at the time of delivery to the purchaser constitutes less than 20 percent of the fair market value of the second product into which the components are incorporated. Thus, cameras sold by a DISC to armed forces personnel stationed in foreign countries were not considered destined for ultimate use within the United States.[112]

Sales from inventory directly to retail customers outside the United States will be considered to be used predominantly outside the United States.[113] Leased property must be used by the lessee predominantly outside the United States for the period of the lessor's taxable year that is included within the term of the lease.[114] Property will be considered used within the United States and thus not qualify as export property if, within three years after it is sold, the purchaser resells the property to another purchaser for use within the United States.

Alternatively, property will not satisfy the foreign use test if, within such a three-year period, the purchaser, for any 365-day period, does not use the property "predominantly outside the United States."[115] Property is generally considered

---

[109] Temp. Treas. Reg. § 1.927(a)-1T(d)(4)(ii); Treas. Reg. § 1.993-3(d)(4)(ii).

[110] Temp. Treas. Reg. § 1.927(a)-1T(d)(4)(ii)(A); Treas. Reg. § 1.993-3(d)(4)(ii)(A).

[111] Temp. Treas. Reg. § 1.927(a)-1T(d)(4)(ii)(B); Treas. Reg. § 1.993-3(d)(4)(ii)(B); *see* Priv. Ltr. Rul. 85-30-003 (April 25, 1985); Temp. Treas. Reg. § 1.927(a)-1T(d)(4)(ii); Treas. Reg. § 1.993-3(d)(4)(ii).

[112] Temp. Treas. Reg. § 1.927(a)-1T(d)(4)(ii)(C); Treas. Reg. § 1.993-3(d)(4)(ii)(C). *See* Rev. Rul. 74-328, 1974-2 C.B. 239.

[113] Temp. Treas. Reg. § 1.927(a)-1T(d)(4)(iv); Treas. Reg. § 1.993-3(d)(4)(iv).

[114] Temp. Treas. Reg. § 1.927(a)-1T(d)(4)(v); Treas. Reg. § 1.993-3(d)(4)(v).

[115] Temp. Treas. Reg. § 1.927(a)-1T(d)(4)(iii); Treas. Reg. § 1.993-3(d)(4)(iii).

used "predominantly outside the United States" if it is located outside the United States for more than 50 percent of the time.[116] For property such as aircraft, vessels, automobiles, and other equipment used for transportation purposes, use "predominantly outside the United States" will be deemed to occur if such property is located outside the United States for more than 50 percent of the time, or more than 50 percent of the miles traversed are outside the United States. Thus, for example, aircraft leased to a U.S. or foreign airline could constitute export property if the aircraft satisfies this 50 percent test.

(c)   Foreign Content Test

To qualify as export property, no more than 50 percent of the fair market value of the property can be attributable to imported items (constituting "foreign content"). For example, flower seeds produced at growing stations outside the United States and returned to the United States for testing and evaluation did not satisfy the foreign content test.[117] The foreign content test is applied on an item-by-item basis. However, the regulations permit large-volume sellers to apply this test on an aggregate basis if the items of property sold contain "substantially identical foreign content in substantially the same proportion." The foreign content test could not be applied on an aggregate basis to camera systems, since such systems were not "substantially identical" and did not have foreign content that was "in substantially the same proportion."[118]

In determining whether the 50 percent test is satisfied, all items constituting foreign content incorporated within the exported property must be valued as of the time such items are imported into the United States.[119] The fair market value of such items of foreign content is computed based on their appraised value as determined under § 403 of the Tariff Act of 1930. The full dutiable value, as computed under these rules, is used without any reduction for special provisions provided under U.S. tariff laws.[120] A taxpayer can, in essence, subtract from the fair market value of imported items the value associated with the U.S. property initially exported if a portion of the imported property was originally manufactured, produced, or grown in the United States.[121]

USCo. purchases computer chips from an unrelated foreign manufacturer that it plans to incorporate into manufacturing equipment that will be sold outside the United States. USCo. agrees to pay a total of $110 per chip, $100 for the chip plus $10 for freight and insurance. For U.S. customs purposes, each chip's dutiable

---

[116] Temp. Treas. Reg. § 1.927(a)-1T(d)(4)(vi); Treas. Reg. § 1.993-3(d)(4)(vi).

[117] Temp. Treas. Reg. § 1.927(a)-1T(e); Treas. Reg. § 1.993-3(e); *see* Rev. Rul. 75-394, 1975-2 C.B. 311.

[118] Temp. Treas. Reg. § 1.927(a)-1T(e)(2); Treas. Reg. § 1.993-3(e)(2); *see* Tech. Adv. Mem. 81-41-016 (Aug. 13, 1979).

[119] Temp. Treas. Reg. § 1.927(a)-1T(e)(4)(i); Treas. Reg. § 1.993-3(e)(4)(i).

[120] Temp. Treas. Reg. § 1.927(a)-1T(e)(4)(i)(A); Treas. Reg. § 1.993-3(e)(4)(i).

[121] Temp. Treas. Reg. § 1.927(a)-1T(e)(4)(i)(B). For special valuation rules applicable to this election, *see* Temp. Treas. Reg. § 1.927(a)-1T(e)(4)(ii)(B).

value is $100, because USCo. is permitted under the customs laws to exclude the cost of foreign freight and insurance in computing such value. The equipment into which chips are incorporated is manufactured in the United States. After the chips are incorporated, the equipment is sold to foreign persons for $215 per unit.

Since the foreign content of the equipment is determined by reference to the fair market value of any imported components *without reduction for special provisions provided under the United States tariff laws,* the equipment will have foreign content for purposes of the FSC rules of $110, not $100. This is because the reduction of $10 for freight and insurance permitted under customs law in determining net dutiable value would not be taken into account for purposes of the FSC foreign content test. Since this amount exceeds 50 percent of the equipment's unit price, the equipment will not qualify as export property.

Arguably, a "special provision" under U.S. tariff laws for computing dutiable value could be the "first sale method." In general, under the first sale method, provided certain conditions are satisfied, U.S. importers are able to compute U.S. duties on imported items by reference to the price paid by the foreign distributor/seller to the original manufacturer, rather than the price paid by the U.S. importer to the foreign distributor/seller. In this way, U.S. importers can avoid paying U.S. duties on the value of imported items attributable to the foreign distributor's profit margin. However, based on a strict reading of the regulations, a position might be taken that any customs benefits derived from the first sale method would likely not be considered a "special provision" reducing dutiable value. This is because if the first sale method is used, the initial dutiable value would be the "first sale" value. Accordingly, no special provisions under the customs laws would be necessary to reflect a lower dutiable value relating to the first sale.

(i) Evidence of Valuation. The appraised value of imported components may be demonstrated by the amount shown on the customs invoice issued upon importation.[122] If the person incorporating the imported components was not the importer, the appraised value of the items may be evidenced by a certificate summarizing the information contained in the customs invoice, provided that person is supplied with such information by the importer.

The evidentiary requirement is particularly problematic when the exporter is not the importer of record. In practice, if the importer of record is an unrelated supplier of the exporter, that supplier may be reluctant to disclose the customs invoice information, which would contain dutiable value amounts, since such information would provide the exporter with an indication of the supplier's markup and profitability. If the customs invoice or the aforementioned certificate cannot be obtained, it is necessary to otherwise "establish" that no more than 50 percent of the fair market value of the exported property relates to foreign content.[123] If such documentation is not available, the exporter could attempt to identify the profit

---

[122] Temp. Treas. Reg. § 1.927(a)-1T(e)(4)(ii); Treas. Reg. § 1.993-3(e)(4)(ii).

[123] Temp. Treas. Reg. § 1.927(a)-1T(e)(4)(ii); Treas. Reg. § 1.993-3(e)(4)(ii).

markup applicable to products sold in the seller's industry and "back into" the seller's import price to establish the fair market value of exported property. As additional evidence, industry or trade pricing publications could be consulted to determine the import price. The exporter could also attempt to obtain independent price quotes for comparable products from the original foreign distributors or manufacturers.

The tax regulations specifically sanction the use of a customs invoice to determine the value of imports for purposes of the foreign content test. However, the regulations do not generally distinguish between goods purchased from a related or unrelated foreign manufacturer or distributor. When goods are purchased from a foreign related party, it is uncertain how an IRC § 482 transfer pricing adjustment should affect valuation. If the IRS were to make an incremental pricing adjustment as to the price paid to the foreign related party for product components, that adjustment should also be reflected in the foreign content analysis.

(ii) Substitution Rule and Interchangeable Component Parts. It is common practice for U.S. manufacturers to utilize both U.S.- and foreign-made component parts in their manufacturing processes. For such manufacturers that also sell goods both within and without the United States, a seemingly logical way of maximizing their production of export property would be to incorporate the foreign-made components in the products sold in the U.S. market, and incorporate U.S.-made components in the products sold outside the United States. In this way, such export products would not violate the foreign content restrictions described earlier.

The regulations, however, do not permit manufacturers to track which components (domestic or foreign) are incorporated in which products (sold within or without the United States). Rather, the regulations state that determination of whether imported components are incorporated into products that are exported shall be made on a "substitution basis," as in the case of the rules relating to duty drawback accounts under the custom laws. Under the substitution rules, U.S. manufacturers that incorporate either an imported component or, alternatively, a similar or identical U.S.-made component into finished products, are deemed to incorporate the imported component first for their export sales, whether or not through a FSC. Under the substitution rule, if an imported component constitutes more than 50 percent of the value of the finished good sold, then the U.S. exporter can have export property only to the extent the number of finished products exported exceeds the number of imported component products. This idea is illustrated in the example in the following paragraph.

USCo. manufactures industrial trucks that incorporate engines purchased from both U.S. and foreign manufacturers. The engines are worth more than 50 percent of the value of the trucks. USCo. purchases 100 engines from a foreign manufacturer and 200 engines from a U.S. manufacturer. In the current year, USCo. sold 50 trucks to foreign construction companies and 250 trucks to U.S. construction companies. Under the substitution rules, notwithstanding which engines are incorporated into which trucks, the 50 trucks sold to foreign manufacturers are deemed to incorporate the imported engines. Thus, given these facts, none of the export trucks would qualify as export property (even if they had actually incorporated the U.S.-made engines). USCo. sold 125 trucks to foreign construction companies, then 25 of those trucks could potentially satisfy the foreign content test (i.e., the first 100 trucks exported would be deemed to incorporate U.S.-made engines and the last 25 would be deemed to incorporate the foreign-made engines).

This example illustrates the seemingly harsh results to U.S. exporters when the substitution rules are applied in a FSC context. As enacted under the customs laws, the duty drawback and substitution rules were intended to encourage U.S. companies to compete more effectively in international markets. In broad terms, under the duty drawback rules, U.S. exporters can recover virtually all of the customs duties paid on imported goods that are incorporated into other products sold to foreign purchasers. The obvious objective of these rules is to put U.S. businesses on an equal footing with foreign competitors. However, the application of the substitution rules in a FSC context, while not necessarily putting U.S. exporters in a worse position than foreign competitors, goes against the underlying incentives intended by the FSC rules.

Perhaps a better approach would be to enable U.S. exporters to otherwise establish which components (foreign- or U.S.-made) are incorporated into exported products. The U.S. exporter would bear the burden of proof. If the exporter cannot establish that the U.S.-made, rather than the foreign-made, components were incorporated into the exported products, then the substitution rules would apply. If adopted in future regulations, this approach would provide a more reasonable result and would be consistent with the legislative intent behind the FSC rules.

(iii) Service and Parts Contracts. A service contract, under which the seller or lessor agrees to provide replacement parts, may be entered into. The 50 percent test will be applied on an aggregate basis to both the property and parts if the purchase price does not distinguish between the property and the parts.[124] Alternatively, if the exporter "separately states" the purchase price for the property and for the parts, the 50 percent test will be applied to each separately. Based on the language of the regulations, it would appear that the exporter is free to determine which alternative (aggregate or separate prices) should be the basis for applying the 50 percent test. The exporter decides by either "separately stating" the prices for each item or using an aggregate price. Thus, in structuring service contracts relating to sales through a FSC, an exporter should consider the impact on the application of 50 percent test produced by separately stating the prices for the property and parts as compared with using an aggregate amount. For example, if it is desirable to use imported replacement parts, the exporter should probably use an aggregate price so that both the property and the replacement parts may qualify as export property.

---

[124] Temp. Treas. Reg. § 1.927(a)-1T(e)(3); Treas. Reg. § 1.993-3(e)(3).

3.4   Excluded Property

The definition of export property under FSC rules closely parallels that used under the DISC regime.[125] As under the DISC rules, there are certain statutory exclusions from the definition of export property that reflect certain policy decisions as to the types of items that should, and should not, be encouraged for export. Services provided by a FSC may not qualify as export property.[126] Although not qualifying as export property, certain services provided by a FSC may, nevertheless, generate FTGR.

The determination of whether a particular item constitutes property or services is based on all the relevant facts and circumstances.[127] Thus, property that symbolizes or embodies the results of activities more in nature of services will not qualify as export property. For example, preparation of a map for a particular construction site would constitute services, whereas the sale of standard maps to customers would constitute export property.[128] A report prepared in connection with management services rendered to a foreign subsidiary or specific client would not qualify as export property, and fees earned by a DISC for the conversion of raw materials into liquid extract were not considered to be the sale or exchange of export property.[129]

Certain specific categories of property are excluded from the definition of export property. In addition to certain enumerated items, the IRC authorizes the president to exclude by executive order any other type of property if the supply of such property is considered "insufficient to meet the requirements of the domestic economy."[130] In this case, any property so declared in short supply will not be eligible to qualify as export property for the period in which the executive order is in effect. In the Omnibus Budget Reconciliation Act of 1993, Congress added raw timber as another category excluded from the definition of export property. This exclusion was enacted to discourage the export of raw timber, which, it was believed, contributed to job loss in the United States for wood-processing activities.[131]

(a)   Property Leased or Rented Within a Controlled Group

Property that is leased or rented to members of the same "controlled group" will not generally qualify as export property.[132] For purposes of FSC rules, "controlled

---

[125] *See* IRC § 993(c)(1).

[126] Temp. Treas. Reg. § 1.927(a)-1T(b); Treas. Reg. § 1.993-3(b). *See, e.g.,* IRC § 924(a)(3); IRC § 993(a)(1)(C) (services related and subsidiary to sale or lease of export property); IRC § 924(a)(5); IRC § 993(a)(1)(II) (certain managerial services). *See* discussion of these categories of FTGR in Section 3.2 (d)–(e) of this chapter.

[127] *See* Temp. Treas. Reg. § 1.927(a)-1T(b); Treas. Reg. § 1.993-3(b).

[128] *See id.* (illustrating distinction between property and services).

[129] *See* Rev. Rul. 74-216, 1974-1 C.B. 194.

[130] IRC § 927(a)(3); IRC § 993(c)(3).

[131] *See The Omnibus Budget Reconciliation Act of 1993 and Repeal of Tax Benefits for Log Exports,* Cong. Res. Serv., Aug. 10, 1993, CRS 93-896 E.

[132] IRC § 927(a)(2)(A); IRC § 993(c)(2)(A).

group" is generally defined to include any group of corporations, 50 percent of the vote and value of all classes of stock of which is owned, directly or indirectly, by a common parent corporation.[133] This restriction on intergroup leasing is intended to prevent U.S. corporations from using a FSC to convert income that would otherwise be foreign manufacturing or operating income (as compared with selling income) to income eligible for partial exemption under FSC rules. This conversion could occur, for example, by having a U.S. corporation, or one of its subsidiaries, sell assets that are used outside the United States to a FSC and then having the FSC lease the property back. In this way, income could be shifted from foreign operating subsidiaries to the FSC, which is eligible for the partial FSC tax exemption. This exclusion does not apply to subleasing arrangements within a controlled group where the property is ultimately leased to a third party and is used predominantly outside the United States. Thus, products leased to foreign subsidiaries for sublease to foreign customers are not excluded from the definition of "export property."[134]

Example

X, FSC, leases movie rights to Y, a foreign corporation and member of the same controlled group as X; Y, in turn, subleases the same rights to Z, an unrelated foreign corporation. Because the rights are ultimately leased to an unrelated foreign corporation that is not part of the controlled group, the movie rights might qualify as export property.[135] This export property exclusion would also apply to *indirect* leasing arrangements to members of the same controlled group. Given the facts of this example, if X were to lease the movie rights directly to Z, rather than Y, and Z were to then, in turn, sublease those rights to Y, such rights would not qualify as export property.[136]

(b) Intangible Property

Intangible property is excluded from the definition of export property. Intangible property includes "patents, inventions, models, designs, formulas, or processes whether or not patented, copyrights (other than films, tapes, records, or similar reproductions, for commercial or home use), goodwill, trademarks, trade brands, franchises, or other like property." A copyrighted article (e.g., a book or standardized mass-marketed computer software), if not accompanied by a right to reproduce that article for external use, may potentially qualify as export property.[137] However, a license of a master recording tape for reproduction outside the United States is not disqualified from being export property.[138]

---

[133] IRC § 927(d)(4); Treas. Reg. §§ 1.993-3(a)(4), 1.993-1(k) (incorporating by reference IRC § 1563(a) but not IRC § 1563(b)).

[134] Temp. Treas. Reg. § 1.927(a)-1T(f)(2); Treas. Reg. § 1.993-3(f)(2); *see* Rev. Rul. 74-217, 1974-1 C.B. 195.

[135] Temp. Treas. Reg. § 1.927(a)-1T(f)(2)(iii); Treas. Reg. § 1.993-3(f)(2)(iii).

[136] *Id.*

[137] Temp. Treas. Reg. § 1.927(a)-1T(f)(3); Treas. Reg. § 1.993-3(f)(3).

[138] *Id.; see, e.g.,* Priv. Ltr. Rul. 81-23-112 (Mar. 13, 1981).

(i) **Computer Software.** The ability to distribute software through a FSC has been the subject of several IRS rulings as well as the focus of recent congressional hearings. Interpreting the FSC and analogous DISC provisions, the IRS issued several private letter rulings, stating that standardized software that is mass marketed and sold or licensed without reproduction rights may constitute export property,[139] ruling that master tapes and records were export property. However, if the contract under which software is sold or licensed entitles the purchaser or licensee to make, use, or sell the technology, then such property would likely not constitute export property.[140]

In Technical Advice Memorandum (TAM) 93-44-002,[141] the IRS addressed the specific question of whether the language in the code and regulations which parenthetically excludes from the definition of intangible property "films, tapes, records or similar reproductions for commercial or home use" can be read to sanction computer software as export property. In addition, the IRS considered whether the regulation that permits a FSC's licensing of a "master recording tape" could include computer software. The IRS focused on whether the term "tape," as used in these regulations, could include magnetic tapes used in the computer software industry.

In its analysis, the IRS first looked to the legislative history of the analogous DISC provision (on which the FSC provision was modeled) and noted that these exceptions to the definition of intangible property were intended to provide the film industry with a tax incentive. Further, the IRS observed that, in an earlier draft of the DISC provision, the language had been narrowly drafted to exclude only "films, tapes or records for the commercial showing of motion pictures or used for radio or television broadcasting or to provide background music." Apparently, based on this legislative history, the IRS concluded that the term "tapes" does not include magnetic tapes holding computer software; rather, the term should be "interpreted to include only audio or video tapes used in the entertainment industry." Based on this finding, the IRS held that, under the facts of the ruling, a magnetic tape master that enabled the licensee to reproduce copies of original software did not constitute export property.

Although TAM 93-44-002 is generally consistent with the teachings of prior IRS rulings and technical memoranda, it crystallizes the stark difference in treatment accorded computer software versus analogous video and audio mediums used in the entertainment industry. In the latter case, master recording tapes licensed or sold for reproduction outside the United States can qualify as export property. With the development and proliferation of new software and software-based technologies, the negative treatment accorded such items under FSC rules has come under intense scrutiny. In recent congressional hearings, the IRS has indicated that it would not oppose providing software companies with expanded

---

[139] *See, e.g.,* Priv. Ltr. Rul. 92-10-015 (Dec. 6, 1991); Tech. Adv. Mem. 86-52-001 (July 31, 1986); Tech. Adv. Mem. 85-49-003 (Aug. 16, 1985).

[140] *See* Priv. Ltr. Rul. 92-10-015 (Dec. 6, 1991).

[141] Nov. 5, 1993.

FSC benefits. However, the IRS also indicated that legislative change would be necessary to achieve this result.

(ii) Legislation Affecting Software. While legislative change appears necessary to enable software exporters to take full advantage of FSC provisions, current law does permit certain forms of software exports. For example, as noted earlier, standardized, mass-marketed computer software can qualify as export property. Thus, "shrink-wrap" or "box-top" software products should, provided that other tests are met, qualify as export property.

Another form of software export that could arguably qualify as export property is a site license. A site license generally entails the transfer of a computer disk with a right to reproduce a limited number of copies for the customer's internal use only. This should be the case even if the customer decides to make additional copies, provided such copies are for its internal use only.

The export property issue becomes less distinct when the medium on which the software is transmitted is not in tangible form, such as a disk, tape, or compact disk. Although the regulations state that software meeting the "mass marketed" standard can be on "any medium" and still qualify as export property, it is not clear whether the electronic transmission of software, for example, would constitute a "medium." These and other software issues should be clarified by legislative enactment. Until that time, however, there will likely be uncertainty and, as a result, underutilization of the FSC incentive by software exporters.

(c) Oil and Gas Products

Oil and gas, including any "primary product" derived therefrom,[142] are excluded from qualifying as export property. "Primary products" of oil are "crude oil and all products derived from the destructive distillation of crude oil," which include volatile products, light oils (e.g., motor fuel and kerosene), distillates, lubricating oils, greases and waxes, and residues.[143] Primary products of gas are "all gas and associated hydrocarbon components from gas wells or oil wells," which include natural gas, condensates, liquefied petroleum gases (e.g., ethane, propane, and butane), and other liquid products.[144] A particular primary product that has undergone additional processing to convert it to a compound of a medicinal or cosmetic nature would likely be no longer disqualified as export property. Primary products do not include "petrochemicals, medicinal products, insecticides, and alcohols."[145] Primary products of oil that are processed to become products classified as drugs by the Food and Drug Administration could qualify as export property.[146]

---

[142] IRC § 927(a)(2)(C); Temp. Treas. Reg. § 1.927(a)-1T(g)(1). The DISC provision excludes "depletable products." Treas. Reg. § 1.993-3(g).

[143] Temp. Treas. Reg. § 1.927(a)-1T(g)(2)(i); Treas. Reg. § 1.993-3(g)(3)(i).

[144] Temp. Treas. Reg. § 1.927(a)-1T(g)(2)(ii); Treas. Reg. § 1.993-3(g)(3)(ii).

[145] Temp. Treas. Reg. § 1.927(a)-1T(g)(2)(iv).

[146] *See* Tech. Adv. Mem. 87-07-002 (Oct. 20, 1986).

(d)   Export Controlled Products

An "export controlled product" is a product or commodity that is restricted from export under Section 7(a) of the Export Administration Act of 1979. This exclusion from the definition of export property is intended to protect the U.S. economy from "excessive drain of scarce materials and to reduce the serious inflationary impact of foreign demand."[147]

3.5   Conclusion

One of the primary objectives of the enactment of the FTGR requirements was to ensure that FSC tax benefits encourage the export of *U.S.-manufactured* goods. Because of the need to achieve this objective while also satisfying the concerns of GATT trading partners, the FTGR requirements address many issues and contain numerous rules and restrictions. On their face, these requirements are seemingly burdensome and clearly complex. However, when viewed from a practical perspective, the FTGR requirements should not create any substantial additional work for U.S. exporters. With moderate effort and careful documentation, these requirements can be satisfied by most U.S. exporters that sell U.S.-manufactured goods.

---

[147] Temp. Treas. Reg. § 1.927(a)-1T(h)(1); Treas. Reg. § 1.993-3(h)(1).

CHAPTER 4

Export Property

Michael N. Schwartz
Roland Ryan Davis

4.1 Introduction

This chapter discusses the statutory requirements that determine qualified export property under foreign sales corporation (FSC) and domestic international sales corporation (DISC) regulations. To qualify for the tax benefits of a FSC, it is necessary to have foreign trade income, the gross income of a FSC attributable to foreign trading gross receipts.[1] To qualify for DISC tax benefits, it is necessary to have qualified export receipts.[2] Since most foreign trading gross receipts, or qualified export receipts[3] arise from or relate to export property, it is appropriate to deal first with the definition of *export property*.

Export property is:[4]

1. Property that is manufactured, produced, grown, or extracted in the United States by a person other than a FSC or a DISC;

2. Property that is held primarily for sale, lease, or rental for direct use, consumption, or disposition outside the United States; *and*

3. Property of which not more than 50 percent of the fair market value is attributable to articles imported into the United States.

---

[1] IRC §923(b).

[2] IRC §993(a).

[3] Foreign trading gross receipts and qualified export receipts are later defined in this chapter.

[4] IRC §927(a)(1). The DISC rules define "export property" in IRC §993(c)(1)(A)-(C), which are identical to IRC §927(a).

All three requirements must be met for property to be considered "export property" for FSC and DISC purposes. Each requirement is technically constructed. As a result, a careful analysis of the statute, regulations, cases, and IRS rulings is necessary to ensure that the taxpayer complies with the statutory language.

Each requirement is discussed in detail in the following sections.

4.2   Manufactured, Produced, Grown, or Extracted in the United States Requirement

Under the first statutory requirement for export property, the property must be manufactured, produced, grown, or extracted in the United States by a person who does not qualify as a FSC or a DISC.[5] Property held by a FSC or DISC that was manufactured, produced, grown, or extracted by it at a time when it did not qualify as a FSC or DISC is not export property of the FSC or DISC. The export property must be "manufactured" or "produced."[6] Property is considered manufactured or produced if one of the three following tests are met:[7]

The definitions of "manufactured" and "produced" are also discussed in the Subpart F regulations under Treas. Reg. §1.954-3. IRC §954(d)(1) defines foreign base company sales income as income derived from certain purchases from, or sales of property to, related persons provided that the property purchased or sold is manufactured, produced, grown or extracted outside the controlled foreign corporation's country of incorporation and is sold for use, consumption, or disposition outside that country.

(a)   Substantial Transformation

Manufacturing includes the substantial transformation of property prior to sale. Substantial transformation includes dismantlement of old railroad cars, shearing and baling scrap steel, and cutting of old railroad rails.[8]

The Subpart F regulations contain an example of the substantial transformation test under Reg. §1.954-3(a)(4)(ii), Example 1. Controlled foreign corporation A, incorporated under the laws of foreign country X, operates a paper factory in foreign country Y. Corporation A purchases from a related person wood pulp grown in country Y. Corporation A, by a series of processes, converts the wood pulp to paper, which it sells for use in foreign country Z. The transformation of wood pulp to paper constitutes the manufacture or production of property.

The Subpart F regulations also describe substantial transformation under Reg. §1.954-3(a)(4)(ii) in Example 2. Controlled foreign corporation B, incorporated

---

[5] IRC §§927(a)(1)(A) and 993(c)(1).

[6] Rev. Rul. 73-279, 1973-1 C.B. 363.

[7] Reg. §§1.927(a)-1T(a)(2) and 1.954-3(a)(4).

[8] Reg. §1.993-3(c)(2)(ii). For a discussion of export property, *see* Robert Feinschreiber, *Domestic International Sales Corporations* (New York: Practicing Law Institute, 1978), Chapter 4; and Robert Feinschreiber, *FSC: The Foreign Sales Corporation* (Corporate Tax Press, 1984), Chapter 8.

under the laws of foreign country X, purchases steel rods from a related person that produces the steel in foreign country Y. Corporation B operates a machining plant in country X in which it utilizes the purchased steel rods to make screws and bolts. This transformation of steel rods to screws and bolts constitutes the manufacture or production of property.

The canning of fish is considered to be a substantial transformation, as illustrated in Reg. §1.954-3(a)(4)(ii), Example 3. Substantial transformation occurs when a controlled foreign corporation, incorporated under the laws of foreign country X, purchases tuna fish from unrelated persons who own fishing boats that catch such fish on the high seas. Corporation C receives such fish in country X in the condition in which they are taken from the fishing boats, and in that country corporation C processes, cans, and sells the fish to related person D, incorporated under the laws of foreign country Y, for consumption in foreign country Z. The transformation of such fish into canned fish constitutes the manufacture or production of property.

The transformation of ore concentrate into ferro alloy also constitutes substantial transformation.[9] X, a controlled foreign corporation incorporated in foreign country M, and contract manufacturer Y were incorporated in country O. X and Y were unrelated. X and Y entered into an arm's-length contract whereby Y processed the ore concentrate that X had purchased in the United States and Canada into ferro alloy. Under the terms of the contract, X paid Y a conversion fee. The ore concentrate, before and during processing, and the finished product remained the sole property of X at all times. X alone purchased all raw material and other ingredients necessary in the processing operation and bore the risk of loss throughout the conversion process. X retained complete control of the production process and the quality of the product. Y was at all times required to use such processes as were directed by X. In addition, X had the right to send its personnel to Y's plant to inspect, correct, or advise with regard to the process. The IRS stated that these procedures constituted substantial transformation.

A further example illustrates operations that do not meet the substantial transformation test. Controlled foreign corporation C, incorporated under the laws of foreign country X, purchases from related persons radio parts manufactured in foreign country Y. Corporation C designs radio kits, packages component parts required for assembly of such kits, and sells the parts in a knocked-down condition to unrelated persons for use outside country X. These packaging operations of corporation C do not constitute the manufacture, production, or construction of property.[10]

(b)   Operations Are Substantial in Nature[11]

The second test that can be used to determine whether property is considered manufactured or produced is whether the operations are substantial in nature and

---

[9] Rev. Rul. 75-7, 1975-C.B. 244.

[10] Reg. §1.954-3(a)(4)(iii), Example 3.

[11] Reg. §1.993-3(c)(2)(iii).

are generally considered to constitute manufacturing, production, or construction. Examples of substantial operations are the assembly of industrial engines and the assembly of automobiles.

Assembly of industrial engines: Assume controlled foreign corporation A, incorporated under the laws of foreign country X, sells industrial engines for use, consumption, and disposition outside country X. Corporation A, in connection with the assembly of such engines, performs machining and assembly operations. In addition, corporation A purchases components manufactured in foreign country Y from related and unrelated persons. On a per-unit basis, corporation A's selling price and costs of such engines are as follows:[12]

Selling price	$400
Cost of goods sold:	
Material	
Acquired from related persons	$100
Acquired from others	40
Total material	$140
Conversion costs (direct labor and factory burden)	70
Total cost of goods sold	$210
Gross profit	$190
Administrative and selling expenses	50
Taxable income	$140

The conversion costs incurred by corporation A are more than 20 percent of total costs of goods sold ($70/$210, or 33 percent). Although the product sold, an engine, is not sufficiently distinguishable from the components to constitute a substantial transformation of the purchased parts, corporation A will be considered to have manufactured the product under this second test.

Assembly of automobiles: Controlled foreign corporation B, incorporated under the laws of foreign country X, operates an automobile assembly plant. In connection with such activity, Corporation B purchases from related persons assembled engines, transmissions, and certain other components, all of which are manufactured outside country X. Corporation B purchases additional components from unrelated persons; conducts stamping, machining, and subassembly operations; and has a substantial investment in tools, jigs, welding equipment, and other machinery and equipment used in the assembly of an automobile. On a per-unit basis, corporation B's selling price and costs of such automobiles are as follows:[13]

---

[12] Reg. §1.954-3(a)(4)(iii), Example 1.

[13] Reg. §1.954-3(a)(4)(iii), Example 2.

Selling price	$2,500
Cost of goods sold:	
Material	
Acquired from related persons	$1,200
Acquired from others	275
Total material	$1,475
Conversion costs (direct labor and factory burden)	325
Total cost of goods sold	$1,800
Gross profit	$ 700
Administrative and selling expenses	300
Taxable income	$ 400

The product sold, an automobile, is not sufficiently distinguishable from the components purchased (the engine, transmission, etc.) to constitute a substantial transformation of purchased parts. Although the conversion costs of corporation B are less than 20 percent of total cost of goods sold ($325/$1,800, or 18 percent), the operations conducted by corporation B in connection with the property purchased and sold are substantial in nature and are generally considered to constitute the manufacture of a product. As a result, corporation B will be considered to have manufactured the automobile under this second test.

However, the design of radio kits, the packaging of component parts required for assembly of such kits, and the sale of the parts in a knocked-down condition do not constitute substantial operations. Controlled foreign corporation C, incorporated under the laws of foreign country X, purchases radio parts manufactured in foreign country Y from related persons. Corporation C designs radio kits, packages component parts required for assembly of such kits, and sells the parts in a knocked-down condition to unrelated persons for use outside country X. These packaging operations of corporation C do not constitute the manufacture, production, or construction of property.[14] In *Garnac Grain*,[15] the cleaning, drying, aerating, fumigating, and blending of grain did not constitute manufacturing, based on industry nomenclature and perception.

(c)   20 Percent Test[16]

The third test that can be used to determine whether property is considered to be manufactured or produced is whether the property conversion costs account for 20 percent or more of the cost of goods sold. The calculation of conversion costs includes direct labor, factory burden, and assembly and packaging, but does not include the value of parts provided pursuant to a service contract. Note that this is

---

[14] Reg. §1.954-3(a)(4)(iii), Example 3.

[15] *Garnac Grain v. Comr. of Internal Revenue*, 95 T.C. 7 (1990).

[16] Reg. §1.993-3(c)(2)(iv).

different from the Subpart F provisions, which do not consider assembly, packaging, and minor assembly as conversion costs.[17] In addition, under Rev. Rul. 75-394,[18] research expenses are not included as conversion costs. If the property at issue is leased, the adjusted basis, rather than the cost of goods sold, is used as the denominator for the 20 percent calculation.[19]

As an illustration of this third test,[20] suppose a U.S. corporation acquired previously manufactured machine components from foreign businesses at a nominal price. The U.S. corporation then completely reconditioned the components, which were sold to foreign customers. If the costs of reconditioning and restoration accounted for 95 percent of the cost of goods sold of the restored machine components, the reconditioned components would qualify as export property under the DISC rules.

If any one of the three aforementioned tests is met, then the property is considered to be manufactured or produced under the first of the three requirements for export property.[21] Moreover, the property need not have been manufactured or produced by a related supplier and need not be new property.[22] Therefore, export property can be manufactured or produced by a third party or can be used property.

(d) Services

To qualify as export property, a property cannot simply represent the manifestation of a service; for example, the preparation of a map of a specific site would not qualify. However, standard maps prepared in the United States for sale to customers generally do qualify.[23] Thus, the determination as to whether an item is considered property or services is based on the facts and circumstances surrounding the development and disposition of the item.[24] In the DISC context, the value of parts provided pursuant to a related services contract[25] is not taken into account in applying this test.[26]

(e) "In the United States"

The statute requires export property for FSC and DISC purposes to be manufactured, produced, grown, or extracted "in the United States." The definition of

---

[17] Reg. §1.927(a)-1T(c)(2).

[18] 1975-2 C.B. 311.

[19] Reg. §1.927(a)-1T(c)(2).

[20] In Rev. Rul. 76-272, 1976-2 C.B. 236.

[21] Under IRC §927(a)(1).

[22] Rev. Rul. 72-455, 1972-2 C.B. 460.

[23] Reg. §1.927(a)-1T(b).

[24] Reg. §1.993-3(b).

[25] Related services are detailed in Reg. §1.993-1(d)(3). In general, a service is related to a sale or lease of export property if such service is customarily furnished with the particular sale or lease. Reg. §1.993-1(d)(3)(i).

[26] Reg. §1.993-3(c)(2)(iv).

"United States" is discussed in the statute as well as in various IRS rulings. Goods manufactured in a foreign trade zone within the geographic area of the United States are considered manufactured in the United States, even though the foreign trade zone is outside U.S. customs territory.[27]

Within the statute, the definition of "United States" includes Puerto Rico.[28] However, possessions of the United States (e.g., Guam, American Samoa, the Commonwealth of the Northern Mariana Islands, and the Virgin Islands of the United States) are considered part of the United States for *DISC purposes, but not for FSC purposes.*[29]

(f)   Further Manufacture or Production Outside the United States

If property is manufactured or produced in the United States, but then undergoes further manufacture or production outside the United States prior to sale, it must be reimported for further manufacturing or production to qualify as export property. If there is no further manufacturing or production outside the United States prior to sale after the property is originally manufactured or produced in the United States, then the property qualifies as export property.

For example, a taxpayer described in Priv. Ltr. Rul. 78-15-004[30] was a U.S. semiconductor company that fabricated silicon wafers in the United States. The wafers were sent to an unrelated company in Korea on consignment. The Korean company scribed the wafers into chips, attached lead wires, and encapsulated the chips and their containers. The assembled semiconductor devices were returned to the United States for stabilization, final testing, and packaging. The fee paid to the Korean company for its assembly operations was approximately 10 percent of the total cost of goods sold for these devices.

The activities performed by the Korean company were found to not result in a substantial transformation of the chips, to not be substantial in nature, and not generally considered to be manufacturing. The postimportation activities of the taxpayer were also held not to constitute manufacturing. Even though there was no postimportation "manufacturing," the completed semiconductor devices were considered to have been manufactured in the United States. This is because there was no further manufacturing or production outside the United States following the original U.S. wafer fabrication. As a result, the chips constituted export property.

(g)   Conversion Costs of at Least 20 Percent of Total Cost

If property is manufactured or produced in the United States and then further manufacture or production occurs outside the United States, the property will be considered manufactured in the United States if it is reimported and has conver-

---

[27] Rev. Rul. 82-115, 1982-1 C.B. 108, and Priv. Ltr. Rul. 81-42-117 (July 23, 1981).

[28] IRC §927(d)(3).

[29] IRC §993(g).

[30] Dec. 1, 1977.

sion costs of at least 20 percent of the cost of goods sold.[31] Rev. Rul. 78-228[32] illustrates this rule, describing a taxpayer that produced electronic devices in the United States and shipped them on consignment to a foreign country for assembly for a fee equal to 20 percent of the taxpayer's total cost of goods sold for the devices. The devices were then returned to the United States for further processing, evaluation, and testing. The costs incurred in these postimportation activities exceeded 20 percent of the taxpayer's total cost of goods sold for the devices.

Since the fee paid to the foreign assembler was at least 20 percent of the total cost of goods sold of the devices, further manufacture outside the United States was considered to have taken place. Nevertheless, the completed devices were held to have been manufactured in the United States because postimportation conversion costs were at least 20 percent of the total cost of goods sold. The taxpayer was allowed to apply the 20 percent test to the devices on an aggregate basis, because it sold a substantial volume of substantially identical devices with substantially identical costs.

(h)   " . . . Other Than a FSC (or DISC)"

Another requirement to consider in the classification of property as export property is that the property must be manufactured, produced, grown, or extracted by a person *other than a FSC (or DISC)*.[33] This phrase in the definition[34] of export property requires that the FSC not be the entity that engages in the manufacture, production, growth, or extraction activity.[35]

The DISC legislation contains an identical restriction.[36] The relevant rulings in this area are in the DISC context, which were the precursors to the FSC legislation. As such, these rulings are indicative of the IRS position in respect to similar fact patterns in the FSC area. The facts in Priv. Ltr. Rul. 79-47-021[37] involved a rather uncommon related-supplier/DISC relationship. The related supplier manufactured a product that underwent certain "finishing operations" after it left the assembly line. The DISC then purchased the product as it left the assembly line and contracted with the related supplier to perform the finishing operations on behalf of the DISC. The "finishing fee" paid by the DISC was less than 20 percent of its cost of goods sold for the products on an item-by-item basis. The product was sold by the DISC to export customers. Since the finishing operations were not considered to constitute substantial transformation nor to be substantial in nature, and because the DISC's conversion costs were less than 20 percent of its cost of goods sold, the

---

[31] Reg. §§1.954-3(a), 1.927(a)-1T(c)(1), and 1.993-3(c)(2)(iv).

[32] 1978-1 C.B. 252.

[33] IRC §993(c)(1)(A).

[34] Reference is to the IRC §927(a) definition.

[35] The DISC statute, IRC §993(c)(1), likewise requires that the DISC not be the entity that engages in the manufacture, production, growth, or extraction activity.

[36] IRC §993(c)(1)(A).

[37] Aug. 21, 1979.

DISC was not considered to have manufactured the products. The reason for handling the transaction in this manner, presumably, was to maximize the profit of the DISC.

The special intercompany pricing rules applied to the "unfinished product" sold to the DISC. The DISC would use the "Section 482 method" as to value added by the finishing operations. Presumably, the taxpayer had determined that there was significant potential in using the Section 482 method on a portion of the product. The same rationale would apply to a FSC. However, FSC rules relative to nonadministrative (i.e., IRC §482) pricing would make such a structure less appealing in the FSC context, particularly since the exemption is only 30 percent.

In another DISC situation, *Webb Export Corporation v. Comr. of Internal Revenue,*[38] a corporation organized as a DISC bought standing timber, had a logging crew fell the trees, clean the branches, and cut the trees into veneer logs, which were then exported. The Tax Court concluded that the DISC's timber "harvesting" activities were substantial in nature and generally considered to constitute production. However, since the logs were produced by the DISC, they did not qualify as export property. The taxpayer should have had a related corporation perform the timber harvesting activities and pay a commission to the DISC. Thus, although the three tests were met, the logs failed to qualify as export property because the production activities were performed by a nonqualified corporation (the DISC in this situation).

These DISC cases are relevant to demonstrate the potential pitfalls in the FSC context. Taxpayers must remember that the manufacturing and production of export property is not to be performed by the FSC nor by a DISC (in the DISC context). If the taxpayer can successfully demonstrate that the property is manufactured, produced, grown, or extracted in the United States by a person other than FSC (or DISC), the second requirement for the property to qualify as export property must also be met.

4.3 Foreign Use, Consumption, or Disposition

The second requirement under the statute is that export property must be held primarily for sale, lease, or rental, in the ordinary course of trade or business, by or to a FSC for direct use, consumption, or disposition outside the United States.[39] This rule applies without regard to the FOB point or place of passage of title, whether the purchaser is a U.S. or foreign purchaser, or whether the property is for the use of the purchaser or for resale.[40]

The property must, in fact, be exported at some point. For example, in Priv. Ltr. Rul. 82-12-043,[41] the taxpayer obtained a $20 million contract to build equipment in the United States for a foreign government. After the taxpayer had received

---

[38] 91 T.C. 131 (1988).

[39] IRC §§927(a)(1)(B) and 993(c)(1)(B).

[40] Reg. §1.993-3(d)(2)(i).

[41] Dec. 23, 1982.

$11 million in progress payments, the U.S. government denied the taxpayer's renewal application for an export license. Commissions had been paid to the taxpayer's DISC based on the percentage of completion method of accounting. However, because the equipment was never exported, it could not qualify as export property and no commission was allowable.

(a)   Destination Test: "Outside the United States"

Property is sold or leased for direct use, consumption, or disposition outside the United States if the sale or lease satisfies the destination test,[42] the proof of compliance requirement, and the "outside the United States test."[43] The destination test is met if the property is delivered by the seller or lessor, or by an agent of the seller or lessor:

1.   Within the United States to a carrier or freight forwarder for ultimate delivery outside the United States;[44]

2.   Within the United States to a purchaser or lessee if the property is ultimately delivered outside the United States within one year after the sale or lease;[45]

3.   To an unrelated FSC or interest-charge DISC;[46]

4.   From the United States, to a purchaser or lessee outside the United States by the seller or lessor's owned, leased, or chartered ship, aircraft, or delivery vehicle;[47]

5.   From a foreign warehouse, storage facility, or assembly site to a foreign purchaser or lessee, if the property had previously been shipped from the United States by the seller or lessor;[48] or

6.   To a foreign buyer or lessee at the termination of a qualifying export lease.[49]

(i)   Grain.   The destination test has proven particularly problematic for fungible commodities, such as grain. This is indicated in Rev. Rul. 77-484[50] and Priv. Ltr. Rul. 78-05-004,[51] in which the taxpayer was a farmer who sold grain to a cooperative. The cooperative placed the grain in its storage facilities, mixing it with grain purchased from other farmers. Most of the grain was, in fact, exported by the cooperative. In the letter ruling, the cooperative certified to the taxpayer that his

---

[42] Under Reg. §1.927(a)-1T(d)(2) for FSC purposes.

[43] For DISC purposes, the identical test is stated in Reg. §1.993-3(d)(2).

[44] Reg. §1.993-3(d)(2)(i)(A).

[45] Reg. §1.993-3(d)(2)(i)(B).

[46] See Rev. Rul. 73-229, 1973-1 C.B. 362.

[47] Reg. §1.993-3(d)(2)(i)(D).

[48] Reg. §1.993-3(d)(2)(i)(E).

[49] Reg. §1.993-3(d)(2)(i)(F).

[50] 1977-2 C.B. 289.

[51] Sept. 29, 1977.

particular grain was exported. The IRS held that because "export" grain was combined with "domestic" grain, the taxpayer farmer could not establish that his grain actually met the destination test. Accordingly, it did not qualify as export property.

Certain personnel in the national office of the IRS have informally indicated that they would not enforce this harsh rule. If, for example, 95 percent of the grain was exported, then 95 percent of the sales to a cooperative or other middlemen should qualify as sales of export property. However, there is as yet no official pronouncement to support this position.

In another situation involving grain, Priv. Ltr. Rul. 78-29-038[52] concerned a grain elevator operator who purchased grain from unrelated farmers. Most of the grain elevator operator's sales were exported, but some of the grain was sold for domestic use. Since the grain elevator operator could state specifically whether a particular shipment of grain was sold for domestic or foreign consumption, its foreign sales qualified as export property for the grain elevator operator's DISC.

Therefore, where a cooperative sells to, or pays a commission to, its own FSC, the commingling problem cited in Rev. Rul. 77-484[53] is avoided, as the cooperative is in the same position as the grain elevator operation described in Priv. Ltr. Rul. 78-29-038.[54]

(ii) Further Use. The destination test is not satisfied if the property is subject to any use, manufacture, assembly, or other processing (other than packaging) by any person between the time of sale or lease and ultimate delivery outside the United States.

An illustration of how it is possible to meet the destination test is discussed in Priv. Ltr. Rul. 84-36-028,[55] which concerned the sale of "Product M," for which a DISC commission was paid. In this ruling, some of Product M was shipped directly overseas and some was sold to an unrelated U.S. manufacturer for installation on its products. The installation process consisted of inserting Product M into a rack and plugging it into a socket. The unrelated manufacturer's product containing Product M was subsequently shipped to a foreign buyer for use outside the United States. Product M was apparently a "black box" installed on an airplane. The IRS concluded that the installation of Product M did not constitute use, manufacture, assembly, or other processing in the United States. The IRS also concluded that because the "operational use" of Product M did not take place until the product in which it was installed had left the United States, it was first "used" outside the United States. Product M met the destination test, and therefore was considered export property.

General Electric Co. v. Comr. of Internal Revenue[56] addressed an important DISC destination issue that is also applicable under the FSC regime. General Elec-

---

[52] Apr. 19, 1978.

[53] 1977-2 C.B. 289.

[54] Apr. 19, 1978.

[55] June 5, 1984.

[56] T.C. Memo. 1995-306.

tric (GE) manufactured sophisticated aircraft engines and thrust reversers and sold these parts to Boeing and McDonnell Douglass, who manufacture airframes.[57] GE sold the engines and reversers through its wholly owned subsidiary, General Electric International Sales Co. (International), which qualified as a DISC during the years at issue. Boeing and McDonnell Douglass installed the engines and reversers and delivered the finished aircraft to foreign purchasers for use, consumption, or disposition outside the United States. GE stated that the engines and reversers were fully assembled before delivery to Boeing and McDonnell Douglass and, therefore, the products were not subject to any use, manufacture, assembly, or other processing before delivery outside the United States. The court disagreed and held that GE was not entitled to additional DISC commission deductions because the engines and reversers were "subject to . . . assembly" after GE sold them to the manufacturers and therefore did not qualify as export property.

A situation illustrating the failure of a taxpayer to meet the destination test is discussed in Rev. Rul. 72-581,[58] which concerned a paint company that sold paint to unrelated purchasers to be used on ships primarily engaged in foreign commerce and offshore oil drilling. Where the purchaser painted a ship while it was in the United States, the paint was "used" in the United States and could not qualify as export property, even though the ship subsequently spent most of its time outside the United States. However, where the purchaser applied the paint to a ship outside U.S. territorial waters, the destination test was met.

(b)   Property Located Outside the United States

If property is located outside the United States at the time of purchase or lease, it can constitute export property for the purchaser or lessee *only* if the property is reimported into the United States and subject to further manufacture or production.[59] For example, assume a U.S. person acquires a used U.S.-manufactured airplane from a foreign airline, taking delivery in a foreign country. Even though the airplane was manufactured in the United States, it cannot qualify as export property, unless it is brought back to the United States and subjected to further manufacture (which might be a difficult test to meet). However, assume the used U.S.-manufactured airplane was delivered to the U.S. person in the United States before that person took title. If the airplane is thereafter exported, it might qualify as export property even if it is not subjected to further manufacture.

Several private letter rulings have addressed this issue. Priv. Ltr. Ruls. 86-49-024,[60] 86-49-025,[61] and 86-49-026[62] involved the foreign lease of U.S.-manufactured equipment. A FSC's related supplier had completed all the negotiations and

---

[57] Airframes are the full aircraft less the engines and reversers.

[58] 1972-2 C.B. 461.

[59] Reg. §1.927(a)-1T(d)(2)(iv) and Reg. §1.993-3(d)(2)(iv).

[60] Sept. 8, 1986.

[61] Sept. 8, 1986.

[62] Sept. 8, 1986.

preliminary paperwork necessary to become the purchaser/lessee of the equipment. However, the equipment was shipped by the manufacturer to a foreign country for inspection by the lessee. Title then passed to the purchaser/lessee in the foreign country. The IRS concluded that, in substance, the equipment had been purchased by the lessee while it was located in the United States. As a result, the property qualified as export property.

(c) Proof of Compliance With the Destination Test

A FSC or DISC must also be prepared to prove compliance with the destination test.[63] There are several statutory methods that can be used to prove compliance. Proof of compliance may be established by providing:

1.   A facsimile or carbon copy of the export bill of lading issued by the carrier who delivers the property;[64]

2.   A certificate of an agent or representative of the carrier disclosing delivery outside the United States;[65]

3.   A facsimile or carbon copy of the certificate of lading executed by the customs officer in the country of delivery;[66]

4.   If the country of destination has no customs administration, a written statement by the person to whom foreign delivery was made;[67]

5.   A copy of the Shipper's Export Declaration, or a magnetic tape filed in lieu of the Shipper's Export Declaration;[68] or

6.   Any other proof sufficient to satisfy the IRS that the property was ultimately delivered outside the United States within one year after the sale or lease.[69]

As part of the proof of compliance, the name of the ultimate consignee of the goods and the price paid for the goods can be marked out of a bill or certificate of lading, or from the Shipper's Export Declaration, provided the country of the ultimate consignee is still shown.[70] In addition, in the case where export sales are made to an unrelated U.S. broker/consolidator, the IRS will ordinarily accept a written statement from the broker/consolidator that all of the goods purchased by it have been shipped overseas within one year from their acquisition by the broker/consolidator.[71]

---

[63] Reg. §§1.927(a)-1T(d)(3) and 1.993-3(d)(3).

[64] Reg. §§1.993-3(d)(3)(i)(A) and 1.927(a)-1T(d)(3)(i)(A).

[65] Reg. §§1.993-3(d)(3)(i)(B) and 1.927(a)-1T(d)(3)(i)(B).

[66] Reg. §§1.993-3(d)(3)(i)(C) and 1.927(a)-1T(d)(3)(i)(C).

[67] Reg. §§1.993-3(d)(3)(i)(D) and 1.927(a)-1T(d)(3)(i)(D).

[68] Reg. §§1.993-3(d)(3)(i)(E) and 1.927(a)-1T(d)(3)(i)(E).

[69] Reg. §§1.993-3(d)(3)(i)(F) and 1.927(a)-1T(d)(3)(i)(F).

[70] Reg. §1.927(a)-1T(d)(3)(ii); Rev Rul. 73-70, 1973-1 C.B. 361.

[71] Rev. Rul. 77-249, 1977-2 C.B. 265.

Failure to provide proof of compliance with the destination test will result in the property not being treated as export property.[72] Although it is not difficult to meet the compliance tests, it is important that the taxpayer retain the necessary information so that proof is readily available in the event of an IRS examination.

(d) Use Outside the United States Test

Another aspect of the second requirement[73] is that the exported property cannot be sold or leased for ultimate use in the United States. FSC and DISC regulations both state that the property will not qualify as export property if the purchaser is a related person and either uses, or resells for use, the property of a second product into which it is incorporated in the United States, within three years of the purchase, or if the purchaser or subsequent purchaser fails, for any period of 365 consecutive days, to use the property or second product predominantly outside the United States.[74] Property is used predominantly outside the United States for any period if, during that period, the property is located outside the United States more than 50 percent of the time.[75]

For example, a U.S. company manufactures component parts that are sold to an offshore subsidiary. The offshore subsidiary then incorporates the component parts into a finished product. Fifty percent of the finished products are sold back to the U.S. company for resale in the United States. The other 50 percent are sold outside the United States by the offshore subsidiary. The 50 percent of the components sold to the offshore subsidiary should qualify as export property, even though a specific component cannot be identified at the time of export as to whether it will ultimately be used within or without the United States. This is because the other 50 percent of the products are not to be sold or leased for ultimate use in the United States.

In *FMC Corp and Subsidiaries v. Comr. of Internal Revenue,*[76] the Tax Court held that industrial cranes used on oil drilling platforms that were attached to the Outer Continental Shelf of the United States in the Gulf of Mexico were not used outside the United States. Thus, the Outer Continental Shelf of the United States is included in the term "United States" for export property purposes.

(e) Disqualifying Agreement or Understanding

An export property will be disqualified if, at the time of the sale, there is an agreement or understanding that the buyer will use, or resell for use, in the United States, the property, or a second product into which it is incorporated, within three years from the time of sale.[77] Such an agreement or understanding may be written

---

[72] Reg. §1.927(a)-1T(d)(3)(v) and Reg. §1.993-3(d)(3)(v).

[73] IRC §927(a), for FSC purposes, and IRC §993(c)(1), for DISC purposes.

[74] Reg. §§1.927(a)-1T(d)(4)(ii)(A) and 1.993-3(d)(4)(iii).

[75] Reg. §1.927(a)-1T(d)(4)(iv).

[76] 100 T.C. 595 (1993).

[77] Reg. §§1.927(a)-1T(d)(4)(ii)(B) and 1.993-3(d)(4)(ii)(B).

or oral.[78] However, such an agreement or understanding does not result from the mere fact that a second product into which the property is incorporated is sold in substantial quantities in the United States, provided the product is also sold outside the United States.[79] There is an agreement or understanding that property will ultimately be used in the United States if a component is sold overseas under an express agreement with the foreign purchaser that the component is to be incorporated into a product to be sold in the United States.[80] Another example is the foreign purchaser indicated at the time of sale, or previously, that the component is to be incorporated into a product that is designed principally for the United States market.[81]

The agreement/understanding issue was raised in Priv. Ltr. Rul. 85-30-003,[82] in which U.S.-produced components were exported to an unrelated company in Country A. The components were incorporated into Product Y by the unrelated company. Agreements between the U.S. exporter and the Country A company contained no terms or understanding concerning the destination of Product Y. The components represented less than 20 percent of the fair market value of the finished product. A trade association published public statistics reporting that 72 percent of Product Y, manufactured in Country A, was sold in the United States. The examining IRS agent argued that there was an "understanding" that the exported components would be incorporated into a product to be sold in the United States. Their reasoning was that there were public statistics establishing that Product Y was principally designed for the U.S. market. The IRS National Office, however, held that a "reasonable belief" is not encompassed in the concept of "understanding." Thus, even though 72 percent of the exported components were ultimately returned to the United States (incorporated in Product Y), all of the exported components qualified as export property.

(f) Reasonable Person Standard

The regulations have addressed the destination test issue by stating a "reasonable person" standard.[83] Under this standard, a property will be disqualified if a reasonable person would have believed that the property, or product into which it is incorporated, would be used or sold for use in the United States within three years from the date of the export sale. This reasonable person standard does not apply to components that constitute less than 20 percent of the fair market value of the product into which they are incorporated.[84] The regulations, however, do not

---

[78] Reg. §§1.927(a)-1T(d)(4)(ii) and 1.993-3(d)(4)(ii).

[79] Reg. §§1.927(a)-1T(d)(4)(ii) and 1.993-3(d)(4)(ii).

[80] Reg. §§1.927(a)-1T(d)(4)(ii)(C) and 1.993-3(d)(4)(ii).

[81] Reg. §§1.927(a)-1T(d)(4)(ii)(C) and 1.993-3(d)(4)(ii).

[82] Apr. 25, 1985.

[83] Reg. §§1.927(a)-1T(d)(4)(ii)(C) and 1.993-3(d)(4)(ii)(c).

[84] Reg. §§1.927(a)-1T(d)(4)(ii)(C) and 1.993-3(d)(4)(ii)(c).

state how this 20 percent test is to be determined or substantiated. Presumably, a written statement from the manufacturer of the second product would suffice.

Property sold to a retailer whose principal business consists of sales from retail outlets outside the United States will be considered used outside the United States, even if the retail customers bring the property into the United States.[85] In Rev. Rul. 74-328,[86] the IRS ruled that U.S.-made cameras sold by mail order by a U.S. company directly to U.S. servicemen stationed overseas qualified as export property.

(g)   Property Must Be Outside the United States More Than 50 Percent of the Time

Another aspect of the definition of export property is that the property must be located outside the United States more than 50 percent of the time.[87] For example, an aircraft, railroad rolling stock, vessel, motor vehicle, container, or other property used for transportation purposes is deemed to be used predominantly outside the United States for any period if, during that period, either the property is located outside the United States more than 50 percent of the time, or more than 50 percent of the miles traveled in the use of the property are traversed outside the United States.[88]

The 50 percent test for export property applies to any period of 365 consecutive days within the three-year period from the date of the export sale.[89] This 50 percent test is made for each taxable year of the lessor for the lease of export property.[90] Leased property could qualify as export property during one year of a lease but not others.[91]

Property located outside the planet is also considered in the definition of property located outside the United States. For example, an orbiting satellite is deemed to be located outside the United States.[92]

4.4   Not More Than 50 Percent of the FMV Is Attributable to Imported Articles

(a)   Foreign Content Test

Once the taxpayer has satisfied the first and second requirements[93] as discussed in the preceding sections, the third and final requirement must be met. The third

---

[85] Reg. §§1.927(a)-1T(d)(4)(iv) and 1.993-3(d)(4)(iv).

[86] 1974-2 C.B. 239.

[87] Reg. §§1.927(a)-1T(d)(4)(vi) and 1.993-3(d)(4)(vi).

[88] Reg. §§1.927(a)-1T(d)(4)(vi) and 1.993-3(d)(4)(vi).

[89] Reg. §§1.927(a)-1T(d)(4)(iii) and 1.993-3(d)(4)(iii).

[90] Reg. §§1.927(a)-1T(d)(4)(v) and 1.993-3(d)(4)(v).

[91] Reg. §§1.927(a)-1T(d)(4)(v) and 1.993-3(d)(4)(v).

[92] Reg. §1.927(a)-1T(d)(4)(vi).

[93] Under IRC §927(a)(1) (as a FSC) or IRC §993(c)(1) (as a DISC).

requirement for the determination of export property is the foreign content test. The foreign content test requires that not more than 50 percent of the fair market value (FMV) of export property can be attributable to articles imported into the United States.[94] In this context, articles imported into the United States are referred to as "foreign content."[95] The fair market value of export property that is sold to a person who is not a person related to the seller is the sale price for such property, not including interest, finance or carrying charges, or similar charges.[96] The 50 percent foreign content test is generally applied on an item-by-item basis. However, where a large volume of substantially identical export property with substantially identical foreign content in substantially the same portion is sold or leased, the 50 percent test may be applied on an aggregate basis.[97]

The foreign content requirement was addressed in Priv. Ltr. Rul. 81-41-016,[98] which concerned a U.S. motion picture camera manufacturer. Most of the camera components were made in the United States, but all the lenses for the cameras were manufactured outside the United States. Each lens was made to fit only one type of camera, but there was more than one type of lens available with each camera. The U.S. camera manufacturer assembled and tested all complete camera systems, including lenses, prior to sale. When a camera system was shipped, the lens was packaged separately in order to prevent damage to the camera and to retain the precise alignment of the lens.

The 50 percent foreign content test applied separately to each camera because the camera systems were not substantially identical and did not contain substantially identical foreign content in substantially the same portion. Where a foreign-made lens constituted not more than 50 percent of the fair market value of a camera system, the entire camera system, including the lens, qualified as export property.

(b) Parts Pursuant to a Services Contract

Where export property is sold or leased and the seller or lessor agrees to furnish parts pursuant to a services contract, application of the 50 percent foreign content test depends on whether the price for the parts is separately stated.[99] Therefore, if the price for the parts is separately stated, the 50 percent test is applied separately to the property and to the parts. If not separately stated, the 50 percent test is applied on an aggregate basis to the property and parts. This rule generally applies to parts furnished under a warranty.

---

[94] IRC §927(a)(1)(C) and Reg. §1.993-3(e)(1).

[95] Reg. §§1.927(a)-1T(e)(1) and 1.993-3(e)(1).

[96] Reg. §§1.927(a)-1T(e)(1) and 1.993-3(e)(1).

[97] Reg. §§1.927(a)-1T(e)(2) and 1.993-3(e)(2).

[98] Apr. 13, 1979.

[99] Reg. §§1.927(a)-1T(e)(3) and 1.993-3(e)(3).

(c)   Valuation for Foreign Content Purposes

To determine whether the 50 percent test is met, it is necessary to determine the fair market value of all articles that constitute foreign content of the property.[100] The fair market value of imported articles is generally their full dutiable value, determined without regard to any special provision in U.S. tariff law that results in a lower dutiable value.[101] For example, assume that U.S.-made products are shipped to a maquiladora for further processing. After processing, the products are reimported into the United States. At the time of importation, the full dutiable value of a processed product is $125, of which $100 is attributable to U.S. content and $25 to value added in Mexico. Under the U.S. tariff laws, duty is paid only on the $25 value added. For FSC purposes, the general rule is that the "foreign content" is $125.

The appraised value may be used for purposes of proving fair market value of imported articles.[102] Such appraised value may be shown by the customs invoice issued on the importation of the articles into the United States. If the holder of the articles is not the importer (or a related person as to the importer), the appraised value of the articles may be evidenced by a certificate based on information contained in the customs invoice and furnished to the holder by the person from whom the articles (or property incorporating the articles) were purchased. If a customs invoice or certificate is not available, the taxpayer is to establish that no more than 50 percent of the fair market value of such property is attributable to the fair market value of the articles that were imported into the United States.[103]

(d)   Election to Exclude

A special election can be made, in certain circumstances, to exclude U.S. manufactured or produced articles from the measure of foreign content at the time of importation.[104] For purposes of this election, if the initial export is made to a controlled person within the meaning of IRC §482, the fair market value of the imported articles and of the portion of the articles that are manufactured, produced, grown, or extracted within the United States is to be established by the taxpayer in accordance with the rules and regulations under IRC §482.[105] If the initial export is not made to a controlled person, the fair market value must be established by the taxpayer under the prevailing facts and circumstances.[106]

The special election is available only if the imported product is further manufactured or produced in the United States. The excludable U.S. content is based on the fair market value at the time of initial export. Where available, it would seem

---

[100] Reg. §§1.927(a)-1T(e)(4)(i) and 1.993-3(e)(4)(i).

[101] Reg. §§1.927(a)-1T(e)(4)(i)(A) and 1.993-3(e)(4)(i).

[102] Reg. §§1.927(a)-1T(e)(4)(ii)(A) and 1.993-3(e)(4)(i).

[103] Reg. §§1.927(a)-1T(e)(4)(ii)(A) and 1.993-3(e)(4)(i).

[104] Reg. §1.927(a)-1T(e)(4)(i)(B).

[105] Reg. §1.927(a)-1T(e)(4)(ii)(B).

[106] Reg. §1.927(a)-1T(e)(4)(ii)(B).

that the special election *should always be made,* as it can only be favorable to the taxpayer.

The special election is a creation of the FSC regulations, in response to language in the Committee Reports to the FSC legislation. *There is no comparable election for DISC purposes,* even though the statutory language is the same in both cases.

If a person acquires interchangeable component articles, some of which are made in the United States and some of which are made outside the United States, the foreign-made articles are deemed to be the first exported.[107] As an illustration, assume a manufacturer produces 20,000 electronic devices, of which 16,000 are exported. Each device contains a tube that represents 60 percent of its value. Furthermore, assume 8,000 of the tubes were imported, while 12,000 were produced in the United States. The imported tubes are deemed to be contained in the first 8,000 exported electronic devices. Since the 50 percent foreign content test is not met as to the 3,000 tubes, only the remaining 8,000 exported devices qualify for FSC benefits.[108]

The fair market value test is performed by comparing the full dutiable value of the imported article (generally the invoice price) to the fair market value of the exported product (generally the sales price).[109] Where the export is to an unrelated person, the export sales price establishes its fair market value. Where the export is to a related person, the intercompany transfer price should be considered the fair market value, unless the IRS makes an adjustment to the price under IRC §482 (or accepts a transfer pricing adjustment by a foreign government). In effect, a "markup" on an imported component is treated as U.S. content.

For example, assume the import price of components is $100. They are assembled into a finished product at a cost of $125. The product is exported at a price of $200. Although the U.S. portion of cost of goods sold in this example is only 20 percent (25/125), the product passes the 50 percent foreign content test, because the fair market value of the import ($100) does not exceed 50 percent of the fair market value of the export ($200).

It is also important to remember the interplay of the "manufactured in the United States" test and the "foreign content" test. This is illustrated by the following example. Assume a U.S. personal computer company has all the components for its computer manufactured abroad. The components for one computer are imported into the United States at a total dutiable value of $900. The computer is then assembled in the United States at a cost of $100. The completed computer is then exported at a sales price of $2,000. The foreign content test is met, as the import value ($900) is not more than 50 percent of the export value ($2,000).

The next issue is whether the computer has been manufactured or produced in the United States. The 20 percent conversion costs "safe haven" has not been met.

---

[107] Reg. §§1.927(a)-1T(e)(4)(iii) and 1.993-3(e)(4)(iii).

[108] Reg. §1.927(a)-1T(e)(4)(iii)(B). A similar example is contained in the DISC regulations under Reg. §1.993-3(e)(4)(iii)(B), Example.

[109] Reg. §1.927(a)-1T(e)(1).

It is certainly possible that at least 20 percent of the total costs of the computer have occurred in the United States if related research and experimental expenditures are taken into account. However, because research expenditures are not an inventoriable cost,[110] they cannot be considered in the 20 percent cost of goods sold test.[111] In addition, it is doubtful that the assembly of the computer would be considered substantial transformation.[112] The issue then becomes whether the activities performed by the computer company are substantial in nature and generally considered to constitute manufacturing. If they are, then the computer will be considered to be export property.

(e) Use of a Foreign Subcontractor

Where U.S.-produced goods are sent outside the United States for further assembly or processing, it can make a substantial difference whether the goods are sold or are consigned to the foreign subcontractor. As an example, assume that a U.S.-manufactured product with a total cost of $100 (all U.S. content) is sent to a maquiladora for further processing. The maquiladora earns $20 for its activities, which do not involve substantial transformation and are not generally considered manufacturing. Assume the full dutiable value of importation, excluding the special tariff exclusion from U.S. content, is $120. The U.S. company incurs an additional $5 in testing and packaging the product. The product is then exported at a price of $300.

If the product had been *consigned* to the maquiladora, then the taxpayer has manufactured a product in the United States that has not undergone further manufacture outside the United States prior to export. The $20 fee to the maquiladora is less than 20 percent of the total cost of goods sold for the product.[113] If the product had been *sold* to the maquiladora, the taxpayer has to "start fresh" after reimportation.[114] The testing and packaging incurred at a cost of $5 are not sufficient to constitute manufacturing. Consequently, the product will not qualify as export property.

(f) Content Determined Based on Where Good Was Grown

The foreign content test is also applied to agricultural products. Rev. Rul. 75-394[115] describes the activities of a seed company and how the export property rules apply to such a taxpayer. The taxpayer sells flower seeds throughout the world. The seeds are produced from plants developed by the taxpayer in its laboratory in the United States. The process of developing new varieties of hybrid seeds entails an extensive amount of development and testing work. When a new variety is ready

---

[110] Reg. §§1.471-11(c)(2)(ii)(F) and 1.263A-1T(a)(6)(iv).

[111] *See* Rev. Rul 75-394.

[112] *See* Reg. §1.954-3(a)(4)(iii), Examples 1 and 2.

[113] *See* Priv. Ltr. Rul. 78-15-004 (Dec. 1, 1977).

[114] *See* Rev. Rul 78-228, 1978-1 C.B. 252.

[115] 1975-2 C.B. 311.

for mass production, the taxpayer ships the stock seed to a growing station in for-eign country X that is operated by a wholly owned foreign subsidiary corporation of the taxpayer. Country X is used as a growing station to provide additional seeds because its climate permits flowers to be grown on a year-round basis. This method provides the taxpayer with a consistent year-round fresh stock of seeds. After the seeds are produced at the country X growing station, they are returned to the tax-payer's laboratory in the United States. At this time, the seeds are again tested and thoroughly evaluated prior to marketing, but the costs of direct labor and factory burden do not exceed 20 percent of the inventory of the cost of goods sold.

The ruling concludes that the seeds are not manufactured, produced, grown, or extracted in the United States. The fact that the "parent seeds" were developed in the United States is seen as irrelevant. The place where the actual seed being sold was grown determines its content. Although not explicitly stated, implicit in the rul-ing's conclusion that the 20 percent cost of goods sold test is not met is a determi-nation that research expenditures cannot constitute part of the cost of goods sold.

(g)   Related FSC Transactions

Property sold, leased, or rented by a FSC, or with a FSC as commission agent, to a related FSC cannot qualify as export property.[116] This provision appears to be based on IRC §924(f)(1)(C), as in effect prior to the Tax Reform Act of 1986, which provided that such related FSC receipts could not be included in foreign trading gross receipts. However, the Tax Reform Act of 1986 amended IRC §924(f)(1)(C) (on a retroactive basis) to permit such related FSC receipts, provided none of the FSCs use the 1.83 percent gross receipts pricing method with respect to the transaction.

Reg. §1.927(a)-1T(a)(4) was issued subsequent to enactment of the Tax Reform Act of 1986. Its blanket prohibition on related FSC sales is apparently an over-sight. Similarly, the wording of Reg. §1.924(a)-1T(g)(6)(B), which prohibits a FSC from having two related suppliers on the same sales transaction (even if the 23 percent combined taxable income method is used with respect to each supplier), is also apparently an oversight.

4.5   Specific Exclusions from Export Property

Five types of property are specifically excluded from the definition of "export property."[117] The first category is property that is leased or rented by FSC for use by a related person (whether or not FSC).[118] A "related person" is any member of the same controlled group of corporations of which the FSC is a member, as de-

---

[116] Reg. §1.927(a)-1T(a)(4).

[117] IRC §927(a)(2).

[118] IRC §927(a)(2)(A). IRC §993(c)(2)(A) states that property leased or rented by a DISC for use by any member of a controlled group (as defined in IRC §993(a)(3)) includes the DISC.

fined in IRC §1563(a), except that "more than 50 percent" is substituted for "at least 80 percent."[119]

Property that is leased to an unrelated person who subleases the property for use by a person related to the FSC (or DISC) is disqualified from being export property.[120] For example, if a FSC (or DISC) leases a movie film to a foreign corporation that is not a member of the same controlled group and the foreign corporation then subleases the film to persons that are members of the controlled group for showing to the general public, the film is not export property.[121]

However, property leased to a related person will be considered export property if the related person subleases the property to an unrelated person predominantly for use outside the United States.[122] Therefore, if a FSC (or DISC) leases a movie film to a foreign corporation that is a member of the same controlled group and the foreign corporation then subleases the film to another foreign corporation that is not a member of the same controlled group for showing to the general public, the film is considered to be export property (provided it meets the other definitional requirements[123]).[124]

(a)   Intellectual Property Issues

Export property excludes *patents, inventions, models, designs, formulas,* and *processes,* whether or not patented, *copyrights* (other than films, tapes, records, and similar reproductions, for commercial or home use), *goodwill, trademarks, trade names,* and *other like property.*[125] A copyrighted article, such as a book or standardized mass-market computer software, can qualify as export property if it otherwise qualifies, if it is not accompanied by a right to reproduce the property for external use.[126] Computer software can be on any medium, including, but not limited to, magnetic tape, punched cards, disks, semiconductor chips, and circuit boards.[127]

(b)   Technology Issues

In Priv. Ltr. Ruls. 85-49-003,[128] 86-52-001,[129] and 92-10-015,[130] the IRS National Office similarly held that standardized computer software that is mass

---

[119] IRC §§927(d)(4) and 993(a)(3).

[120] Reg. §§1.927(a)-1T(f)(2)(iii) and 993(f)(2)(iii).

[121] Reg. §§1.927(a)-1T(f)(2)(iii) and 993(f)(2)(iii).

[122] Reg. §§1.927(a)-1T(f)(2)(i) and 993(f)(2)(i).

[123] Under IRC §927(a)(1) for a FSC or IRC §993(c)(1) for a DISC.

[124] Reg. §§1.927(a)-1T(f)(2)(iii) and 993(f)(2)(iii).

[125] IRC §§927(a)(2)(B) and 993(c)(2)(B).

[126] Reg. §1.927(a)-1T(f)(3).

[127] Reg. §1.927(a)-1T(f)(3).

[128] Aug. 16, 1983.

[129] Sept. 3, 1986.

[130] Dec. 6, 1991.

marketed outside the United States without reproduction rights constitutes export property. Moreover, in TAM 9344002,[131] the IRS addressed the issue of whether software reproduction royalties are eligible for FSC benefits. In this TAM, the taxpayer licensed foreign distributors to duplicate software programs that were to be sold overseas through these foreign distributors. The taxpayer granted nontransferable and nonexclusive licenses to these distributors to duplicate and to distribute the software. These distributors were also granted the right to publish instruction materials for the software. The U.S. company provided the distributors with a master disk containing the software. The IRS found that the computer software conveyed by the licenses was excluded from export property; thus, the royalties were not eligible for FSC benefits.

The term "tapes"[132] refers to audio or video tapes used in the entertainment industry and does not apply to magnetic tapes used in the computer software industry. Computer software conveyed through a licensing agreement that gives the licensee the right to reproduce the software therefore is excluded from the term "export property." As a result, the royalties from the taxpayer's licensing agreements are not eligible for FSC benefits.

A license of a master recording tape for reproduction outside the United States can qualify as export property.[133] It would seem that the same rationale should apply to a license of a software master for duplication outside the United States. The IRS position, however, is that a software master license cannot qualify as export property. Notwithstanding the apparent IRS position, taxpayers have a reasonable position to treat a master software license as export property, based on the regulation's treatment of a master recording tape license. IRC §6662 disclosure should be made if this position is taken.

In a case currently before the United States Tax Court, *Borland International Inc. v. Comr. of Internal Revenue,*[134] Borland is contesting the determination that the commission attributable to reproduction royalties for computer software and related instruction books do not qualify as foreign trading gross receipts. Borland is the successor in interest to Ashton-Tate Corp., which granted licenses to certain foreign distributors to reproduce and sell its software programs and related instruction books. Ashton-Tate treated the royalties it received as foreign trading gross receipts from the sale or lease of export property, for purposes of computing the commission to its wholly owned foreign sales corporation.

The IRS has determined that the commissions attributable to the reproduction royalties do not qualify as foreign trading gross receipts, ruling that the computer software conveyed through a licensing agreement that gives the licensee the right to reproduce the software is excluded from the term "export property" under IRC §927(a)(2)(B), and that the term "tapes" contained in the parenthetical exception

[131] May 27, 1993.

[132] *In* IRC §927(a)(2)(B).

[133] Reg. §1.927(a)-1T(f)(3). *Also see* Priv. Ltr. Rul. 81-23-112 (March 13, 1981).

[134] Docket No. 1605-94.

refers to audio or video tapes used in the entertainment industry and does not apply to magnetic tapes used in the computer software industry. Borland is claiming that the IRS's interpretation of the statute is erroneous and that the reproduction royalties qualify as foreign trading gross receipts.

(c)   Oil and Gas

Export property does not include *oil, gas, or any primary product thereof.*[135] Primary products from oil are crude oil and products derived from the destructive distillation of crude oil, including:[136]

1. Volatile products;
2. Light oils, such as motor fuel and kerosene;
3. Distillates such as naphtha;
4. Lubricating oils;
5. Greases and waxes; and
6. Residues such as fuel oil.

Primary products from gas are all gas and associated hydrocarbon components from gas wells or oil wells, including:[137]

1. Natural gas;
2. Condensates;
3. Liquefied petroleum gases such as ethane, propane, and butane; and
4. Liquid products such as natural gasoline.

Petrochemicals, medicinal products, insecticides, and alcohol, however, are not considered primary products from oil or gas and therefore can potentially be export property if the statutory definition is met. In addition, in Priv. Ltr. Rul. 87-07-002,[138] white mineral oils, petroleum jelly, and micro-crystalline waxes were found not to be primary products from oil or gas. Accordingly, they could qualify as export property as well.

(d)   Export Controlled Products

Several types of property, not commonly encountered, are not treated as export property for FSC (or DISC) purposes. Exported products that are prohibited or curtailed by the Export Administration Act of 1979 cannot qualify as export property. This prohibition emanates from the necessity to protect the domestic economy

---

[135] IRC §§927(a)(2)(C) and 993(c)(2)(C).

[136] Reg. §§1.927-1T(g)(2)(i) and 1.993-3(g)(3)(i).

[137] Reg. §§1.927-1T(g)(2)(ii) and 1.993-3(g)(3)(ii).

[138] Oct. 20, 1986.

from an excessive drain of scarce materials and to reduce the serious inflationary impact of foreign demand.[139]

Export property also excludes property that the president has designated by executive order as being in short supply.[140] A Commodity Control List (CCL) is detailed and explained in approximately 200 pages of Part 799 of Chapter VII, Title 15 of the Code of Federal Regulations (CFR). This list is updated daily, when necessary, in the Federal Register. The CCL is separated into 10 groups. Each item within a group is given a four-digit export control commodity number and is followed by a code letter that determines the level of documentation requested.

4.6   Qualified Foreign Trading Gross Receipts

Once a taxpayer's property has met the three-prong definition of export property under IRC §927(a)(1), the property will qualify for FSC benefits if it also falls under one of the categories of foreign trading gross receipts. There are five general categories of foreign trading gross receipts:[141]

1. Receipts from the sale, exchange, or other disposition of export property;
2. Receipts from the lease or rental of export property for use by the lessee outside the United States;
3. Receipts for services that are related and subsidiary to a sale or lease of export property;
4. Receipts from engineering or architectural services for foreign construction projects; and
5. Receipts from managerial services for an unrelated FSC or DISC.

The *principal* category is receipts from the sale, exchange, or other disposition of export property.[142]

(a)   Sale, Exchange, or Other Disposition of Export Property

One of the predominant uses of a FSC is the sale of export property. The term "sale" includes an exchange or other disposition.[143] In Rev. Ruls. 73-228,[144] and 76-338,[145] the IRS seized upon the literal wording of the statute to hold that commissions received by a DISC from its foreign parent company for arranging for the

---

[139] IRC §§927(a)(2)(D) and 993(c)(2)(D).

[140] IRC §§927(a)(3) and 993(c)(3).

[141] In the DISC context, qualified export receipts are identically identified.

[142] IRC §924(a)(1).

[143] Reg. §1.924(a)-1T(a)(2).

[144] 1973-1 C.B. 362.

[145] 1976-2 C.B. 233.

purchase of U.S.-produced property, did not constitute qualified export receipts.[146]
The rationale was that the commissions were received as to the purchase, rather than
sale, of export property. The validity of the rulings, however, is open to question.

Priv. Ltr. Rul. 81-12-001[147] involved a situation that, in substance, was essentially the same as discussed in Rev. Ruls. 73-228 and 76-338, with a slight varia-
tion in form. The foreign parent company had a non-DISC U.S. subsidiary that
purchased U.S. products and resold them to the parent company and other foreign
purchasers. The U.S. subsidiary, in turn, had a DISC subsidiary. The DISC received commissions on the sale of products by the non-DISC. The DISC commissions were held to constitute qualified export receipts. Given the nature of the activity, it is probable the DISC in Priv. Ltr. Rul. 81-12-001 received all the net
income from exports under the 4 percent method. Thus, the result (other than the
IRS's blessing) is likely to be the same as in Rev. Ruls. 73-228[148] and 76-338.[149]

In Priv. Ltr. Rul. 83-25-020,[150] the IRS recast the form of transactions involving
a buy/sell DISC into a commission arrangement in order to fit the transactions
within Rev. Ruls. 73-228 and 76-338. A foreign trading company had an operating
U.S. subsidiary which, in turn, owned all the stock of a DISC. A foreign customer
would order U.S.-made equipment from the foreign trading company, which in
turn sent the order to its U.S. subsidiary as the agent for the DISC. The U.S. manufacturer would sell the equipment to the DISC, which then resold it to its foreign
grandparent trading company at a markup of 1.2 percent to 1.5 percent above cost.
The IRS concluded that the DISC's sales markup was, in substance, a purchasing
commission and, accordingly, did not result in qualified export receipts.

Rev. Rul. 74-216[151] concerned a domestic corporation that converted raw materials into a liquid extract on behalf of a foreign corporation. The domestic corporation did not take title to the raw materials but, rather, received a conversion fee from
the foreign corporation. The domestic corporation proposed to pay a commission to
a DISC subsidiary as to the conversion fee. The ruling concluded that no DISC
commission would be paid, because the conversion fee was not receipts from the
sale, exchange, or other disposition of export property. Receipts from the sale of
U.S.-produced textbooks to schools sponsored by U.S. citizens in foreign countries
are considered to be foreign trading gross receipts under Rev. Rul. 76-458.[152]

Export property can include the receipts from sales to the United States or an instrumentality. These receipts can qualify as foreign trading gross receipts if made
pursuant to the regulations, which contain the following:[153]

---

[146] *Under* IRC §993(a).

[147] Nov. 13, 1981.

[148] 1973-1 C.B. 362.

[149] 1976-2 C.B. 233.

[150] Mar. 15, 1983.

[151] 1974-1 C.B. 195.

[152] 1976-2 C.B. 237.

[153] Reg. §1.924(a)-1T(g)(4)(iii).

1. A program under which the U.S. government purchases property for resale on commercial terms, to a foreign government or agency, or

2. A program under which sales to the U.S. government are open to international competitive bidding.

For purposes of qualifying as foreign trading gross receipts under the first category of receipts from the sale exchange, or other disposition of export property,[154] there must be a contract with the FSC, or assigned to the FSC, prior to the shipment of the property to the purchaser. However, the contract or contract assignment can be oral.[155] The FSC must, in fact, qualify as a FSC at the time of shipment to the purchaser in order for proceeds therefrom to constitute foreign trading gross receipts.[156]

(b) Lease or Rental of Export Property

The second category of qualified foreign trading gross receipts is the lease or rental of export property for use by the lessee outside the United States.[157] To be classified as export property under this category, the property must be held by the FSC, or by its principal if the FSC acts as commission agent. This relationship must apply as owner or lessee at the beginning of the term of the lease, and the FSC must qualify as a FSC for its taxable year in which the term of the lease begins.[158] It is not necessary for the FSC to have been in existence at the time the property was previously shipped from the United States.[159]

Prepaid lease receipts are considered foreign trading gross receipts if it is reasonable to expect that the leased property will be export property throughout the term of the lease.[160] However, if prepaid lease receipts are received in a year in which it is expected that the leased property will not be export property, those receipts are not considered foreign trading gross receipts.[161] For example, if a lessee makes a prepayment of the first and last years' rent, and it is reasonably expected that the leased property will be export property for the first half of the lease period but not for the second half of that period, the amount of the prepayment that represents the first year's rent will be considered foreign trading gross receipts if it would otherwise qualify, whereas the amount of the prepayment that represents the last year's rent will not be considered foreign trading gross receipts.[162]

---

[154] IRC §924(a)(1).

[155] Reg. §1.924(a)-1T(b).

[156] Reg. §1.924(a)-1T(b).

[157] IRC §924(a)(2).

[158] Reg. §1.924(a)-1T(c)(1).

[159] Rev. Rul. 75-311, 1975-2 C.B. 310.

[160] Reg. §1.924(a)-1T(c)(2)(i).

[161] Reg. §1.924(a)-1T(c)(2)(ii).

[162] Reg. §1.924(a)-1T(c)(2)(ii).

(c) Related and Subsidiary Services

The third category of foreign trading gross receipts includes receipts for services that are related and subsidiary to a sale or lease of export property.[163] A service is related to a sale or lease of export property if it is of a type customarily and usually furnished.[164] Qualifying services may be performed either within or without the United States, although they are generally performed at a foreign location.[165] Related services that qualify include, but are not limited to, warranty, maintenance, repair, installation, and transportation.[166] In addition, the contract to furnish the service must be:[167]

1. Expressly or implicitly provided for in the sale or lease contract;
2. Offered to the purchaser or lessee by the time of shipment of the property and entered into within two years of the date of the sales or lease contract; or
3. A renewal of either of the above.

Cumulative expected receipts for the services must be recalculated each time the FSC, or person under contract with the FSC, enters into a renewal contract for related services.[168]

Services are considered subsidiary to a sale or lease of export property if it is reasonably expected, at the time of the sale or lease, that the gross receipts from all related services furnished by the FSC (or a person under contract with the FSC) will not exceed the gross receipts from the sale or lease.[169] The "reasonable expectation" is based on related services expected to be performed during the 10-year period following the date of an export sale, or throughout the term of the lease of an export lease.[170] For example, assume that export property is sold for $100, and that related services are expected to be $100. Receipts from these related services are foreign trading gross receipts. Contrast this example with a scenario in which the export property is sold for $100, and related services are expected to be $101. In this case, none of the receipts from the related services are foreign trading gross receipts.

Where services are "bundled" into the export sale or lease price, an allocation of the value of the services is required to determine if the services meet the "subsidiary" requirement.[171] Where more than one item of export property is sold or leased in a

---

[163] IRC §924(a)(3).

[164] Reg. §1.924(a)-1T(d)(3)(i).

[165] Reg. §1.924(a)-1T(d)(1).

[166] Reg. §1.924(a)-1T(d)(3).

[167] Reg. §1.924(a)-1T(d)(3)(ii).

[168] Reg. §1.924(a)-1T(d)(1)(iv).

[169] Reg. §1.924(a)-1T(d)(4)(i).

[170] Reg. §1.924(a)-1T(d)(4)(i).

[171] Reg. §1.924(a)-1T(d)(4)(ii).

single transaction, the comparison of receipts from services to sale or lease receipts is done on an aggregate basis for that transaction, provided the various items of export property fall within the same product line.[172] Receipts related to the furnishing of parts under a services contract are not considered to be received for services.[173]

The services may be performed by the FSC, the related supplier, another member of the same controlled group, or an unrelated person under contract with the FSC.[174] In each case, it is necessary that the FSC act as principal or commission agent on the underlying sale or lease, as discussed in Rev. Rul. 75-322.[175] In this ruling, P, a domestic corporation, exported machines manufactured by X, an unrelated corporation. P paid a commission to a DISC on the export sales. Employees of X provided installation and warranty services to the foreign purchasers under contract with P. Receipts received by P for the services provided by X's employees under contract with P were held not to be for related and subsidiary services. The receipts would have qualified if the contract had been directly with the DISC.

The determination as to whether gross receipts from the sale or lease of export property constitute foreign trading gross receipts does not depend on whether services connected with the sale or lease are related and subsidiary to the sale or lease.[176] For example, assume that the FSC receives gross receipts of $1,000 from the sale of export property and gross receipts of $1,100 from the installation and maintenance services, which are to be furnished by the FSC within 10 years after the sale and which are related to the sale. The $1,100 that the FSC receives for the services would not be foreign trading gross receipts since the gross receipts from the services exceed 50 percent of the sum of the gross receipts from the sale and the gross receipts from the related services furnished by the FSC. The $1,000 that the FSC receives from the sale of export property would be foreign trading gross receipts if the sale otherwise meets the export property requirements of Reg. §1.924(a)-1T(b).[177]

(d) Engineering or Architectural Services for Foreign Construction Projects

The fourth category of foreign trading gross receipts are receipts for engineering or architectural services for foreign construction projects.[178] These services may be performed within or without the United States.[179] For purposes of this category, engineering services in connection with any construction project[180] include any pro-

---

[172] Reg. §1.924(a)-1T(d)(4)(iii).

[173] Reg. §1.924(a)-1T(d)(4)(v).

[174] Reg. §1.924(a)-1T(d)(2).

[175] 1975-2 C.B. 310.

[176] Reg. §1.924(a)-1T(d)(6).

[177] Reg. §1.924(a)-1T(d)(6).

[178] IRC §1.924(a)(4).

[179] Reg. §1.924(a)-1T(e)(1).

[180] As defined in Reg. §1.924-1T(e)(8).

fessional services requiring engineering education, training, and experience and the application of special knowledge of the mathematical, physical, or engineering sciences to those professional services as consultation, investigation, evaluation, planning, design, or responsible supervision of construction for the purpose of assuring compliance with plans, specifications, and design.[181] Similarly, architectural services that qualify as foreign trading gross receipts include the offering or furnishing of any professional services such as consultation, planning, aesthetic and structural design, drawings and specifications, or responsible supervision of construction (for the purpose of assuring compliance with plans, specifications, and design) or erection, in connection with any construction project as defined[182] in the regulations.[183]

For example, engineering and architectural services in connection with a feasibility study for a proposed foreign construction project would qualify as foreign trading gross receipts.[184] For purposes of this category, a "construction project" includes:[185]

1.   Erection, expansion, or major repair of buildings or other physical facilities such as roads, dams, canals, bridges, tunnels, railroad tracks, and pipelines; and

2.   Site grading and improvement and equipment installation.

These services may be performed by the FSC, by another person under contract with the FSC acting as principal, or by another person where the FSC acts as commission agent.[186] The persons performing the services may be nonresident aliens.[187] However, qualifying services exclude:[188]

1.   Services connected with exploration for oil or gas; and

2.   Technical assistance or know-how, including activities or programs designed to enable business, commerce, industrial establishments, and governmental organizations to acquire or use scientific, architectural, or engineering information.

(e)   Receipts from Managerial Services for an Unrelated FSC or DISC

The fifth category of foreign trading gross receipts is one that is rarely encountered, the managerial services for an unrelated FSC or DISC.[189] To qualify under

---

[181] Reg. §1.924(a)-1T(e)(5).

[182] As defined in Reg. § 1.924(a)-1T(e)(8).

[183] Reg. §1.924(a)-1T(e)(6).

[184] Reg. §1.924(a)-1T(e)(2).

[185] Reg. §1.924(a)-1T(e)(8).

[186] Reg. §1.924(a)-1T(e)(7).

[187] Rev. Rul. 75-69, 1975-1 C.B. 253.

[188] Reg. §1.924(a)-1T(e)(3).

[189] IRC §924(a)(5).

this category, the FSC providing the managerial services must derive at least 50 percent of its total gross receipts from export sales and leases and related and subsidiary services to those sales and leases.[190] The services may be provided by the FSC or by another person under contract with the FSC.[191] "Managerial services" include such things as conducting export market studies, making shipping arrangements, and contacting foreign purchasers, but do not include legal, accounting, scientific, or technical services.[192]

4.7 Nonqualified Foreign Trading Gross Receipts

Examples of transactions that specifically would not qualify as foreign trading gross receipts and would not be eligible for FSC benefits are included in the statute. For instance, receipts from a transaction that is for ultimate use by the United States or any instrumentality thereof, are not foreign trading gross receipts if the use of export property or services is required by law or regulation.[193]

(a) Sales to the Department of Defense

A sale of export property to the Department of Defense does not produce foreign trading gross receipts if the property is purchased from appropriated funds subject to a provision that requires the items purchased to have been grown, reprocessed, reused, or produced in the United States.[194] Receipts from items purchased by the Department of Defense for resale in post or base exchanges and commissary stores located on U.S. military installations in foreign countries are *not* disqualified under this provision.[195] Rev. Rul. 73-71[196] had held that purchases by the Department of Defense for resale at foreign commissary stores gave rise to disqualifying receipts. However, the holding of Rev. Rul. 73-71 was *overruled* by Rev. Rul. 88-11[197] as having been based on a mistake of fact.

(b) Subsidies

Subsidies are excluded from qualifying as foreign trading gross receipts. A subsidy is a receipt from a transaction accomplished by a subsidy from the United States or an instrumentality thereof.[198] The relevant subsidies are as follows:[199]

---

[190] IRC §924(a).

[191] Reg. §1.924(a)-1T(f)(1).

[192] Reg. §1.924(a)-1T(f)(2).

[193] IRC §924(f)(1)(A)(ii).

[194] Reg. §1.924(a)-1T(g)(4)(i).

[195] Reg. §1.924(a)-1T(g)(4)(i).

[196] 1973-1 C.B. 361.

[197] 1988-1 C.B. 296.

[198] IRC §924(f)(1)(B).

[199] Listed in Reg. §1.924(a)-1T(g).

1. The development loan program, or grants under the technical cooperation and development grants program of the Agency for International Development, or grants under the military assistance program administered by the Department of Defense, pursuant to the Foreign Assistance Act of 1961, as amended,[200] unless the FSC shows to the satisfaction of the Commissioner that, under the conditions existing at the time of the sale (or at the time of the lease or at the time the services were rendered), the purchaser (or lessor or recipient of the services) had a reasonable opportunity to purchase (or lease or contract for services) on competitive terms and from a seller (or lessor or performer of services) who was not a U.S. person, goods (or services) that were substantially identical to such property (or services) and that were not manufactured, produced, grown, or extracted in the United States (or performed by a U.S. person);

2. The Public Law 480 program authorized under Title I of the Agricultural Trade Development and Assistance Act of 1954, as amended;[201]

3. The Export Payment program of the Commodity Credit Corporation authorized by Section 5(d) and (f) of the Commodity Credit Corporation Charter Act, as amended;[202]

4. The Section 32 Export Payment Program authorized by Section 32 of the Act of August 24, 1935, as amended;[203]

5. The Export Sales Program of the Commodity Credit Corporation authorized by Sections 5(d) and (f) of the Commodity Credit Corporation Charter Act, as amended (15 USC 714c(d) and (f)) other than the GSM-4 program provided under 7 CFR 1488, and Section 407 of the Agricultural Act of 1949, as amended,[204] for the purpose of disposing of surplus agricultural commodities and exporting or causing to be exported agricultural commodities; and

6. The Foreign Military Sales Direct Credit Program[205] or the Foreign Military Sales Loan Guaranty Program[206] if

   a. The borrowing country is released from its contractual liability to repay the United States government as to those credits or guaranteed loans;

   b. The repayment period exceeds 12 years; or

   c. The interest rate charged is less than the market rate of interest as defined in 22 USC 2763(c)(B); unless the FSC shows to the satisfaction of the Commissioner that, under the conditions existing at the time of the sale,

---

[200] 22 USC 2151.

[201] 7 USC 1961, 1701–1714.

[202] 15 USC 714c(d) and (f).

[203] 7 USC 612c.

[204] 7 USC 1427.

[205] 22 USC 2763.

[206] 22 USC 2764.

the purchaser had a reasonable opportunity to purchase, on competitive terms from a seller who was not a U.S. person, goods that were substantially identical to this property and that were not manufactured, produced, grown, or extracted in the United States.

Information as to whether an export is financed, in whole or in part, with funds derived from the programs identified in this subdivision may be obtained from the Comptroller, Defense Security Assistance Agency, Department of Defense, Washington, DC 20301.

(c) Receipts from Related Parties

When a corporation has more than one FSC, receipts from a related FSC are not foreign trading gross receipts if either FSC uses the 1.83 percent of gross receipts pricing method.[207] This multiple FSC rule also applies if the FSC receives a commission from more than one related supplier with respect to the same export property.[208] As an illustration, assume R and S are domestic corporations that are members of the same controlled group as FSC. Assume that R sells export property in the United States to S for $100, and S immediately ships the property to a foreign customer at a price of $110. If the 1.83 percent of gross receipts method is used in determining the FSC's commission from R or from S, then the intercompany sale from R to S will not produce foreign trading gross receipts. This rule prevents a "pyramiding" of FSC benefits. However, if the 23 percent of combined taxable income method is used for both parts of the transaction, the FSC can receive a commission from both R and S. The example in Reg. §1.924(a)-1T(g)(6)(B) is in need of revision to reflect the addition of the flush language to IRC §924(f)(1) by the Tax Reform Act of 1986.

4.8 Conclusion

The tests under IRC §924(a), relating to foreign trading gross receipts, and IRC §927(a), relating to the definition of export property, must be met for a taxpayer to have qualified foreign trading gross receipts. Once the taxpayer has determined that the gross receipts qualify for FSC benefits, the other FSC requirements must also be met. Details regarding the other FSC requirements are discussed in other chapters of this book. In the DISC context, the tests under IRC §993(a) for qualified export assets, and IRC §993(c), which contains the definition of export property, must be met to qualify for the tax benefit.

---

[207] IRC §924(f)(1)(C).

[208] Reg. §1.924(a)-1T(g)(6)(B).

CHAPTER 5

FSC and DISC Benefits for Services

Lisa T. Fair
Mark C. Thompson

5.1 Introduction

Foreign sales corporations (FSCs) and domestic international sales corporations (DISCs) can provide tax benefits from three types of services:

1. Related and subsidiary services
2. Engineering or architectural services
3. Managerial services provided to an unrelated FSC or DISC.

This chapter discusses each of the three types of services, related planning ideas, and practical issues that may arise.

5.2 Related and Subsidiary Services

Related and subsidiary services qualify for FSC or DISC benefits. The services must be related and subsidiary to any sale or lease of export property by the FSC or DISC, whether directly or through a commission arrangement, and may be provided within or outside the United States.[1]
The services must be provided by:

1. The person who sold or leased the applicable export property;
2. The FSC or DISC as principal; or
3. A person with whom the FSC or DISC has contracted to provide such services.

Services provided by a member of the FSC or DISC's controlled group are eligible if the sale or lease was made by another member of the controlled group. The FSC or DISC must be the principal or commission agent for the sale or lease of the property in all cases.[2] The services must both be "related" and "subsidiary."

(a) Related Services

To be a related service, the service must be of a type customarily provided as part of the trade or business in which the sale or lease arose and must be provided for, either expressly or implied, by warranty under the sale or lease. Prior to the first shipment of the related property, the provider of the service must give the purchaser a written offer or option to furnish the services. The contract to furnish the service must be entered into within two years of the contract to sell or lease. The services contract may be renewable.[3]

---

[1] Treas. Reg. §§ 1.924(a)-1T(d)(1) and 1.993-1(d)(1).

[2] Treas. Reg. §§ 1.924(a)-1T(d)(2) and 1.993-1(d)(2); *for more information, see* Robert Feinschreiber, *Domestic International Sales Corporation* (New York: Practicing Law Institute, 1978), Chapter 9.

[3] Treas. Reg. §§ 1.924(a)-1T(d)(3) and 1.993-1(d)(3).

Related services include, but are not limited to, warranty service, maintenance service, repair service, and installation service. Transportation service (including transportation insurance) will qualify as related and subsidiary service if the cost of the transportation is included in the sale price or rental of the property. Transportation services qualify if they are paid directly by the FSC or DISC to the person furnishing the transportation. Financing services are not considered related.[4]

The related services rule is illustrated by the following example:

Example

P, a U.S. corporation, exported machinery that was manufactured by X, an unrelated corporation. P paid a commission to a DISC for the export sales. Employees of X provided installation and warranty services to the foreign purchasers under a contract with P. Receipts received by P for the services provided by X's employees under contract with P were held not to be related and subsidiary services.[5] These services would have qualified as related services if the contract services pertained directly to the DISC.

(b) Subsidiary Services

Services are considered subsidiary to the sale or lease if, at the time of such sale or lease, it is reasonable to expect that the gross receipts from all related services will not exceed 50 percent of the sum of the gross receipts from the sale or lease of export property and the gross receipts from related services furnished by the FSC or DISC ("50 percent test").

$$\frac{GR_S}{GR_E + GR_S} \leq 50\%$$

$$GR = \text{gross receipts}$$
$$E = \text{export property}$$
$$S = \text{services}$$

In the case of a sale, reasonable expectations are based on the gross receipts from services that may reasonably be expected to be performed within 10 years after the sale. For leased property, the time period is the term of the lease without regard to renewals.[6]

Subsidiary services rules are illustrated by the following example:

Example

P, a U.S. corporation, sold machinery for $100,000 to F, a foreign purchaser. P agreed to provide warranty service to F for the first five years of ownership. The terms of the warranty stated that P would provide to F all labor required at a flat fee of $10 per hour. If P, at

---

[4] Treas. Reg. §§ 1.924(a)-1T(d)(3) and 1.993-1(d)(3).

[5] Rev. Rul. 75-322, 1975-2 CB 310.

[6] Treas. Reg. §§ 1.924(a)-1T(d)(4)(i) and 1.993-1(d)(4)(i).

the time of the sale, could reasonably expect the amounts received for labor under the warranty to be $50,000 or less over the entire warranty period, then the services would meet the 50 percent test.

Services that are part of a renewed service contract will qualify as subsidiary services if the contract is renewable within 10 years for a sale, or within the lease term in the case of a lease. In addition, it must be reasonable to expect that, at the time of renewal, the 50 percent test will be met as to all related services that have been and which are to be furnished by the FSC or DISC. The cumulative expected receipts for the services must be recalculated.[7]

If more than one item of export property is sold or leased under the same contract and the items are from the same product line, the 50 percent test is calculated on the gross receipts from the entire transaction. If the items are not from the same product line, separate tests must be run based on product line.[8] Product lines could be determined by using either recognized trade or industry standards or the two-digit major groups of the Standard Industrial Classification (SIC) published by the Office of Management and Budget (OMB). In any given taxable year, any one item must be included in the same product line classification for all transactions.[9]

The amount of applicable gross receipts are determined without regard to whether the services are furnished under the particular sale or lease contract or under a separate contract. Nor is it relevant whether the cost of the services is specified in the contract.[10] Receipts related to parts furnished under the services contract are not considered to be received for services.[11]

(c)   Practical Problems and Planning Points

The following practical problems are often encountered in attempting to obtain a benefit for related and subsidiary services:

1. *Unavailability of benchmarks for the value of services.* In most cases, it will be necessary for an exporter to compile support for the pricing of the services. With unrelated services, this would not seem to be a problem. However, if the services are furnished by another member of the control group other than the exporter of the property, presumably the principles set forth under § 482 would apply.[12]

2. *Failure to tie the related services to the contract for export sale or lease.* The exporter may be providing services that would otherwise result in a

---

[7] Treas. Reg. §§ 1.924(a)-1T(d)(4)(i) and 1.993-1(d)(4)(i).

[8] Treas. Reg. §§ 1.924(a)-1T(d)(4)(iii) and 1.993-1(d)(4)(iii).

[9] Treas. Reg. §§ 1.925(a)-1T(c)(8)(ii) and 1.994-1(c)(7)(ii).

[10] Treas. Reg. §§ 1.924(a)-1T(d)(4)(ii) and 1.993-1(d)(4)(ii).

[11] Treas. Reg. §§ 1.924(a)-1T(d)(4)(v) and 1.993-1(d)(4)(v); *for more information, see* Robert Feinschreiber, *FSC: The Foreign Sales Corporation* (Corporate Tax Press, 1984), Chapter 10, pp. 95–110.

[12] Treas. Reg. §§ 1.925(a)-1T(c)(6)(ii) and 1.994-1(c)(6)(ii).

FSC or DISC benefit, but such services may not in fact be "related" by contract. All services to be provided or available to be provided should be reviewed prior to the sale or lease and documented in a manner that meets the requirement that the services be related.

3. *No separate charge for related services.* U.S. exporters include the charge for installation and warranty services in the sale price of the property. They may view these services as an item of cost and not as an item that generates a separate profit for the exporter. As a result, many businesses show no profit attributable to the providing of warranty services. Exporters should rethink this consideration in light of the FSC or DISC benefit.

4. *Documentation related to the 50 percent test.* For subsidiary services, the benefit will not be available if it is *reasonable* to expect that the value of the services are such that the 50 percent test will not be met. Documentation should be kept to support the determination of reasonableness.

5. *Commonly overlooked services.* Many sales of export property include some type of services. Services that relate to an export should be reviewed for possible classification as related and subsidiary services. The most commonly overlooked services are transportation, the act of insuring of goods, and the installation and warranty of property. Exporters should make sure that these amounts are not already included with other items as part of the FSC or DISC calculation. Such services may be candidates for both commercial profit and FSC or DISC benefit enhancement.

6. *Extended warranty services.* Many U.S. exporters provide significant warranty services to their U.S. customer base, but none to their foreign customers. These exporters often believe that the cost of providing warranty services abroad would make their products too expensive. However, failure to provide a warranty with the product when sold outside the United States may, in fact, put the product at a disadvantage relative to local offers. In addition, as a product matures and its life cycle continues, the failure to offer any type of after-market support may also make the product noncompetitive. Therefore, extending warranty coverage to these products sold abroad can make sense commercially as well as create a possible FSC or DISC benefit.

(d) Structure

For U.S. companies that have no foreign presence other than the FSC or DISC, a sales structure is shown in Exhibit 5.1.

Within the structure provided in the example, P, the U.S. parent, sells export property to a foreign customer and pays a commission to a FSC or DISC in the normal course of business. P also provides warranty service to its foreign customer through a foreign service branch of a new U.S. subsidiary. P compensates the new U.S. subsidiary for its branch expenses by paying a service fee. The FSC or DISC is then entitled to a commission related to the services, which are performed entirely outside of the United States.

Exhibit 5.1

SALES STRUCTURE

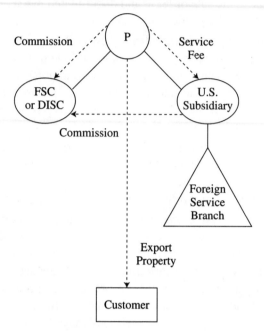

This fairly straightforward structure has a number of advantages for a U.S. parent:

1. A FSC or DISC benefit can be derived in connection with the service fee paid to the U.S. subsidiary.

2. The parent may generate additional gross receipts because of an increased price for property sold with the warranty and may also avoid losing a competitive advantage.

3. Warranty activity concerning the foreign export products is captured within the affiliated group. As long as the service fee is adequate for transfer pricing purposes, there should be little additional U.S. tax risk associated with the new operation.

4. P may enjoy state tax benefits from separate reporting in connection with the payment of the service fee to the U.S. subsidiary. For example, if P were established in a state that does not tax on a unitary basis, an additional state tax deduction may be available for the service fee. The benefits could be significant if most of the services are performed outside of the United States and, therefore, are subject to little state tax at the U.S. subsidiary level.

For a FSC, the branch should be established in a nontax jurisdiction to avoid dilution of the FSC benefit. If the warranty services cause establishment of a foreign office, the U.S. subsidiary would likely lose treaty protection and incur a foreign tax that would be noncreditable, thus eliminating the FSC benefit entirely. The structure will be most successful in those cases where warranty service can be handled by a team of traveling technicians who are not permanently based in the country where the services are performed. Of course, a country may aggregate these activities. Where a foreign tax is inevitable, consideration may be given to structuring the activity so that the FSC benefit is claimed for the activities of the traveling technicians. The foreign tax should be associated with those activities of individuals coordinating the warranty service.

5.3 Engineering or Architectural Services

Gross receipts earned by a FSC or DISC from engineering and architectural services that are related to construction projects are eligible for FSC or DISC benefits.

(a) Construction Projects

The term "construction project" includes the erection, expansion, and repair of new or existing buildings or other physical facilities. The term also includes site grading and improvement and installation of equipment necessary for the construction. The equipment itself does not qualify for FSC or DISC benefits unless the property is export property.[13]

For engineering and architectural services to qualify for FSC or DISC benefits, the services must be provided by either the FSC or DISC, an agent of the FSC or DISC (with the FSC or DISC acting as principal), or another person with the FSC or DISC acting as a commission agent.[14] The services may be provided inside or outside the United States, but must relate to construction projects located outside the United States.[15]

Feasibility studies for a proposed construction project overseas will qualify for export benefits even if the project is not ultimately pursued.[16] However, services connected with the exploration for oil or gas or with technical assistance or know-how will not qualify. For purposes of these rules, technical assistance or know-how includes activities designed to facilitate the acquisition or use of scientific, architectural, or engineering information.[17] Receipts from the performance of construction services other than engineering and architectural services may qualify for FSC or DISC benefits to the extent they are related and subsidiary services.[18]

---

[13] Treas. Reg. §§ 1.924(a)-1T(e)(8) and 1.993-1(e)(8).

[14] Treas. Reg. §§ 1.924(a)-1T(e)(7) and 1.993-1(h)(7).

[15] Treas. Reg. §§ 1.924(a)-1T(e)(1) and 1.993-1(h)(1).

[16] Treas. Reg. §§ 1.924(a)-1T(e)(2) and 1.993-1(h)(2).

[17] Treas. Reg. §§ 1.924(a) -1T(e)(3)(i)-(ii) and 1.993-1(h)(3)(i)-(ii).

[18] Treas. Reg. §§ 1.924(a)-1T(e)(4) and 1.993-1(h)(4).

(b) Engineering Services

Engineering services include any services requiring engineering education, training, and experience and the application of special knowledge of a mathematical, physical, or engineering nature. These services may be provided in the form of consultation, investigation, evaluation, planning, design, or responsible supervision of construction for the purpose of assuring compliance with plans, specifications, and design.[19]

(c) Architectural Services

Architectural services include consultation, planning, aesthetic and structural design, drawings and specifications, or responsible supervision of construction or erection, in connection with any construction project.[20]

(d) Planning Points

(i) Engineering Services. A commonly overlooked fact is that it is not necessary for engineering or architectural services to be related and subsidiary in order to qualify for a FSC benefit.[21] Therefore, companies with no export property tie-in can utilize a FSC if they provide services within one or more of the defined areas.

For example, a U.S. company that commands a technical advantage for equipment related to power generation may charge an amount (in addition to the equipment cost) for the evaluation of a foreign project's specific requirements and the suitability of the equipment for a specific application. The amount charged would qualify for a FSC benefit. This would be true even if the property is never exported, as long as the U.S. manufacturer is paid for its preliminary services.

In addition, engineering and architectural services are often free from the burden of foreign tax because the services are either provided in the United States, or are eligible for treaty protection because no permanent establishment exists under the construction project article of a U.S. double tax treaty.

(ii) Architectural Services. Many U.S. architectural firms overlook the opportunity for a FSC or DISC benefit in connection with their efforts related to foreign projects. This is true even though a number of architectural firms have found their most lucrative contracts abroad where more and more U.S. companies are becoming involved in infrastructure projects in developing countries, such as power plants and wastewater treatment facilities, and with environmental protection-related equipment such as incineration units.

---

[19] Treas. Reg. §§ 1.924(a)-1T(e)(5) and 1.993-1(h)(5).
[20] Treas. Reg. §§ 1.924(a)-1T(e)(6) and 1.993-1(h)(6).
[21] Sections 924(a)(4) and 993(a)(1)(G).

Many architectural firms are currently organized as S corporations and are ineligible to own a FSC or DISC.[22] In situations where firms are either founded as, or evolving to, specialty operations for foreign customers, an analysis of the potential FSC or DISC benefit should be included in the determination of whether the new company should be a C corporation rather than an S corporation. Obviously, this choice is only one of many considerations in making such a determination. Where foreign fees are significant but do not constitute 100 percent of a project, consideration should be given to isolating the non-U.S.-related project work in a separate, segregated C corporation, rather than within an S corporation, to obtain FSC or DISC benefits.

(iii)   Joint Venture Opportunities.   It is becoming more common for foreign customers who purchase large-ticket export items to require that installation and warranty be provided as part of the purchase package. At the same time, U.S. manufacturers are focusing on core competencies and may make contractual arrangements with unrelated parties to provide the necessary service installation and warranty services.

For large contracts, where substantial services may be required, manufacturers should consider entering into a joint venture arrangement to provide the collective package. This joint venture could be located in the United States or in a foreign country, depending on the location of the unrelated party and other tax considerations, but should be set up to qualify for partnership treatment under U.S. tax rules. The manufacturer could then set up a FSC which would, in turn, contract with this joint venture to provide the relevant services. In this case, the contractual relationship between the customer and the U.S. partnership would have to be closely monitored to ensure that the services are indeed furnished by the FSC.[23] An example of a possible structure is shown in Exhibit 5.2.

(iv)   Turnkey Contracts.   It is quite common for purchasers of equipment that requires a high degree of expertise to maintain and operate to outsource such maintenance and operation to third parties through so-called turnkey contracts. For the purchaser, this provides a cost-effective way to operate and maintain complex equipment. For the U.S. exporter, it may provide a way to increase its FSC or DISC benefit.

(v)   The 50 Percent Test for Related and Subsidiary Services.   Related and subsidiary services can be expressly stated in the contract with the customer. It is important to segregate the services that are related and subsidiary from those that may be of an operational nature. This may prevent problems with the 50 percent test that could cause the services to be other than subsidiary to the sale or lease.[24]

---

[22] IRC § 1361(b)(2)(A).

[23] Treas. Reg. §§ 1.924(a)-1T(d)(2) and 1.993-1(d)(2).

[24] Treas. Reg. §§ 1.924(a)-1T(d)(4) and 1.993-1(d)(4).

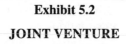

Exhibit 5.2

JOINT VENTURE

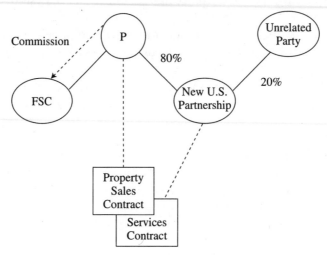

(vi)   Sale Versus Lease.   On a case-by-case basis, it will be necessary to determine whether the contract will be treated as a sale or a lease. In the case of a sale, the 50 percent related and subsidiary test is based on a reasonable expectation at the time of the sale. The "reasonable expectation" must be based on gross receipts from all related services that may reasonably be performed at any time before the end of a 10-year period following the date of the sale.[25] In the case of a lease, the relevant time frame is the term of the lease.

Since, in most turnkey contracts, the customer may not be interested in purchasing the equipment, the transaction will be structured as a lease. Although at first glance this may seem to make determination of reasonableness for the 50 percent test more difficult than if the transaction were a sale, in practice it may be much easier because of the uncertainty associated with 10-year projections and the potential for renewed service contracts. Under a renewed service contract, the determination of whether the services are subsidiary depends on whether it is reasonably expected, at the time of the *renewal,* that the gross receipts from all services that have been and that are to be furnished by the FSC or DISC will not exceed 50 percent of the sum of gross receipts from the sale or lease and the gross receipts from related services furnished by the FSC or DISC, as so described.[26]

---

[25] Treas. Reg. §§ 1.924(a)-1T(d)(4)(i) and 1.993-1(d)(4)(i).

[26] Treas. Reg. §§ 1.924(a)-1T(d)(4)(iv) and 1.993-1(d)(4)(iv).

(vii) Parts. Typically, a turnkey contract requires the seller or lessor of the property (who may also be the provider of the services) to furnish any necessary parts. Gross receipts from the parts should not be taken into account in calculating whether the 50 percent related and subsidiary test were met. However, the gross receipts from the sale of these parts may qualify for FSC or DISC benefits under the export property provisions.[27]

(viii) Final Demise of the Equipment. At the time FSC or DISC benefits are claimed, consideration must be given to whether there is a high likelihood that the property will be returned to the United States at the end of the turnkey arrangement. To avoid any uncertainty, the contract should address this issue specifically to prevent deemed use of the property in the United States.

A purchaser of property is deemed to use the property in the United States if, at the time of the sale, there is an agreement or understanding that the property will be ultimately used in the United States. Usage in the United States occurs if, at any time within three years after the purchase of such property, the property is resold by the purchaser for use by a subsequent purchaser within the United States or the purchaser or subsequent purchaser fails for any period of 365 consecutive days to use the property predominantly outside the United States.[28]

The same rules apply in the case of a lease, except that this determination—as to whether the ultimate use of the leased property is in the United States—is made for each taxable year of the lessor during the lease term. Property may be export property in one year, yet not in the next.[29]

(ix) Accounting. Given all the different requirements and the need to show qualification under the percent related and subsidiary test, proper accounting for the property and services provided under a turnkey contract is critical. This may be the key to maximizing the FSC or DISC benefit.

For example, if more than one item of export property is sold or leased in a single transaction pursuant to one contract, the total gross receipts from the transaction and the total gross receipts from all services related to the transaction are taken into account in determining whether the services are subsidiary to the transaction. However, after reviewing the accounting for the sale or lease of property, the exporter may determine that each item of export property and the related and subsidiary services should be contained within a single contract. This may prevent one set of services from jeopardizing the total FSC benefit available for a group of export property items.

---

[27] Treas. Reg. §§ 1.924(a)-1T(d)(4)(v) and 1.993-1(d)(4)(v).

[28] Treas. Reg. §§ 1.924(a)-1T(d)(4)(ii) and 1.993-1(d)(4)(ii).

[29] Treas. Reg. § 1.927(a)-1T(d)(4)(v).

5.4   Managerial Services

Although rarely encountered, receipts for managerial services provided by one FSC to another unrelated FSC or interest charge DISC will qualify for FSC benefits, provided the services aid the unrelated FSC or DISC in deriving foreign trading gross receipts (FTGR).[30]

Managerial services include all staffing and operational services necessary to operate the unrelated FSC or interest charge DISC, but do not include legal, accounting, scientific, or technical services.[31] For the receipts to qualify, the FSC providing the managerial service must derive at least 50 percent of its FTGR for such year from the sale or lease of export property and the provision of related and subsidiary services.[32]

As with engineering and architectural services, for managerial services to qualify for FSC benefits, the services must be provided by the FSC, by an agent of the FSC (with the FSC acting as principal), or by another person (with the FSC acting as a commission agent).[33] In addition, the FSC providing managerial services must know that the entity to whom the services are provided is a FSC or interest charge DISC. This is best accomplished by requesting a copy of the receiving company's election for FSC or DISC status along with a signed statement that the election was timely filed.[34]

5.5   Special Pricing Considerations

Special considerations apply to pricing of services provided by a FSC.

(a)   Pricing Methods

The rules regarding the transfer pricing for export property are directly applicable only in the case of sales or exchanges of export property, but are applicable by analogy to relevant services. FSC regulations provide that if services are *not* includable in the *same* taxable year as the income from the export transaction, the amount of taxable income that the FSC may derive for any taxable year will be determined under the arrangement between the FSC and its related supplier and will be computed in a manner consistent with the rules that apply for computing the transfer price in the case of sales for resale of export property.[35]

---

[30] Treas. Reg. §§ 1.924(a)-1T(f)(1) and 1.993-1(i)(1).

[31] Treas. Reg. §§ 1.924(a)-1T(f)(2) and 1.993-1(i)(2).

[32] Treas. Reg. §§ 1.924(a)-1T(f)(1) and 1.993-1(i)(1).

[33] Treas. Reg. §§ 1.924(a)-1T(f)(1)(i)-(iii) and 1.993-1(i)(1)(i)-(iii).

[34] Treas. Reg. §§ 1.924(a)-1T(f)(3) and 1.993-1(i)(3).

[35] Treas. Reg. §§ 1.924(a)-1T(d)(3)(ii) and 1.993-1(d)(3).

(b) Grouping

Related and subsidiary services are grouped according to the time at which they are provided. If provided in the same year as the export transaction, the services are grouped with the relevant export property. For all later years, the services are grouped with the product or product line to which they relate, based on either year of export grouping or year of service grouping.[36] Engineering and architectural services and certain managerial services are not considered related to a product and are, therefore, treated as separate types of income.[37]

Applying the grouping rules to services, while providing opportunities for greater FSC or DISC benefit, may also be problematic in cases where products or product lines change from one year to the next as new products are introduced or old products are discontinued, or where the related supplier and the FSC or DISC undertake redetermination procedures that result in changes in the product groupings as originally reported on the tax return. Because of the consistency requirement, it is necessary to track from prior year groupings to determine the appropriate combined taxable income from related and subsidiary services.

(c) Architectural and Engineering Services

Architectural and engineering services for construction projects located or proposed for location outside the United States and FSC managerial services may not be grouped. The determination of combined taxable income for these transactions must be made only on a transaction-by-transaction basis.[38]

(d) Marginal Costing

The marginal costing rules do not apply to performance of services even if they are related and subsidiary services.[39] As a result, in those situations where marginal costing would be expected to provide significant benefits on the sale or exchange of the export property, the related and subsidiary services may have to be excluded from the FSC or DISC calculation. This is because the gross receipts for related and subsidiary services must be treated as part of the receipts from the export transaction to which the services are related and subsidiary, but only if the income from such services is includable for the same taxable year as income from the export transaction.[40] If such a situation occurs, the exporter should consider the feasibility of exporting the property in one year and providing the services in the next year.

---

[36] *See* Robert Feinschreiber, *Transfer Pricing Handbook* (New York: John Wiley & Sons, 1993), Chapter 13.

[37] Treas. Reg. §§ 1.925(a)-1T(d)(3) and 1.994-1(d)(3).

[38] Treas. Reg. §§ 1.924(a)-1T(d)(3)(ii) and 1.993-1(d)(3)(ii).

[39] Treas. Reg. §§ 1.925(b)-1T(a) and 1.994-2(a).

[40] Treas. Reg. §§ 1.925(a)-1T(d)(3) and 1.994-1(d)(3).

5.6 Conclusion

As with most tax-saving opportunities, some "roll up the sleeves" work may be required to obtain a FSC benefit for services (or to maximize it). However, the effort can lead to increased tax efficiency which may, in turn, enhance competitiveness in the global marketplace.

CHAPTER 6

Foreign Economic Process Requirements

Jeffrey A. Levenstam
Rafeal E. Brown

6.1 Introduction

A foreign sales corporation (FSC) has foreign trading gross receipts (FTGR) from any transaction only if certain economic processes occur outside the United States. The foreign economic process requirements have two parts: sales activities and foreign direct cost activities. The FSC must participate outside the United States in the sales portion of the transaction and satisfies either a 50 percent or 85 percent foreign direct cost test.[1]

The specific foreign economic process requirements, both sales activity requirements and foreign direct cost requirements, are discussed in this chapter. Planning for the most cost-efficient manner of meeting each of these requirements is a factual determination, which must take into account each company's method of selling its products for export.

6.2   Sales Activities Test

A transaction qualifies as generating foreign trading gross receipts if the FSC, or a person under contract with the FSC, has participated outside the United States in the solicitation (in a manner other than advertising), the negotiation, or the making of the contract relating to the transaction.[2] For the purposes of this test the term "solicitation" refers to communication (by telephone, telegraph, mail, or in person) by the FSC or its agent to a specific, targeted, potential customer regarding a transaction. The term "negotiation" includes any communication by the FSC or its agent to a customer or potential customer concerning the terms of the sale. The term "making of a contract" includes the performance by the FSC, or its agent, of any of the elements necessary to complete a sale.

The elements necessary to complete a sale include making or accepting an offer or written confirmation by the FSC or its agent to the customer of an oral agreement that confirms verbal contract terms. To facilitate the FSC's compliance with these requirements, the FSC may act on standing instructions from its principal (generally the related supplier).[3] Furthermore, a sale need not occur in order for the solicitation or negotiation tests to be satisfied. Once the FSC has participated outside the United States in an activity that constitutes the solicitation, negotiation, or the making of a contract for a transaction, any prior or subsequent activity will be disregarded for purposes of determining whether the FSC has met the requirements.

The regulations give the example of a FSC selling a product to a foreign customer, first meeting with the customer in New York to discuss the product and subsequently mailing a product brochure to the foreign customer from a place outside the United States. The initial meeting is to be disregarded, and only the mailing is considered in determining whether the FSC participated outside the United States in the solicitation of this sales transaction.[4] Generally, the location of any activity

---

[1] Reg. § 1.924(d)-1(c). For background, including the legislative history, *see* Robert Feinschreiber, *FSC: The Foreign Sales Corporation* (Corporate Tax Press, 1984), Chapters 6 and 7.

[2] IRC § 924(d)(1)(A).

[3] General explanation of the Revenue Provisions of the Deficit Reduction Act of 1984 (H.R. 4170, 98th Congress Public Law 98-369).

[4] Reg. § 1.924(d)-1(c)(1).

is determined by the place where the activity is initiated by the FSC, not by the location of the person transmitting instructions to the FSC.[5]

The sales activities referred to in the preceding paragraph are generally measured on a transaction-by-transaction basis. However, the FSC may make an annual election whereby any of the sales activity tests may be applied on the basis of a group of transactions. The election should be made on the FSC's annual tax return. It is recommended that an affirmative written election statement be included in the return as a method of documenting the choices made for this purpose. The elections made on the original FSC tax return may be changed by filing an amended tax return before the expiration of the statute of limitations for the tax year.

A group of transactions for this purpose may be based on the sale or lease of a particular product or products that are either recognized as similar by standard trade or industry usage, or on a two-digit major group or any inferior classification (or combination of such inferior classifications) within a major group under the Standard Industrial Classification system. The rules governing the grouping of transactions for purposes of compliance with the foreign economic process requirements are a separate and distinct from the grouping of transactions for purposes of the transfer pricing rules. In addition, a choice by the FSC to group transactions may be made separately for each of the required sales activities, as well as each of the five categories of activities under the direct cost test. Groupings chosen for this purpose will have no relationship to or bearing on groupings used for other purposes, such as satisfying the direct costs test.[6] However, it is important to note that although the choice by a FSC to group transactions generally applies to all transactions within the scope of such groupings, the choice of the grouping applies only to transactions covered by the grouping. Accordingly, for transactions not covered by the grouping, determinations may be made on a transaction-by-transaction basis or other grouping basis.[7]

For example, Sneeker Corporation manufactures two products in the United States that are fully produced from U.S. source materials. Sneeker Corporation's wholly owned FSC has elected to determine satisfaction of the sales activity tests of the foreign economic process requirements on a group basis for its first product, High-Traction Gym-Shoes for preteens. Therefore, the determination as to whether the foreign economic process requirements were met for all sales of High-Traction Gym-Shoes for preteens will be based on all sales during the tax year. For Sneeker Corporation's second product, Super-Fast Ten-Keys, no grouping election was made. Therefore, in respect to sales of Super-Fast Ten-Keys, the determination as to whether the sales activity tests of the foreign economic process requirements have been met will be made on a transaction-by-transaction basis.

---

[5] Reg. § 1.924(d)-1(a).

[6] Reg. § 1.924(d)-(1)(c)(5)(iii).

[7] Reg. § 1.924(d)-1(c)(5)(ii). *See, The Export Handbook*, Chapter 8.

6.3   Solicitation

A FSC can comply with the sales activity test to generate foreign trading gross receipts. "Solicitation" refers to any communication (by any method) by the FSC during the 12-month period immediately preceding the initiation of a contract, as it relates to the transaction with a specific customer or potential customer. The communication must specifically address the customer's attention to the product or service that is the subject of the transaction.[8] The transmission of a qualified communication that is used to satisfy this solicitation test may not also be used to satisfy the advertising activity requirement within the direct cost tests, discussed later in this chapter.

In general, solicitation is the most cost-effective means of meeting the sales activity requirement. Once each year a brochure (or similar item) listing the export products available for sale by the FSC and its related supplier is mailed to each export customer from a location outside the United States. This mailing to each export customer each year will meet or exceed the minimum coverage threshold.

If the FSC elects to group transactions of products or product lines within a two-digit Standard Industrial Classification (SIC) code, solicitation must be performed outside the United States for customers with sales representing either:

- Twenty percent or more of the foreign trading gross receipts of each product or product line grouping during the current year; or
- Fifty percent or more of the foreign trading gross receipts of the product or product line grouping for the prior year, irrespective of whether any sales occurred within the current year to prior year customers.[9]

For some taxpayers, the required effort in meeting these solicitation requirements may be substantial because of fluctuations in sales by customers. In such cases, taxpayers generally pursue the 50 percent threshold, since this test is based on prior year customers and is a fixed target. For each year, the FSC or its related supplier will examine its qualified export sales for the previous year and ensure that an appropriate mailing from a location outside the United States is sent to customers representing at least 50 percent of the prior year's qualified sales. This test is preferable to the 20 percent test in cases where the population is unknown at the beginning of the tax year. The selection of this technique allows a taxpayer to send its mailings early in the tax year. It also avoids the possibility that this solicitation activity would not be accomplished owing to an oversight during the rush of activity that often occurs just before year end.

A corporation that has not been treated as FSC in the prior year does not have to meet either the 20 percent test or the 50 percent test for the first year in which it is

---

[8] Reg. § 1.924(d)-1(c)(2).
[9] Reg. § 1.924(d)-1(c)(5)(i)(1)(A).

treated as a FSC.[10] Therefore, in the first fiscal year of the FSC's existence, a single brochure mailed from a location outside the United States to one of the export customers will satisfy the solicitation requirement.

6.4   Negotiation

A FSC can comply with the sales activity test by negotiating the contract with a potential customer. "Negotiation" is any communication by the FSC to a customer or potential customer that is aimed at creating an agreement concerning one or more of the "terms of a transaction." Terms of a transaction include price, credit terms, quantity, time of delivery, and manner of delivery. Communications may be in any form, as was the case for the solicitation test.[11]

A communication should be sent by the FSC to the customer from the FSC's location outside the United States, even if the specific instructions or an original draft of a written communication has been sent from the related supplier's U.S. office to the foreign office. Negotiations may take place at the same time as, and in conjunction with, another sales activity. Additionally, it may take place with any person, whether domestic or foreign, and whether or not related to the FSC. Negotiation does not include the mere receipt of a communication from a customer (such as an order) that includes terms of a sale. The 20 or 50 percent tests apply to negotiations as they do to solicitation.

6.5   Making of a Contract

A FSC can comply with the sales activity test by "making the contract." The "making of a contract" refers to the elements necessary to complete a sale. The elements of making a contract include such components as making or accepting an offer.[12] The location of an activity is determined by the location from which it is initiated by the FSC, and not by the location of anyone transmitting instructions to the FSC.[13] The communication sent by the FSC must originate from a foreign location. It does not matter if this activity takes place based on instructions received from a source within the United States, nor if the communication is sent from the FSC's foreign location to someone within the United States.

The acceptance of an order on a requirements contract will qualify for purposes of making of a contract. A requirements contract is considered an open offer, to be accepted from time to time, when a customer submits an order for a specified quantity. The written confirmation, by the FSC to the customer, of the acceptance of the open order will also be considered the making of a contract. Acceptance of an

---

[10] Reg. § 1.924(d)-1(c)(5)(i)(1)(A).

[11] Reg. § 1.924(d)-1(c)(3).

[12] Reg. § 1.924(d)-1(c)(4).

[13] Reg. § 1.924(d)-1(a).

unsolicited bid or order is considered the making of a contract, even if no solicitation or negotiation occurred as to the transactions. The written confirmation, by the FSC to the customer, of an oral or written agreement that confirms variable contract terms, such as price, credit terms, quantity or time or manner of delivery, or specifies (directly or by cross-reference) additional contract terms will be considered the making of a contract. Consider the following example:

Example

A FSC earns commissions on the sale of export property by its domestic related supplier to U.S. wholesalers for final sale to foreign customers. The related supplier receives an order from one of its U.S. wholesalers. The related supplier telephones the U.S. wholesaler to inform it of the new price and the probability of another price increase. The U.S. wholesaler orally agrees to the new price, and the related supplier instructs the FSC to fax a written confirmation to the wholesaler from its foreign office that the product will be sold at the current new price. The written confirmation, by the FSC, of an oral agreement on a variable contract term constitutes the making of a contract.[14]

A written confirmation is any confirmation expressed in writing, including a letter sent by facsimile or mail, telex, or other similar written communication. The making of a contract may take place at the same time as, and in conjunction with, another sales activity. The 20 or 50 percent tests for solicitation and negotiation also apply for purposes of making of a contract.

6.6   Foreign Direct Cost Test

A FSC does not earn foreign trade gross receipts from a transaction unless the foreign direct costs incurred by the FSC attributable to the transaction meet the foreign direct cost test. This test can be met in either of two ways. The foreign direct costs must either equal or exceed 50 percent of the total direct costs incurred by the FSC for the transaction or the FSC must meet an alternative 85 percent test. The specific facts and circumstances of each situation should be examined to determine which of the two alternatives could be more easily achieved. Before addressing these alternatives in greater detail, it is necessary to consider the costs that are taken into account for purposes of this analysis.

The term "total direct costs" means, as in any transaction, the costs that are incident to and necessary for the performance of any of the required activities relating to the disposition of export property. These required activities consist of five statutorily defined categories of activities:[15]

1. Advertising and sales promotion
2. The processing of customer orders and arranging for delivery of the export property

---

[14] Reg. § 1.924(d)-1(d)(6)(i), Example 3.
[15] IRC § 924(e).

3. Transportation
4. Determination and transmittal of invoice and the receipt of payment
5. The assumption of credit risk[16]

The activities are those performed at any location within or without the United States by the FSC or any person acting under contract with the FSC. If costs are identified with more than one of the aforementioned categories of activities, the taxpayer must allocate the costs among such activities. This allocation must be consistently applied and, if possible, reflect the relative costs that would have been incurred if the activities were independently performed.

(a) Foreign Direct Costs

The term "foreign direct costs" means the portion of the total direct costs incurred by the FSC that are attributable to activities performed outside the United States. Although the activities must be performed outside the United States, either the FSC or any person acting under contract with the FSC may perform the activities. If a person acting under contract with the FSC is to be employed for this purpose, a written agency contract should be signed by both parties in advance of the performance of these services. Often, an independent FSC management company is employed for this purpose.

(b) Alternative 85 Percent Test

The requirement that foreign direct costs incurred by the FSC equal or exceed 50 percent of the total direct costs incurred by the FSC attributable to a transaction may be satisfied by an alternative 85 percent test. Under this alternative test, a corporation will be treated as satisfying the requirement that economic processes take place outside the United States if the foreign direct costs incurred by the FSC equal or exceed 85 percent of the total direct costs. Both the foreign direct costs and the total direct costs of the FSC must be attributable to at least two of the five activities relating to the disposition of export property.[17] It is generally recommended the FSC attempt to satisfy three of the five categories as additional assurance that it will be in compliance if there are unexpected events that cause failure to meet the test in one of the selected categories.

Only the direct costs paid or accrued by the FSC or its agent will be taken into consideration in meeting the direct cost test. It is not necessary to incur expenses in all categories to use either the 50 percent or the 85 percent test. If no costs are incurred for activities in a certain category, that category will not be taken into account in meeting the requirement. However, if any amount of direct costs are incurred in a particular category, that category will be taken into account. Thus,

---

[16] IRC § 924(e).
[17] IRC § 924(d)(1)(B).

under either foreign direct cost test, the qualification of a transaction depends not only on incurring foreign direct costs, but also on minimizing domestic direct costs.

The direct cost tests will be applied on a transaction-by-transaction basis or by alternatively grouping transactions, based on product or product lines, according to either recognized industry or trade usage, or on a two-digit major grouping (or on any inferior classification or combination of inferior classifications) of the SIC; customer groupings (all transactions with a particular customer); contract groupings; or product or product line groupings within a customer or contract grouping. Different direct cost tests may be used for different transactions or groupings. Congress intended that a FSC will be allowed to group transactions differently for the various purposes for which grouping is permitted.[18] Thus, the groupings of transactions elected for this purpose may be different from those selected for purposes of meeting the sales activity tests. Both of these groupings may be different from the groupings used for purposes of determining the appropriate transfer pricing. The election of groupings for the direct cost tests, similar to the election for the sales activity test, is an annual election that is to be made on the FSC's annual tax return and may be changed by filing an amended tax return before the expiration of the statute of limitations for the year in question.

Most taxpayers choose to meet the 85 percent foreign direct costs test since the 50 percent test requires the management and monitoring of costs in all five categories. Furthermore, some companies have significant domestic costs in one or more categories, which makes compliance with the 50 percent test difficult, at best. The direct cost categories chosen for compliance with the 85 percent test will vary, depending on the nature of the taxpayer's business. The goal is to meet at least two categories that do not involve significant costs or efforts that would not otherwise be expended. Again, a FSC should achieve compliance within at least three categories. Of course, there must be a cost-benefit analysis of meeting additional categories. This extra-category approach is a prudent way to provide some protection in the event the 85 percent threshold is inadvertently missed in one of the other two categories. The regulations underlying the FSC statutory provisions offer very specific information regarding the definition of these categories and what constitutes a "foreign" direct cost. The following sections of this chapter describe the five statutory direct cost categories.

6.7 Activity Categories

Five activity categories describe the disposition of export property under the direct cost test:

1. Advertising and sales promotion
2. Processing of customer orders and arranging for delivery of the export property

---

[18] General explanation of the Revenue Provisions of the Deficit Reduction Act of 1984 (H.R. 4170, 98th Congress Public Law 98-369), § 1.924(1)(e)(3).

3. Transportation

4. Determination and transmittal of a final invoice or statement of account and the receipt of payment

5. Assumption of credit risk

(a) Advertising and Sales Promotion

The first part of the direct cost test includes two distinct activities: advertising and sales promotion. The costs of both activities are aggregated for purposes of measuring the foreign and total direct costs in this category. "Advertising" is an appeal that is related to a specific product or product line, made through any medium, and directed toward all or a part of the general population of potential export customers in order to induce multiple customers or potential customers to buy or rent export property from the FSC or its related supplier. This appeal must take place in some medium of mass communication, such as radio, television, newspapers, trade journals, mass mailings, or billboards. Advertising not related to a specific product or product line, such as the cost of corporate image building, is not included in the definition of advertising. Advertising primarily directed at customers in the United States is not considered advertising for this purpose, nor is any advertising not related to export property.[19] Thus, for purposes of this test, much of the existing advertising costs will likely be ignored.

Special rules exist where the FSC's customer is a distributor. To qualify, the FSC must either incur 20 percent or more of the total advertising costs of the distributor related to the FSC's products, or pay (directly or indirectly) the total charge for a specific advertisement. This latter approach, reimbursing the distributor for the cost of one specific advertisement, is often a cost-effective method of meeting this test and is generally viewed favorably by the distributor. These rules apply, regardless of whether the distributor itself is located in the United States or in a foreign jurisdiction and whether the distributor is a related party or an independent person. The FSC may incur costs for advertising (as described earlier) to the distributor's foreign customers or potential customers.

"Sales promotion" is an appeal to an export customer or potential export customer for the sale or rental of a specific qualifying FSC product or service, made in person within the context of a trade show or customer meeting. A "customer meeting" is a periodic (at least annual) meeting at which 10 or more existing or potential customers are reasonably expected to be present. The costs of trade shows and annual customer meetings are included in the total direct cost of sales promotion. The costs of trade shows and customer meetings do not include the cost of salaries and commissions of direct sales people, but do include payments to organizers or other persons hired for the event, as well as costs for travel, meals, and lodging of direct sales people if these costs are paid by the FSC or the related supplier.[20]

---

[19] Reg. § 1.924(e)-1.

[20] Reg. § 1.924(e)-1(a)(2).

In determining foreign direct costs, the location of the advertising activity is determined by the place where the advertising is transmitted, displayed, distributed, mailed, or otherwise conveyed to the potential customer. Fees paid to an independent advertising agency to develop the announcement or description, translation costs, or costs of preparing the announcement or description of the export property for potential use as advertising are not considered direct costs of advertising.[21] The location of the trade promotion activity is determined by the place where the customer meeting or trade show is held.

For purposes of meeting either the 50 percent or the 85 percent direct cost test described earlier, it is essential that the location of advertising set forth in the regulations is understood so that the direct costs can be properly identified as foreign or domestic. As a general rule, the location of advertising is the place to which the advertising is transmitted, displayed, distributed, mailed or otherwise conveyed to the customers or potential customers. The FSC may rely on the distribution statistics of the publisher of print media or the broadcaster of broadcast media in making this determination.[22] All direct costs incurred in connection with the advertisement will be considered foreign if the distribution statistics show 85 percent or more of the readership, listenership, or viewership is outside the United States.[23] Note that this 85 percent test should not be confused with the 85 percent alternative direct cost.

Costs related to advertising in English-language foreign editions of U.S. publications, as well as advertising in any publication in a foreign language, are foreign direct costs.[24] In contrast, costs related to advertising in the U.S. edition of a publication are not treated as direct costs, even if the publication also has a foreign edition in English.[25] For example, a United States weekly magazine publishes, in addition to its U.S. edition, a Canadian edition in English and a Mexican edition in Spanish. A FSC incurs costs of $200 X for a one-page display in each of the three editions for a total advertising cost of $600 X. The $200 X cost relating to the advertising in the United States edition is not a direct cost because it relates to U.S. sales. The total cost of $400 X relating to advertising in the English-language Canadian edition and the Spanish-language Mexican edition is a foreign direct cost.[26]

One way in which domestic advertising costs could inadvertently be incurred is by placing an advertisement in a foreign journal, published in English, with a U.S. readership of more than 15 percent. An example of a scenario designed to meet the advertising test is to incur costs in connection with placing one foreign advertisement per group of transactions each year. This must be continued each year to en-

---

[21] Reg. § 1.924(e)-1(a)(1)(ii).

[22] Reg. § 1.924(e)-1(a)(1)(iii)(A).

[23] Reg. § 1.924(e)-1(a)(1)(ii).

[24] Reg. § 1.924(e)-1(a)(1)(iii)(B).

[25] Reg. § 1.924(e)-1(a)(1)(iii)(C).

[26] Reg. § 1.924(e)-1(a)(1)(v), Example 2.

sure qualification of export sales for a FSC benefit. In some cases, this extra advertisement may be viewed favorably by the product sales management group.

Generally, the direct costs of sending sales literature to customers may be treated as solicitation or advertising, but not both. However, if the taxpayer engages in first and second mailings to customers, a distinction may be made between the two mailings. This distinction will allow one mailing to be treated as advertising and the other to be treated as solicitation. To meet the requirement of the "second mailing rule," the two mailings must be substantially different. A second mailing in which a product description and price list are different from the items in the first mailing would meet the requirements of the second mailing rule. However, simply amending the price list in the second mailing would not meet this requirement.[27]

The location of a sales promotion activity is the place where the trade show or customer meeting is held. Taxpayers must take great care if trade shows directed at export customers or meetings with foreign customers are located within the United States. For example, if the taxpayer conducts a meeting with its foreign customers at its U.S. headquarters, the costs of the meeting will be included in the determination of *total direct costs,* but not *foreign direct costs.* For those businesses that have a need to hold trade shows or customer meetings in the United States for export customers, this category may not be an appropriate one to use for meeting the 85 percent test. Depending on the extent of the costs in all categories, such meetings held in the United States may also make it impractical for a FSC to comply with the 50 percent test. The need to hold U.S. sitused trade shows or customer meetings for export customers and products is the primary reason taxpayers do not rely on the "advertising and sales promotion" category of activity when meeting the alternative 85 percent test for satisfying the economic process requirements. One technique is to mix export and nonexport customers.

(b) Processing of Customer Orders and Arranging for Delivery of the Export Property

This category of direct costs encompasses two distinct activities: processing of customer orders and arranging for delivery of the export property, which are combined. "Processing of customer orders" means notification, by the FSC to the related supplier, of the order and of the requirements for delivery of the export property.[28] Notification is required even if the related supplier may already have independent knowledge of such order and delivery. This direct cost test is met if the FSC succeeds in meeting a "20 percent coverage" threshold during the year.[29] The percentage test could be satisfied if, within each grouping, customers representing 20 percent or more of the foreign trade gross receipts for the current year

---

[27] Reg. §§ 1.924(e)-1(a)(1)(iv) and 1(a)(2)(iii).

[28] Reg. § 1.924(e)-1(b)(1)(i).

[29] Reg. § 1.924(e)-1(b)(1).

are requested to send their orders and delivery information in duplicate, one copy to the FSC (or an agent of the FSC) and one copy to the related supplier. The FSC or its agent can then fax a copy of this order to the related supplier and thus satisfy this test. Transactions may be "grouped" by election, as with all categories of activities for purposes of the direct cost tests.

"Arranging for delivery" means taking necessary steps to have the export property delivered to the customer in accordance with the requirements of the order, but does not include packaging, crating, and similar pretransportation costs. The direct costs of arranging for delivery do not include shipping expenses. The direct costs in this category do include salaries for clerks and telephone, telegraph, and documentation expenses. Delivery, for purposes of this test, can occur within or outside the United States since the location of arranging for delivery is the place where the activity is initiated by the FSC. The cost of arranging for delivery can be met by the 20 percent coverage test (by grouping) and may be easy to qualify. Consider the following example:

Example

An FSC earns commissions through its domestic related supplier to foreign customers on the sale of export property. The shipment term of all sales of the related supplier is FOB manufacturing plant. Thus, under the FSC regulations, there is no transportation. The related supplier telephones carriers to arrange for delivery from its shipping department at the plant and notifies the FSC, by mail, of the time and place of delivery of the orders placed by the customer. The FSC transmits the received information to the customer from its office outside the United States. Because there is no transportation to be arranged, this communication alone—by the FSC to the customers to notify them of the time and place of delivery—constitutes arranging for delivery.[30]

Assume the same facts given in preceding example, except that the shipment term of all the related supplier's sales is CIF (cost, insurance, and freight) and the commission relationship for transportation begins after the export property leaves U.S. customs territory. The related supplier telephones a trucking firm from its plant to ascertain information about transporting its property by truck to the docks. Then the related supplier telephones an overseas carrier from the docks to the location at which the customer takes possession. Upon receiving the necessary information, the related supplier electronically transmits to the FSC the shipping information, including the time and place of delivery to the customer. In addition, the related supplier instructs the FSC to communicate the necessary shipping information to the carriers to ensure shipment, and to notify the customer of the time and place of delivery. The FSC performs both activities from its office located outside the United States. The communications by the FSC to the carriers and the customer constitute arranging for delivery.[31]

---

[30] Reg. § 1.924(e)-1(b)(2).

[31] Reg. § 1.924(e)-1(b)(2), Example 2.

If foreign customers within each group represent 20 percent of current year FTGR are contacted in this manner, all such costs are foreign direct costs. U.S. costs are disregarded. Both the processing costs component and arranging for delivery costs component must qualify to use the direct cost category. This category often requires the use of outside personnel to perform the activities. In such cases, it is rare for a FSC to select this as a category to meet the 85 percent test. Only where a company has its own personnel, through a foreign branch or subsidiary, is this activity selected for compliance as part of the 85 percent test.

(c) Transportation

Transportation is one of the five components of the direct cost test. Transportation that is taken into account for this purpose is the activity undertaken by the FSC or its agent for shipping the export property. This transportation is taken into account during the period under which the FSC owns the export property or is responsible for such property. If the FSC is acting as a commission agent, the transportation costs taken into account toward this activity are transportation costs that are incurred for the export property only after the commission relationship begins. This severance rule applies even if the relationship begins after the property leaves U.S. customs territory.[32] The regulations allow the FSC and its related supplier to specify a specific time at which the commission agency begins for purposes of this transportation category. The written commission agreement between the related supplier and the FSC could specifically provide that the commission arrangement does not begin until after the property leaves U.S. customs territory.

The FSC's commission agency status does not begin until the product leaves U.S. customs territory if this relationship is properly defined in the written FSC agency agreement. Thus, it will be necessary to develop a methodology for accumulating the direct costs of transportation after such time. Total direct costs of transportation are expenses incurred by the FSC or its agent for transporting the export property. Direct costs of transportation are the expenses of shipping, such as fees paid to carriers and freight forwarders, costs of freight insurance, and documentation fees.

The FSC or its agent will not be considered to undertake transportation activity as to this export property if the customer pays the cost of transportation directly. However, the ultimate transfer of costs paid by the FSC to the customer will not disqualify the transaction. For example, the FSC or its agent could directly pay the transportation costs to the carrier, but include the cost of the transportation as a separate item on the invoice the FSC sends to its foreign customers. In this way, the costs will be included in meeting the foreign direct cost computation of this activity, even though the customer has economically borne the expense.

The cost of arranging for delivery is not included in the definition of total direct costs of transportation. For fungible commodities, total direct costs include only

---

[32] Reg. § 1.924(e)-1(c)(1).

those transportation costs that are incurred after goods have been identified to a contract. Goods are treated as leaving U.S. customs territory when they have been tendered to an international carrier for shipment to a foreign location, so long as the goods are not removed from the carrier's custody before they reach a point outside U.S. customs territory.

The amount of total direct costs treated as foreign direct costs is determined on the basis of the ratio of mileage outside U.S. customs territory to total transportation mileage. For example, if 50 percent of the mileage associated with a particular shipment is outside U.S. customs territory, 50 percent of the transportation expenses will be considered foreign direct costs. Only the direct costs that relate to the time after the FSC's commission agency begins are taken into account. Therefore, proper planning and a well-written commission agency agreement should ensure that all costs in this category are foreign direct costs. Thus, "transportation" is a commonly used category for purposes of the 85 percent test.

For the related supplier to incur transportation costs, the related supplier must make at least one shipment a year for which it bears the risk of loss or insures the property during shipment. Examples of methods of shipping that qualify as transportation include FOB destination, CIF, Ex Ship, and Ex Quay. Only one shipment per year will be required to qualify *all* export sales made during the year. Use of these foreign title passage techniques can also benefit the related supplier, since they may result in an increased foreign tax credit limitation.

(d)   Determination and Transmittal of a Final Invoice or Statement of Account and the Receipt of Payment

Two distinct activities, the determination and transmittal of the final invoice and the receipt of payment, are combined in measuring foreign and total direct costs under the direct cost test. "Determination and transmittal" means both assembly and forwarding: the assembly of the final invoice or the statement of account, and the forwarding of the document to the customer. The "final invoice" is the invoice upon which payment is made by the customer. An invoice that is transmitted after payment is made, as a receipt for payment, would satisfy this definition.[33] A "statement of account" is any summary statement transmitted to a customer giving the status of transactions occurring within an accounting period that does not exceed one taxable year. A single final invoice or statement of account can cover more than one transaction with one customer.

The costs of office supplies, office equipment, clerical salaries, mail, and miscellaneous similar expenses that are directly attributable to the assembly and transmittal of a final invoice or statement constitute direct costs for this activity. For example, the cost of assembling the final invoice at the FSC's foreign office and mailing the invoice from the FSC's foreign office to the customer would meet this requirement. A FSC may elect to send either final invoices or statements of ac-

---

[33] Reg. § 1.924(e)-1(d)(1)(iii)(B).

count. Costs associated with item not selected can be disregarded. Assembly and transmittal do not include the engineering or cost accounting functions involved in the establishment of a price.

A minimum coverage rule applies to assembly and forwarding activities.[34] The FSC could rely on the minimum coverage test by assembling and forwarding either statements of account or a final invoice from outside the United States to current or prior year customers, representing 50 percent of the current or prior year's foreign trading gross receipts as applicable within a product or product line grouping.[35] Foreign costs can be incurred by the FSC, the FSC management company, or the FSC's other agents. For example, the related supplier could send either the final invoice or statement of account to the applicable customers, to the extent of 50 percent coverage within each group, to the foreign office of the FSC management company. In turn, the management company would fold such documents, place each document in an envelope, address and affix postage, and mail the envelopes from the foreign location. The result is that 100 percent of the direct costs of this activity qualify as foreign direct costs.

The second activity within the determination and receipt rule is receipt of payment. The receipt test is accomplished by timely depositing into the FSC bank account an amount that is not less than 1.83 percent of foreign trade gross receipts. Direct costs include bank maintenance charges, service fees, and transfer fees associated with the bank account. The location (foreign or domestic) of the costs is dictated by the timing of the payment.

The FSC is considered to have received payment outside the United States if payment is made by the purchaser directly to the FSC or the related supplier in the United States, and the FSC or related supplier transfers the gross receipts amount associated with the transaction to a FSC bank account outside the United States after receipt of payment (i.e., cash, check, wire transfer, etc.) within 35 calendar days after receipt of good funds (i.e., the clearance of the check).[36] All transfer fees and the costs of the foreign bank account are treated as foreign direct costs. The bank costs in the United States are disregarded. If, however, the related supplier does not transfer the gross receipts amount within 35 calendar days, United States bank costs are not disregarded and are considered domestic direct costs. In any case, the transfer costs, currency conversion charges, and foreign bank costs remain foreign direct costs.

Year-end "offsetting" entries cannot be made if this receipt rule is used by the taxpayer to qualify as direct costs. Instead, payment must actually occur for the commission to be earned. A practical method of compliance with the 35-day rule is to make a monthly sweep, on the fourth day of the following month, in the amount of 1.83 percent or more of the export gross receipts for a given month. This sweep technique presupposes customers pay amounts directly to the U.S. bank

---

[34] Reg. § 1.924(e)-1(d)(1).

[35] *Ibid.*

[36] Reg. § 1.924(e)-1(d)(2)(iii).

account of the related supplier, as is often the case. It is important to make appropriate arrangements with the bank and to fully understand the bank charges that will be incurred because of the funds transfers between the FSC and its related supplier. These charges for banking transactions may make this category a costly one to utilize for purposes of the 85 percent test.

(e)   Assumption of Credit Risk

The "assumption of credit risk" means bearing the economic risk of nonpayment as to a transaction. If the FSC is acting as a commission agent for the related supplier, this risk is borne by the FSC if the written commission agency agreement transfers the costs of the economic risk of nonpayment in the transaction from the related supplier to the FSC. The FSC may elect on its annual return to bear the economic risk of nonpayment from the transaction during a taxable year through one of the five following methods:[37]

1. Assuming the risk of a bad debt,
2. Obtaining insurance to cover nonpayment,
3. Investigating the credit of a customer or a potential customer,
4. Factoring trade receivables, or
5. Selling by means of letters of credit or banker's acceptance.

The location of the activity concerning the assumption of the credit risk is the location of the customer whose payment is at risk. However, the location of investigating the credit is the location of the credit agency or association performing the investigation. Thus, a foreign branch of a United States credit agency can investigate the credit of the foreign purchaser, and this activity would be a foreign direct cost. This result applies even though the same credit report can be obtained from a U.S. branch of the same agency and that activity would result in a domestic direct cost.

The assumption of credit risk consists of the bearing of the economic risk of nonpayment in a transaction. However, in some circumstances, a taxpayer may not have any export receivables that become uncollectable. For example, all exports may be sold to large and well-financed (and possibly related-party) distributors and (OEMs). None of these distributors or OEMs would be in a position in which it could not meet its obligations. Even though the FSC is contractually assuming the risk of loss, there would be no actual loss or bad debt expense. In such cases, the FSC will be considered to bear the risk of loss only if it incurs an actual loss (or is allowed to deduct an addition to a bad debt reserve under present law) in at least one year within a three-year period. If a FSC contractually assumes the risk of loss but incurs no bad debt expense in the first two years of operations as a FSC, it can-

---

[37] Reg. § 1.924(e)-1(e)(2)(i) through (v).

not satisfy the assumption of credit risk activity in the third year unless it actually incurs a loss in that year. The FSC cannot use one of the other four bad debt methods in year three. For this reason, it does not make sense for some companies to use the first alternative for the bad debt test.

Even if the FSC does not incur a loss in the third year, it would still be treated as having satisfied the assumption of a credit test in the first two years.[38] If the FSC then incurs a loss in the fourth year, it could use the credit test in the fourth, fifth, and sixth years. However, the FSC could not use the loss in year four to cover years three, four, and five and by doing so retroactively cure its lack of compliance for the bad debt category in year three.

A bad debt deduction applies when the customer cannot or does not pay its valid obligation. Credits given for returned merchandise, defective merchandise, and disputes with customers do not count as bad debt expenses.

6.8 Foreign Military Sales

Congress recognized that certain foreign military sales must be made through the U.S. government, typically to foreign governments. Since negotiation and other activities performed in connection with the sale must occur between the taxpayer and the U.S. government, many of the expenses incurred by a FSC in connection with such sales will be incurred within the United States. Therefore, for the purposes of the foreign presence and economic process tests, such expenses (and the expenses of the U.S. government in connection with the sale) will not be taken into account.[39]

6.9 Conclusion

The foreign economic process test is unique to FSCs, having no DISC background. Moreover, both the sales activity test and the direct cost test are complex, especially the direct cost test. Taxpayers should focus on the potential and risks of those provisions.

---

[38] *Ibid.*

[39] Reg. § 1.924(d)-1(f).

CHAPTER 7

Foreign Sales Corporation's Foreign Management Requirements

Edward Tanenbaum

7.1 Introduction

To ensure compliance with the General Agreement on Tariffs and Trade (GATT), a foreign sales corporation (FSC) is required to have a foreign presence, and activities that relate to export income must have economic substance and must be performed by the FSC outside United States customs territory. The United States interprets this exception as applying to transactions in which the economic processes that give rise to the income take place outside the United States. As a result, the FSC must comply with the foreign management rules.

7.2 Qualification of FSC

FSC must have a foreign presence. The foreign management rules require FSC to demonstrate its foreign presence through the following measures:

1. The FSC must maintain an office in an eligible U.S. possession or qualifying foreign jurisdiction at all times during the taxable year.[1]
2. The FSC must maintain a set of permanent books of account at its qualifying foreign office.[2]
3. The FSC must maintain, at a location within the records that are required to be kept by a U.S. corporate taxpayer.[3]
4. The FSC's board of directors must have at least one member who is not a U.S. resident.[4]

7.3 Foreign Office

A FSC is considered as having an "office" in an eligible U.S. possession or qualifying foreign jurisdiction if the purported office satisfies all of the following requirements:

1. The office must have a fixed location. A transient location will not suffice.[5]
2. The office must be a building or a portion of a building consisting of at least one room. A room is a "partitioned" part of the inside of a building.[6] The term "partition" implies that something less than a conventional walled enclosure will satisfy the room requirement. The room used as the corporation's office, however, must be large enough to accommodate the required communication equipment described below.[7]

   The regulatory definition of an office is not limited to a room with communication equipment or an adjacent room. Noncontiguous space within a building will also constitute an office of a FSC if it is equipped for the retention of the documentation required to be maintained by FSCs and if access to the necessary communication equipment is available to the FSC.[8]

3. The office must be equipped for the performance of the corporation's business, equipped for the communication and retention of information, and must be supplied with communication services.[9]

---

[1] IRC § 922(a)(1)(D)(i). For legislative history and background, *see* Robert Feinschreiber, *FSC: The Foreign Sales Corporation* (1984), Chapter 4.

[2] IRC § 922(a)(1)(D)(ii).

[3] IRC § 922(a)(1)(D)(iii).

[4] IRC § 922(a)(1)(E).

[5] Treas. Reg. § 922-1(h), Q&A 9, (i).

[6] Treas. Reg. § 922-1(h), Q&A 9, (ii).

[7] *Id.*

[8] *Id.*

[9] Treas. Reg. § 922-1(h), Q&A 9, (iii).

4. The office must be regularly used for some business activity of the cor-
    poration.[10] For this purpose, a corporation's business activities include
    (a) the solicitation, the negotiation, or the making of contracts concerning
    the sales of export property by the corporation or a related supplier, and
    (b) the preparatory or ancillary activities of the corporation.

    The maintenance of books of account are an activity that must be regu-
    larly conducted.[11] Documentation activities may be performed by any per-
    son, whether or not related to the FSC, at the office, if the activity is per-
    formed pursuant to an oral or written contract.[12] However, documentation
    activities do not have to be performed at the office.[13]

5. The office must be operated, and owned or leased, by the corporation or by
    a person, whether or not related, who is under contract to the corporation.[14]
    The required business activity, therefore, may be conducted by the FSC or
    by the FSC's dependent or independent agent. For example, an indepen-
    dent management company can perform the required activities. In addi-
    tion, the regulations require that the office be maintained by the corpora-
    tion or by the independent or dependent agent at all times during the
    taxable year.[15]

A FSC is likely to be established in a jurisdiction that has adequate banking facilities, but FSC can be established in a jurisdiction that does not have these facilities. A FSC does not have to locate its office in the country or possession of its incorporation so long as it has at least one office in a qualifying U.S. possession or
foreign country that is a party to a treaty with the requisite exchange of information provisions to which the FSC is subject.[16] In the case of a newly organized
FSC, there is a 30-day grace period that runs from the time the corporation is organized as a FSC, that is, the effective date of the FSC election, and the time the
office is first maintained.[17]

7.4 Documentation Requirements

An FSC must maintain a "set of the permanent books of account" of the corporation.[18] The following documentation must be maintained at the FSC's qualifying

---

[10] Treas. Reg. § 922-1(h), Q&A 9, (iv).

[11] *Id.*

[12] *Id.*

[13] *Id.*

[14] Treas. Reg. § 922-1(h), Q&A 9, (v).

[15] Treas. Reg. § 922-1(h), Q&A 9, (vi).

[16] Treas. Reg. § 1.922-1(h), Q&A 10, 11.

[17] Treas. Reg. § 1.922-1(h), Q&A 9 (iv).

[18] IRC § 922(a)(1)(D)(ii).

foreign office; however, such documentation need not be prepared by the FSC or at the FSC's office.[19]

The FSC must provide quarterly income statements, a final year-end income statement, and a year-end balance sheet.[20] Quarterly income statements must contain, at a minimum, a "reasonable estimate" of the corporation's income and expense items.[21] If the corporation is a commission FSC, 1.83 percent of the related supplier's gross receipts will be considered a reasonable estimate of the FSC's income.[22]

The FSC must provide all final invoices, a summary of all final invoices, and statements of account concerning sales by the FSC and sales by any related person if the FSC realizes income from such sales.[23] A document will constitute a "final invoice" if it contains the customer's name or identifying number and the date, products, or product code or service or service code, quantity, price, and amount due.[24] Alternatively, in the absence of any of the preceding enumerated data, an invoice will be considered final if the FSC establishes that the document is considered a final invoice under normal commercial practices.[25] A summary of final invoices may be in any reasonable form, provided that the summary contains all substantive information from the invoices, that is, the customer's name or identifying number, the invoice number, date, product or product code, and amount owed, or a summary of the information that is included on documents considered to be final invoices under normal commercial practice.[26]

A "statement of account" is defined as any summary statement that apprises a customer of, or confirms the status of, transactions within a period of a month or longer within a taxable year.[27] Such a statement, as compared with a final invoice, must contain the customer's name or identifying number, date of the statement of account, and the balance due as of the last day of the accounting period covered by the statement.[28] If any required information is lacking, a FSC may establish that the documents are considered statements of account under normal commercial practice.[29] If a document is sent to domestic as well as export customers to inform them of the status of accounts, the document will be considered a statement of account under normal commercial practice.[30]

---

[19] Treas. Reg. § 1.922-1(i), Q&A 12 (iii).

[20] Treas. Reg. § 1.922-1(i), Q&A 12 (i).

[21] Treas. Reg. § 1.922-1(i), Q&A 12 (iii).

[22] Id.

[23] Treas. Reg. § 1.922-1(i), Q&A 12 (ii).

[24] Id.

[25] Id.

[26] Treas. Reg. § 1.922-1(i), Q&A 12 (iii).

[27] Treas. Reg. § 1.922-1(i), Q&A 12 (iii).

[28] Id.

[29] Id.

[30] Id.

The documentation required to be maintained by the office may be originals or duplicates.[31] Such documentation may be maintained in the form of punch cards, magnetic tapes, disks, and other machine-sensible media used for recording, consolidating, and summarizing accounting transactions and records within a taxpayer's automatic data processing system.[32]

If the FSC does not prepare the required documentation itself, the documentation must be forwarded to the FSC office within the regulatory time period. Generally, the quarterly income statements for the first three quarters must be "maintained" at the FSC office no later than 90 days after the end of the quarter. The quarterly statement for the fourth quarter, as well as the year-end income statement, balance sheets, and final invoices, summaries, or statements of account must be "maintained" no later than the due date, including extensions, of the FSC's income tax return.[33] The required documentation for a particular taxable year must be maintained at the FSC's office until the statutory period of limitations for assessment of tax for the taxable year has expired.[34]

As long as a FSC makes a good faith effort to maintain the required final invoices, summaries, or statements of account, a failure to comply properly with the documentation requirements will not be fatal if such failure is cured within a reasonable time of discovery of the failure.[35] FSCs must maintain in the records that are required to be kept by a corporate taxpayer under IRC § 6001.[36]

7.5 Nonresident Board Member

For FSC purposes, the "board of directors" is "the body that manages and directs the corporation according to the law of the qualifying foreign country or eligible possession under the laws of which the corporation was created or organized."[37] The FSC foreign presence rules require the FSC's board of directors to include at least one member who is not a U.S. resident.[38] The nonresident board member can be a citizen of the United States so long as a person would not otherwise be classified as a U.S. resident for tax purposes.[39] A nonresident alien individual who elects to be treated as a resident of the United States for a taxable year under the provision relating to joint filing of tax returns with a spouse who actually is a resident of the United States[40] can be considered a nonresident of the United States for FSC purposes.[41]

---

[31] Treas. Reg. § 1.922-1(i), Q&A 14.

[32] *Id.*

[33] Treas. Reg. § 1.922-1(i), Q&A 13.

[34] Treas. Reg. § 1.922-1(i), Q&A 15.

[35] Treas. Reg. § 1.922-1(i), Q&A 12 (iv).

[36] IRC § 922(a)(1)(D)(iii); Treas. Reg. § 1.922-1(i), Q&A 16.

[37] Treas. Reg. § (j), Q&A 17.

[38] IRC § 922(a)(1)(E).

[39] Treas. Reg. § 1.922-1(j), Q&A 18.

[40] *See* IRC § 6013(g).

[41] Treas. Reg. § 1.922-1(j), Q&A 20.

There was some concern among practitioners that if the board of directors had only one such nonresident member, FSC status would terminate if the lone nonresident board member were to die or resign. Regulations issued in connection with this requirement added some degree of flexibility by permitting a FSC to rectify the situation by appointing a new board member who is a nonresident of the United States within 30 days after the death or resignation of the former nonresident member.[42] Because the grace period is limited to 30 days, frequent contact between the FSC and the director is advantageous. Moreover, the FSC should ascertain whether resignation would require the consent of the FSC. If not, a disgruntled director could preclude FSC benefits.

7.6   Foreign Management Rules

A portion of a FSC's foreign trade income (FTI) is excluded from taxation in the United States. FTI is gross income earned by a FSC arising from foreign trading gross receipts.[43] A FSC is considered as having foreign trading gross receipts for any taxable year only if the management of the FSC during such taxable year takes place outside the United States.[44] A FSC satisfies the foreign management requirement for a taxable year if:

1.   All meetings of the board of directors and all meetings of the shareholders are outside the United States;[45]

2.   The principal bank account of the FSC is maintained outside the United States at all times during the taxable year;[46] and

3.   All dividends, legal and accounting fees, and salaries of officers and members of the board of directors are disbursed during the taxable year out of foreign bank accounts.[47]

Many taxpayers use a management company to perform these services. A FSC management company typically handles all day-to-day activities and any foreign management or foreign economic requirements.

A taxpayer can exempt itself from the foreign management requirements and still generate receipts that qualify as foreign trading gross receipts by electing small FSC status.[48] The small FSC provisions afford administrative convenience, but they allow the small FSC to take only up to $5 million of annual foreign trad-

---

[42] Treas. Reg. § 1.922-1(j), Q&A 19.

[43] IRC § 923(b).

[44] IRC § 924(b)(1)(A).

[45] IRC § 924(c)(1).

[46] IRC § 924(c)(2).

[47] IRC § 924(c)(3).

[48] IRC § 922(b)(1), 924(b)(2)(A).

ing gross receipts income into account in any taxable year.[49] Foreign trading gross receipts beyond $5 million are not exempt.

7.7 Foreign Shareholders and Directors Meetings

A FSC must hold all meetings of its board of directors and shareholders outside the United States.[50] The regulations relax this stringent requirement by providing that the nexus requirement applies only in connection with board or shareholder meetings that are "formally convened."[51] Whether a meeting is "formally convened" is determined in reference to local law. The phrase "formally convened" apparently relates only to actual board or shareholder meetings where the appropriate persons congregate to accomplish a stated purpose. Local laws determine whether such a meeting must be held, when and where it must be held, quorum requirements, use of proxies, and so forth. For example, if the law of the FSC's jurisdiction of incorporation allows written consents in lieu of formal meetings, the fact that the individuals are present in the United States when executing their consents does not constitute a meeting within the United States.[52]

If the participants in a meeting, as defined by local law, are not all physically present in the same location (and under local law do not need to be physically present in the same location), the location of the meeting is determined by the location of the persons exercising the majority of the voting power (including proxies) participating in the meeting.[53] For example, assume that the country of organization requires a majority of directors, but does not require that the meeting take place in that country or that the directors be physically present. If one director is in country X, another in country Y, and another in the United States, and these three directors participate in a meeting by telephone (which constitutes a meeting under local law), the meeting takes place outside the United States because the persons exercising a majority of the voting power participating in the meeting are located outside the United States.[54]

7.8 Principal Bank Account

The principal bank account of a FSC must be maintained at all times during the taxable year in any country in which it could be organized or in any eligible United States possession.[55] The principal bank account of a FSC is the account utilized to

---

[49] IRC § 924(b)(2)(B)(i).

[50] IRC § 924(c)(1).

[51] Treas. Reg. § 1.924(c)-1(b).

[52] *Id.*

[53] Treas. Reg. § 1.924(c)-1(b).

[54] *See* Treas. Reg. § 1.924(c)-1(b).

[55] IRC § 924(c)(2).

disburse certain payments, such as dividends, legal and accounting fees paid to independent persons, and salaries of officers and directors.[56] Any account from which any such payments are disbursed is treated as a principal bank account.[57]

A FSC can have multiple principal bank accounts. All principal bank accounts must be so designated on the FSC's income tax return with the name of the banks and the account numbers.[58] In addition, a FSC may have other bank accounts in any location (even in the United States).[59]

The principal bank account must be maintained with a company that is carrying on a banking, financing, or similar business.[60] While the principal bank account must be maintained outside the United States, the account can be kept and reflected on the books of the foreign branch of a U.S. bank.[61] Notwithstanding the foreign account location, instructions governing the account are permitted to originate in the United States.[62] When a FSC is first organized, the FSC is granted 30 days following the effective date of its FSC election to open its principal bank account, provided that the FSC maintains that principal bank account for the remainder of the year.[63]

In Rev. Rul. 90-108,[64] the IRS addressed a situation in which a corporation revoked its small FSC status and elected regular FSC status. The IRS held that the corporation was treated as a newly formed corporation for purposes of the principal bank account requirement. As a result, the corporation had 30 days following the date its FSC election was effective to open its principal bank account.

In Technical Advice Memorandum (TAM) 9344002, a new FSC made a FSC election. One week later a principal bank account was opened in a bank located outside the United States. No funds were deposited. No deposits were made into the account for the first 34 months of operation. A related company made all disbursements (including accounting fees, salaries, etc.) on the behalf of the FSC. A few days after the extended due date for the new FSC's tax return for its second year of existence, funds were deposited into its principal bank account and transferred to the related company as a reimbursement of expenses.

The IRS noted that the statute and the regulations do not require that funds be deposited into the bank account, only that the account be opened and maintained on the books and records of the banking institution. Since the FSC's account had been obtained and maintained, the FSC had complied with the principal bank account requirements.

---

[56] Treas. Reg. § 1.924(c)-1(c)(1).

[57] Treas. Reg. § 1.924(c)-1(d)(1).

[58] Treas. Reg. § 1.924(c)-1(c)(1).

[59] Treas. Reg. § 1.924(c)-1(c)(5).

[60] Treas. Reg. § 1.924(c)-1(c)(2).

[61] Id.

[62] Treas. Reg. § 1.924(c)-1(c)(4).

[63] Treas. Reg. § 1.924(c)-1(c)(4).

[64] Rev. Rul. 90-108, 1990-2 C.B 185.

However, the regulations require that a related person be reimbursed no later than the last date prescribed for filing the FSC's tax return (including extensions) for the taxable year which the reimbursement relates.[65] In this case, the FSC's accounting fees and other expenses were paid by a related person. The FSC did not reimburse the related party for these expenses until after the extended due date for its tax returns. Therefore, the FSC's reimbursements were not timely.

Nevertheless, the IRS held that the regulatory good faith exception[66] applied. This provision states that if it is determined that fees or salaries were paid by a related person and reimbursements were not made, the FSC may still satisfy the foreign management requirements if reimbursements are effected within 90 days of determination. The IRS reasoned that the FSC's reimbursements to the related person were late by not more than a few days and the FSC had attempted to make these payments in a timely fashion. Further, the facts indicated that the FSC's tax department was understaffed and in a formative period and that, consequently, it was difficult to establish and maintain consistent disbursement procedures. The following year, the FSC hired a full-time, in-house tax professional that revised the payment procedures so that accounting fees and other direct expenses were paid directly from the account.

7.9 Dividend Distributions and Certain Expenses

A FSC must disburse all dividend distributions, legal and accounting fees, and salaries of officers and directors out of its bank accounts that are located outside the United States.[67] If the FSC is owed money by a related supplier, the FSC can offset such amount by making book entries to reflect dividend distributions.[68] For these purposes, dividends are cash dividends actually paid pursuant to a declaration or authorization of the FSC. Constructive dividends, regardless of source, and distributions of property are not considered.[69]

A related party can pay on behalf of the FSC its legal and accounting fees, as well as salaries to its officers and directors, provided, however, that the FSC reimburses the related party.[70] Inadvertent disbursements by a FSC (with the exception of distributions of dividends) can be made from an account other than its principal bank account (a "secondary account"), provided the principal bank account reimburses the secondary account within a reasonable period of time following the date it discovers the mistaken disbursement.[71]

---

[65] Treas. Reg. § 1.924(c)-1(d)(2).

[66] Treas. Reg. § 1.924(c)-1(d)(3).

[67] IRC § 924(c)(3).

[68] Treas. Reg. §§ 1.924(c)-1(d)(1) and 1.924(c)-1(d)(4)(i), (ii).

[69] Treas. Reg. § 1.924(c)-1(d)(4).

[70] Treas. Reg. §§ 1.924(c)-1(d)(1) and 1.924(c)-1(d)(2).

[71] Treas. Reg. § 1.924(c)-1(d)(1).

Legal and accounting fees include payments paid to independent third parties, but not to employees of the FSC or any related persons.[72] Salaries of officers and salaries or fees of directors are only those salaries or fees paid for services as officers or directors of the FSC.[73] If an officer, director, or employee of a related person is also an officer or director of a FSC who receives additional compensation for other services performed for the FSC, the portion of compensation paid to that individual for services performed for the FSC must be disbursed (or reimbursed to the related person) out of the FSC's principal bank account.[74] In light of this requirement, the FSC should pay its directors directly.

7.10 Conclusion

Foreign management is complex in its own right, but must also be coordinated with the election requirements and the economic process requirements. The economic process and foreign management affect permanent establishment issues, advertising rules, banking relationships, and professional services. Foreign management issues are relatively easy to audit, necessitating that the taxpayer remain vigilant.

---

[72] Treas. Reg. § 1.924(c)-1(d)(5).

[73] Treas. Reg. § 1.924(c)-1(d)(6).

[74] *Id.*

CHAPTER 8

Pricing and Grouping Strategies

Robert Feinschreiber

8.1   Introduction

The grouping of transactions is complex for a foreign sales corporation (FSC) than for a domestic international sales corporation (DISC). Grouping can diminish tax benefits in some situations and increase tax benefits in others. FSC grouping applies to the sales test, the direct cost test, and the transfer price between the FSC and its related supplier. In contrast, DISC grouping applies only to pricing.

8.2   Three Types

The FSC provisions enable three types of grouping to take place. In the FSC context, three separate grouping techniques are examined: sales activities, direct costs, and administrative pricing.[1] Both DISCs and FSCs utilize transfer pricing, but FSC grouping also applies to the sales test and the direct cost test.

(a)   Sales Activities

Sales activities comprise solicitation, negotiation, and making of the contract as part of the economic process test. The FSC must participate, directly or indirectly, in one or more of these sales activities outside the United States. However, the sales activity test does not have to be met on a transaction-by-transaction basis. A grouping rule enables the sales activities to be grouped to determine whether these activities take place outside the United States.

(b)   Direct Costs

Non-sales activities are subject to a direct cost test. The economic process tests are met if direct costs incurred by the FSC equal or exceed 50 percent of the direct costs.[2] Alternatively, the FSC can meet the 85 percent test as to two categories.[3] These tests are advertising and sales promotion, order processing, transportation, invoicing and receipt, and credit risk.[4] However, these rules can be met through using grouping rules.

(c)   Administrative Pricing

Administrative pricing is permitted between the FSC and its related supplier. Excluding marginal costing or loss transaction, the FSC can receive 1.83 percent

---

[1] IRC §§ 921–927, 991–997, and 994. *See* Robert Feinschreiber, *Domestic International Sales Corporations* (PLI, 1978), Chapter 11; "How to Aggregate DISC Sales to Make Most Effective Use of the Deferral," *Journal of Tax* 36 (1972):300; "New Strategies for Increasing DISC Benefits," *Finance Executive* 44 (1976):32.

[2] § 924(d)(1)(B).

[3] § 924(d)(2).

[4] § 924(e).

of foreign trading gross receipts[5] or 23 percent of combined taxable income of the FSC and its related supplier,[6] whichever is higher. The gross receipts method is limited to 46 percent of combined taxable income.[7] Grouping rules apply to determine the FSC income.

8.3 Economic Processes

Sales activities and direct costs are economic processes[8] that apply on a transaction-by-transaction basis or on a group basis. A grouping can be based on products or product lines, customers, contracts, or products or product lines within customer or contract groupings.[9] Product or product line groupings can be based on a recognized trade or industry usage or on a two-digit major SIC group. (SIC is the Standard Industrial Classification system prepared by the Statistical Policy Division of the Office of Management and Budget.) A FSC can use classifications or combination of inferior SIC classifications within a major group.[10]

Different groupings can be used for different purposes. The FSC can choose to group transactions separately for each of the sales activities or for each of the direct cost tests.[11] Groupings need not have relationship to groupings used for other purposes. The choice to group transactions applies to all transactions within the scope of that grouping. For transactions not encompassed by the grouping, the determination is made on a transaction-by-transaction or other grouping basis.[12] A FSC may elect a product grouping for one product and the transaction-by-transaction method for another product.

(a) Sales Activities

The sales activity test can be met through solicitation (other than advertising), negotiation, and making of the contract, outside the United States.[13] This test is met if the sales activities are performed in regard to customers with sales representing 20 percent or more of the foreign trading gross receipts of the product or product line grouping during the current year.[14] Alternatively, the sales activity test can be met by 50 percent or more of the foreign trading gross receipts (FTGR) of

---

[5] § 925(a)(1).

[6] § 925(a)(2).

[7] § 925(d).

[8] IRC § 924(d); Reg. § 1.924(d)-1.

[9] Reg. §§ 1.924(d)-1(e)(1) and 1.924(d)-1(c)(5)(i).

[10] Reg. §§ 1.924(d)-1(c)(5)(i)(A) and 1.924(d)-1(e)(1)(i).

[11] Reg. §§ 1.924(d)-1(c)(5)(iii) and 1.924(d)-1(e)(3).

[12] Reg. §§ 1.924(d)-1(e)(2) and 1.924(d)1-1(c)(5)(ii).

[13] IRC § 924(d)(1)(A); Reg. § 1.924(d)-1(c).

[14] Reg. § 1.924(d)-1(c)(5)(A)(i).

the product or product line grouping for the prior year.[15] In the following situation, ungrouping of transactions is advantageous. A company has two products, X and Y, within the same two-digit SIC. The FSC performed 19 percent of the sales activities and did not meet the 20 percent test. Because of the sales activity test, FSC grouping did not qualify.

Product	Sales FTGR	Total FTGR
X	$300,000	$1,000,000
Y	$80,000	$1,000,000
Total	$380,000	$2,000,000

If Product X and Product Y are treated separately, the sales activity test is met for Product X (30 percent of foreign trade gross receipts), but not for Product Y (8 percent of foreign trade gross receipts).

In another situation, a company could benefit from grouping, rather than treating each product separately. Suppose Product M meets the 20 percent sales activity test, but Product N does not. If Products M and N are grouped, the group as a whole qualifies for the 20 percent sales test. Thus, Product N qualifies for the sales activity pertaining to Product M.

Product	Sales FTGR	Total FTGR
M	$250,000	$1,000,000
N	$170,000	$1,000,000
Total	$420,000	$2,000,000

(b) Foreign Direct Costs

FSC sales qualify as foreign trading gross receipts only if the foreign direct costs equal or exceed 50 percent of the total direct costs incurred by the FSC, or equal or exceed 85 percent of total direct costs in two categories.[16] The direct cost tests are ascertained transaction-by-transaction unless the FSC elects to group these transactions. The product or product line groups that are established for purposes of determining combined taxable income may be different from the groups that are established in regard to economic processes.

(c) The 50 Percent Test

In some situations grouping can cause some transactions to qualify as foreign direct costs even though they would qualify on their own, because the entire group

---

[15] Reg. § 1.924(d)-1(c)(5)(A)(ii).

[16] Reg. §§ 924(d)(1)(B), 924(d)(2), and 924(d)-1(d)(1).

qualifies as foreign direct costs. In other situations grouping can cause an entire group to be disqualified, even if an individual item would qualify separately as foreign direct costs.

In a particular situation, foreign direct costs (FDC) were 65 percent of the total direct costs (TDC) for Product A and 40 percent of direct costs for Product B. Separately, Transaction A would meet the direct cost test, but Transaction B would not. Together, however, A and B would meet the 50 percent test.

Transaction	FDC	TDC
A	65	100
B	40	100
Total	105	200

In another situation, foreign direct costs were 55 percent of the total direct costs for Product C and 40 percent of direct costs for Product B. Separately, Transaction C would meet the direct cost test, but Transaction B would not. Together, B and C do not meet the 50 percent test.

Transaction	FDC	TDC
B	55	100
C	40	100
Total	95	200

The primary grouping, for meeting the direct cost test, is to meet the 50 percent test or the 85 percent test. In this situation, the company has already ascertained that it will group all of its direct cost categories rather than selecting two categories of direct cost.

(d) The 85 Percent Test

Situations arise in which a FSC appears not to be in compliance with the direct cost test, because the FSC failed either the 50 percent test or the 85 percent test, but the ungrouping of transactions can enable the direct cost tests to qualify. In other situations, grouping is beneficial.

In the following situation, 45 percent of the foreign direct costs of Total Group AB were total direct costs, so that 50 percent of the direct cost test failed. Only one category, credit, met the 85 percent test for AB, so the two-category requirement was not satisfied. In this instance ungrouping is beneficial. When the FSC uses its inferior classifications, each meets the 85 percent test. Thus, Group A meets the first and third direct cost test and Group B meets the second and fourth direct cost test.

Total Group AB

Category	FDC	TDC	Qualifies
1	9	20	No
2	6	20	No
3	0	25	No
4	25	30	No
5	5	5	Yes
Total	45	100	

· Group A

Category	FDC	TDC	Qualifies
1	9	10	Yes
2	1	15	No
3	0	15	No
4	11	15	No
5	5	5	Yes
Total	26	60	

Group B

Category	FDC	TDC	Qualifies
1	0	10	No
2	5	5	Yes
3	0	10	No
4	14	15	Yes
5	0	0	No
Total	19	40	

In the next situation, grouping is beneficial. Group C meets only one test under the 85 percent rule, as does Group D. However, Combined Group CD meets the 85 percent test in the two categories.

Group C

Category	FDC	TDC	Qualifies
1	8	10	No
2	1	5	No
3	2	10	No
4	1	10	No
5	10	10	Yes
Total	22	45	

Group D

Category	FDC	TDC	Qualifies
1	10	10	Yes
2	2	5	No
3	3	20	No
4	2	10	No
5	8	10	No
Total	25	55	

Group CD

Category	FDC	TDC	Qualifies
1	18	20	Yes
2	3	10	No
3	5	30	No
4	3	20	No
5	18	20	Yes
Total	47	100	

If a FSC elects to utilize the 85 percent direct cost test, it can benefit from a second tier of grouping possibilities. Three of five direct costs pertain to grouping, but each of these grouping rules are different from the others.

8.4 FSC and DISC Transfer Pricing Methods

Exporters who qualify can claim favorable tax benefits under the FSC provisions. If the exporter establishes a separate entity that meets organizational and operative requirements, the entity can qualify as a FSC and can use one or more transfer pricing options. A portion of the income is taxed at a lower tax rate. An IC-DISC remains available.

Pricing rules enable a FSC to benefit from safe haven pricing and provide some measure of certainty between the U.S. manufacturer or other related supplier and the FSC. (A related supplier is a related party who directly participates in these transactions.) Transactions between the related supplier and the FSC should be pursuant to a written agreement, specifying the buy-sell or commission arrangements, pricing methods, reimbursement, and correlative aspects of the arrangement.

A FSC has to meet numerous requirements, such as foreign incorporation, export trading gross receipts, export property, foreign management, and economic processes (including foreign sales activities and foreign costs).[17] Nevertheless, a

---

[17] Bruce and Lieberman, 264-4th T.M., *Foreign Sales Corporations;* Robert Feinschreiber, *FSC: The Foreign Sales Corporation* (Corporate Tax Press, 1984).

FSC provides "form with substance" in many cases. Safe haven rules are necessary because the FSC's share of this income would be very limited on an arm's length basis.

These pricing rules started with the domestic international corporation (DISC), the predecessor of the FSC, which was first suggested in 1969.[18] The DISC proposal was included in the Trade Act of 1970, which was not enacted,[19] and was also included in the Revenue Act of 1971.[20] FSCs substantially replaced DISCs under the Deficit Reduction Act of 1984.

There are two primary safe haven pricing rules for DISCs. A DISC is a sales entity, and it should earn half of the income, with the other half retained by the manufacturer, following IRC § 863(b). At the time of DISC enactment, companies earned nearly 8 percent of sales as income, so that exporters were entitled to 50 percent of that amount, or 4 percent of gross receipts. Under the second safe haven alternative, a 4 percent rate of gross receipts was adopted instead of 50 percent of combined taxable income.

8.5 Transfer Pricing Rules

FSCs supplanted DISCs, largely because of attacks by members of the General Agreement on Tariffs and Trade (GATT), but DISCs remain as interest charge DISCs. As a consequence, DISC safe haven pricing under IRC § 994 was partially replaced with FSC administrative pricing under IRC § 925. DISCs provided only tax deferral, but FSCs provide a tax rate reduction. Accordingly, DISC benefits were reduced in the DISC-FSC conversion. The DISC safe haven rates were multiplied by the then-applicable 46 percent tax rate.

Thus, the 50 percent tax haven rate under DISC rules became 23 percent (50 percent times 46 percent) under the FSC administrative pricing rules. Similarly, the 4 percent tax haven rate under DISC rules would have been 4 percent times 46 percent, or 1.84 percent, under FSC administrative pricing rules. Because of a computational error, however, the gross receipts rate is 1.83 percent, not 1.84 percent, for FSC administrative pricing purposes. (See Exhibit 8.1.)

(a) Sale Price Charged

The transfer price or the commission may be determined under IRC § 482 in lieu of the 1.83 percent rate or the 23 percent rate. If this alternative is elected, all of the usual rules of IRC § 482 apply. Presumably, a FSC will establish that it can be recognized as a separate entity, but its share of the total income is uncertain at

---

[18] Robert Feinschreiber, "The DISC Proposal: Tax Measure Seen as Boost to American Exports," NAM *National Association of Manufacturers Reports* (20 April 1970).

[19] HR. 18392, introduced July 9, 1970. *See* Robert Feinschreiber and Reale, DISC, 70-15th T.M. July 27, 1970.

[20] *See* Robert Feinschreiber, "Electing DISC Benefits," 50 *Taxes* 304 (1972); Robert Feinschreiber, "Tax Benefits for Domestic International Sales Corporations (DISCs)—Pricing, Profits and Dividends," 40 *CPA J.* 221 (1972).

Exhibit 8.1

FSC PRICING ALTERNATIVES

Gross Revenue (GR)	Combined Taxable Income (CTI)	1.83% of GR	23% of CTI	Limitation	FSC Income
100	10	1.83	2.30*	0	2.30
100	9	1.83	2.07*	0	2.07
100	8	1.83	1.84*	0	1.84
100	7	1.83*	1.61	0	1.83
100	6	1.83*	1.38	0	1.83
100	5	1.83*	1.15	0	1.83
100	4	1.83*	0.92	0	1.83
100	3	1.83	0.69	1.38*	1.38
100	2	1.83	0.46	0.92*	0.92
100	1	1.83	0.23	0.46*	0.46

*Maximum FSC Income

best, even if it performs its economic process functions. If a FSC earns profit that exceeds the profit under the administrative pricing rules, the IRS is likely to object to this pricing split and will give "special scrutiny" to such a transaction.

An independent trading entity that buys U.S. goods from unrelated parties and sells these goods overseas to unrelated parties can also be a FSC. Such a FSC is not subject to the general intercompany transfer pricing rules of IRC § 482, nor to the specific FSC pricing rules. The price charged by such a FSC, or the commission paid to such a FSC, may be set as determined by the parties.

(b)   Gross Receipts Method

A FSC can earn 1.83 percent of the foreign trading gross receipts derived from the sale of export property.[21] "Foreign trading gross receipts" are gross receipts of the FSC from the sale, exchange, or other disposition of export property, the lease or rental of export property, related and subsidiary services, engineering or architectural services, and managerial services. These amounts can be determined on a transaction-by-transaction basis or on a grouping basis.

"Gross receipts" includes total receipts from the sale, lease, or rental of property held primarily for sale, lease, or rental in the ordinary course of a trade or business, and gross income from all other sources. Thus, gross receipts includes such other items as the furnishing of services, dividends, interest, and tax-exempt interest.

---

[21] See Reg. 1.925(a)-1T(c)2; Robert Feinschreiber, "Proposed Regulations Define Gross Receipts," DISCussion 1 (1972) 4.

There are two differences between the FSC provisions and the DISC provisions regarding the definition of "gross receipts." For both DISCs and FSCs, gross receipts includes interest, but the FSC provisions make clear that tax-exempt interest includes gross receipts. The DISC provisions are silent on this issue. Also, returns and allowances are treated differently for DISC and FSC purposes. For DISC purposes, gross receipts are not reduced by returns and allowances, while for FSC purposes gross receipts are reduced.

(c) Combined Taxable Income Method

The taxable income of the FSC and its related supplier are combined under the 23 percent combined taxable income method.[22] This taxable income can be applied on a transaction-by-transaction basis or on a grouping basis. Combined taxable income is computed by determining gross receipts, then subtracting the sum of the cost of goods sold, the related supplier's expenses, and the FSC's expenses. Gross receipts are the foreign trading gross receipts. (These receipts could also be used for the 1.83 percent of gross receipts method.) Combined taxable income includes inventory amounts, such as FIFO (first in, first out) or LIFO (last in, first out), to determine cost of goods sold.[23] In addition, noninventory costs must be included for FSC purposes,[24] and UNICAP amounts must be included in cost of goods sold.[25]

Expenses must be allocated and apportioned between combined taxable income of the FSC and other classes of gross income.[26] In addition, these expenses must be apportioned for each transaction. Expenses pertaining to the FSC must be included, whether or not these expenses pertain to economic process requirements. These expenses normally include direct and indirect expenses and should be determined for each transaction. An example of computing combined taxable income follows:

Foreign trading gross receipts	100
Cost of goods sold	(60)
Related supplier's expenses	(30)
FSC's expenses	(6)
Combined taxable income	4

---

[22] Reg. §§ 1.925(a)-IT(c)(3) and -IT(c)(6); *see also* Robert Feinschreiber, "New Regulations Affect DISC Pricing," *International Tax Journal* 1 (August 1975):325.

[23] IRC §§ 471 and 472; Reg. §§ 1.925(a)-IT(c)(6)(i) and -IT (c)(6)(iii)(C); Robert Feinschreiber, "How Extensive Are the Absorption Costing Requirements in the Final Inventory Regs?" *Journal of Taxation* 39 (1973):338.

[24] Reg. §§ 1.471-1(c)(2)(ii) and 1.61-3; *see also* Robert Feinschreiber, "Inventory Costing Rules Affect DISC Status and Profitability," *International Tax Journal* 1 (1974):14.

[25] IRC § 263A.

[26] Reg. § 1.925(a)-1T(c)(6)(iii)(D); Reg. § 1.861-8; Robert Feinschreiber, "Final Regulations for Allocating and Apportioning Deductions," *International Tax Journal* 3 (1977):344.

(d) Limitation and Customary Margin Rules

The gross receipts computation is limited to twice the combined taxable income or 46 percent of combined taxable income. The FSC income is the lower of the gross receipts amount or the gross receipts limitation, or the higher of these two amounts and the 23 percent of combined taxable income amount. This FSC limitation rule is analogous to the DISC rule, but the DISC rule was simpler to apply because it was based on 100 percent of combined taxable income (twice the 50 percent rate).[27]

If the related supplier and the FSC have negative combined taxable income, the related supplier incurs the entire portion of the loss and the FSC breaks even.[28] The customary margin rule, or special no-loss rule, was used under DISC, but was not carried forward to FSC. This omission by the IRS may be erroneous. The following example shows how loss sales are allocated:

Foreign trading gross receipts	100
Cost of goods sold	(60)
Related supplier's expenses	(30)
FSC's expenses	(15)
Combined taxable income	(5)
FSC income	0
Related supplier's income	(5)

(e) Choosing the Best Method

Which method—gross receipts, combined taxable income, or combined taxable income limitation—is the "best method" depends on the profit margin. Exhibit 8.1 shows the maximum amounts[29] when combined taxable income is up to 10 percent of gross receipts.

For high-profit transactions, the 23 percent of combined taxable income alternative is preferable. For simplicity, these transactions are referred to as Type A transactions. For the next group of transactions, the 1.83 percent of foreign trading gross receipts is preferable. These transactions are referred to as Type B transactions (Exhibit 8.2). For low-profit transactions, the optimal approach is to use the gross receipts method subject to the combined taxable income limitation. These transactions are referred to as Type C transactions. Under the DISC provisions, the dividing point between Type A and Type B was 8 percent; between Type B and Type C it was 4 percent.

---

[27] Robert Feinschreiber, "New Strategies for Increasing DISC Benefits," *Fin. Executive* 44 (August 1976):32 .

[28] Reg. §§ 1.944-1(e), 1.994-2(d) and 1.925(a)-1T(e)(1); *see also* Robert Feinschreiber, "The 'No Loss Rule' Restricts DISC Profits," *DISCussion* 1 (December 1972):2; Robert Feinschreiber, "Loss Sales Can Be Used to Maximize DISC Profit," Int'l Tax Inst. Proc. 8 (1973):139.

[29] Robert Feinschreiber, "Intercompany Pricing Rules for DISC Increase Complexity, Curtail Benefits," *Int'l Tax Inst. Proc.* 8 (1973):101; Feinschreiber, "How to Aggregate DISC Sales to Make Most Effective Use of the Deferral," *J. Tax* 36 (1972):300.

Exhibit 8.2

FSC PROFIT MARGIN ANALYSIS

Transaction	Minimum %	Maximum %	Method
A	7.95652174	100.00	.23 CTI
B	3.97826087	7.95652174	1.83 GR
C	0	3.97826087	.46 CTI

Profit as a percentage of gross receipts

8.6   Grouping: Administrative Pricing

Grouping rules apply to a transfer from a related supplier to a FSC in the case of a sale of export property.[30] Significant changes from the DISC rules pertain to the no-loss rule and marginal costing.

The gross receipts method is limited to exceed 1.83 percent of the foreign trading gross receipts.[31] The gross receipts amount is limited to twice the profit determined under the combined taxable income method. Using the marginal costing rules, because of the no-loss rule, profit earned by the FSC is limited to 100 percent of the full costing combined taxable income.

Under the combined taxable income method, the FSC's income is limited to 23 percent of the full costing combined taxable income.[32] Full costing combined taxable income of the FSC and its related supplier is based on foreign trading gross receipts less the total costs of the FSC and related supplier.

(a)   Grouping Transactions

Pricing is made on a transaction-by-transaction basis. The related supplier can choose the pricing each year. Pricing may be made wholly or partially on the basis of groups consisting of products or product lines.[33]

Pricing will be accepted by the IRS if the pricing conforms to recognized trade or industry usage, or the two-digit major groups or any inferior classifications or combinations within a major group SIC code. A product can be included in only one product line for this grouping if that product otherwise falls within more than one product line classification.[34]

---

[30] Reg. § 1.925(a)-1T(c)(8).

[31] Reg. § 1.925(a)-1T(c)(2).

[32] Reg. § 1.925(a)-1T(c)(3).

[33] Reg. § 1.925(a)-1T(c)(8)(i).

[34] Reg. § 1.925(a)-1T(c)(8)(ii).

A related supplier can choose to group transactions for a taxable year on a product or product line basis. The related supplier can select all transactions pertaining to that product or product line consummated during the taxable year. The choice of a product or product line grouping applies only to transactions covered by the grouping. As to transactions not encompassed by the grouping, determinations are made on a transaction-by-transaction basis.[35] For example, the related supplier may choose a product grouping with respect to one product and use the transaction-by-transaction method for another product within the same taxable year.

(b) Pricing Examples

Consider a situation in which there are two transactions that could be kept separate or grouped at the taxpayer's option. The first transaction has foreign trading gross receipts (FTGR) of 100 and combined taxable income (CTI) of the manufacturer (the related supplier) of 11. The FSC's income is maximized for that transaction by utilizing 23 percent of CTI, which is 2.53. The second transaction has foreign trading gross receipts of 100 and combined taxable income of 5. The FSC's income is maximized by that transaction by utilizing the gross receipts method, or 1.83.

For the group, foreign trade income is 200 and combined taxable income is 16. The FSC income of the group uses the combined taxable income method—23 percent of 16, or 3.68. In contrast, the separate transaction method for the FSC is 4.36 (2.53 plus 1.83).

Transactions	FTGR	CTI	FSC
A	100	11	2.53
B	100	5	1.83
Ungrouped	200	16	4.36
Grouped	200	16	3.68

Using the transaction method rather than grouping is not advantageous in this situation. The solution is not to use the transaction method. In a number of situations, grouping increases FSC income.

In the following example, Transaction C has foreign trade gross receipts of 100 and combined taxable income of 7, so its FSC income is 1.83 of gross receipts, or 1.83. Transaction D has foreign trade gross receipts of 100 and combined taxable income of 1, so its FSC income is 46 percent of CTI, or 0.46.

The sum of these transactions is FSC income of 2.29 (1.83 plus 0.46). On a combined basis, foreign trade gross receipts are 200 and combined taxable income is 8; FSC income is 23 percent of FTGR 3.66.

---

[35] Reg. § 1.925(a)-1T(c)(8)(iii).

Transactions	FTGR	CTR	FSC
C	100	7	1.83
D	100	1	0.46
Ungrouped	200	8	2.29
Grouped	200	8	3.66

The decision as to whether a company should use grouping or ungrouping is more complex. There are many groupings of products or product lines, SIC codes, and industry groupings.

(c) Loss Sales

Transactions in which combined taxable income is negative can be excluded from FSC computations or can be included with other transactions. Companies can either group or ungroup their transactions; such strategy depends on the circumstances of the transactions.

Loss Sales—Grouping Can Help

Transactions	FTGR	CTI	FSC
E	100	7	1.83
F	100	−1	0
Ungrouped	200	6	1.83
Grouped	200	6	2.76

Loss Sales—Grouping Can Hurt

Transactions	GR	CTI	FSC
G	100	3	1.38
H	100	−1	0
Ungrouped	200	2	1.38
Grouped	200	2	.96

Because there are so many variations of grouping, grouping benefits have to be achieved by each company on an individual basis.

Many companies group their FSC transactions, whenever possible, to minimize computations and paperwork. However, in some situations, grouping does not maximize FSC benefits, and taxpayers should ungroup and utilize the transactions individually.

8.7 FSC Marginal Costing

Marginal costing enables a foreign sales corporation to increase income from export sales.[36] Marginal costing limits costs when determining combined taxable

---

[36] IRC § 925(b)(2); Robert Feinschreiber, "Introduction to FSC Marginal Costing," *U.S. Taxation of International Operations* 7527 (1990):218.

income of a FSC and its related supplier, thereby increasing combined taxable income that is available to the FSC.[37] Marginal costing enables a FSC and its related supplier to eliminate fixed costs and a significant portion of their other costs and expenses, but is limited by profitability standards.

The theoretical standard for marginal costing is that the FSC must be seeking to establish or maintain a market for export property.[38] Neither the Internal Revenue Code nor the regulations define establishing or maintaining a market.[39] This criterion emanates from requirements imposed by GATT that predate the FSC enactment. The overall profit percentage limitation (OPPL) serves as the "establish or maintain" test,[40] but this calculation applies imperfectly in many situations. Under the OPPL test, FSC sales provide marginal costing benefits only when export sales are less profitable than domestic sales in the relevant grouping.

FSC pricing emanates from the DISC program, but some significant changes in marginal costing rules have taken place since the DISC program was proposed more than 20 years ago. First, the definition of "costs" to be included in the marginal costing computation has been modified.[41] Second, the focus has shifted away from "export promotion expenses."[42] Third, a new limitation, called the 100 percent limitation or full cost method, restricts FSC marginal costing benefits.[43] Eligibility for marginal costing is based on "an item, product, or product line," so that grouping rules apply.[44] Selection of marginal cost grouping can be made each tax year.[45]

Any change in gross receipts, whether by increasing or decreasing these amounts, changes combined taxable income (CTI). The gross receipts method, which generally applies to the FSC with income equal to 1.83 percent of foreign trading gross receipts, has no direct impact on marginal costing, but the gross receipts formula affects various aspects of marginal costing.

(a) Costs and Expenses

Under marginal costing rules, only direct production costs are used in computing CTI, and other costs are excluded.[46] Direct production costs are defined as "direct material and labor costs."[47] These costs are included if they are "incident to and necessary for" production or manufacturing.

---

[37] Reg. § 1.925(b)-1T(b)(1).

[38] Reg. § 1.925(b)-1T(c)(1).

[39] *See* Robert Feinschreiber, *Domestic International Sales Corporations* (New York: Practicing Law Institute, 1978), Chapter 12, pp. 275–284, PLI (1978).

[40] Reg. § 1.925(b)-1T(b)(1); Reg. § 1.925-1T(b)(1).

[41] *See* Reg. § 1.471-11; Reg. § 1.861-8.

[42] Reg. § 1.994-1(e)(1)(i).

[43] Reg. § 1.925(b)-1T(b)(4)(iii).

[44] Reg. § 1.925(b)-1T(c)(1).

[45] Reg. § 1.925(b)-1T(b)(3).

[46] Reg. § 1.925(b)-1T(b)(1).

[47] Reg. § 1.471-11(b)(2)(i); *See also* Robert Feinschreiber, "How Extensive Are the Absorption Costing Requirements?" 338–341; Meyer and Robert Feinschreiber, "Taxpayers Electing LIFO Face Additional Taxes and Administrative Burdens," *J. Tax* 41 (1974):214; Feinschreiber, "Inventory Costing Rules Affect *DISC* Status."

The regulations define material costs as:

1. Materials that become an integral part of the product; or
2. Materials that are consumed in the ordinary course of manufacturing and associated with that product.

These direct material amounts are based on cost.[48] In this regard, uniform capitalization (UNICAP) rules are applicable.[49]

Direct labor costs include labor that can be identified with products. Labor costs encompass:

1. Basic compensation;
2. Overtime;
3. Vacation and holiday pay;
4. Some types of sick leave;
5. Shift differential;
6. Payroll taxes; and
7. Payment for supplemental insurance plans.

Marginal costs include costs that pertain to CTI of the FSC and its related supplier.[50] These costs are determined for a particular item, product, or product line[51] using grouping rules.[52] Some costs are excluded in determining combined taxable income for marginal costing purposes. These excluded costs are deductible by the FSC if they pertain to nonforeign trade income.[53] Ordinarily, the manufacturer is the related supplier.[54] However, if the related supplier is not the manufacturer or producer of the export property that is sold, the related supplier's purchase price is used.[55]

For example, M incurs material costs of $2, labor costs of $3, and other costs and expenses of $15, and sells the product to W, an unrelated party, for $20. W sells the item through the FSC. The marginal cost amount is $20, not $5 ($2 plus $3), because W is the related supplier of the FSC, and its cost is $20.

(b)   Overall Profit Percentage Limitation

The overall profit percentage limitation (OPPL) restricts marginal costing benefits because the CTI of the FSC and its related supplier, using the marginal cost-

---

[48] Reg. § 1.471-3.

[49] Reg. § 1.263A-1T.

[50] IRC § 925(a)(2).

[51] Reg. § 1.925(b)-1T(b)(1).

[52] Reg. § 1.925(b)-1T(b)(3).

[53] Reg. § 1.925(b)-1T(b)(1).

[54] IRC § 927(a)(1)(A).

[55] Reg. § 1.925(b)-1T(b)(1).

ing rules, cannot exceed the OPPL.[56] For this purpose, CTI is gross receipts less direct material costs and direct labor costs, so that other costs and expenses are excluded. The OPPL is the product of the overall profit percentage (OPP)[57] times the FSC's foreign trading gross receipts (FTGR) from export property. This formula can be expressed as:

$$OPPL = FTGR \times OPP$$

If the FSC operates as a commission agent, the related supplier's gross receipts are used for this purpose. If the FSC is a buyer and seller, its gross receipts from these sales are used.[58]

The OPP combines the domestic and export sales percentage, determined on a product or product line basis for each tax year of the FSC.[59] This percentage is net income divided by gross receipts. The numerator includes two separate net income amounts:[60]

1. CTI of the FSC and its related supplier from the sale of export property; and
2. All other taxable income of the related supplier from all sales, domestic and foreign, based on full costing combined taxable income (FCCTI).[61]

The denominator is total gross receipts (TGR)[62] of the FSC and its related supplier from all export and domestic sales.[63]

The computation can be expressed by the following formula:

$$OPP = \frac{CTI + FCCTI}{TGR}$$

Example

Company X engages in domestic and export activities. Export activities yielded CTI of $80 on gross receipts of $950. Domestic activities yielded full costing income of $620 on gross receipts of $3,050. The OPP is:

$$\frac{\$80 + \$620}{\$950 + \$3,050} = \frac{\$700}{\$4,000} = 17.5 \text{ percent}$$

Because Company X has foreign trading gross receipts of $950 and the OPP is 17.5 percent, the OPPL is $166.25.

---

[56] Reg. § 1.925(b)-1T(b)(2).

[57] Reg. § 1.925(b)-1T(c)(2).

[58] Reg. § 1.925(b)-1T(b)(2).

[59] IRC § 925(c)(2)(i).

[60] Reg. § 1.925(b)-1T(c)(2)(i)(A).

[61] Reg. § 1.925(b)-1T(c)(3).

[62] Reg. § 1.927(b)-1T.

[63] Reg. § 1.925(b)-1T(c)(2)(i)(B).

Taxpayers can aggregate OPP data. This election is made by the related supplier,[64] not by the FSC itself. Under this aggregate approach, amounts of CTI, full costing income,[65] and total gross receipts[66] for the FSC are combined with the total amounts from the domestic members of the controlled group[67] of which the FSC is a member. This election is made annually for the FSC's tax year and for tax years of members ending with or within the FSC's tax year.

The aggregate method is a one-way election. It applies only to the FSC and its related supplier, not to its affiliates. Even though those amounts are used in the computation, the affiliates do not have to use the aggregate method to determine their OPPL.

An exclusion applies to the general percentage computation[68] and to the aggregate percentage computation.[69] For purposes of these computations, a sale of property between a FSC and its related supplier is not taken into account until the property is ultimately sold to a nonaffiliated party or to a related foreign person.[70] If the item remains in inventory at the end of the FSC's tax year, or at the end of the tax year of the member ending within the FSC's tax year, the transaction is treated as having taken place when the item was sold to a nonaffiliated party or a related foreign person.[71] This rule was designed to prevent a taxpayer from artificially maximizing OPP.

The taxable income amount under OPPL is illustrated by the following example: Company X has domestic and export activities as indicated in the following table.

	Export		**Domestic**		**Total**	
Gross receipts		950		3,050		4,000
Direct labor	(200)		(600)		(800)	
Direct materials	(400)		(1,200)		(1,600)	
Other inventory costs	(50)		(280)		(330)	
Cost of goods		(650)		(2,080)		(2,730)
Gross income		300		970		1,270
Related supplier's expense	(100)		(350)		(450)	
FSC's expense	(120)		(0)		(120)	
		(220)		(350)		(570)
Total taxable income		$ 80		$ 620		$ 700

---

[64] Reg. § 1.925(b)-1T(c)(2)(ii).

[65] Reg. § 1.925(b)-1T(c)(2)(i)(A).

[66] Reg. § 1.925(b)-1T(c)(2)(i)(B).

[67] IRC § 927(d)(4); Reg. § 1.924(a)-1T(h).

[68] Reg. § 1.925(b)-1T(c)(2)(i).

[69] Reg. § 1.925(b)-1T(c)(2)(ii).

[70] Reg. § 1.925(b)-1T(c)(2)(iii).

[71] Id.

The FSC's income is maximized under marginal costing:

Method	Income
Gross receipts method	$17.39
Combined taxable income method	$18.40
Marginal costing income	$38.24

Under the marginal costing rules, the FSC earns $38.24, as shown in the preceding list. Under the gross receipts method, foreign trading gross receipts are $950, resulting in FSC income of $17.39 ($950 × 1.83 percent). Under CTI, which is $80, the FSC income would be $18.40 (23 percent of $80).

From a marginal costing standpoint, the marginal costing amount is $350, computed as follows:

Gross receipts	$950
Direct labor	(200)
Direct materials	(400)
Marginal CTI amount	$350

The OPPL is $166.25 (see the preceding example). The marginal amount is the lower of marginal CTI ($350) or OPPL ($166.25). Thus, the overall percentage limitation is used as the combined taxable amount, resulting in the FSC earning $38.24 ($166.25 × 23 percent).

(c)   "No Loss" Rules

Two "no loss" rules apply to FSC income, and both provide a "no profit" exception. If there is a combined loss between the FSC and its related supplier, the marginal costing rules do not apply.[72] This combined loss is determined by the regular marginal costing rules.[73] The second limitation applies to full costing combined taxable income.[74] If this amount is higher than 23 percent of marginal costing income, the FSC would have a loss to its related supplier.[75] This rule applies only to FSC tax years after 1986.

If either of these "no loss" rules apply, the FSC can break even.[76] The related supplier may charge a transfer price, or pay a commission, that will allow the FSC to recover an amount that does not exceed full cost. This adjustment is acceptable

---

[72] Reg. § 1.925(b)-1T(b)(4).

[73] Reg. § 1.925(b)-1T(b)(1).

[74] Reg. § 1.925(b)-1T(b)(4).

[75] Reg. § 1.925(b)-1T(c)(3); Reg. § 1.925(a)-1T(c)(6).

[76] Reg. § 1.925(b)-1T(b)(4).

even if it would create or increase a loss to the related supplier. The combined effect of the "no loss" rule and the OPPL is to limit the FSC's profit under these marginal costing rules to the lesser of these amounts:[77]

1. Under the marginal costing rules, 23 percent of maximum CTI;[78]
2. 23 percent of the OPPL;[79]
3. 100 percent of full costing CTI determined under the regular full costing CTI computation.[80]

The third test applies to FSC tax years after 1986.

(d)   Marginal Cost Grouping

Grouping rules for marginal costing,[81] including definitions for "product" and "product line,"[82] are identical to nonmarginal costing rules.[83] Any product or product line grouping[84] that is permissible under the grouping rules[85] may be used for OPP purposes.[86] The FSC can choose its grouping annually, but a grouping used for OPP purposes must be as broad as the regular grouping rules.[87]

A FSC can include this product in only one product group, even if it would otherwise fall into more than one group. Marginal costing rules do not permit regrouping if it does not include the product or products that are included for full cost purposes. For example, Product A is included in Group AB and in Group ABC, so product A cannot be included in Group ACD. Grouping is advantageous in some situations, but disadvantageous in others, so careful planning is necessary.[88]

---

[77] Reg. § 1.925(b)-1T(b)(4).

[78] Reg. § 1.925(b)-1T(b)(4)(i).

[79] Reg. § 1.925(b)-1T(b)(4)(ii).

[80] Reg. §§ 1.925(a)-1T(c), 1.925(a)-1T(c)(6), and 1.925(b)-1T(b)(4)(iii).

[81] Reg. § 1.925(b)-1T(b)(3)(i).

[82] Reg. § 1.925(a)-1T(c)(8).

[83] Reg. §§ 1.925(b)-1T(c)(3) and 1.926(a)-1T(c)(6).

[84] Reg. § 1.925(b)-1T(b)(3)(ii).

[85] Reg. § 1.925(a)-1T(c)(8).

[86] Reg. § 1.925(b)-1T(c)(2).

[87] Reg. § 1.925(b)-1T(b)(3)(ii).

[88] Robert Feinschreiber, *Domestic Sales Corporations;* "How to Aggregate DISC Sales"; "Intercompany Pricing Rules for DISC Increase Complexity, Curtail Benefits," *International Tax Institute Proceedings* 8 (1973):101; "Maximizing DISC Profits Through Quantitative Pricing Techniques," *International Tax Journal* 2 (1975):28; "New Regulations Affect DISC Pricing"; "Export Incentives: The Use of Grouping Strategies to Maximize Foreign Sales Corporation Benefits," *Tax Notes International* 2 (May 1990):449.

8.9 Grouping Strategies

Pricing can be done on a transaction-by-transaction basis, on a product basis, or on a product-line basis.[89] The related supplier can choose its pricing strategy for each year, after the year has ended. The choice of a product or product line grouping applies only to transactions covered by the grouping. As to transactions not encompassed by the grouping, the determinations are made on a transaction-by-transaction basis. For example, the related supplier may choose a product grouping with respect to one product and still be able to use the transaction-by-transaction method for another product within the same taxable year.

Grouping will be accepted by the IRS if the pricing conforms to recognized trade or industry usage, or if the two-digit major groups or any inferior classifications or combinations are within a major group, based on the government's Standard Industrial Classification (SIC) Manual. A product can be included in only one product line for this particular grouping if a product otherwise falls within more than one product-line classification.

Consider an example in which two transactions could be kept separate or grouped, at the taxpayer's option. In this situation, grouping is advantageous. W has foreign trading gross receipts of 100 and combined taxable income of 6. The FSC's income is maximized for that transaction by using the gross receipts method, or 1.83. X has foreign trading gross receipts of 100 and combined taxable income of 2. The FSC's income is maximized in that transaction by using the gross receipts method, limited to the combined taxable income limitation, which computes to 0.92.

For the group, foreign trade income is 200 and combined taxable income is 8. The FSC income of the group is 3.66 (200 times 1.83 percent). In contrast, the separate transaction method for the FSC yields 2.75 (1.83 plus 0.92).

Transaction	GR	CTI	1.83 GR	23 CTI	FSC Profit
W	100	6	1.83	1.38	1.83
X	100	2	.92	.46	.92
Ungrouped	200	8	2.75	1.84	2.75
Grouped	200	8	3.66	1.84	3.66
Grouping Benefit	—	—	—	—	.91

Keeping transactions separate can be more beneficial than grouping in some situations, as the next example indicates: Transaction Y has foreign trade gross receipts of 100 and combined taxable income of 10. The Y FSC income is 23 percent of combined taxable income, or 2.30. Transaction Z has foreign trade gross receipts of 100 and combined taxable income of 6. The Z FSC income is 1.83

---

[89] Robert Feinschreiber, "Maximizing DISC Profits Through Quantitative Pricing Techniques"; "Choosing the Best FSC Pricing Options," *J. Int'l Tax* 2 (1990):218.

percent of gross receipts, or 1.83. The sum of these separate transactions for FSC income purposes is 4.13 (2.30 plus 1.83). On a combined basis, foreign trade gross receipts are 200, and combined taxable income is 3.68 under the 23 percent of combined taxable income method.

Transaction	FTGR	CTI	1.83 GR	.23 CTI	FSC Profit
Y	100	10	1.83	2.30	2.30
Z	100	6	1.83	1.38	1.83
Ungrouped	200	16	3.66	3.68	4.13
Grouped	200	16	3.66	3.68	3.68
Ungrouping benefit	—	—	—	—	.45

Loss sales can sometimes be used advantageously for grouping purposes. This can be illustrated as follows:

Transaction	FTGR	CTI	FSC Profit
M	100	7	1.83
N	100	(1)	0
Ungrouped	200	6	1.83
Grouped	200	6	2.76
Grouping benefit	—	—	.93

The decision as to whether a company should use grouping is more complex. There are many groupings of products or product lines, SIC codes, and industry groupings. Transactions in which combined taxable income is negative can be excluded from FSC computations or can be included with other transactions. Companies can group or keep their transactions separate. Which strategy is chosen depends on the circumstances of the transactions involved.

Because there are so many variations of grouping, whether or not to group must be decided by each company. Many companies group their FSC transactions whenever possible, to minimize computations and paperwork, but this is not necessarily advantageous. Often, grouping does not maximize FSC benefits, and taxpayers should treat the transactions individually.

The FSC methods provide a large measure of certainty from a pricing standpoint. The 1993 transfer pricing regulations provide much less.

CHAPTER 9

Foreign Sales Corporations and Their Service Providers

Robert Feinschreiber

9.1   Introduction

Companies that perform activities on behalf of a foreign sales corporation (FSC), known as "service providers," have become an important part of the export process.[1] A service provider typically provides a variety of FSC services, encompassing basic FSC requirements,[2] management,[3] sales activities,[4] and direct cost tests.[5] Off-shore FSC incorporation and banking functions are sometimes included. As a result, relationships between FSCs and service providers have become increasingly important to both.

9.2   Selecting an FSC Management Company

A FSC almost always needs an offshore trust or management company, since it probably cannot operate offshore on its own. The management company functions as the FSC's agent, ensuring that it meets the requirements of the Internal Revenue Code (IRC), and performing other business-related services. This analysis examines 10 fundamental criteria for an exporter to consider in selecting a FSC management company.

For the gross receipts of the FSC (unless it is a small FSC) to qualify as foreign trading gross receipts under the Code, the FSC must satisfy both a foreign management test and a foreign economic processes test.

The foreign management test is satisfied if:

- All board of directors meetings and all shareholders meetings are held outside the United States;
- The FSC's principal bank account is located outside the United States; and
- All dividends, legal and accounting fees, and the salaries of officers and directors are paid from FSC bank accounts located outside the United States.

---

[1] Reg. §1.924(d)-(1)(d)(2)(i).

[2] IRC §922(a)(1).

[3] IRC §924(c).

[4] IRC §924(d)(1)(A).

[5] IRC §924(d)(1)(B), (d)(3).

The foreign economic processes test is satisfied for gross receipts from certain categories of activities relating to export property if the FSC participates outside the United States in solicitation, negotiation, or making of the contract for the transaction, and either

- The direct costs attributable to activities performed outside the United States (foreign direct costs) are at least 50 percent of the total direct costs for the transaction; or
- For at least two of the five categories of activities, the foreign direct costs are at least 85 percent of the total direct costs for that category of activity.

The activities relating to export property are as follows:

1. Advertising and sales promotion;
2. Processing customer orders and arranging delivery of export property;
3. Transporting the export property to the customer;
4. Transmitting or determining a final invoice or statement of account, and the receipt of payment; and
5. Assuming credit risk.

These and other FSC requirements can be overseen and handled by the FSC management company.

(a) Business Experience

A management company to a FSC must offer many different services to exporters with diverse business practices and financial needs. So when selecting a management company, the exporter should strongly weigh the breadth and depth of the management company's business and financial experience.

Historically, management companies were often established as trust companies by international financial institutions, and many still are such trust companies. But recently, more management companies have been formed by private individuals who do not meet the requirements of the financial institutions. Because these companies were formed recently to take advantage of the new FSC provisions, they lack the decades of extensive experience of their more established competitors.

In selecting a management company, it is important to determine the number of years it has been in business, the size of its staff, and the type of business activities it handles. In choosing between companies, experience should be a strong positive factor.

(b) Financial Resources

A management company must incur substantial start-up and implementation costs in order to provide the FSC a full range of services. While some companies have spent millions of dollars to provide these services, and are able to make additional expenditures to expand services to their customers, including FSCs, such financial resources should not be assumed—some management companies are prepared to spend only a few thousand dollars, or even less. When selecting a management company, the exporter should examine the audited financial statements of the management company or its parent.

The FSC and its parent should make sure that, in the event that the management company makes a serious error of omission or commission, the management company will be capable of assuming the liability. This "deep pocket" rule should not be overlooked.

(c) Bank Account Management

One typical responsibility of the management company is to monitor the flow of funds. It can make sure the FSC meets the principal bank account requirement, and can facilitate compliance with the receipt of payment portion of the fourth economic process test.

The FSC will probably make frequent distributions to its parent, and the management company can transfer the funds quickly. Cash management experience is an important attribute so that the management company can protect the FSC from disqualification and loss of use of the funds.

(d) Telecommunications Network

Communication between the management company and the business is important to making a FSC successful. The communications link should include an extensive computer facility, telecommunications, and on-line hook-ups between the United States and the country in which the FSC is managed.

Management companies that have not yet established a communications network must depend on mail delivery or messenger services. A good telecommunications network is essential to meeting the requirements for solicitation, negotiation, and making of the contract.

(e) FSC Experience

While some management companies began working with the FSC provisions when Congress first considered them in 1983, others did not review these provisions until much later. FSC experience is, therefore, another important factor in the selection of a management company. The company must understand the complexities of the statute, Committee Reports, and the regulation.

(f) Convenience

Convenience is an important factor. Some management or trust companies and their affiliates have offices throughout the United States, while others have few, if any, U.S. offices.

(g)   Wire Transfer Capability

Transmitting funds to and from the United States is important to many FSCs, but particularly for companies that seek to meet the fourth economic process requirement, which includes the foreign receipt of payment.

A management company with extensive wire transfer facilities will enable businesses and their FSCs to use funds more effectively than can be accomplished with checks.

(h)   Reinvoicing Capability

Many FSCs will have their management companies provide reinvoicing services in order to meet the fourth foreign economic process requirement, which includes billing or annual statements of account. Whether the management company has experience providing a large volume of reinvoicing should be a factor in any decision to retain it.

(i)   Credit Review

The sales activity assets of the foreign economic processes requirements will be difficult for many FSCs to meet, but these may sometimes be satisfied if the management company can establish credit terms to foreign customers as part of "making the contract" or "negotiation" with those foreign customers. Not all management companies are capable of providing this credit review.

(j)   Reliability and Integrity

The management company should show a proven record of reliability and integrity.

Its potential for continuity of services and personnel also is valuable to the exporter. If the management company is small, run principally by one person or with a limited staff, the death or incapacity of that key person will endanger the quality and continuity of the work. Thus, size is a positive factor in determining the management company's reliability.

9.3   Implementation

Considerable flexibility in performing these services is possible within the confines of the FSC regulations.[6] Although a FSC can perform the myriad of tax-related activities and off-shore corporate law functions by itself, almost every FSC uses one or more service providers. The alternative is to establish off-shore physical facilities and hire employees at the FSC locality, which is seldom cost-effective.

---

[6] Robert Feinschreiber, "The Use of Grouping Strategies to Maximize Foreign Sales Corporation Benefits," *Tax Notes International* 2(1990):449.

A new industry of service providers has developed since 1983. Then it was contemplated that FSCs would replace DISCs. Many potential service providers anticipated that there would be as many FSCs as there were domestic international sales corporations (DISCs). Eventually, fewer than the anticipated number of FSCs were established, and subsequent competition and attrition has narrowed the number of service providers. As service providers decline in number but become more significant in scope, FSCs should take a closer look at their contracts with service providers.

9.4   Preliminary Considerations

Before signing or renewing an agreement with a service provider, a FSC should consider 10 factors, which are described in the following paragraphs.

(a)   Standard Forms

Most service providers establish a standard-form contract between themselves and the FSC or the FSC's owner. Because the standard contract is prepared by the service provider, it tends to favor the service provider rather than the FSC. For this reason, FSCs should take care before signing these agreements.

The contract may be based on the FSC's export data, business experience, accounting procedures, and/or mode and method of doing business. A standardized data form may be used as the basis for the contract. Counsel should review the data for accuracy.

(b)   Negotiations

The IRS does not prepare standard contracts and FSC data forms. Consequently, the FSC and its owner need not use these standard forms and service contracts. Many arrangements may be negotiated by the FSC and the service provider, but the service provider may have the upper hand because of the limited number of service providers. Moreover, time constraints for activating the FSC may foreclose both negotiations and a search for an alternate service provider.

(c)   Legal Approval

The export data forms and analysis should be prepared or reviewed by individuals who are familiar both with the company's mode of doing business and with FSC requirements. Then the contract between the service provider and the FSC should be developed. It should include legal substantive issues that affect FSC requirements. Legal counsel—either attorneys within the tax or legal department, or special counsel—should review these issues. Relying on nonlegal personnel from the tax department is not the best approach.

(d) Timing

A substantial period of time may be needed to negotiate the contract and implement the FSC. Because of these time constraints, it is advisable to select the tentative FSC jurisdiction and the tentative service providers long before actual FSC operations commence. The FSC should begin this negotiation and implementation process many months before the FSC's taxable year begins.

(e) Changing the Service Provider

A FSC may need to change service providers because of changes in circumstances. While some service providers have thrived, others have not and are closing shop. Some service providers are effective; others, ineffectual.

A service provider could conceivably hinder the FSC's ability to change providers. It might indirectly impair the mechanics of the management test, fail to meet the economic process requirements, or fail to retain records for the correct time period if the contract is not renewed. As a result, a FSC should carefully review all timing and grouping requirements. The contract should provide for completing the ongoing FSC requirements for some period (such as the remainder of the taxable year) after either party terminates the agreement.

(f) Representation of Expertise

An FSC expects a service provider to be proficient in providing FSC services. Similarly, a FSC may expect the service provider to have expertise in implementing FSC activities. These expectations may not be realized. FSC service providers are not regulated by the U.S. government, so the FSC is on its own in selecting one.

If a service provider fails to meet the management tests or economic process requirements, the service provider might claim exculpation based on its lack of tax expertise. If the service provider had previously claimed expertise, the FSC could hold the service provider to a higher legal standard. Before signing the contract, the FSC should ask the service provider to state in writing its claim of expertise. Then the FSC should ask for a written statement that includes the number of large and small FSCs the provider has contracted.

(g) Applicable Substantive Law

In establishing the FSC-service provider contract, both parties should establish which law applies. A number of alternatives exist: The FSC's contract with the service provider could be interpreted according to the laws of the situs of the service provider, the situs of the FSC owner, the place where the contract was signed, or another alternative. Determining the choice of law is important because substantive contractual law may differ from jurisdiction to jurisdiction. Needless to say, the choice of law should be specified by the contract itself. It should not be left to the choice-of-law rules of whatever jurisdiction becomes the site of any subsequent litigation.

(h) Applicable Forum

If a dispute arises between the service provider and the FSC, they will need to determine where the dispute will be resolved. Conceivably, the service provider could make the FSC defend itself at the FSC's off-shore headquarters, or the FSC might be able to compel the service provider to defend itself at the FSC's owner's location. Arbitration could be the exclusive dispute-resolution device. The best resolution is for the FSC and the service provider to agree by contract to use a mutually convenient forum.

(i) Financial Statements

It may be feasible to obtain the service provider's financial statement by contract. The contract should specify whether these financial statements will be provided annually or quarterly, and when they will be furnished. For the FSC's protection, the financial statement should be certified by a certified public accountant in the United States. At a minimum, financial statements should indicate any actual or potential claims against the service provider.

(j) Abandonment or Bankruptcy

A service provider could become bankrupt or abandon its FSC business (which has happened in a number of instances), especially during the inception of the FSC program. If this situation occurs, the service provider might not continue to meet the FSC's requirements. The FSC should inquire early on about alternatives for continuing FSC services, especially the ongoing requirements, in the event of abandonment or bankruptcy. A contingency should be established by contract in advance of any abandonment or bankruptcy. Transfer of FSC contracts between one service provider and another sometimes takes place; if the service provider has this kind of agreement, it should give a copy to the FSC. Above all, the FSC should retain the power to veto any assignment of the contract to the extent that this is consistent with the Bankruptcy Act.

9.5 Specific Clauses

(a) Enumerate Required Activities

The FSC's contract with the service provider should clearly enumerate the specific functions the FSC expects, the service provider to perform, such as basic requirements, direct cost activities, management activities, and sales functions. Articulating specific Code and regulations sections in the contract will lessen chances of ambiguity.

(b)   Standard of Care

The contract could articulate the standard of care the FSC expects from the service provider. If the contract is silent as to the standard of care, the service provider could be subject to an ordinary negligence standard. However, the service provider could attempt to change the threshold by contracting to limit its liability to a gross negligence standard. This provision would excuse the service provider for ordinary negligence performed for the FSC, as well as failures to start or complete various tasks. Since ordinary negligence could take place in the FSC context, the FSC should, if possible, avoid a gross negligence clause.

(c)   Liability

In some situations, FSCs have a difficult time establishing (1) that negligence has in fact taken place, (2) the consequences of the negligence, or (3) that the service provider knew the consequences of a lack of adequate performance. To avoid these difficulties, the FSC could establish with the service provider an anticipated cost of any negligence based on FSC projections for the year. A clause such as the following might be appropriate: "We recognize that our failure to perform these activities for this year could cost the FSC an amount of $4 million." Because the amount of the potential liability could be large in comparison with the FSC fee that the service provider receives, the scope of the liability should be established by contract. Otherwise, the service provider might allege that its activities were akin to those of a messenger service, thereby attempting to diminish its liability.

(d)   Liability Insurance

A service provider may be insured against its malpractice liability or other potential liability; on the other hand, the cost of this liability insurance may be prohibitive. If the service provider has such a policy, the FSC should examine the limits of this coverage and ascertain the wherewithal of the insurance company. As a service organization, the service provider may have few assets, so insurance may be advantageous for the FSC. Insurance with a company with few assets may be equally worthless.

(e)   Confidentiality

A FSC may contract with its service provider to solicit sales,[7] invoice those sales, or collect payment[8] for the FSC. In so doing, the service provider may have access to customer lists. Protecting the customer list is likely to be important. A clause should be inserted in the contract, whereby the service provider promises to hold confidential this and all other information received in the course of providing services.

---

[7] IRC §924(d)(1)(A).
[8] IRC §924(e)(4).

(f) Fees

Service providers expect fees for their services in addition to an annual fee (which, in the first year, should include the FSC's incorporation). These fees are usually expressed as an hourly rate. Cost factors in setting the fees, such as employee categories of the service provider, specific FSC functions to be performed, and fees for each function, should be specified in the contract.

(g) Foreign Director

A prerequisite for FSC status is the continued presence of a foreign director,[9] and the FSC should specifically contract with the service provider to assure this presence. The service provider should maintain the foreign status of the director and should replace the director if necessary.

(h) Tax Audits

In the event of audit by the IRS or state tax authorities, the facilities to hold the audit and data to defend the FSC's position will be necessary. Tax audits could take place at the FSC location, which is likely to be at the service provider's facilities and the FSC owner's headquarters. If a tax audit occurs, collaboration between the FSC and the service provider is essential. The contract should provide for these audit services and a schedule of compensation for needed personnel, regardless of whether the relationship between the service provider and the FSC continues.

9.6 Disputes

The consequences of disputes between FSCs and service providers are evident in the following examples.

Basic Facts: X Company establishes a FSC through AB Service Provider. The contract provides that AB will meet the foreign advertising and credit tests and place an advertisement in a newspaper in Nogales, Mexico. The advertisement, however, is placed in a newspaper in Nogales, Arizona, by mistake. As a result, FSC benefits are lost for the year.

X's FSC had been expected to save $3 million that year. X paid $3,000 to the service provider, while the advertising amount paid to the wrong newspaper was $30. The FSC sues the service provider for the $3 million, but the service provider will not pay more than $30, or perhaps the $3,000 fee.

Companies Y and Z have established FSCs and use AB Service Provider as their service provider. FSC benefits for 1990 are $100,000 for Y and $100 million for Z. The service provider performs its FSC functions for Y and Z without incident.

---

[9] IRC §922(a)(1)(E).

Example 1

The contract between X and AB contains an exculpatory clause limiting damages to the fee paid. If that clause prevails, the service provider avoids 99.9 percent of the amount claimed, and the FSC bears that portion of the loss.

Example 2

A judgment for $3 million is rendered for X against AB. AB goes bankrupt. X is unable to collect its judgment. Other FSCs that use this service provider, including Y and Z, are unable to continue to meet the ongoing FSC requirements, such as maintaining a foreign director. As a result, these companies are disqualified from receiving FSC benefits, with no recourse against the now-bankrupt service provider.

9.7 Conclusion

Structuring and evaluating service-provider agreements is an important facet of FSC operations. After FSC audits are in full bloom, disputes are likely to increase in number and intensity. It is wise to provide for all possibilities in advance by contract and by insurance.

CHAPTER 10

Tax Compliance

Rafeal E. Brown
Jeffrey A. Levenstam

10.1 Introduction

The preparation of a foreign sales corporation (FSC) or domestic international sales corporation (DISC) tax return is complex. Issues that do not arise in a regular Form 1120 apply in the FSC or DISC context.

(a) Foreign Sales Corporation (FSC) Overview

A FSC acts as an intermediary between a United States producer of export property or "related supplier" and the foreign customer. The FSC can sell export property purchased from its U.S. parent to foreign purchasers, or alternatively, it can act as a commission agent for its U.S. parent on foreign sales (a "commission FSC"). Under a commission agreement, the U.S. parent or an independent management company can still perform all sales functions on behalf of the FSC. Thus, the FSC can be a "paper" company, with no employees. The FSC rules represent an exception from the general principle of arm's-length pricing. The benefit of qualifying as a FSC is that a FSC's income from qualified export transactions is eligible for a partial exemption from U.S. taxation.

The net profits of the FSC and its related supplier from the qualified FSC transactions are collectively referred to as "combined taxable income" (CTI). CTI is calculated as the foreign trading gross receipts (FTGR) reduced by the cost of sales and an allocation for expenses. The CTI must then be divided between the related supplier and the FSC. The portion that is deemed earned by the related supplier is fully taxable to the related supplier in its U.S. income tax return. The FSC is allocated sufficient gross income to earn its profit as determined under the FSC transfer pricing rules described in the following paragraphs. The gross income of the FSC attributable to FTGR is called "foreign trading income" (FTI). The exempt portion of the FSC's FTI (exempt FTI) is 32 percent if arm's-length pricing is utilized, or 16/23 of the FTI determined under the administrative FSC pricing rules. If the FSC's shareholder is a C corporation, the exempt FTI amounts are reduced to 30 percent of the arm's-length profit or 15/23 of the FTI determined under the administrative FSC pricing rules. The two administrative pricing rules are as follows:

- *The 1.83 percent FTGR method.* The taxable income of the FSC attributable to the transaction is calculated at 1.83 percent of the FTGR derived from the FSC's sales. However, the taxable income under this method cannot exceed twice the amount determined under the 23 percent CTI method.
- *The 23 percent CTI method.* The FSC's taxable income from a transaction is calculated at 23 percent of the CTI from the FSC's sales. CTI is the combined taxable income of the FSC and its related supplier attributable to the export transaction.

Administrative Pricing Example 1

Related Supplier, Inc. (RS) and its wholly owned FSC subsidiary (FSC) have FTGR for the year in the amount of $1,000. The CTI is $200. The FSC's direct expenses of $100 are already deducted in computing the CTI of $200. Under the 1.83 percent FTGR method, the FSC's taxable income would be $18.30 ($1,000 × 1.83 percent). Under the 23 percent CTI method, the FSC's taxable income would be $46 (23 percent of $200). The FSC's FTI would be $118.30 under the 1.83 percent FTGR method and $146 under the 23 percent CTI method. The FSC should always be reimbursed for its direct expenses, as well as the net profit it is entitled to under the administrative pricing rules.

Administrative Pricing Example 2

A different Related Supplier Corp. (RS2) and its wholly owned FSC subsidiary (FSC2) have FTGR for the year in the amount of $2,000 and their CTI is $50. The FSC's taxable income under the 23 percent CTI method is $11.50 (23 percent of $50). Its taxable income under the 1.83 percent FTGR method would be $36.60 (1.83 percent of $2,000). However, this method has the restriction that limits FSC2's taxable income to twice the amount it would earn under the 23 percent CTI method, or $23.

Once FTI has been determined, this amount is divided into exempt and nonexempt FTI. Exempt FTI is treated as foreign source income not effectively connected with a U.S. trade or business, and provides the basis for the FSC benefit. The amount of exempt FTI (the portion of FTI that is exempt from U.S. tax) depends on the pricing method. If either of the safe harbor administrative pricing rules are used, exempt FTI is computed as 65.217 percent of FTI (69.6 percent for a noncorporate or S corporation shareholder). When the IRC § 482 pricing is used, exempt FTI is computed as 30 percent of FTI (32 percent for noncorporate or S corporation shareholders). However derived, nonexempt FTI determined under the administrative pricing rules is generally treated as U.S. source effectively connected income, and therefore subject to U.S. corporate tax at the FSC level. However, if the traditional arm's-length pricing is used, this nonexempt income may be eligible for tax deferral to the extent it is not effectively connected with a U.S. trade or business. The FSC will be taxed as another foreign corporation on the nonexempt FTI.

Once exempt FTI has been determined, expenses must be allocated and apportioned in order to arrive at taxable income attributable to exempt FTI and, therefore, not subject to U.S. tax. This allocation and apportionment of expenses, which is discussed in detail in Chapter 8 of this book, follows several statutory and regulatory methodologies in determining expenses to be matched with FTGR and is finally apportioned between exempt and nonexempt FTI based on relative amounts.

(b) Definitions

The definitions of certain terms used in this chapter should be understood:

Related supplier. The term "related supplier" means a related party that directly supplies to a FSC any property or services in a transaction producing foreign trading gross receipts, or a related party that uses the FSC as a commission agent in the disposition of any property or services producing foreign trading gross receipts.[1] A FSC may have different related suppliers for different transactions.

Related party. A "related party" means a party owned or controlled directly or indirectly by the same interests as the FSC.[2] Ownership or control is determined by the percentage of a corporation's stock owned by another corporation. Generally, a corporation is owned or controlled if another corporation owns more than 50 percent of its voting stock.[3]

Foreign trading gross receipts. Foreign trading gross receipts (FTGRs). The qualified gross receipts of a FSC that has met the statutory foreign management and foreign economic process rules.[4] Small FSCs are not required to meet certain of these standards. The qualified receipts for this purpose must be from the sale, exchange, or other disposition of export property; the lease, or rental of export property for use outside the United States; the performance of engineering or architectural services for a construction project lo-

---

[1] Temp. Reg. § 1.927(d)-2T(a).

[2] Temp. Reg. § 1.927(d)-2T(b).

[3] Temp. Reg. § 1.924(a)-1T(h).

[4] IRC § 924.

cated (or proposed for location) outside the United States; or the performance of managerial services on behalf of an unrelated FSC or DISC in furtherance of the production of the previously discussed types of transactions that result in FTGRs.[5]

Commission FSC and buy-sell FSC. Both a commission FSC and a buy-sell FSC are required to meet all the FSC requirements discussed throughout this book. The difference between a commission FSC and a buy-sell FSC lies in the nature of the legal relationship between the FSC and its related supplier. A commission FSC is an agent of the related supplier. A buy-sell FSC is similar to a distributor or reseller for the related supplier. A commission FSC is a commission company that receives commissions on the sale of export goods by its related supplier. A buy-sell FSC is a company that purchases and sells goods, actually taking title to the goods before reselling the goods to the foreign purchaser. Both types of FSC may be either a paper company with no employees or a substantive operating company with sufficient employees to conduct an active trade or business. A buy-sell FSC is rare in practice.

Small FSC. A foreign corporation may elect to be treated as a small FSC.[6] The corporation cannot be a member at any time during the tax year of a controlled group of corporations that includes a FSC, unless the other FSC also elects small FSC status.[7]

Small FSCs are not required to meet foreign management and foreign economic process requirements in determining foreign trade gross receipts from which exempt foreign trade income is derived. However, a small FSC must meet the same requirements for use of the administrative pricing rules as a regular FSC. The disadvantage of electing small FSC status is that a small FSC is allowed the FSC benefit from export profit attributable to only $5 million of its foreign trading gross receipts.[8] If a small FSC generates more than $5 million of foreign trading gross receipts, the excess cannot be taken into account in determining exempt foreign trade income.[9] The corporation is, however, allowed to choose which gross receipts qualify for the $5 million limitation in order to derive the maximum FSC benefit from the qualifying sales.[10] If the small FSC exists for only part of the year, the $5 million limitation is prorated on a daily basis. If there are multiple small FSCs in one controlled group, a single $5 million limitation must be split among the various small FSCs.

---

[5] *Id.*

[6] IRC § 927(f)(1).

[7] IRC § 922(b)(2).

[8] IRC § 924(b)(2)(B).

[9] IRC § 924(b)(2)(B)(j).

[10] *Id.*

10.2 FSC Compliance

(a) General Compliance with the Rules Relating to FSCs

A foreign corporation that has elected to be treated as a FSC or a small FSC (the election is made by filing Form 8279) must file a U.S. income tax return, Form 1120-FSC. The return must be filed on or before the 15th day of the third month following the close of the FSC's taxable year. However, an extension of time to file may be requested, using Form 7004.

(b) Income Exempt from U.S. Taxation

Income exempt from U.S. taxation is determined as a portion of a FSC's gross receipts attributable to foreign trading gross receipts, or foreign trade income.[11] The gross receipts of a FSC are the total receipts or the total commissions received from the sale, lease, or rental of property.[12] Gross receipts also include receipts from furnishing services, income from dividends and interest, and the gain on the sale of property not held primarily for sale or lease.[13] Gross receipts do not include proceeds of a loan or from the repayment of a loan, contributions of capital, or the exchange of stock for property.[14]

Foreign trade income includes profits earned directly by the foreign sales corporation from exports and commissions earned from products or services exported by others. The amount of foreign trade income *exempt* from U.S. taxation is determined under the transfer pricing methods determined on Form 1120-FSC, Schedule P. The portion of a FSC's exempt foreign trade income depends on whether the exempt amount of foreign trade income is computed under the general corporate rules relating to transactions between unrelated parties (IRC § 482 rules for arm's-length pricing in transactions between related parties), or the administrative pricing rules.[15]

If the income is computed according to general corporate rules for unrelated parties, only 30 percent of a FSC's foreign trade income will be exempt. If the FSC has a noncorporate shareholder, 32 percent of the foreign trade income attributable to the shareholder's proportionate interest in the FSC will be exempt. If income is computed according to the administrative pricing rules, 65.217 percent (15/23) of its foreign trade income attributable to the corporate shareholder's proportionate interest in the FSC will be exempt. If the FSC has a noncorporate shareholder, approximately 69 percent (16/23) of the foreign trade income attributable to the shareholder's proportionate interest in the FSC will be exempt.[16] Exempt foreign

---

[11] IRC § 923(b); Temp. Reg. § 1.923-1T(a).

[12] *See* Temp. Reg. § 1.927(a)-1T(a) (definition of "export property").

[13] IRC § 923(a)(4).

[14] IRC § 921(d).

[15] IRC § 923(a)(2), (3); Temp. Reg. § 1.923-1T(b).

[16] IRC § 291(a)(4)(B) (corporate preference rules); IRC § 923(a)(3); and Temp. Reg. § 1.923-1T(b)(1)(i).

trade income is treated as foreign source income not effectively connected with a U.S. trade or business.[17]

Types of income (non-foreign trading income) not eligible to be exempt from U.S. taxation under the FSC provisions include:

- Nonexempt foreign trade income computed in the manner described earlier;
- Foreign trade income from intangibles that do not constitute export property;[18]
- Investment income; and
- Carrying charges.[19]

The non-foreign trade income of a FSC is generally treated as U.S. source effectively connected income.[20]

(c) Maintaining FSC Books and Records

The first step in preparing the FSC's tax return is gathering and sorting the information necessary to complete the return. This process is greatly facilitated with FSC compliance and pricing software, which is now available. In addition to compiling often voluminous transactions for tax return preparation, the software can also perform complicated calculations to maximize the FSC's benefit under a myriad of grouping alternatives.

For a commission FSC, periodic books may not have been maintained and it may be necessary to create the company's income statement and balance sheet at year end. The first step in computing the FSC's income will be determining the related supplier's qualified export transactions for the year. The gross receipts from these transactions are aggregated to determine FTGR as the first step in calculating the CTI for the year. Assigning all foreign sales specific account numbers or specific codes is the simplest way to compile this information. In addition, specific costs attributable to export sales should be tracked whenever possible. Similarly, an attempt should be made to isolate costs that have no relationship to export transactions or that have a specific relationship to non-FSC transactions. These costs should not be allocated and apportioned to CTI. Indirect costs that are not directly related to any specific sales are allocated to the FTGR in a manner consistent with the allocation and apportionment rules contained in the regulations for determining net foreign source income and net U.S. source income for purposes of the foreign tax credit calculation (among other things).[21] Other costs or disbursements

---

[17] Temp. Reg. § 1.923-1T(b)(1)(iii).

[18] IRC § 291(a)(4)(A) (corporate preference rules); IRC § 923(a)(2); and Temp. Reg. § 1.923-1T(b)(1)(ii); *see* IRC § 927(a) for definition of export property.

[19] IRC § 921(d); Temp. Reg. § 1.921-3T(a).

[20] IRC § 921(d).

[21] Generally, *see* Reg. § 1.925(a)-1T(c)(6)(iii)(D), which references Reg. § 1.861-8.

that must be specifically identified are the costs that satisfy the direct cost test[22] and the disbursements required to be made out of the FSC's foreign bank account.[23] (A small FSC does not have the foreign bank account requirement.)

The actual profit of a commission FSC is computed on Schedule P of the tax return. With the FSC profit having been determined, the financial statements of the FSC are created. The regulations require that quarterly income statements, a final year-end income statement and balance sheet, and the final invoices (or a summary thereof) or certain statements of account be maintained at the FSC's non-U.S. office.[24] These rules are discussed in greater detail in Chapter 5, which addresses the foreign management test and foreign office requirement of a large FSC.

10.3 Completion of Form 1120-FSC, Schedule P, Transfer Price or Commission

(a) Overview

The preparation of a FSC return generally begins with Schedule P, which determines the FSC transfer price or commission. Schedule P calculates the allowable transfer price to charge a buy-sell FSC or the commission to pay a commission FSC. Schedule P is generally filed for a FSC that had qualified FTGR during the tax year. Schedule P is not required if the arm's-length transfer pricing method is used, or when transactions are incomplete at year's end.

If the administrative pricing methods are not used, the profit of the FSC will be determined using the arm's-length transfer pricing method. In this case, the transfer price for a sale by the related supplier to the FSC is calculated on the basis of the transaction price actually charged, but subject to certain statutory prescribed standards.[25] The FSC determines its profit based on the arm's-length price determined as if the FSC and the related supplier were not related. Thus, the FSC's income is determined in accordance with the economic functions performed and risks undertaken by the FSC for the transactions.

The administrative pricing methods cannot be used if transactions are considered incomplete at year's end. A transaction is incomplete if export property bought during the tax year by the FSC from the related supplier is unsold by the end of the FSC's tax year, or the related supplier's tax year in which the property was transferred. Instead, the transfer price of the property bought by the FSC is the supplier's cost of goods sold for the property.[26] All profit or loss from the transaction to both the FSC and its related supplier is deferred until the year in which the transaction is completed.

---

[22] These costs must be specifically identified on Schedule G of Form 1120-FSC.

[23] *See* Reg. § 1.924(d) for further discussion.

[24] *See* Reg. § 1.922-1(I), Question 13 and Notice 88-93, 1988-2 CB 419.

[25] IRC § 482; Temp. Reg. § 1.925(a)-1T(a)(3)(ii).

[26] *See* Temp. Reg. § 1.925(a)-1T(c)(5)(C) for rules regarding the transfer price of property resold during the subsequent tax year.

(b)   Grouping Transactions

The FSC may file a Schedule P on a transaction-by-transaction basis, by groups of transactions consisting of products or product lines, or report all transactions according to the administrative transfer pricing rules the FSC uses. The grouping of transactions for determining combined taxable income may be different from the groups which have been established with regard to the economic process requirements.[27]

In preparing the return the appropriate box on Line B is checked to indicate the type of transaction that applies to Schedule B. In box 1, the determination may be made on a transaction-by-transaction basis. If box 1 is checked, a separate Schedule P must be filed for each of the FSC's transactions.

In box 2, an annual election may be made to group transactions consisting of products or product lines. The product or product lines must be entered on Line A. The product or product lines must conform to the two-digit major groups (or any classifications or combinations within a major group) of the Standard Industrial Classifications, or a recognized industry or trade usage. If box 2 is checked, a separate Schedule P must be filed for each of the FSC's product or product line groups of transactions. In some cases, the ability to group by product or product line can significantly increase the tax benefit achieved through the use of a FSC. This is a planning opportunity that should not be overlooked. The use of FSC tax compliance software enhances the ability to undertake this type of planning.

To aggregate transactions, box 3 is checked. A single Schedule P is filed for all aggregated transactions if this box is checked. Under this method, the FSC and its related supplier are required to maintain a supporting schedule for each transaction or group of transactions in their records.

(c)   Computation of Combined Taxable Income

After determining the amount of the qualifying sales, combined taxable income (CTI) must be computed. The full costing or marginal costing rules provide a mechanism of allocating expenses to FTGR. Under Part I, Section A, of Schedule P, combined taxable income is calculated according to the full costing or marginal costing rules. Under the administrative transfer pricing rules, both full costing and marginal costing may be used in the same tax year for separate transactions or separate groups of transactions. Generally, CTI refers to the excess of the FSC's gross receipts on a sale over the sum of the related costs of the FSC and the supplier. The regulations define CTI with reference to a single transaction, but transactions may be aggregated or grouped.

(d)   Full Costing CTI Rules

Full costing CTI rules may be applicable. If the FSC is the principal in the sale of export property, the full costing combined taxable income of the FSC and its

---

[27] Temp. Reg. § 1.925(a)-1T(c)(8)(viii).

related supplier is the excess of the FSC's FTGRs from the sale over the total costs of the FSC and related supplier. These costs include the supplier's cost of goods sold, and the supplier's and the FSC's noninventoriable costs that relate to the FTGRs.[28]

Costs and expenses may be deductible. Expenses of the related supplier that are definitely related to the FTGRs must be allocated to those receipts in computing CTI. Expenses that are not specifically related to a particular item of income must be apportioned to FTGR ratably. These apportioned costs must also be considered in computing CTI. All allocations and apportionments are to be determined in a manner consistent with the rules set forth in the Treasury Regulations.[29]

The allocation and apportionment of expenses should be given careful consideration to avoid overapportionment of expenses to FTGR. Special rules exist for allocating and apportioning several types of expenses, such as the following:

- Interest expense;
- Research and development expenses;
- State or local income taxes; and
- General and administrative expenses.

Generally, a net operating loss (NOL) deduction is treated as a deduction definitely related and allocable to a particular class (or classes) of gross income. The class to which the NOL is allocated is the same class as the activity that generated the NOL. Once allocated to the particular class or classes of gross income, the NOL deduction is apportioned between the statutory and residual groupings of gross income within each class. This apportionment is based on the relative amounts of the NOL attributable to the respective groupings of income in the year when the NOL arose. Depending on the specific facts and circumstances, a NOL may or may not be allocated or apportioned to a statutory grouping of gross income that gives rise to foreign trade gross receipts and, thus, reduces the FSC benefit.[30]

(e) Marginal Costing CTI Rules

A related supplier may elect to use the marginal costing rules to calculate CTI if the FSC is treated as seeking to establish or maintain a foreign market for sales of export of property.[31] A FSC is treated as seeking to establish or maintain a foreign market if marginal costing CTI is greater than full costing CTI (as discussed in the preceding section).[32]

---

[28] *See* Treas. Reg. § 1.471-11(c)(2)(ii); *also see* Temp. Reg. § 1.925(a)-1T(c)(6)(iii) for special rules regarding gross receipts and total costs.

[29] Treas. Reg. § 1.861–8.

[30] *See* PLR 8911022.

[31] Temp. Reg. § 1.925(b)-1T(c)(1).

[32] Temp. Reg. § 1.925(b)-1T(c).

Under the marginal costing rules, CTI is calculated by subtracting from FTGRs the direct material and direct labor costs of producing a particular item, product, or product line.[33] Other indirect and allocated costs are not included. Costs incurred by the FSC not taken into account in computing CTI on a marginal costing basis are deductible by the FSC only to the extent of non-foreign trade income.[34] CTI may, however, be limited under the marginal costing rules (discussion to follow).

Certain limitations on the use of the marginal costing rules do exist. The marginal costing rules do not apply to:

- Income from leasing property;[35]
- Income from services that are related and subsidiary to the sale of export property;[36] and
- Sales of export property that would produce foreign base company income in the hands of the seller unless the *de minimis* or high-tax exceptions apply.[37]

In addition to these exceptions, marginal costing CTI is limited under the overall profit percentage limitation (OPPL). Under the OPPL, marginal costing CTI may not exceed the overall profit percentage multiplied by foreign trading gross receipts.[38] The overall profit percentage is the ratio of full costing CTI to the total gross receipts of the FSC and related supplier from all sales of a product or product line as the denominator. If the FSC is a member of a controlled group, the related supplier may elect to determine the OPP by aggregating amounts, for the numerator and the denominator, of the FSC and all domestic members of the controlled group.[39]

The calculation of marginal costing CTI for a product or product line is determined as follows:

Step One: *Compute marginal costing CTI:*

Qualified foreign trading gross receipts

Less:

Direct production costs (labor and materials)

Equals:

Marginal costing CTI before application of the overall profit percentage limitation (OPPL)

---

[33] *See* Treas. Reg. § 1.471-11(b)(2)(ii).

[34] Temp. Reg. § 1.925(b)-1T(b)(1).

[35] Temp. Reg. § 1.925(b)-1T(a).

[36] *Id.*

[37] *Id.*

[38] Temp. Reg. § 1.925(b)-1T(b)(2).

[39] *Note* that under Temp. Reg. § 1.925(b)-1T(c)(2)(ii) and recent case law, it is possible for an aggregation election to be made by a related supplier without a conforming election by other domestic members of the controlled group making a conforming election.

Step Two: *Compute overall profit percentage (OPP):*

Taxable income from worldwide sales on a full cost basis
Divided by:
Worldwide gross receipts
Equals:
Overall profit percentage

Step Three: *Compute overall profit percentage limitation (OPPL):*

FTGR (used in Step One)
Multiplied by:
OPP (as determined in Step Two)
Equals:
OPPL

Step Four: *Marginal costing CTI is:*

The lesser of marginal costing CTI (as determined in Step One)
or the OPPL (as determined in Step Three).

(f)   Administrative Pricing Rules

The FSC's portion of CTI as determined using the marginal costing method is computed under the same administrative transfer pricing rules as CTI determined under the full costing method. These administrative pricing methods have previously been discussed and illustrated in this chapter.

Through application of these administrative pricing methods, the allowable transfer price charged the FSC or the commission paid to the FSC is determined. The key to maximizing the amount of exempt income is in the application of these rules and the grouping of transactions by the controlled group. The pricing calculations for a commission FSC and a buy-sell FSC are identical.

The 23 percent of combined taxable income method is applied on Schedule P, Section B. The FSC's profit is 23 percent of either full costing CTI or marginal costing CTI, as calculated in Section A on Schedule P.

In Section C of Schedule P, the 1.83 percent of foreign trading gross receipts method is applied. By using the 1.83 percent method, the FSC determines its profit by multiplying 1.83 percent by the FTGRs of the FSC. However, the FSC's profit cannot exceed 46 percent of the FSC's combined taxable income.

In the preparation of Schedule P, if there is a loss on line 3 and line 12 (or just line 3 if marginal costing is not used), the FSC may not earn a profit under either the 23 percent CTI method or the 1.83 percent FTGR method. Under the 1.83 percent FTGR method, the FSC's profit on line 19 may not exceed the full costing CTI reported on line 3. The related supplier may, however, set a transfer price or rental payment or pay a commission in an amount that will enable the FSC to recover its costs, if any, even if the result is a loss for the related supplier. See Part II, Transfer Price from Related Supplier to FSC, or Part III, FSC Commission from Related Supplier on the form.

If the FSC recognizes income while the related supplier recognizes a loss on a sale under the IRC § 482 method, neither the 23 percent method nor the 1.83 percent method may be used by the FSC and the related supplier (or by an FSC in the same controlled group and the related supplier) for any other group or groups of sales, during the tax, year falling within the same three-digit Standard Industrial Classification as the subject sale.[40]

The combination of the "no-loss rules" and the marginal costing rules dictate that the FSC profit is the greater of the profit derived under the following two administrative pricing methods:

Combined Taxable Income Method

FSC profit is limited to the lesser of:

- 23 percent of marginal costing CTI; or
- 23 percent of the overall profit percentage limitation; or
- 100 percent of the full costing CTI.

Gross Receipts Method

FSC profit is 1.83 percent of qualifying gross receipts, limited to the lesser of:

- 46 percent $\times$ CTI; or
- 100 percent of full costing CTI.

10.4 Completion of Form 1120-FSC

(a) Overview

Once the required Schedule Ps have been completed and the FSC profit thus determined, the taxpayer must complete the basic six pages of Form 1120-FSC. Form 1120-FSC is used to report the basic information relative to income, gains, losses, deductions, and credits of a foreign sales corporation. The FSC return includes a balance sheet, a reconciliation of book income to taxable income, and an analysis of unappropriated retained earnings.

(b) Computation of Cost of Goods Sold

Schedule A of Form 1120-FSC is completed by a buy-sell FSC to determine the cost of goods sold deduction related to foreign trading gross receipts reported on

---

[40] Reg. § 1.925(a)-1T(e)(1)(iii).

lines 1 through 5 of Schedule B. A commission FSC would not ordinarily have expenses related to inventory and would not complete Schedule A. A FSC completing Schedule A should consult the full costing and uniform capitalization rules, as well as observe the arm's-length standards imposed by the code whenever necessary.

Column (a) of Schedule A determines the cost of goods sold for inventory acquired in transactions using the administrative pricing rules. Column (b) of Schedule A determines the cost of goods sold for inventory acquired in transactions that use an arm's-length standard for determining the cost of goods sold.

(c) Computation of Taxable Income (or Loss)

Schedule B of Form 1120-FSC is used to compute taxable income or loss of the FSC from all sources. Part I of Schedule B computes net income attributable to nonexempt foreign trade income. Nonexempt foreign trade income is used to compute a FSC's tax liability.

Foreign trade gross receipts reflect the type of qualifying FSC transaction on lines 1 through 5 of Schedule B. Schedule B, like Schedule A, has two columns. Column (a) of Schedule B is used if the administrative pricing rules were used to determine the FSC profit. Column (b) of Schedule B is used if the administrative pricing rules were not used. The cost of goods sold amounts from Schedule A flow to their respective columns on line 7 of Schedule B.

Schedule B ultimately divides the FSC's foreign trade income (foreign trade gross receipts less the cost of goods sold) into two groups, exempt and nonexempt income. The division of foreign trade income into exempt and nonexempt income foreign trade income is accomplished by multiplying the total amount by the "exemption percentage." The exemption percentage is computed on Schedule E of Form 1120-FSC (subsequently discussed in this chapter). After determining nonexempt foreign trade income, Schedule B subtracts from such amount the deductions attributable to nonexempt foreign trade income. The deductions attributable to nonexempt foreign trade income are determined on Schedule G of Form 1120-FSC (also subsequently discussed in this chapter). Net income attributable to nonexempt foreign trade income having been determined, the final step in arriving at total net income attributable to nonexempt foreign trade income is the addition of certain types of net income computed on Schedule F.

Schedule F of Form 1120-FSC calculates the amount of net income from additional types of nonexempt foreign trade income. These additional sources of nonexempt foreign trade income are 50 percent of receipts from transactions involving military property and related services, receipts of international boycott income, and receipts of illegal payments, bribes, or kickbacks paid to government officials, employees, or agents. Like Schedules A and B, these amounts are reported according to whether profit from them are related to transactions using the administrative pricing rules or to transactions in which the profit is determined without regard to the administrative pricing rules. These amounts reported on Schedule F are offset by the amount of cost of goods sold and other costs related to them. A schedule calculating such offsetting costs must be attached to the return. The net income attributable to the nonexempt foreign trade income computed on Schedule F, having been added to the amounts calculated in the preceding paragraph, equals the total net income attributable to nonexempt foreign trade income.

(d) Small FSCs

Schedule B calculates the $5 million foreign gross receipt limitation on small FSCs. This amount is prorated for short taxable years or for the apportionment of the single gross receipts limitation among multiple small FSCs in a controlled group. Income from foreign trade gross receipts in excess of the limitation do not receive any FSC benefit, which may result in an underpayment of the FSC's estimated tax liability. Often, the related supplier will have overpaid its estimated tax liability by a like amount. This "mismatching" may be avoided by a well-worded commission agreement between the FSC and its related supplier. The agreement should generally provide for a FSC commission not to exceed the maximum amount of such commission that qualifies for the FSC benefit. It may benefit the controlled group to have the FSC earn less than the maximum benefit allowed where there are foreign tax credit limitations, expiring net operating losses, or other tax attributes or alternative minimum tax situations.

The remainder of Schedule B calculates the taxable income or loss of the FSC. The first step in this computation is the combining of total net income attributable to nonexempt foreign trade income as computed under both the administrative and nonadministrative pricing rules. To this amount is added the nonforeign trade income of the FSC, computed in the second part of Schedule F. Non-foreign trade income is generally investment income of the FSC, for example, items such as interest and dividends. From this sum is subtracted the FSC's net operating loss deduction and the dividends received deduction to arrive at the FSC's taxable income or loss for the year.

(e) Computation of Percentages for Exempt Foreign Trade Income

Schedule E calculates the exemption percentage applied to foreign trade income reported on Schedule B in determining the exempt and nonexempt pieces of foreign trade income. Practitioners should not look for Schedules C and D, as there are no such schedules on this form.

If the FSC is owned entirely by either C corporations or noncorporate or S corporation shareholders, the computation is somewhat simplified. If all shareholders of the FSC are C corporations, the exemption percentage for foreign trade income determined without regard to the administrative pricing rules is 30 percent; for foreign trade income determined using the administrative pricing rules, the exemption percentage is 65.217 percent. If all of the FSC's shareholders are shareholders other than C corporations, the percentages are 32 percent and 69.565 percent, respectively.

(f) Schedule G

Schedule G of Form 1120-FSC reports the deductions allocated or apportioned to the income of the FSC. As previously discussed in this chapter, the allocation of the FSC and related supplier's expenses is a detailed process governed by various provisions of the IRC.

Line 1 of Schedule G is of special importance. The foreign direct costs, used in the satisfaction of the foreign economic process requirements are reported here. As was done with the foreign trade income of the FSC, the total deductions of the FSC are divided between exempt and nonexempt deductions (these amounts were used in the discussion of Schedule B).

(g) Schedule J, Computation of Tax Liability

Schedule J of Form 1120-FSC computes the FSC's tax liability as to the amount of taxable income calculated on Schedule B. The generally simple computation of tax is somewhat complicated if the FSC is a member of a controlled group. When a controlled group adopts or amends a plan that apportions bracket deductions, each member of the controlled group must attach to its tax return a copy of its consent to this plan. If no apportionment plan is adopted, the members of a controlled group must divide the amount in each taxable income bracket equally among themselves. This arbitrary allocation could have a significant effect on the overall tax liability of the controlled group.

The taxable income of the FSC may be subject to the tax rate that applies to personal service corporations. In addition, the foreign tax credit rules, the alternative minimum tax rules, and the rules imposing the environmental tax may all apply to a FSC.

(h) Balance Sheet

Schedule L of Form 1120-FSC presents the balance sheet of the FSC. The balance sheet of a Form 1120-FSC is similar to the balance sheet of any other corporate return. However, the primary complication in maintaining a FSC's balance sheet is the posting of entries relating to the intercompany charges between the FSC and its related supplier. It is important to post the entries of the FSC so accurate books and records may be maintained. If the dividend to the parent corporation is offset against commissions receivable in the succeeding year, this offset should be reflected on the balance sheet and on the Analysis of Unapportioned Retained Earnings (Schedule M-2).

(i) Reconciliation of Income per Books with Income per Return

Although Schedule M-1 of Form 1120-FSC is substantially similar to the Schedule M-1 of a Form 1120, certain computational modifications are required. The need for these modifications arises as a result of excluding a portion of the

FSC's income and deductions from tax. Schedule M-1 provides a line for each of these adjustments.

(j)   Form 5471 Filing Requirements

U.S. citizen or resident shareholders, officers, or directors do not have to file Form 5471 and a separate Schedule O to report the initial organization of a FSC. Subsequent transfers, reorganizations, acquisitions, or dispositions must be reported by such persons. U.S. shareholders of a FSC who own more than 10 percent of the FSC's stock for an uninterrupted period of 30 days *and* own the FSC stock on the last day of the FSC's taxable year must include on Schedule H, I, and J of Form 5471 all FSC income other than exempt FTI and nonexempt FTI other than nonexempt FTI from transactions in which the FSC taxable income is determined under arm's-length pricing (so-called Section 923(a)(2) nonexempt income). Stated another way, the amounts not reported on Schedules H, I, and J are all exempt FTI and nonexempt FTI determined under administrative pricing rules. Deductions that are apportioned or allocated to income that is not reported on these schedules are similarly not reported on these schedules. Conversely, the income of a FSC that is nonexempt FTI determined under arm's-length pricing, investment income of a FSC, carrying charges, and any other income earned by a FSC must be reported on Schedules H, I, and J. Similarly, any deductions apportioned or allocated to such income are reported on these schedules. The result of these requirements is that Form 5471 does not reflect the types of income of a FSC that could be taxable as a subpart F income inclusion or upon actual distribution to the FSC's shareholder.

10.5   DISC Overview

(a)   Compliance Overview

An interest-charge domestic international sales corporation (IC-DISC) is not taxed on its export profits, but defers U.S. taxation on profits from specified export-related transactions until the profits are distributed or deemed distributed to the shareholder. The IC-DISC's shareholder(s) must pay an annual interest charge to the IRS based on the tax that is deferred. IC-DISC profits are invested in a manner that allows the IC-DISC to maintain the required level of qualified export assets (QEA). 95% or more of the year-end total adjusted basis of the assets on the IC-DISC's balance sheet must comprise QEAs. The IC-DISC provides long-term tax deferral interest at a low charge, effectively, a form of loan financing from the U.S. government. There is no ultimate tax benefit or reduction inherent in the IC-DISC rules, although in some cases the effect may be a savings of corporate taxes (i.e., where income of the related supplier would be subject to corporate tax and the IC-DISC's shareholder is not subject to corporate level tax). The IC-DISC, however, does not have a permanent tax exemption benefit.

A domestic corporation that has elected to be treated as an interest-charge domestic international sales corporation (IC-DISC) and has satisfied the various statutory requirements for treatment as an IC-DISC[41] is required to file a U.S. income tax return on Form 1120-IC-DISC. The return is due on or before the 15th day of the ninth month following the close of the taxable year, with no opportunity for extension of time.

(b)   Deferred Tax Liability

An IC-DISC may defer up to 50 percent of its U.S. income tax on income attributable to $10 million or less of "qualified export receipts."[42] Qualified export receipts (QER) generally relate to the sale, exchange, or other disposition of export property. QERs may also relate to the lease of export property and certain specified services. The term *QER* also includes interest on any obligation that is a qualified export asset. The single $10 million annual QER limitation must be prorated on a daily basis for a short taxable year end and must be apportioned between multiple IC-DISCs in a single controlled group.

10.6   Completion of Schedule P

(a)   Overview

Schedule P calculates taxable income that is used in computing the allowable transfer price that the related party may charge the buy-sell IC-DISC or the commission the related supplier pays to a commission IC-DISC. Schedule P is normally used for transfer pricing purposes. However, Schedule P is not required if the IRC § 482 method of transfer pricing is used. The administrative pricing rules are inapplicable or a taxpayer does not choose to use them. Schedule P does not apply when transactions are incomplete at year-end or when some or all property in a transaction remains unsold at the end of the year. Each transaction or group of transactions requires its own Schedule P. The annual election to group transactions by product or product line may be a powerful planning exercise. Each taxpayer utilizing an IC-DISC should review the opportunity to save taxes inherent in the DISC pricing. DISC software can be of assistance (see Chapter 8).

(b)   Qualified Export Receipts

The application of the IC-DISC rules necessitates its own terminology. A *related supplier* is a related party that engages in a qualified export transaction with an IC-DISC.[43] A *related party* is a person owned or controlled directly or indirectly by the same interest as the IC-DISC, within the meaning of IRC § 482.[44]

---

[41] *See* IRC § 992 for these requirements.

[42] IRC § 995(b).

[43] Treas. Reg. § 1.994-1(a)(3)(ii).

[44] Treas. Reg. § 1.994-1(a)(3)(i).

QERs are the gross receipts that determine taxable income under the transfer pricing methods. QERs are derived from the sale, lease/rental, or disposition of export property or qualified export assets, or from qualified services, dividends, and interest on any obligation that is a qualified export asset. Receipts that are excluded from the 95 percent computation include amounts from capital contributed to an IC-DISC, stock issued by an IC-DISC for money or other property, funds borrowed by an IC-DISC, and loan repayments to an IC-DISC.

(c) Export Promotion Expenses

Export promotion expenses (EPEs) are expenses incurred by an IC-DISC to advance the sale, lease, or other distribution of export property for use, consumption, or distribution outside the United States.[45] EPEs include the costs of packaging, depreciation on certain property owned and used by the IC-DISC, marketing expenses, general and administrative costs (including payments to independent contractors), and other similar expenses. EPEs do not include interest, bad debts, income and franchise taxes, freight insurance, and cost of goods sold. One half of the freight costs will qualify as EPEs if the property is shipped aboard a U.S. flag carrier where laws or regulations do not mandate the use of a U.S. flag carrier. Certain EPEs, such as salaries of the IC-DISC's employees, costs of the space used by its employees, and depreciation on property used by its employees, must be directly incurred by the IC-DISC.[46]

(d) Commission DISC and Buy-Sell DISC

Both a commission DISC and a buy-sell DISC are required to meet all DISC requirements discussed throughout this book. The difference between the commission DISC and the buy-sell DISC lies in the nature of the legal relationship between the DISC and its related supplier. A commission DISC is an agent of the related supplier. A buy-sell DISC is similar to a distributor or reseller for the related supplier. A commission DISC is a commission company that receives commissions on the sale of export goods by its related supplier. A buy-sell DISC is a company that purchases and sells goods, actually taking title to the goods before reselling the goods to the foreign purchaser. Both types of DISCs may be either a paper company with no employees or a substantive operating company with sufficient employees to conduct an active trade or business. The latter case is rare in practice.

(e) Computation of Combined Taxable Income

Combined taxable income (CTI) is the excess of the IC-DISC's gross receipts on a transaction over the sum of the costs of the IC-DISC and the supplier related

---

[45] IRC § 994(c).

[46] Treas. Reg. § 1.994-1(f)(7).

to the gross receipts from the transaction. The computation of taxable income under the intercompany pricing rules will not be permitted to the extent that their application would result in a loss to the related supplier.

Section A must be completed if the marginal costing rules (discussed subsequently) do not apply. The appropriate apportionment of deductions that are not directly allocable, such as interest expenses, stewardship expenses, and R&D expenditures, must be included.[47] Alternatively, Section A-2 should be completed if the marginal costing rules apply.

The regulations define CTI with reference to a single transaction. However, transactions may be aggregated or grouped. The IC-DISC may make an annual election to group transactions by product or product line. The election need not be affected by elections made in prior years. The goal is to classify sales into products or product lines with clearly differentiated gross profit percentages. If the group basis is elected, then all transactions for that product or product line must be grouped. Each group is limited to one type of transaction (i.e., sales, leases, or commissions). As stated earlier, proper use of groupings may lead to a significant increase in a taxpayer's DISC benefit. Grouping all transactions together is rarely permitted, or advantageous.

The determination of a product or product line will be accepted if it conforms to either a recognized industry or trade usage, or the two-digit major groups (or any subclassifications within a major group) of the principal business activity groups listed in the instructions for Form 1120-IC-DISC. The taxpayer may choose a product grouping for one product and use the transaction-by-transaction method for another product within the same tax year.

(f) Marginal Costing Rules

The marginal costing method applies if the IC-DISC is characterized as seeking to establish or maintain a foreign market. The requirement of "seeking to establish or maintain a foreign market" will be met so long as the computed CTI under the marginal costing rules, as determined in the following paragraph, is greater than taxable income in domestic and export sales combined. The marginal costing rules may be used whether or not the related supplier is the manufacturer or producer of the export property.

To determine CTI under the marginal costing method, *direct* production costs (material and labor costs incident to production or manufacturing processes) and EPEs are subtracted from gross receipts other costs are not taken into account. The taxpayer may elect not to subtract all or part of the EPEs from CTI. By excluding some of the EPEs from the computation, the marginal CTI is increased. In some factual situations, the benefit of increasing IC-DISC taxable income by excluding EPEs outweighs the loss of the IC-DISC to earn an extra profit of 10 percent of the

---

[47] *See* Reg. §§ 1.861-8, 1.861-11T(a), 1.861-14T(e), and 1.861-17 for an explanation of appropriate allocation and apportionment of these expenses.

EPEs actually incurred by the IC-DISC. However, if this choice is made, the EPEs cannot be used in calculating the extra profit of 10 percent under the safe harbor methods of IC-DISC transfer pricing. However, combined taxable income determined through the use of marginal costing is limited to an overall profit percentage based on taxable income.

The combined taxable income determined by using marginal costing may not exceed a percentage of gross receipts calculated as the overall profit percentage limitation (OPPL). OPPL is derived by comparing the combined taxable income on all foreign and domestic sales of each item, product, or product line with the total gross receipts from those sales.[48] Since the OPP can be measured on the sales of items, products, or product lines, the taxpayer has an almost free choice in grouping transactions for purposes of determining the OPP. The objective is to classify sales into products or product lines with clearly differentiated gross profit percentages. In addition, the transactions reflected in the OPP may include not only those of the related supplier, but also those of other members of a controlled group. The inclusion of these other sales contrasts with the OPP under the "special" 4 percent no-loss rule, where only the related supplier's sales may be considered.[49]

(g)   Expense Allocation and Apportionment Rules

Consistency with the accounting rules is required. The determination of CTI and OPP in the application of the no-loss rules and marginal costing limitations require the allocation and apportionment of expenses between QERs and other statutory classes of gross income, both by the IC-DISC and the related supplier, in a manner consistent with the rules used for purposes of the foreign tax credit calculation.[50]

The related supplier is to allocate and apportion its expenses among export sales, nonexport sales, and other income. The IC-DISC allocates and apportions its costs between export sales and other income. The computations under Treas. Reg. § 1.861-8 are made on a separate company basis, then combined for purposes of CTI and the various OPP limitations. The goal is to minimize the allocation of expenses to CTI. The following expenses are subject to the allocation and apportionment rules:

- Interest expense;
- Research and development costs;
- Foreign taxes;
- State income taxes; and
- All other expenses.

---

[48] Treas. Reg. § 1.994-2(c)(2).

[49] *See* the section, *infra*, on Transfer Pricing Methods for a discussion of the "special" 4 percent no-loss rule.

[50] *See* Treas. Reg. § 1.994-1(c)(6)(iii), which references Reg. § 1.861-8. *See also* the Regulations that expand on § 1.861-8, as cited at footnote 46, *supra*.

(h)   Administrative Pricing Rules

The intercompany pricing methods allocate income between the IC-DISC and its related supplier. The related supplier may be the IC-DISC's parent corporation or any other person described in IRC § 482. The transfer pricing rules do not apply in the case of sales to an IC-DISC by a person other than a related supplier or in the case of sales by an IC-DISC. The rules apply both to a buy-sell IC-DISC and a commission IC-DISC. Specifically, if a related person sells export property to an IC-DISC, the selling or transfer price is that which will allow the IC-DISC to derive taxable income that is the greater of the two safe harbor (or administrative) intercompany pricing methods. These two methods are:

- The 50/50 combined taxable income method; and
- The 4 percent gross receipts method.[51]

The key to maximum deferral is in the application of the intercompany pricing rules, which will also be crucial to maximize the IC-DISC's investments in QEAs. The administrative pricing methods apply only to transactions between a related supplier and an IC-DISC, the most common of which is a sale (or exchange) of export property in which the IC-DISC acts as a broker or commission agent.[52] In addition, leases, rendition of services related or subsidiary to an IC-DISC sale (such as installation or repair services), and architectural and engineering services for foreign construction projects are also covered by the administrative pricing methods. The regulations permit the administrative pricing methods to be applied in either a basic or modified form. Under the modified form, the 4 percent special no-loss method and marginal costing will be referred to as the variant methods. Moreover, all of the costs and expenses of the IC-DISC and the exporter are taken into account in determining the transfer price or commission using the administrative pricing methods. These costs and expenses offset the gross receipts from transactions and resales between an IC-DISC (or related supplier) and a third party in calculating CTI. The administrative pricing rules allow an IC-DISC to earn an extra profit of 10 percent of the EPEs actually incurred by the IC-DISC.[53]

Under the 4 percent gross receipts method, a basic or special method may be used in calculating the transfer price. In preparing the return, Part I, Section C should not be completed if the 50/50 method in Part I, Section B is used. The "basic" 4 percent method allows an IC-DISC to earn a profit of 4 percent of its gross receipts plus 10 percent of its EPEs, so long as the profit earned by the IC-DISC does not cause the related supplier to incur a loss on the transactions (or group of transactions). Where there is profit of less than 4 percent of QERs, the en-

---

[51] IRC § 994; *see* the "working" set of pricing rules under Treas. Reg. §§ 1.994-1 and 1.994-2.

[52] Treas. Reg. §§ 1.994-1(b) and Treas. Reg. § 1.861-15.

[53] Treas. Reg. § 1.994-1(f)(1).

tire CTI may be allocated to the IC-DISC and the related supplier may break even on the transaction or transactions.[54] The "special" no-loss method allows the IC-DISC to compute a 4 percent profit when the CTI is less than 4 percent plus 10 percent of the EPEs, but more than 4 percent on all export and domestic sales of the product.[55] The profit earned from this transaction may not exceed the aggregate percentage profit on all sales, export or domestic, of the same product or product line.[56]

Under the 50/50 CTI method, the transfer price or commission is 50 percent of the IC-DISC's and related supplier's CTI attributable to the QERs from the transaction, plus 10 percent of the IC-DISC's EPEs attributable to the QERs. In preparing the return, complete Part I, Section C, if the 50/50 method in Part I, Section B, is used. The key to maximizing deferral of income under this method is the calculation of CTI. As mentioned earlier, CTI must reflect the allocation or apportionment of all relevant deductions in a manner consistent with the principles of Treas. Reg. § 1.861-8 *et seq.*

If the marginal costing rules are used where only direct expenses are taken in account, combined taxable income calculated under the marginal costing rules will always exceed combined taxable income determined by taking all costs and expenses into account.

In sum, the choice of the optimum pricing method will always depend on the amount of profit on export sales as compared with the amount of profit on combined export and domestic sales under any of the grouping alternatives. The following table presents some of the pricing method.

CTI Export	OPPL Combined	Pricing Method
1. Less than 4%	More than 4% and less than 8%	4% Special no-loss
	More than 8%	Marginal costing
2. More than 4% and less than 8%	Less than 8%	4%
	More than CTI%	Marginal costing
3. More than 8%	Less than CTI%	50/50
	More than CTI%	Marginal costing

Part II and Part III of Schedule P calculate the transfer price or commission charged if CTI is less than zero, in the same manner as it is calculated on Form 1120-FSC, Schedule P. In addition, if the commission or transfer price calculated is used on more than one line of Form 1120-IC-DISC, a schedule explaining the amounts used must be attached to the return.

---

[54] Treas. Reg. § 1.994-1(e)(1)(i).

[55] Treas. Reg. § 1.994-1(e)(1)(ii).

[56] Treas. Reg. § 1.994-1(e)(1)(ii).

10.7 Preparing the DISC Return

(a) Overview

Form 1120-IC-DISC reports income, gains, losses, deductions, and credits of an Interest Charge Domestic International Sales Corporation (IC-DISC), former DISCs, and former IC-DISCs. For example, an IC-DISC has elected to be an IC-DISC and that election is still in effect. An IC-DISC is not taxed on its deferred income from qualified export receipts. The percentage of qualified export receipts that is deferred is determined under the administrative pricing rules (see the earlier discussion of Schedule P). The amount of deferred income is calculated on Schedule J.

Form 1120-IC-DISC figures an IC-DISC's taxable income, although the IC-DISC does not pay most taxes. Generally, an IC-DISC is subject only to the tax imposed on certain transfers to avoid tax.[57] An IC-DISC is exempt from the corporate income tax, the alternative minimum tax, and the accumulated earnings tax.

An IC-DISC and its shareholders are not entitled to the possessions corporation tax credit.[58] Further, an IC-DISC cannot claim the general business credit or the credit for fuel produced from a nonconventional source. Nor can these credits be passed through to shareholders of the corporation.

(b) Schedule A, Computation of Cost of Goods Sold

The cost of goods schedule calculates the cost of goods sold deduction for a buy-sell IC-DISC. If the IC-DISC acts as another person's commission agent on a sale (a commission IC-DISC), the corporation need not complete Schedule A. The buy-sell IC-DISC must report actual purchases from a related supplier. Line 4, additional Section 263A costs, need be completed only if the IC-DISC elected a simplified method of accounting.

(c) Schedule B, Computation of Gross Income

Schedule B calculates the corporation's gross income. The IC-DISC's income is reported according to the type of receipts received from the transaction. If an income item falls into two or more categories, report each part on the applicable line. For example, if interest income consists of qualified interest from a foreign international sales corporation and nonqualified interest from a domestic obligation, enter the qualified interest on an attached schedule for line 2g and the nonqualified interest on an attached schedule for line 3f. When qualified export assets are sold, attach a separate schedule in addition to the forms required for lines 2h and 2i. Accrual basis taxpayers need not accrue certain amounts to be received from the performance of services which, on the basis of the experience of the taxpayer, will not

---

[57] *See* IRC §§ 1491 through 1494.

[58] *See* IRC § 936.

be collected.[59] Corporations should attach a schedule showing total gross receipts, amount not accrued, and net amount accrued. The net amount should be entered on the applicable line of Schedule B. If the IC-DISC received commissions on selling or renting property or furnishing services, list in column (b) the gross receipts from the sales, rentals or services on which the commissions arose, and in column (c) list the commissions earned. In column (d) report receipts of property or furnishing of services, as well as all other receipts.

For purposes of completing line 1a and line 1b, related purchasers are members of the same controlled group as the IC-DISC.[60] All other purchasers are unrelated. On line 1, report qualified export receipts which are received from the sale of property, such as inventory, that is produced in the United States for direct use, consumption, or disposition outside the United States. These sales are qualified export sales. The sale of any unprocessed log, cant, or similar form of timber that is softwood after August 10, 1993, produces nonqualified export receipts that are reported on line 3 of Schedule B. On line 1a, enter the IC-DISC's qualified export receipts from export property sold to foreign, unrelated buyers for delivery outside the United States. Do not include amounts entered on line 1b. Enter on line 1b the IC-DISC's qualified export receipts from export property sold for delivery outside the United States to a related foreign entity for resale to a foreign, unrelated buyer, or an unrelated buyer when a related foreign entity acts as commission agent.

On lines 2a through 2j, the IC-DISC reports income from other qualified export receipts. Enter the gross amount received from leasing or subleasing export property to unrelated persons for use outside the United States on line 2a. Receipts from leasing export property may qualify in some years and not in others, depending on where the lessee uses the property. Enter only qualifying receipts for the tax year. Use Schedule E to deduct expenses such as repairs, interest, taxes, and depreciation. On line 2b, report the income from services related and subsidiary to a qualified export sale or lease. A service connected to a sale or lease is related if the service is usually furnished with that type of sale or lease. A service is subsidiary to a sale or lease if it is less important than the sale or lease.[61]

Include on line 2c receipts from engineering or architectural services on foreign construction projects abroad or proposed for location abroad. These services include feasibility studies, design and engineering, and general supervision of construction, but do not include services connected with mineral exploration. On line 2d, include receipts for export management services provided to unrelated IC-DISCs. Qualified dividends calculated on Schedule C, line 15, are reported on line 2e. Nonqualified dividends calculated on Schedule C, line 16, are reported on line 3e.

On line 2f, include interest received on any loan that qualifies as a producer's loan,[62] on line 2g enter interest on any qualified export asset other than interest on

---

[59] *See* IRC § 448(d)(5).

[60] *See* IRC § 993(a)(3) for definition of a controlled group.

[61] *See* Reg. § 1.994-1(b).

[62] *See* Schedule Q (Form 1120-IC-DISC), Borrower's Certificate of Compliance with the Rules for Producer's Loans and Treas. Reg. § 1.993-4.

producer's loans. For example, include interest on accounts receivable arising from sales in which the IC-DISC acted as a principal or agent, and interest on certain obligations issued, guaranteed, or insured by the Export-Import Bank, or by the Foreign Credit Insurance Association.

On line 2h, report capital gain net income calculated on Schedule D (Form 1120). Schedule D (Form 1120) must be attached to the return. In addition to Schedule D, attach a separate schedule computing gain from the sale of qualified export assets.

On line 2i, enter the net gain or loss from line 20, Part II, Form 4797, Sales of Business Property. In addition to Form 4797, attach a separate schedule computing gain from the sale of qualified export assets. Enter on line 2j any other qualified export receipts for the tax year not reported on lines 2a through 2i. These receipts include the IC-DISC's allocable portion of an adjustment to income required because of a change in accounting methods.[63]

On lines 3a through 3f, the IC-DISC reports income from nonqualified gross receipts. The total gross income calculated on line 4 goes to line 1, on page 1 of the return in the section entitled "Taxable Income." Receipts from selling products subsidized under a U.S. program (if they have been designated as excluded receipts) are entered on line 3b. On line 3c, enter receipts from selling or leasing property or services for use by any part of the U.S. government if law or regulations require U.S. products or services to be used. On line 3d enter receipts from any IC-DISC that belongs to the same controlled group.[64] Finally, include in an attached schedule any nonqualified gross receipts not reported on lines 3a through 3e and report them on line 3f. Do not offset any income item against a similar expense item.

(d)   Schedule C, Computation of Dividends and Special Deductions

Schedule C calculates dividend income from qualified and nonqualified dividends, and the dividends received deduction. Qualified and nonqualified dividends are calculated on lines 15 and 16, respectively, and are reported on Schedule B. Nonqualified dividends are calculated by subtracting from the total dividend amount on line 14 the qualified dividends reported on line 15. Qualified dividends are dividends that qualify as qualified export receipts. This amount includes all dividends includible in gross income that are attributable to stock of related foreign export corporations and other amounts includible in income of U.S. shareholders of controlled foreign corporations.[65]

(e)   Schedule E, Deductions

The deduction schedule calculates the total deductions allowed to offset gross income in computing the IC-DISC's tax liability on page 1 of the return. Total de-

---

[63] See IRC § 481(a).

[64] See IRC § 993(a)(3) for the definition of a controlled group.

[65] See IRC § 951 relating to these amounts.

ductions calculated on Schedule E are reported on page 1, line 4. Export promotion expenses (EPEs) are entered on lines 1a through 1m. As discussed earlier, EPEs are an IC-DISC's ordinary and necessary expenses paid or incurred to obtain qualified export receipts. EPEs often arise only in those situations where the IC-DISC has its own employees or operating assets. Do not include federal income taxes as a deduction. Enter on lines 2a through 2g any portion of an expense not incurred to obtain qualified export receipts.

(f) Schedule J, Computation of Deemed and Actual Distributions, and Deferred Income

After the deductions have been calculated on Schedule E and forwarded to line 4 on page 1, calculate the IC-DISC's taxable income. The IC-DISC's taxable income, as calculated on page 1, is used on Schedule J to calculate the corporation's deemed distributions to its shareholders.

Schedule J calculates deemed and actual distributions to shareholders for the current year, deemed distributions for the prior year, and the corporation's deferred income. A separate Copy A of Schedule K (Form 1120-IC-DISC) must be attached to Form 1120-IC-DISC for each shareholder who received an actual or deemed distribution during the tax year or to whom the corporation reported deferred DISC income for the tax year. Schedule K is the Shareholder's Statement of IC-DISC Distributions.

Schedule J, Part I, calculates the deemed distributions for the current year and allocates the distribution based on the type of shareholder that owns the stock. Part II calculates the taxable income attributable to qualified export receipts that exceed $10 million. The $10 million limit is prorated on a daily basis. This proration is made on lines 4 and 5. Any taxable income of the IC-DISC attributable to qualified export receipts that exceed $10 million will be deemed distributed. The taxable income calculated on line 7 is reported on line 6 of Part I.

Part III calculates deemed distributions for the prior year. This calculation is made if the corporation is a former IC-DISC that revoked IC-DISC status or lost IC-DISC status for failure to satisfy one or more of the DISC requirements.[66] Under these circumstances, each shareholder is deemed to have received a distribution taxable as a dividend on the last day of the tax year. The deemed distribution equals the shareholder's prorated share of the IC-DISC's income accumulated during the years just before IC-DISC status ended. The shareholder will be deemed to receive the distribution in equal parts on the last day of each of the 10 tax years of the corporation following the year of the termination or disqualification of the IC-DISC, but in no case more than twice the number of years the corporation was an IC-DISC.

Part IV calculates the source of actual distributions from the accumulated earnings DISC actual distributions. This calculation takes into account distributions

---

[66] *See* IRC § 992(a)(1) for the requirements.

required to be qualified as an IC-DISC and other actual distributions. These two amounts are totaled on line 3. On lines 4a through 4d, the amount on line 3 is allocated among previously taxed income, accumulated IC-DISC income (including IC-DISC income for the current year), and other earnings and profits.

Finally, Part V calculates deferred IC-DISC income. Generally, deferred IC-DISC income is accumulated IC-DISC income (for periods after 1984) of the IC-DISC as of the close of the computation year reported on line 1, over the amount of distributions-in-excess-of-income for the tax year of the IC-DISC following the computation year reported on line 2.[67] For line 2, distributions-in-excess-of-income means the excess (if any) of: actual distributions to shareholders out of accumulated IC-DISC income, over the amount of IC-DISC income for the tax year following the computation year.[68]

The amount on line 3, Part V, is allocated to each shareholder on line 2, Part III, of Schedule K (Form 1120-IC-DISC). Shareholders of an IC-DISC must file Form 8404, Interest Charge on DISC-Related Deferred Tax Liability, if the IC-DISC reports deferred DISC income.

(g) Other Schedules

Schedule L should generally be prepared on a tax basis to avoid unnecessary questions regarding compliance with the gross asset test. Accumulated pre-1985 DISC income is reported on line 12. If the corporation was a qualified DISC as of December 31, 1984, the accumulated pre-1985 DISC income will generally be treated as previously taxed income (exempt from tax) when distributed to DISC shareholders after December 31, 1984.[69] Accumulated IC-DISC income (for periods after 1984) is accounted for on line 13 of Schedule L. The balance of this account is used in figuring deferred DISC income in Part V, Schedule J.

Differences between the book income and taxable income of the supplier must be taken into account in computing combined taxable income and the various profit limitations for Schedule M-1, Reconciliation of Income per Books with Income per Return. Schedule M-2 analyzes other earnings and profits reported on line 10, Schedule L. Schedule M-3 analyzes previously taxed income reported on line 11, Schedule L, while Schedule M-4 analyzes accumulated IC-DISC income reported on line 13, Schedule L.

Schedules N and O report certain other information. On Schedule N, the IC-DISC reports export gross receipts of the IC-DISC and related parties for the current and prior taxable year. On Schedule O, the IC-DISC reports certain information relating to the corporation's activities and ownership. These items reflect, among other things, the basic corporate requirements necessary to qualify as an IC-DISC.

---

[67] *See,* generally, IRC § 995(f) and Prop. Reg. § 1.995(f)-1 for a definition of computation year, examples, and other details on figuring deferred DISC income.

[68] *See* IRC § 996(f)(1) for definitions of divisions of earnings and profits.

[69] *See* Temp. Reg. § 1.921-1T(a)(7) for an exception to the exemption.

CHAPTER 11

Litigating FSC and DISC Cases

Robert J. Cunningham

11.1   Introduction

This chapter describes the litigation of tax issues arising from a foreign sales company (FSC) or domestic international sales company (DISC).[1] It should be noted that much of the discussion is based on the highly contentious (and more highly developed) litigation involving IRC § 482 and transfer pricing. Developments in the litigation of transfer pricing cases are driving developments in the litigation of FSCs and all other types of tax litigation.

For purposes of this chapter, it is assumed that the Internal Revenue Service (IRS, or Service) has completed its examination of the taxpayer and is preparing to issue a notice of deficiency concerning an issue arising from the qualification of the FSC or the calculation of the taxable income of a FSC. Furthermore, the taxpayer has determined that it must undertake to prepare the issues raised, on the assumption that the issues will have to be tried. Based on this background, this chapter first describes the requirements of litigating a FSC case, then discusses the choice of the appropriate forum in which to litigate the case, and finally elaborates on the actual process of preparing for and litigating a FSC case before the United States Tax Court (Tax Court).

A FSC case can involve both legal and factual issues. If the issue raised by the IRS principally involves *facts,* such as the calculation of the appropriate transfer pricing[2] or the determination of whether a specific activity constitutes "manufacturing,"[3] the case will require a tremendous time commitment by the taxpayer and

---

[1] For ease of reference and unless specifically required, this chapter refers only to FSCs. Portions of this chapter were first published as Chapter 19, "Litigating Transfer Pricing Cases," in Robert Feinschreiber, ed., *Transfer Pricing Handbook* (New York: John Wiley & Sons, 1993).

[2] IRC §§ 925 and 994.

[3] See *Webb Exports Corp. v. Commissioner,* 91 T.C. 131 (1988), and *Garnac Grain Co. v. Commissioner,* 95 T.C. 7 (1990).

outside tax counsel for full factual development *of its case.* Since the Service must rely on the taxpayer to provide most of the facts needed to prepare for litigation, a substantial amount of time will be involved in answering the IRS's factual questions. Therefore, if it has not been done before the examination was begun, the taxpayer must conduct an in-depth factual review of its particular factual issue and carefully apply the relevant legal principles to the facts. A complete and objective legal analysis of the issue should also be performed before deciding to proceed into the IRS's controversy resolution process. The taxpayer must establish, at the beginning, reasonable goals as to the defense of the FSC issue in question.

The taxpayer should demonstrate to the Service its commitment to obtain the correct long-term and potentially multiyear results, rather than merely a short-term settlement of the issue. FSC issues can impact multiple years under audit and often carry over into subsequent taxable years. The taxpayer's settlement of one audit cycle may have a significant impact on the Service's approach to that issue during future audits. Projecting the results of today's settlement into future taxable years is needed to determine properly the appropriate strategy at any time.

The goal is always to settle a tax controversy at the earliest possible level. Nevertheless, the taxpayer must deal from strength in that process. This position toward controversies requires that the taxpayer undertake to prepare the issue as if litigation were inevitable. The taxpayer should demonstrate to the examination team, the Appeals Officer, or IRS counsel, the taxpayer's commitment to litigate and ability to litigate the FSC issue if it is not fairly and correctly resolved at the lower level. Thus, an understanding of what is required to litigate an issue is likely to have a significant positive impact on the taxpayer's ability to obtain the optimum settlement of the issue.

This chapter focuses on a taxpayer's preparation to litigate a FSC case and on those situations in which settlement is not possible. Furthermore, because the most significant issues arising in the litigation of a tax controversy involve the development and presentation of facts at trial, much of the discussion focuses on such a case. Trial of legal issues is discussed, including strategies for expediting resolution of such issues.

The IRS has been concerned regarding its results in litigation and continues to modify its internal procedures to better evaluate and coordinate the audit and trial of large cases.[4] During May 1992, the IRS Office of Chief Counsel published an internal notice regarding the coordination of large cases, both at the audit and docketed stages. For this purpose, the definition of a large case is any case involved in:

1. The Coordinated Examination Program;
2. The Industry Specialization Program;
3. A disputed liability of at least $10 million; or
4. An issue of potential significance to tax administration.

---

[4] N (35) 000-114, 89 DTR G-11, L-1 (5/11/93).

Many FSC cases fall within one or more of these definitions and will be subject to the IRS notice.

The Chief Counsel issued new procedures as to:

1. The active coordination of the identification and handling of large cases between the IRS's National Office and its Field Offices; and
2. The direct involvement of senior IRS executives in the development and management of large cases, including decisions regarding litigation and trial strategies.

The goals of the Chief Counsel will be implemented through:

1. The development of large case work plans;
2. The deployment of litigation teams; and
3. The careful monitoring of all aspects of the case through opinion and appeals.

These changes should assist taxpayers in more easily resolving cases that should be resolved. However, these changes will result in better prepared and trained IRS counsel handling the large cases.

11.2   Basic Considerations

(a)   Organization of the Trial Team

The corporation must commit to provide any support needed to locate and develop the factual and testimonial needed to prevail in FSC tax litigation. A litigation team should consist of members of the taxpayer's tax, operating, financial, and legal groups and tax counsel. Early identification and organization of the litigation team is necessary to maximize the advantage that a taxpayer has in knowing the facts better than anyone else.

The litigation team should develop a detailed plan for the defense of the taxpayer's FSC policies and results. This litigation plan should include

1. identifying the critical facts supporting the taxpayer's position,
2. determining how to prove facts to a court (documents, testimonial witnesses, experts, videos and so forth), and
3. establishing reasonable time lines to achieve these goals within the pretrial schedule.

The litigation plan must also anticipate the Service's approach to the taxpayer's FSC and should develop strategies for demonstrating that the IRS's approach is incorrect. Depending on the issue, it may be necessary to identify and retain various experts early in the process. The Service is expanding its use of expert witnesses, some of whom also testify occasionally for both the Service and taxpayers. This trial plan becomes the most important single document prepared by the litigation team. The trial plan should be continually revised and updated as preparation for the litigation continues.

(b) Fact Preparation

Facts can be the lifeblood of a FSC case. Thus, the taxpayer, either through its own resources or with the assistance of outside advisors, should undertake to locate and organize all of the relevant facts. For this purpose, facts include all of the relevant contemporaneous documents, individuals familiar with the transaction, and the financial records underlying the transaction. This process will require a major commitment on behalf of the taxpayer to locate *"everything"* relating to the operation of the FSC.

Control of the facts developed as part of the preparation of a case is critical. Most of these facts consist of documents gathered from the taxpayer's files, either by the taxpayer or by the taxpayer and its outside counsel. Initially, procedures must be developed to keep a record of the files reviewed and their contents. The taxpayer may need to demonstrate to the court at a later date the extent of its search for relevant documents, and the taxpayer's file audit trail can be an important piece of proof in this regard. Second, to the extent that documents are pulled from files, a record of the file from which *each* document was pulled must be kept to meet evidentiary requirements if the Service refuses to stipulate to the document. It is typically best to make a copy of the relevant document, mark it so that the original can be located in the future, and leave the original in its file.

The taxpayer should send instructions to everyone who is likely to have copies of documents relevant to the pricing issue, stating that they are not to dispose of any documents without the prior approval of the Tax Department or someone else involved directly in the tax case. This instruction should require retention of all documents, hard copy and electronic, that are potentially relevant to the transactions to be tested under the FSC or DISC rules, including invoices, purchase orders, research and development records, marketing data, and similar items.

Depending on the volume of documents involved, the taxpayer should consider use of document identification procedures, such as the "bates" numbering of all documents, the computerization of its document file and other procedures, and the use of full text and image document retrieval procedures.

(c) Use of Document Privileges

The process of organizing the taxpayer's facts and preparing to contest a FSC case requires an understanding of the various rules as to the preservation and presentation of facts. Thus, effective use of the attorney-client privilege and work product doctrine plays a significant role in management of the case. The attorney-client privilege applies to confidential communications between the client and its lawyers made for the purpose of seeking legal advice.[5] The attorney-client privilege can be potentially applicable to a broad range of communications, including information that is prepared for and provided to counsel to enable counsel to render a legal opinion, and the attorneys' legal opinions and advice.

The attorney-client privilege does not apply to the taxpayer's underlying facts or to the information in the taxpayer's files that may have been used to ask the attorneys for their assistance. Information provided to or by other outside experts, such as accountants or economic experts, is generally not covered by the attorney-client privilege, unless such experts are necessary to enable the attorneys to understand the facts needed to provide legal advice *and* the experts are not expected to testify. Forwarding attorney-client privileged documents to testifying experts or to individuals other than the taxpayer, such as to the taxpayer's outside auditors, will generally waive the attorney-client privilege, both for the confidential communications provided and *all other privileged information covering the same subject matter.* Therefore, extreme care should be used in deciding to disclose attorney-client privileged documents to third parties.

The IRS has announced that it will continue to challenge aggressively the use of attorney-client and work product privileges to prevent the production of information developed by companies for use by outside counsel in providing legal advice to the company and in anticipation of litigation. Much of this litigation has involved pricing studies and other outside advice obtained by taxpayers as to potential IRC § 482 adjustments. In the *Bell*[6] case, the IRS asked the District Court to issue an order against officials of Connor Peripherals, Inc. (Connor) to produce certain reports and other documents prepared by an accounting firm for use by Baker & McKenzie. These documents provided legal advice to Connor as to Connor's compliance with the transfer pricing rules. After an in camera review of the documents, the judge denied the IRS's request for the production of the documents.[7]

The work product doctrine is the other protection against disclosure.[8] The doctrine applies to documents prepared in anticipation of, by, or for the party. The policy underlying the work product doctrine differs from that of the attorney-client privilege in that the former is concerned with protection of the adversary process, while the latter protects the attorney-client relationship. In short, the work product doctrine is intended to prevent one party's attorney from relying on the wits of the other party's lawyer to prepare his case.

The work product doctrine draws a zone of privacy around the lawyer's and his party's preparation of their case. Again, the doctrine does not protect the taxpayer's

---

[5] See *Upjohn Co. v. United States,* 449 U.S. 383 (1981), and *United States v. United Shoe Mach. Corp.,* 89 F. Supp. 357 (D. Mass. 1950).

[6] *United States v. Bell,* C 94-20342 RMW (No. D. Calif.) (Orders dated 11/9/94 and 12/14/94.) (Notice of appeal filed and withdrawn by the IRS.) *See also Adlman v. United States,* 95-2 USTC ¶50,579 (2d Cir. 1995) (Tax planning memorandum prepared by Big Six accounting firm for inside counsel had to be disclosed.)

[7] *Compare Skoog v. United States,* No. 94-H-340 (D. Colo.) (order dated 11/28/94), in which the District Court denied a motion to quash an IRS summons for records held by an accountant.

[8] *Hickman v. Taylor,* 329 U.S. 495 (1947), and *Hartz Mountain Ind. Inc. v. Commissioner,* 93 T.C. 521 (1989).

basic records and documents from discovery by the Service during the litigation process. The doctrine protects the materials that the taxpayer and their advisers prepare in anticipation of the controversy. The potential for litigation as to a particular issue should always be kept in mind, because it can protect documents prepared at the very initiation of a project if the Service's litigating propensity is known at that time.

These two doctrines should be taken into account in a taxpayer's factual development of its FSC case. First, all attorney-client privileged materials should be clearly identified as such by labeling the documents with a legend, such as

PRIVILEGED AND CONFIDENTIAL
ATTORNEY-CLIENT PRIVILEGE

Second, all work product documents also should be identified by stamping the documents with a legend, such as

ATTORNEY WORK PRODUCT
(NAME OF TAXPAYER)
(CASE NAME)
DOCKET NO. _____

Third, all documents relating to the litigation, including documents forwarded to and correspondence with counsel, should be segregated from the taxpayer's main files and neither commingled with other tax documents nor made available to individuals outside of the taxpayer. To the extent that taxpayer records are forwarded to counsel, the taxpayer should retain the originals in their normal location and place copies of those documents in its attorney-client file.

Fourth, to the extent that accounting, economic, and other outside experts are retained to assist in preparing the case, they should be retained directly by counsel to bring their activities within the various privileges. As noted earlier, care should be taken prior to disclosing privileged materials to testifying experts.

(d) Burden of Proof in an FSC Case

The taxpayer in a FSC case has the burden of going forward and demonstrating that its application of the FSC or DISC provisions to its entities was correct. This burden requires that the taxpayer identify the relevant law and marshall the facts in a way that will persuasively demonstrate to the court that its application of the law was correct. A FSC case does not typically involve the extraordinary burden of proof applicable to an IRC § 482 transfer pricing case, where the taxpayer has the burden both of demonstrating that the IRS's adjustment was arbitrary, capricious, and unreasonable, and of proving that what the taxpayer did was correct. This dual burden has resulted in substantial litigation in the transfer pricing area solely on the burden of proof issue.[9]

---

[9] *See National Semiconductor Corp v. Commissioner,* 61 T.C.M. (CCH) 2005 (1991), and *Yamaha Motor Corp. U.S.A. v. Commissioner,* 63 T.C.M. (CCH) 2176 (1992).

11.3 Choice of Judicial Forums

A taxpayer may have a choice of three different courts in which to litigate its FSC case. The taxpayer has the ability to attempt to resolve its FSC case with the IRS Appeals, notwithstanding docketing the case directly in court and not first protesting the proposed adjustment.[10] Nevertheless, the vast majority of all tax cases, including FSC cases, are docketed in and tried before the Tax Court. The following discussion highlights the differences between the various courts and the reasons that most cases are litigated in the Tax Court.

(a) Three Courts

The three courts in which FSC cases can be litigated are

1. the Tax Court,[11]
2. the United States Court of Federal Claims (the Claims Court),[12] and
3. the United States District Courts (the District Court).[13]

The Tax Court is more familiar with the IRS's controversy resolution procedures than the other two courts and is *likely to be more lenient* than other courts in delaying the onset of normal trial preparation while the case is pending before the Appeals Office. Nevertheless, if government counsel in a Claims Court or District Court case is willing to allow the Appeals Office to attempt to resolve the case, the courts will view it as a form of alternative dispute resolution, similar to mediation,

---

[10] *See* Rev. Proc. 87-24, 1987-1 C.B. 720.

[11] Major DISC and FSC cases heard by the Tax Court include: *McCoy Enterprises, Inc. v. Commissioner,* 58 F.3d 557 (10th Cir. 1995), *aff'g* 64 T.C.M. (CCH) 1449 (1992); *Brown-Forman Corp. Commissioner,* 955 F.2d 1037 (6th Cir. 1992), *aff'g* 94 T.C. 919 (1990), *cert. denied,* 113 S.Ct. 87 (1993); *Dresser Ind., Inc. v. Commissioner,* 911 F.2d 1128 (5th Cir. 1990), *rev'g* 92 T.C. 1276 (1989); *Addison Int'l Inc. v Commissioner,* 887 F.2d 660 (6th Cir. 1989), *aff'g* 90 T.C. 1207 (1988); *Gehl Co. v. Commissioner,* 795 F.2d 1324 (7th Cir. 1986), *rev'g* 49 T.C.M. (CCH) 372 (1984); *LeCroy Research Systems Corp. v. Commissioner,* 751 F.2d 123 (2d Cir. 1984), *aff'g* 47 T.C.M. (CCH) 1345 (1984); *CWT Farms, Inc. v. Commissioner,* 755 F.2d 790 (11th Cir. 1985), *aff'g* 79 T.C. 1054 (1982) and T.C. 86 (1982); *Bowater Inc. v. Commissioner,* 101 T.C. 207 (1993); *FMC Corp. v. Commissioner,* 100 T.C. 595 (1993); *Garnac Grain Co. v. Commissioner,* 95 T.C. 7 (1990); *Advance Int'l, Inc. v. Commissioner,* 91 T.C. 445 (1988); *Foley Machinery Co. v. Commissioner,* 91 T.C. 434 (1988); *Gibbons Int'l, Inc. v. Commissioner,* 89 T.C. 1156 (1987); *Sam Goldberger, Inc. v. Commissioner,* 88 T.C. 1532 (1987); *Bentley Laboratories, Inc. v. Commissioner,* 77 T.C. 152 (1981); *Arrow Fastener Co. v. Commissioner,* 76 T.C. 423 (1981); *Longview Fibre Co. v. Commissioner,* 71 T.C. 357 (1978); and *Steiner v. Commissioner,* 69 T.C.M. (CCH) 2176 (1995).

[12] Major DISC and FSC cases heard by the Claims Court's immediate predecessor, the United States Claims Court, include *Dow Corning Corp. v. United States,* 984 F.2d 416 (Fed. Cir. 1992), *aff'g* 90-2 USTC ¶50,359 (Cl. Ct. 1990); *Thomas Int'l, Ltd. v. United States,* 773 F.2d 300 (Fed. Cir. 1985), *rev'g* 6 Cl. Ct. 414 (1984); and *Anchor Hocking Corp. v. United States,* 11 Cl. Ct. 173 (1986).

[13] The DISC and FSC cases heard by the United States District Courts include *Archer-Daniels-Midland Co. v. United States,* 37 F.3d 311 (7th Cir. 1994), *rev'g* 798 F. Supp. 505 (C.D. Il. 1992); *Polychrome Int'l Corp. v. Krigger,* 5 F.3d 1522 (3rd Cir. 1993), *rev'g* unreported decision; *L&F Int'l Sales Corp. v. United States,* 912 F.2d 377 (9th Cir. 1990), *aff'g* unreported decision; *Naporano v. United States,* 834 F. Supp. 694 (N.J. 1995); and *National Electrostatics Corp. v. United States,* 93-1 USTC ¶50,336 (W.D. Wis. 1993).

and allow time to complete that process. Strategies for dealing with the Appeals Office, including when to proceed to the Appeals Office before docketing a case in court, is beyond the scope of this chapter.

At this time, the most significant difference between the courts is that a taxpayer can litigate its FSC case in the Tax Court without having first paid the deficiency proposed by the Service. In contrast, the taxpayer is required to have paid the deficiency resulting from the FSC adjustment and sue for a refund of those taxes in order to use either the Claims Court or the District Court. Furthermore, if the taxpayer has already paid the tax resulting from a FSC adjustment, the taxpayer will be limited to obtaining a refund of the tax through the Claims Court or the District Court and will not be able to utilize the Tax Court.

(b) Impact of "Hot Interest"

The large adjustments that can be proposed by the Service magnify the benefit to a taxpayer of being able to file in the Tax Court without prepayment of the deficiency.[14] Nevertheless, the "hot interest" rates may cause more taxpayers to consider seriously docketing their cases in the Claims Court or the District Court instead of in the Tax Court. The Service has published procedures to enable a taxpayer to stop the running of interest on a proposed deficiency in light of the over-market rate of interest imposed on underpayment in general, and on large corporate underpayment with respect to procedures to stop the accrual of interest. The premium "hot interest" rate is 5 percentage points over the federal short-term rate.

(c) Jury Trials

The actual judicial procedures of the three courts are becoming more alike than they are different and should not be a major factor in choosing between the courts. One difference in procedure is that a taxpayer can obtain a jury trial of the FSC issue in the District Court, but not in the Tax Court or the Claims Court. This difference is unlikely to be of much significance, because few taxpayers will be willing to try a sophisticated FSC case before a jury.

(d) Comparison of Three Courts

In comparing the three courts, a taxpayer should consider the specific FSC precedent available on the issues that are likely to arise. Because the Tax Court has handled the vast majority of the current FSC cases, it has developed a substantial body of published and unpublished procedural rules applicable to the preparation and trial of the FSC case[15] that do not exist in the Claims Court. In addition, the Tax Court has published numerous FSC and DISC opinions and would look to those opinions first in ruling in new cases. The taxpayer should also consider the

---

[14] IRC § 6621(c), Rev. Proc. 84-58, 1984-2 CB 501.

[15] *See* discussion hereafter with respect to the Tax Court's pre-trial order and related rulings.

Appellate Court precedent applicable to the trial court under consideration. For the Tax Court, the taxpayer must review the precedent in the United States Court of Appeals Circuit to which the taxpayer's case would be appealed.[16] The Claims Court would look first to its precedent and then to the precedent in the United States Court of Appeals for the Federal Circuit.

Traditionally, the taxpayer could try a FSC case most quickly and efficiently before the Tax Court, mostly because of the streamlined procedures of the Tax Court, which focused on a stipulation-of-fact process rather than contentious discovery activities. In light of the increased discovery and motion practice in the Tax Court, some of this time differential may disappear. The Tax Court itself, however, is committed to moving large cases through the court as quickly as possible and is developing new procedures to streamline the litigation of large, fact-intensive cases.

As indicated earlier, discovery and other rules in the Claims Court and the District Courts were traditionally more extensive than in the Tax Court, particularly as to the taking of depositions. Although the Tax Court has not yet formally amended its rules, Tax Court judges are forcefully encouraging the parties to agree to depositions, even in those circumstances where the rules would not otherwise require allowing a deposition.[17] To achieve its desired goals of obtaining depositions of employees of the taxpayer, the Tax Court, for example, can simply schedule an evidentiary hearing involving the employees and thus bypass the normal prohibitions of the Tax Court Rules regarding party depositions.

Finally, because the Tax Court is a specialized court dealing solely with federal tax issues, its judges are also tax specialists and are likely to be more sophisticated in tax and financial matters than judges on the Claims Court and, especially, on the District Court. Because of the potentially complicated factual nature of large FSC cases, the sophistication of the Tax Court is likely to be of benefit. This focus on federal tax matters may not impact to any degree the caliber of the government attorneys with which the taxpayer would be dealing. The taxpayer would work with the Service's Chief Counsel lawyers in the Tax Court and Department of Justice tax lawyers in the Claims Court and District Courts. This sophistication may increase the Chief Counsel lawyers' ability to represent their client; it also makes it easier to resolve various issues, including settling the case. In a refund situation, such as would exist in either the Claims Court or the District Court, the government counsel would be viewed as giving something back, rather than collecting something, and may not be as focused on settling the issues.

11.4   Tax Court FSC Litigation

In making the decision to docket the FSC issue in court, the taxpayer still has various decisions to make regarding the methodology. Because taxpayers most fre-

---

[16]*Golsen v. Commissioner,* 54 T.C. 742 (1970), *aff'd,* 445 F.2d 985 (10th Cir.), *cert. denied,* 404 U.S. 940 (1971).

[17] *See* concurring opinion of Judge Swift in *Ash v. Commissioner,* 96 T.C. 459 (1991).

quently litigate their FSC and other cases before the Tax Court, the following discussion focuses on the Tax Court and its rules.

(a) Basic Characteristics

The Tax Court has published its own set of Tax Court Rules, but the Federal Rules of Civil Procedure apply in the absence of a specific Tax Court rule.[18] Furthermore, the Federal Rules of Evidence apply to all trials.[19]

The principal difference between the Tax Court and the other two federal courts that hear federal income tax cases is the Tax Court's commitment to the parties' negotiating and agreeing upon a comprehensive stipulation of all matters not privileged that are relevant to the pending case. Historically, this requirement to prepare a complete stipulation of fact, coupled with the Tax Court's relative informality as compared with the Claims Court or the District Courts, resulted in less contentious and adversarial litigation than in the other courts. The Claims Court has abandoned the stipulation process as too burdensome and unworkable. In light of recent problems in the Tax Court's stipulation process, changes in that procedure may also be necessary. In certain circumstances, it may add to the contentiousness of trial preparation, rather than to the efficiency of the entire process.

The Tax Court is located in Washington, D.C., and generally has nineteen judges, nine senior judges, and fourteen special trial judges. The Tax Court trials are conducted throughout the United States during typically two-week trial schedules. Large tax cases, such as a FSC case, may be placed on a special trial calendar, at the request of either the parties or of the judge, and may be heard in Washington, D.C., notwithstanding the request of the taxpayer regarding a place of trial.

(b) Pleadings: The Initial Outline of the Case

At the conclusion of the examination, or of Appeals Office consideration of the FSC adjustment, the Service prepares a Notice of Deficiency or 90-Day Letter, which it issues to the taxpayer concerning the FSC adjustment. The notice will set forth the Service's description of the FSC adjustment and its computation of the tax liability resulting from that adjustment. In recent years, the Service's description has become quite general, and the best understanding of the adjustment is gained through a close review of the actual computation of the adjustment.

The taxpayer has 90 days from the date on which the notice is mailed within which to file a petition with the Tax Court asking for a redetermination of the deficiency set forth in the notice.[20] Pursuant to Tax Court Rule 34, the petition must comply with the form attached to the Tax Court's Rules, describe the errors made by the Service in the determination of the deficiency, and set forth clearly the facts

---

[18] Tax Court Rule 1.

[19] Tax Court Rule 143 and IRC § 7453.

[20] § 6213 (a).

on which the petitioner bases its assignments of error. The petition typically constitutes the Tax Court's first involvement in the case and should be viewed as an opportunity to begin to educate the court as to the detailed facts relating to the FSC transaction. In this regard, a petitioner should consider the preparation of a complete and detailed petition that clearly frames the FSC issue to be faced by the court.

The taxpayer should file a designation of place of trial with the court at the time of filing its petition. The petition should designate where the taxpayer would prefer the trial to be held. If the petitioner does not file such a request, the Service can do so at the time of filing its answer. The parties by motion can request a change in the place of trial, or the court on its own motion can change the place of trial.

The Service has 60 days from the date of the service of the petition within which to file an answer to the petition. The answer should advise the court and the petitioner fully of the nature of the Service's defense of the notice of deficiency and must respond specifically to each material allegation in the petition. Every material allegation in the petition that is not expressly admitted or denied is deemed admitted for purposes of the case.[21]

The petitioner has 45 days from the date of service of the answer within which to file a reply to the answer. Although not typically filed, respondent should respond to any allegations made by the Service with respect to issues for which the Service has the burden of proof.[22] The petitioner has only 30 days from the date of service within which to file a motion with respect to the Service's answer. The most common motion that should be considered for a large FSC case is a Motion for More Definite Statement, as provided in Tax Court Rule 51, if the Service's answer does not properly respond to the factual allegations set forth in the petition.

Any affirmative allegations of fact contained in the answer that are not expressly admitted or denied are deemed admitted for purposes of the case. If a reply is not filed, any material allegations are deemed denied unless the Service, within 45 days after expiration of the time for filing the reply, files a motion asking that the affirmative allegations be specifically admitted. New material contained in the answer is deemed denied.

(c) Pre-Trial Orders

The Tax Court has aggressively been taking control of the large cases filed in the court, including handling the cases on a last-in, first-out basis. One of the most significant means by which the court is managing these cases is the early issuance of a pre-trial order to the parties to begin to frame and narrow the issues and to set a rapid schedule for discovery and trial.

The typical pre-trial order includes provisions similar to the following, after the parties begin the stipulation of fact process. The parties must prepare pre-trial memoranda and file them with the court, outlining:

---

[21] Tax Court Rule 36.

[22] *See* Tax Court Rule 37.

1. The facts to be stipulated, identifying any issues likely to be unable to be stipulated;
2. The legal authority relevant to the case pending before the court;
3. A statement of the facts to be proved;
4. A proposed timetable for discovery that has been agreed upon by the parties;
5. A list of the witnesses expected to be called;
6. A description of any evidentiary problems expected to be encountered during trial;
7. A proposed list of agreed upon trial dates; and
8. A realistic estimate of the time required to try the case.

Counsel must participate in a pre-trial conference with the court to review the pre-trial memorandum in detail, on the record.

Through its issuance of its pre-trial orders, the Tax Court is taking greater control of the entire pre-trial process, including greater oversight of the discovery and stipulation-of-facts processes. Furthermore, the parties may be required to agree to stipulate documents during the discovery phase of the pre-trial period and to agree upon the textual portion of the stipulation closer to the trial date.

(d) Motion for Summary Judgment

In a case in which the facts are not substantially in controversy, a taxpayer should consider the use of a Motion for Summary Judgment under Rule 121. In *W.L. Gore & Associates Inc. v. Commissioner*[23] a motion was filed for summary judgment as to the question of whether the petitioner controlled a Japanese affiliate. The motion indicated that, in the alternative, if the first motion was denied, the IRS had the burden of proving that the Japanese subsidiary was in fact controlled by the petitioner. In an opinion filed on March 7, 1995, the Tax Court denied the petitioner's motion for summary judgment, finding that there were sufficient areas of potential factual dispute for the case to proceed to trial.

11.5 Discovery

The time between the filing of the initial pleadings and the actual trial is used for the development of the stipulation of facts and the discovery of the relevant facts. This discovery process is basically a one-way street, because the taxpayer possesses most of the facts and must respond to the Service's various discovery requests. This process has become much more contentious and comprehensive. The Tax Court encourages the parties to engage in informal discovery before invoking

---

[23] T.C. Memo. 1995–96, Docket No. 15476-93, filed March 7, 1995.

the court's formalized discovery tools. For this purpose, the stipulation of facts is not a discovery device but, instead, a method to narrow the issues and shorten trial time.

(a)   Informal Tax Court Discovery

Discovery typically begins with the Service's mailing to counsel for the petitioner a letter, plus attachments, asking counsel to respond to an extensive set of questions, with multiple subparts, and to a broad request for documents. These requests are referred to as "Branerton requests," after the Tax Court's opinion in *Branerton Corp. v. Commissioner.*[24] The taxpayer is required to deal with these questions in good faith and to begin the discovery process at this time. In fact, these requests are merely the first stage in an overwhelming wave of discovery that will occur prior to trial. The taxpayer can utilize the Branerton process to obtain information from the Service's administrative files and to clarify its FSC rationale.

(b)   Freedom of Information Act Requests

A taxpayer may wish to consider using a request under the Freedom of Information Act guidelines for certain documents that may be relevant to the litigation, but which may not be readily produced by the Service's counsel. A taxpayer should consider, at the end of its examination, filing a request under the authority of the Freedom of Information Act to review the Service's administrative file as to the pending or just completed examination. Such a request can force the Service to reveal documents and other information that it may have relied on as part of the development of the transfer pricing adjustment, including documents obtained in third-party summons activities.

(c)   Alternative IRS Strategies to Gather Facts

The taxpayer should be sensitive to the Service's using other informal, non-Tax Court procedures to attempt to develop facts to use in the FSC case. These activities include use of its inherent examination powers. The Service's use of these 2 discovery avenues has recently been the subject of extensive litigation and discussion.[25]

In *Universal Mfg. Co. v. Commissioner,* the Tax Court held that information obtained as a result of an administrative summons issued during a concurrent criminal investigation could not be introduced as evidence in a pending civil tax proceeding. The extent to which the Tax Court would exclude information obtained by the Service pursuant to an administrative summons was recently tested in *Ash v. Commissioner.* In the *Ash* opinion, the Tax Court, with two concurring opinions,

---

[24] 64 T.C. 191 (1975).

[25] *See Westreco, Inc. v. Commissioner,* 60 T.C.M. (CCH) 589 (1990), appeal to 6th Circuit dismissed.

refused to issue a protective order to exclude evidence obtained in an administrative summons issued prior to the petition's being filed in the Tax Court. The court limited the normal situation in which it will issue a protective order, to an administrative summons issued to the same taxpayer and for the same taxable year after filing the petition. The Service can avoid a protective order even in this narrow situation if it establishes a sufficient reason, independent of the pending litigation, for issuing a summons.

11.6 Formal Tax Court Discovery Activities

The Tax Court Rules contain a variety of formalized discovery devices. These devices include interrogatories, requests for the production of documents and things, depositions for discovery purposes with and without the consent of the parties, and dispositions of experts. As pointed out below in a later subsection of this chapter, the Tax Court Rules provide for very limited use of depositions. As a result, the Service typically issues hundreds of interrogatories and production requests in large FSC cases. The Tax Court to date has not limited this type of discovery.

Each of these formal discovery techniques is addressed in the following paragraphs, within the context of a FSC case.

(a) Interrogatories

Pursuant to Tax Court Rule 71, either party may issue written interrogatories to be answered by the person served. In FSC cases, hundreds of interrogatories can be issued by the Service, requiring substantial effort to respond in a complete and timely fashion. Each individual interrogatory must be separately answered, or the objection to the interrogatory stated in lieu of an answer.

A party must file its answers and objections to the other party within 45 days of the service of the interrogatories. Although the process has now become more formalized, discussions with opposing counsel as to the proposed response or problems in responding can materially simplify the procedure and potentially reduce the effort to respond. Tax Court Rule 71 also authorizes the use of interrogatories to ask questions of the other party's experts.

(b) Production of Documents and Things

Pursuant to Tax Court Rule 72, a party may request another party to produce or permit the inspection and copying of documents and other physical things and to permit entry onto designated property or other property, including the inspection of buildings. The Service uses Tax Court Rule 72 to require taxpayers to produce all relevant documents and samples of products, to allow the Service to visit plants and other facilities, and to review manufacturing and other operations. Copies of documents are typically satisfactory in response to a document production request.

A taxpayer needs to monitor carefully the documents turned over, including the initial source of the documents, to be in the position of authenticating the documents at a later date during trial. The receiving party must serve a written response within 30 days, responding to the various requests either by agreeing to the requests, offering alternative arrangements, or objecting to them.

(c) Defenses to Formal Discovery Requests

Pursuant to Tax Court Rule 70(b), the court's rules regarding the scope of "relevance" is quite broad and, therefore, most requests must be answered. Only the most irrelevant discovery requests will be limited as a result of an assertion that the interrogatory or production request asks for "irrelevant" materials.[26]

The petitioner, however, may nevertheless properly object to particularly burdensome or onerous requests. Such objections should be set forth in the taxpayer's written response to an interrogatory or production request. The requesting party can then determine whether to file a motion with the Tax Court asking it to rule on adequacy of the responses and the objections made, and asking the court to direct that the discovery request be answered.

The Tax Court will not order compliance with discovery requests that are overly broad or burdensome. Upon receipt of such a request, the responding party may merely state its objection in a written response or contact the requesting party to attempt to limit voluntarily the scope of the request. Because of the tremendous number of requests that can arise in a FSC case, if opposing counsel has shown any willingness to limit the scope of its requests, then an offer to work together to obtain the information properly discoverable should be attempted. Offers to undertake sampling or other methods of responding to overly broad or burdensome requests should be attempted.

Simple inconvenience will not be sufficient to overcome the other party's right to have the interrogatory answered or the documents produced; the party receiving the request must be prepared to describe to the Tax Court judge its problems with complying with the requests. In certain circumstances, it may be appropriate to require the Service to provide its own copying and other services or to charge the Service if the costs of complying with its requests become burdensome.

The attorney-client privilege and work product doctrine[27] may also be properly used to withhold documents falling within the scope of a discovery request. In most FSC cases, both parties have submitted discovery requests that have resulted in the assertion of either or both of the document privileges. Furthermore, as a result of a party's motion to produce the privileged documents, the documents have been submitted to the judge for his or her *in camera* inspection of the documents for purposes of complying with the requirements of the privileges.

---

[26] *See,* for example, *Rosenfeld v. Commissioner,* 82 T.C. 105 (1984).

[27] *See Hartz Mountain Industries, Inc. v. Commissioner,* 93 T.C. 521 (1989).

(d) Depositions

The Tax Court traditionally allowed depositions to preserve testimony, but did not encourage the use of depositions as a regular discovery device. The Tax Court's Rules with respect to the use of depositions for discovery purposes provide that the deposition of either a party or a non-party may be taken with the consent of parties.[28] If the deponent is a non-party, written notice of the deposition must be filed with the deponent, who then has 15 days within which to file an objection to the deposition.

The Tax Court Rules provide that depositions may be used for discovery purposes without the consent of the other party only as "an extraordinary method of discovery and may be used only where a non-party witness can give testimony or possesses documents that . . . practicably cannot be obtained through informal consultation or communication. . . ."[29] No deposition of a party is allowed under this rule unless a party-deponent agrees. This rule has received very careful consideration by the Tax Court during the various FSC cases. The Tax Court judges utilized their skills of persuasion to allow a limited number of party depositions to be held for discovery purposes. The need to encourage the use of both consensual and nonconsensual depositions was emphasized by Judge Swift, particularly as to large, complicated cases, such as transfer pricing cases. As a result of the *active* encouragement of Tax Court judges, counsel for taxpayers in several recent cases have agreed to limited "nonconsensual" depositions, including the number of such depositions, their subject matter, and similar items.[30]

Tax Court Rule 76 provides for the deposition of expert witnesses with the consent of all parties, and the deposition of expert witnesses without the consent of the parties as an "extraordinary method of discovery," requiring an order of the court. To the extent that the court believes that deposing an expert witness prior to trial will assist the parties in preparing for trial and the court in resolving the case, the court is likely to grant such an order.

(e) Trade Secrets and Other Confidential Information

IRC § 6103 causes information concerning the taxpayer given to the IRS to be treated as "tax return" information. Improper disclosure by the IRS or by its contractors or experts is subject to substantial penalties.[31] Information requested by the IRS during discovery can include highly confidential trade secrets, including manufacturing technology and financial data. Pursuant to Tax Court Rule 103, counsel for the petitioner should enter into a closing agreement with IRS counsel, setting forth the guidelines for protection and use of the confidential information.

---

[28] Tax Court Rule 74.

[29] Tax Court Rule 75.

[30] *See Ash v. Commissioner,* 96 T.C. 459, 479–481 (1991), concerning opinion by Judge Swift.

[31] *See* O'Brien and Cunningham, "Protecting Against the Disclosure of Trade Secrets to Independent Experts and Third Party Witnesses During an Internal Revenue Service Examination," *Tax Executive* 44:99.

(f) Narrowing the Issues

A unique aspect of Tax Court litigation is the stipulation of fact procedure set forth in Rule 91. This procedure reflects the Tax Court's historic goal that the parties work together to prepare a comprehensive, complete stipulation of the facts in order to assist the court in handling the case and to reduce trial time and controversy between the parties. The court continues to encourage the stipulation process, although it is becoming more difficult to use in large, complex cases, such as FSC cases. The process of stipulation requires both parties to agree. If they cannot, for whatever reason, a meaningful stipulation may not be prepared. It also can be so replete with evidentiary objections that the proof required to admit the documents may defeat most of the benefit of the stipulation in the first place.

The typical stipulation is a written agreement signed by both parties and filed with the court prior to the start of trial, including the stipulated documents. In the stipulation, the paragraphs are numbered and one matter is stated per paragraph. Documents relevant to the matter contained in a paragraph are separately numbered and attached to the stipulation. The parties attempt to resolve any evidentiary issues as to the documents, prior to stipulating them, but may state relevancy, hearsay, or other objections in the stipulation.

When FSC cases are basically fact cases, the stipulation can become a voluminous agreement, with potentially thousands of documents. Care should be taken to stipulate only relevant documents, but in the pressure of trial deadlines, a "kitchen sink" approach has been seen in some FSC cases. If time permits, the court's assistance in the stipulation process can be helpful. Because of the importance of the stipulation process, the court may attempt to require counsel to prepare and submit to the court at least a preliminary stipulation months before the scheduled trial date.

Facts contained in the stipulation are taken as admitted for all purposes of the trial. Thus, a party must be careful not to "stipulate itself out of court" as a result of the stipulation of an adverse fact.[32]

(g) Requests for Admissions

The Tax Court treats requests for admissions as part of the process of proving facts prior to trial, in the same way that the stipulation of facts narrows and simplifies the trial. Pursuant to Tax Court Rule 90, a party may file a request for admissions after it has attempted and failed to obtain the agreement to the fact informally with the other party. Thereafter, the party may serve on the other party a written request setting forth in separated paragraphs the nonprivileged, relevant matters that were to be admitted for purposes of this case. Each matter is deemed admitted unless, within 30 days, the party to whom the request was directed re-

---

[32] *See Ball v. Commissioner,* 47 T.C.M. (CCH) 1684, 1690–91 (1984).

sponds. The party must respond in writing, admitting the matter in whole or in part, asserting that the matter cannot be admitted or denied and explaining the reasons, or objecting to the request and explaining the reasons.

The request for admissions process has been extremely helpful in FSC cases to clarify the Service's position, both on the facts and on the law.

(h) Motions *in Limine*

The use of motions *in limine* to resolve various issues relating to the scope of trial has increased as a result of the size and complexity of FSC cases. For example, it may be helpful to the court to limit the evidence that can be offered to the taxable years before the court and earlier, rather than to all taxable years, including the current taxable year. A general motion to obtain the court's assistance in achieving the goals of a narrowly focused trial can be very helpful.

(i) Expert Witnesses

The Tax Court is not totally comfortable with the role of expert witnesses and is considering changes in their role. For example, the parties typically have not been able to depose the opposing parties' experts prior to trial. The Tax Court has allowed the parties to depose experts in several recent cases in order to help narrow the issues and improve the development of information during the trial (see Rule 76). In addition, the Tax Court generally has adopted the expert's report as the expert's direct testimony and allowed cross-examination to begin almost immediately without any expert direct testimony. Direct testimony by an expert witness may better assist in understanding the expert's position.

The expert witnesses in an FSC case can include (1) an accounting expert and (2) an industry expert. Multiple experts in these various categories may be required, depending on the particular transaction. The accounting expert would be expected to testify as to product line or other profit split and comparable transactions. The increased emphasis on various economic ratios as set forth in the recently finalized Treasury Regulations under IRC § 482 may increase the role and need for accounting assistance. The industry expert would be expected to testify as to the industry context in which the transaction occurs, such as whether a particular activity constitutes "manufacturing" within the industry.

Each of these experts is likely to file both an original report and a rebuttal report. Under the appropriate circumstances, an expert may file only a rebuttal report as to the other party's expert reports, rather than a main report on his or her own behalf. Counsel must be careful in respect to maintaining the attorney-client privilege and work product doctrine during the preparation of the case so as to limit the information that must be disclosed to the opposing party at the time of the exchange of expert reports. For this reason, it may be helpful in a large FSC case to retain an expert who is scheduled to testify and a second expert who would work closely with the trial team in putting together the actual trial strategy and determining how the testifying expert fits into it.

When the expert reports are exchanged, the experts must disclose and make available to the opposing party information they relied on that would not otherwise be in the possession of the other party. These documents will consist principally of underlying work papers and documents that were either prepared by the expert or provided to the expert by the taxpayer's counsel.

(j) Preparation for Trial

During the final two months before trial, the court will require the filing of the stipulation of facts, the exchange of expert witness reports and rebuttal reports, the exchange of trial memoranda, including witness lists, and identification and resolution of any procedural or evidentiary issues.

11.7   Trial of a FSC Case

The trial of a FSC case is similar to the trial of most other fact-intensive Tax Court cases. It requires tremendous preparation to make a coherent presentation to the Tax Court judge of the evidence developed, which will consist of the stipulation of facts and related exhibits, any requests for admissions, and factual and expert testimony. This presentation must be fitted within the legal framework applicable to the case being made.

(a) Presentation of Petitioner's Case

A clear presentation is particularly important in a FSC case, because the taxpayer has an extraordinary burden of proof to overcome in order to prevail in the Tax Court. Thus, counsel for the petitioner must carefully organize his or her presentation to the judge in order to educate the judge as to the underlying economic framework applicable to the taxpayer's transactions and to the taxpayer's unique facts that fit into that framework. Furthermore, the various fact and expert witnesses must be well prepared to present clearly and succinctly the critical facts necessary to carry the taxpayer's burden. It should be remembered that if the Service is successful in confusing the facts presented to the court, the taxpayer's chances of prevailing are materially reduced.

Potential objections must be anticipated and dealt with quickly and efficiently so as to avoid the creation of any doubts. In this regard, it may be helpful to err on the side of assisting the Service in its attempt to develop and understand the facts, rather than to leave it to blindly struggle until the last date, when the court is likely to allow the Service extra leeway to get prepared.

The IRS in several recent cases has attempted to use the Tax Court's subpoena powers under Rule 147 to gather and develop potentially relevant third-party comparable information. It is unclear how effective this procedure will be in gathering information that would be credible evidence for use during a trial, particularly where the recipient of the subpoena does not cooperate with the issuer of the subpoena.

(b) Demonstrative Evidence

Physical evidence, such as product samples or models, is admissible under the normal rules of evidence. It is important to give the opposing party notice of the intent to introduce such evidence so as to provide that party with access to the evidence prior to its admittance. Prior arrangements with the Tax Court may be required in order to schedule its delivery to the appropriate Tax Court courtroom.

Certain large FSC cases may require the presentation of the relevant "functions" involved in an intercompany transaction. If the sale of a manufactured product is involved, video or other pictorial evidence may be helpful in demonstrating the taxpayer's operations to the judge. With proper notice to the opposing party and care to meet foundational requirements, this type of evidence is admissible in the Tax Court. The opposing counsel may request access to the original site in order to determine the fairness of the video or pictures. The judge can be invited to tour a site personally but generally will not do so for budgetary and other reasons. A video or picture is also likely to be preferred because it gives the party control over the evidentiary presentation. Even if some types of demonstrative evidence do not satisfy admissibility requirements, the demonstrative evidence may nonetheless be used to help explain a witness' testimony. In a bench trial, the difference between full admissibility and the ability to use demonstrative evidence to help explain testimony is often blurred.

Charts, graphs, and other summary evidence may be admissible under the rules of evidence as summaries pursuant to Rule 1006 of the Federal Rules of Evidence. This type of summary evidence can be very helpful in a FSC case, because it helps to simplify and explain the evidence presented. Because of the natural advantage that the taxpayer has over the facts, the taxpayer must be careful to make available to the Service the originals or duplicates of the voluminous documents being summarized at a reasonable time and place. This rule requires that the Service be given access to these documents sufficiently ahead of the introduction of the evidence so that the accuracy of the evidence can be tested, if desired. If the Service refuses to stipulate to the summary evidence, the taxpayer must be prepared to meet the foundational requirements of admissibility under Rule 1006 of the Federal Rules of Evidence.

(c) Proof of Foreign Law

The Tax Court has tended to treat the proof of foreign law as a question of law for which the Tax Court is not required to take judicial notice. The court can consider any relevant material including the testimony of an expert witness on foreign law. As provided in Tax Court Rule 146, the party intending to raise an issue of foreign law must give notice to the other party. While the timing of giving notice is not specified, it must be reasonable in the context of the difficulty of proving foreign law. The issue of the proof of foreign law can become relevant in a FSC case as a result of the need to establish the application of foreign law to various intercompany transactions.

(d)   Post-Trial Activities: Briefing

Typically, in Tax Court cases, simultaneous opening briefs are required 75 days after conclusion of the trial, with simultaneous answering briefs due 45 days thereafter.[33] Because of the size and complexity of most FSC cases, the court will grant extensions of time to file both briefs at the conclusion of trial.

Recently, the Tax Court ordered seriatim briefs in one large case to focus the issues. The opening brief was due three months after the close of trial, the answering brief 60 days thereafter, and the reply brief 30 days after the answering brief. While the Tax Court has not typically set page limits on the size of briefs that can be filed in a FSC case, the Tax Court recently indicated its intent to limit significantly the number of pages allowed in the briefs to force the party to focus on the most important facts.

(e)   Opinion and Rule 155 Computation

After the filing of the briefs, the court takes the case under advisement. Completion of the Tax Court Rule 155 computation will occur following the court's issuance of its opinion. Few issues should arise as to Rule 155, unless the court modifies the transaction in a way that does not easily convert into a tax computation.

(f)   Appeal of Tax Court Decision

A notice of appeal from a Tax Court decision must be filed within 90 days after the decision has been entered. A bond must be posted with the Tax Court in an amount double the amount of the deficiency on or before the date the notice of appeal is filed. Appeal is to the United States Court of Appeals where the corporation has its principal office or where a noncorporate taxpayer has its legal residence.

11.8   Alternatives to a Full Tax Court Trial

The Tax Court has been exploring various methods of handling complicated and large tax cases, such as FSC cases. As indicated earlier, the court is exploring the use of mini-trials to resolve certain critical factual or legal issues, which might then result in the parties's being able to resolve the case.

(a)   Mini-Trial

The Tax Court is considering different means of resolving large cases. One method being considered seriously involves a mini-trial. The purpose of a mini-trial is to resolve a very narrow factual or other question that may be the key to re-

---

[33] *See* Tax Court Rule 151.

solving the larger overall issues being presented to the court. Other creative means to narrow the issues in large FSC cases are likely to be proposed both formally and informally by the court.

(b)   Arbitration

Pursuant to Rule 124, the Tax Court has been encouraging the use of arbitration as a means of resolving transfer pricing and other large, fact-intensive cases. Rule 124, which provides for voluntary binding arbitration, has been used in a dozen or more valuation cases during the past several years. It is being used in one large FSC case and is being considered in other cases. Two aspects of Rule 124 may discourage the use of arbitration. The first is that it must be voluntarily agreed upon by the parties; the Tax Court cannot order the parties to participate in an arbitration proceeding. The second is that it is binding; no appeal or other review of the arbitration proceeding is allowed. Changes in these two aspects of Rule 124 may be proposed by the Tax Court and could result in additional arbitration proceedings.

One transfer pricing case that has been resolved through arbitration involves Apple Computer, Inc. (Apple). On March 5, 1992, the parties filed a joint motion for voluntary binding arbitration and a 40-page stipulation in *Apple Computer, Inc. v. Commissioner*.[34] In summary, the terms of this voluntary binding arbitration were as follows:

1. The issue submitted was framed in terms of the income that Apple's Singapore subsidiary would have earned at arm's length;

2. Each party had to submit its single income amount for each of the taxable years two months prior to the scheduled date of the commencement of the arbitration;

3. The parties could not amend or change the income amount once it has been submitted (i.e., "baseball" arbitration);

4. A three-member arbitration panel was chosen, consisting of a retired federal judge, an industry expert, and an economic expert;

5. Discovery under Tax Court Rules was allowed, except that the Tax Court's pleadings, Apple's tax returns, and other evidence of the parties' prearbitration positions were not to be admitted;

6. The parties were each to make an industry presentation, file limited pre-trial memoranda, and put on direct fact and expert witnesses; and

7. The findings of the board (one income amount per year from those offered by the parties) were to be filed within 30 days, to contain no support, to be final, and to have no value as a precedent.

It will be interesting to determine the effect of this procedure on the manner in which the Tax Court handles FSC cases. Arbitration will be a useful alternative to

---

[34] T.C. No. 21871-90.

a full Tax Court trial if it reduces the overwhelming cost of document production and discovery of a full trial and forcefully encourages the parties to settle the case prior to a full presentation of the facts.

The arbitrators in *Apple Computer, Inc. v. Commissioner*[35] reached a decision during September 1993 in the binding arbitration, selecting IRS's arbitration numbers over the Apple Computer Inc.'s arbitration numbers in this "baseball" arbitration proceeding for each of the taxable years before the panel and transmitted those numbers to the Tax Court. The hearing before the arbitrators began on July 6, 1993, and could last no more than 60 calendar days or 30 hearing days. Thus, the arbitrators' decision was issued within a month of the conclusion of the formal hearing proceedings. Based on this initial binding arbitration proceeding under the Tax Court's Rules of Practice and Procedure, the most significant difference between the trial of a transfer pricing case and the arbitration of that same case appears to be in the prompt issuance of the arbitrators' decision and the absence of an opinion that could be used as precedence in other taxable years.

As compared with the arbitrators' action in the *Apple Computer, Inc.* case, the Tax Court issued a 167-page opinion in *Perkin-Elmer Corp. v. Commissioner,* approximately 25 months after the trial of the case. Discovery and related trial preparation activities appear to have been reasonably comparable. Costs are also quite similar, with the savings on extensive briefing balanced by the high costs of the arbitrators themselves.

In *Fujitsu America Inc. v. Commissioner,* No. 2954-91, the Tax Court approved a stipulation of binding arbitration between the taxpayer and the IRS that would become effective if the parties are unable to resolve the case through the competent authority procedures. Thus, in the event that the competent authority officials cannot resolve the case, the case will be submitted to binding arbitration.

The European Union's (EU) Arbitration Convention became effective on January 1, 1995, providing for binding arbitration to resolve intra-EU transfer pricing disputes. It will be interesting to watch how this procedure works in actual practice, because it also could herald an increased use of arbitration as an alternate dispute resolution process.

(c) Mediation

While the Tax Court has not adopted formal mediation rules, the Tax Court continues to support strongly the use of mediation to resolve transfer pricing cases. The IRS has assisted this process by issuing Announcement 95-86,[36] in which the IRS published procedures to be used by taxpayers to request mediation for certain issues that are pending in an IRS Appeals Office and not docketed in any court. The Announcement established a one-year trial of the mediation resolution process, beginning on October 30, 1995.

---

[35] T.C. Docket No. 21871-90 (stipulation filed 9/22/93).

[36] 1995-44 I.R.B. at 27.

The IRS Chief Counsel's Office in November 1995 indicated that in an appropriate case, it will entertain requests from taxpayers for mediation of issues in docketed court cases, if such issues have not already been subject to mediation before the Appeals Office. Mediation is the intervention of an individual who attempts to work with both parties to identify the actual issues in controversy and thereafter to find common ground for their resolving those issues short of a full trial.

Resolving a case prior to a full trial has generally been the part of the mission of the Appeals Office, which has done a good job and will continue to play a significant role in this regard. The importance of the new procedures, whether mediation or the efforts of the Appeals Office, is that they provide a reality check for both the taxpayer and the Service prior to the trial of an issue.

11.9 Conclusion

As stated initially, the goal is to settle rather than to litigate a FSC case. Being willing to litigate that case and being familiar with the rules applicable to such litigation, however, is critical to achieving the optimum settlement.

Large cases continue to be docketed, and the Tax Court continues to explore ways to reduce this burden on the court. Taxpayers should anticipate further changes in the Tax Court's Rules of Practice and Procedure with respect to the court's discovery rules, and in the Tax Court's pre-trial orders with respect to the management and scheduling of large, complicated FSC and other cases.

CHAPTER 12

Customs Aspects of Exporting

Charles L. Crowley
James Geraghty

12.1 Introduction

Congress has the plenary authority to regulate foreign trade. Nevertheless, the Constitution expressly prohibits duties and taxes on exports. This proscription is the principal difference between export and import transactions. However, the proscription does not preclude an exporter's involvement with United States Customs.

An exporter's involvement with Customs includes:

1. Exporters or their agents must file Shippers Export Declarations (SED) with Customs;
2. Exporters and others who are eligible for duty drawback should file claims with Customs;
3. Exporters who furnish North American Free Trade Agreement (NAFTA) certificates of origin to their customers are subject to customs enforcement.

Newly established customs penalties could apply to exporters who file or furnish inaccurate information, or even fail to maintain pertinent records under NAFTA and drawback. Exporters who are sensitive to their foreign customers' customs regimes might price or structure their transactions accordingly. Therefore, a sophisticated exporter must understand customs principles despite never having paid duty to United States Customs.

This chapter explores an exporter's compliance obligations and potential exposure to various types of customs-related violations. Opportunities under the complex, but lucrative, duty drawback programs include the bases for drawback, procedural requirements, and record keeping, with all its pitfalls. In addition, this chapter covers customs appraisement issues which could affect the duty assessed by foreign customs on customers' imports from the United States.

12.2   Export Customs Compliance

(a)   Shipper's Export Declarations

Commerce Department regulations require exporters to file a Shipper's Export Declaration (SED) with Customs for shipments valued at more than $2,500 to all foreign countries.[1] The purpose of the document is to facilitate the compilation of official export statistics and to assist Commerce in administering the Export Administration Act. The Commerce regulations exempt shipments to Canada that do not otherwise require an export license or declaration issued by a government agency.

The Commerce Department Bureau of Census publishes a booklet entitled *Correct Way to Fill Out the Shipper's Export Declarations,* which addresses specific issues regarding completion of the document. Questions arise as to which party in a back-to-back export transaction is the party responsible for the SED. Generally, the party named on a validated export license, if applicable, or otherwise identified as the shipper on a bill of lading, is deemed to be the exporter. Frequently, the exporter's agent, such as a freight forwarder, actually completes and files the SED.

---

[1] 15 CFR.

The SED requires disclosure of the value of the exported goods, which is the selling price or the cost, if the shipment is not pursuant to a sale. In this context, the price is an FAS-level value and excludes unconditional discounts and commissions. The SED must also identify intermediate and ultimate consignees.

The SED must provide other information, including the Schedule B number, which frequently is congruent to the Harmonized Tariff System (HTS) classification number. Accordingly, exporters as well as importers must be facile in interpreting the HTS. Interestingly, the exporter is required to disclose the "point of origin" of the shipment, that is, the location within the United States at which the shipment commenced. The exporter is not required to disclose the country of origin of foreign goods on the SED itself, but the consignee may require a certificate of origin as a separate document.

The SED requires a certification that the statements are true and that the exporter understands that false statements could lead to civil and criminal penalties. It is the certification that could be the basis for an accusation that the exporter has made a knowingly false statement to a government agency, a predicate for liability. Therefore, care is required in preparing the document or furnishing information to freight forwarders for filing.

(b) Harbor Maintenance Fee

Exporters are not liable for customs duties per se, but Congress has established the assessment of a Harbor Maintenance Fee (HMF) on both imports and exports shipped by vessel.[2] Certain inland shipments too are subject to the HMF. As of the date of publication of this handbook, the HMF is equal to .125 percent of the value of the subject cargo. On imports, the HMF is deposited with duty at the time of entry, that is, transaction by transaction. However, exporters are required to file quarterly declarations on a Customs Form 349 and deposit the fee on the value of all shipments exported from a port facility during the quarter. Since HMF deposits are not made with SEDs, or otherwise assessed at export upon shipment, it is not uncommon for exporters to neglect to pay the HMF. Customs has implemented an enforcement initiative to encourage voluntary compliance. However, the law does not appear to authorize interest or penalty assessments for late payment or nonpayment.

The HMF is a liability of the exporter, arises at the time of loading, and is based on the value of the goods. For this purpose, the value is the amount declared on the SED. The taxpayer is the exporter identified as such on the SED. Accordingly, the SED can affect HMF liability.

There is pending litigation concerning the constitutionality of the HMF on exports. Specifically, dozens of exporters have filed actions claiming that the HMF violates Article 1, Section 5, Clause 9, of the Constitution of the United States, which prohibits taxes on exports. The lower court has declared the HMF unconstitutional, but the decision is on appeal.

---

[2] 19 CFR § 24.24.

(c)   North American Free Trade Agreement

Under the North American Free Trade Agreement (NAFTA), certain products originating within the United States, Canada, or Mexico may be imported duty free or at a reduced duty rate into the territory of a NAFTA country.[3] To qualify, goods must meet the complex and product-specific rules of origin and must be shipped directly to a NAFTA country with a special certificate of origin (CO). Exporters who tout their products' NAFTA eligibility, or who otherwise are required to do so by their customers, must determine that their goods are NAFTA-qualified and must properly prepare and furnish their customers with NAFTA COs. NAFTA documents are not submitted to Customs in the United States, but are submitted by the exporters' customers to the customs authorities in Mexico or Canada. The NAFTA legislation requires exporters who issue NAFTA COs to retain records to substantiate that the goods were NAFTA-qualified. Such exporters can be penalized for issuing false COs and/or for failing to maintain substantiating documents.

12.3   Duty Drawback

Duty drawback refunds 99 percent of the duty paid on imported merchandise that is:

1.   Used in the production of articles subsequently exported;
2.   exported unused; or
3.   exported under other qualifying circumstances.[4]

Customs has estimated that tens of millions of dollars in potential drawback are unclaimed each year because potential claimants are unaware that their transactions qualify or believe that the claims procedure is too complex to warrant the effort.

Drawback procedures are strict and require the maintenance of extensive records. Nevertheless, the potential refunds can be viewed as a means to remove a disincentive to export by making exported products more price-competitive in foreign markets. Alternatively, drawback can be viewed as an additional source of revenue that goes right to the final line. In either event, any exporter who does not explore potential drawback eligibility misses an opportunity to evaluate the benefits of this export-driven duty refund program.

(a)   Types of Drawback

Section 313 of the Tariff Act provides for discrete drawback bases, the most significant of which is manufacturing drawback. Under these provisions, a claimant can recover duty paid on imported materials and components used in the produc-

---

[3] 19 CFR, Parts 102 and 181.

[4] 19 USC § 1313; 19 C F R, Part 191.

tion of merchandise ultimately exported from the United States. The concept is simple, but the record-keeping requirements are strict so as to permit a Customs auditor to trace the imported "designated merchandise" through a production bill-of-materials to evidence of exportation.

A unique feature of the drawback program is the substitution principle, by which a manufacturer may substitute, in production, domestic or other imported merchandise of the same kind and quality as the designated merchandise. The manufacturer can claim drawback on the quantity of such merchandise used in the manufacture of the exported product, even though none of the designated merchandise is actually contained in the exported product. This substitution provision avoids the need to physically segregate inventory in order to facilitate drawback claims. Potential drawback rights can be transferred when a drawback-eligible product is transferred to a third party for use in production or for exportation. A transferee should inquire whether the purchased products involve potential drawback eligibility.

(b)   Unused Merchandise Drawback

Imported merchandise exported without having been used in the United States is eligible for a drawback. Under prior law, such merchandise had to be in the same condition as when imported. Thus, unused merchandise precluded eligibility for goods that had deteriorated after importation or that had not been altered sufficiently to qualify for manufacturing drawback. However, Congress removed this requirement so as to close what was perceived to be a gap between manufacturing drawback and what had been referred to as "same condition" drawback. The imported merchandise may be subject to incidental operations such as packing, sorting, fumigating, and the like, which are not considered to be disqualifying uses. Here, too, the substitution principle is applicable for domestic or other imported merchandise that is "commercially interchangeable" with the imported merchandise. Unused merchandise drawback allows an importer to dispose of unsold inventory without resorting to a distress sale in the domestic market.

(c)   Other Drawback Bases

Unordered merchandise and merchandise that fails to conform to sample or specification may be drawback eligible if exported within three years of importation. Specific products are drawback eligible, such as meats cured with imported salt, materials for the construction and equipment of vessels built for foreigners, and jet aircraft engines, among other things. Certain Internal Revenue taxes are also subject to drawback.

Under NAFTA, there are drawback phaseout provisions for exports to Canada and Mexico. All drawback qualifying for exportations must be made within five years of importation of the designated merchandise, except as to unused merchandise drawback, for which the time frame is three years. The business must substantiate books and records for three years after Customs remits the drawback payment.

Claims must be filed and completed within three years of exportation. In most instances, merchandise may be destroyed under Customs supervision rather than exported to be drawback eligible. Exporters commonly retain customs brokers who specialize in drawback. Many of these customs brokers charge a percentage of recovery on a sliding-scale contingent fee basis.

12.4   Liabilities

Exporters are potentially liable for a variety of penalties and other sanctions in connection with export transactions. Although their discussion in this chapter is not meant to be exhaustive, the major pitfalls that exporters must avoid are addressed in the following paragraphs.

(a)   Export Licensing

Customs is authorized to enforce various regulations promulgated by other agencies. Customs may seize merchandise that a business exports or attempts to export contrary to law, such as merchandise for which special Commerce Department or State Department licensing is required.[5] Furthermore, merchandise to be exported directly or indirectly to a proscribed destination and transactions prohibited under the Foreign Assets Control regulations are also within Customs' jurisdiction.[6] Such transactions generally involve countries hostile to the United States, such as Cuba or Iran, or countries that are targeted for boycott, which until recently included South Africa. Proscribed merchandise typically includes armaments and munitions. These prohibitions are subject to change, and a prudent exporter will know in advance whether a product or destination is subject to sanction. Apart from criminal prosecution for intentional violations, an exporter's goods may be subject to seizure even though a transgression was unintentional. Customs has guidelines for releasing such goods for lawful disposition. However, the exporter will be subject to monetary penalties.

(b)   Drawback Violations

The intentional filing of a false drawback claim may subject an exporter to criminal prosecution,[7] but, the basis for civil penalties for negligent violations has been murky. The law is in a state of transition. Previously, it was thought that an exporter could be liable under the False Claims Act for knowingly filing a false

---

[5] *See,* generally, *Operational Handbook of Other Agency Requirements,* U.S. Customs Service Office of Operations/Duty Assessment Division.

[6] 31 CFR, Part 500 *et seq.*

[7] 18 USC.

drawback claim.[8] However, the authors know of no case in which an actual False Claims Act action was filed against an exporter, although Customs has threatened such actions. Under the Customs Modernization Act legislation which accompanied the implementation of NAFTA, Congress has fashioned a new civil penalty provision for false drawback claims under which penalties are based on level of culpability, including ordinary negligence.[9] As with Customs' civil penalties generally, the sanctions can be multiples of the loss or potential loss of revenue for intentional violations, and 20 percent of the loss of revenue in negligence cases. Thus, a negligent drawback claim can result not merely in the denial of the claim, but in the imposition of a monetary penalty.

(c) NAFTA Record Keeping

Exporters who execute NAFTA certificates of origin are required to maintain records for five years from signing the certificates. Failure to comply with the certificate could result in the loss of NAFTA eligibility for exported products. False or negligent certifications of noncomplying goods can expose an exporter to the same liability as would apply to an importer who has committed a comparable violation. This liability could be forfeiture value, four times the loss of revenue, or twice the loss of revenue for fraud, gross negligence, or negligence, respectively. If an exporter discovers that goods believed to be NAFTA eligible actually failed to qualify, there are no penalties if the exporter notifies the customer within 30 days that the certification was inaccurate.

An exporter unsure of eligibility may request a ruling from Canadian or Mexican Customs authorities. U.S. Customs will not issue NAFTA rulings to exporters. Exporters with little importing experience will find NAFTA to be unusual, inasmuch as issuing a CO brings the exporter within Customs' enforcement jurisdiction. Civil penalties are multiples, not percentages, of the loss of revenue. Exporters could face exposure under the laws of Mexico or Canada.

(d) False Statements

It is an indictable offense to make a knowingly false statement to a government official.[10] The statement need not be under oath, can be oral or written, and may be made to a representative of any federal government agency. This false statement provision can be invoked in cases involving false SEDs. As to the SED, a separate provision proscribes giving false trade statistics to the federal government.[11] Consequently, even preparing the standard SED can be the source of some risk if the document is inaccurate.

---

[8] 31 USC §§ 3729 *et seq.*

[9] 19 USC 1593A.

[10] 18 USC 1001.

[11] 13 USC 305.

12.5   Customs Implications of Export Pricing

Tariff classification and appraisement are two components of duty assessment. Most countries with whom the United States engages in significant trade adhere to the Customs Valuation Agreement (or "the Code") concluded during the 1979 Tokyo Round Multilateral Trade Negotiations concluded under the auspices of the General Agreement on Tariffs and Trade.[12] The Code was implemented by Congress and has been the law in the United States since 1980.[13] Although other countries departed from the Code prescriptions in certain respects, the basic principles have been effected in the European Community (EC) countries, Brazil, Japan, the Scandinavian countries, Turkey, and Australia, among others. Exporters need to understand the Customs valuation aspects of their pricing and distribution decisions so that transactions can be structured to minimize the duty burden on customers and to make export products more competitive.

Under the valuation Code, merchandise is appraised under hierarchically arranged bases of appraisement, each of which includes criteria or elements of value. The primary basis, transaction value, is the price paid or payable for the merchandise undergoing appraisement. Generally, invoice value represents the transaction basis if the parties are unrelated. Transaction value still can apply to related parties if the price is comparable to certain test values or if there is other evidence that the relationship did not affect the price, that is, that the parties dealt as if they were at arm's length.

If the primary basis does not apply, the next bases in sequence are transaction value of identical merchandise and transaction value of similar merchandise. There are standards for determining the existence of identical or similar merchandise. Suffice it to say that neither basis reflects a price in the country of export or prices charged by other producers in third countries.

If the goods are not sold for exportation, or if there are no transactions that would meet the secondary or tertiary basis criteria, the next basis in sequence is deductive value, which is the price in the country of importation with deductions that yield what might have been an FOB-level sales price if one had existed. If deductive value does not exist, the following basis is computed value, which is not a price but, rather, the sum of the cost of production. If cost data is unavailable, customs authorities may resort to a residual basis known as derivative value, which reflects a prior basis as to which an element of value cannot be established.

All bases of appraisement are subject to adjustments for elements of value not included in the price, such as selling agent's commissions, packing, certain royalties, "assists," and resale proceeds that inure to the benefit of the foreign seller. There are other potential adjustments that may vary from country to country, depending on how the Code was implemented and has been interpreted by the courts. The appraisement issues discussed in the following paragraphs have been contro-

---

[12] *Multilateral Trade Negotiations, International Codes Agreed to in Geneva, Switzerland, April 12, 1979,* Joint Committee Print 96th Cong. 1st Sess., April 23, 1979, WMCP:96-18.
[13] 19 USC § 1401a, 19 CFR, Part 152.

versial in the United States and could create either problems or opportunities for a U.S. exporter. Therefore, exporters should be aware of the issues and consult with their customers to determine the rules that apply in their countries.

(a) Price Adjustments

Ocean freight and insurance are nondutiable elements in the United States. However, in other countries, such as those of the European Community, these expenses are dutiable regardless of whether they are included in the price. Therefore, an exporter who arranges the lowest freight possible provides advantages for customers by the extent of the savings and its impact on duty.

Foreign inland freight, finance charges, and quota payments are not dutiable under certain circumstances in the United States. The rules may vary in other countries. Exporters should be sensitive to these distinctions and offer to structure sales transactions and pricing so as to minimize the customer's duty payment. For example, selling ex-factory and facilitating a foreign customer's direct payment to carriers or to financial institutions may help the customer reduce duty.

Price adjustments may be treated differently in various countries; the Code does not address this issue. In the United States, post-importation price reductions are disregarded in determining transaction value. However, formula pricing is recognized, provided that the parties do not have control over the variables used to calculate the price. Customs recognizes quantity discounts, but not deferred discounts that involve a price reduction or credit based on volume purchased over a period of time. Preexportation price changes should not be a difficulty. Goods sold in a currency other than the currency of the country of importation must be adjusted, based on an exchange rate. Each country adhering to the Code may utilize either the date of exportation or the date of importation for this purpose. The difference can be considerable, so the expected conversion rate should be taken into account in negotiating prices.

(b) First Sale Rule

United States Customs does not recognize in-transit sales as transaction value, although the rule may differ in other countries. Nevertheless, there are circumstances in which there may be more than one potential transaction value, especially in the case of so-called back-to-back sales, both consummated prior to exportation. The United States and the European Community, as well as some other countries, recognize what is sometimes referred to as the "first sale" rule. Under the first sale rule the earlier of two sales, presumably the price from the factory, will be deemed to be the appropriate transaction value if there is evidence that the sale was for exportation. Each Customs jurisdiction has its own criteria for determining when the first sale rule applies.

Appraisement under this first sale principle can result in a substantial duty savings since, as a practical matter, the reseller's markup would be factored out of appraised value. When parties are unrelated, cooperating in a first sale appraisement means revealing what otherwise would be confidential information about sources of supply and prices. Nevertheless, exporters should be mindful of the principle, because a customer's potential duty savings could be the decisive factor in realizing a sale.

12.6   Antidumping/Subsidies

Although other countries have not been as militant as the United States in invoking its antidumping and countervailing duty laws, exporters should be aware that competitors in foreign countries may request an investigation, the result of which could virtually close a market to United States exporters who sell at a margin of dumping. Generally, dumping is the difference between the price for export and prices at the same level of sale in the home market or to third countries or, in certain circumstances, below the cost of production. Under the international antidumping code, sales at a margin of dumping must cause or threaten to cause injury to an industry in the importing country before antidumping duties may be imposed. A discussion of dumping margin calculations and adjustments is beyond the scope of this handbook. However, exporters should be aware of the potential risk when attempting to penetrate a price-sensitive market by engaging in marginal cost pricing, selling "loss leaders," or other price reduction mechanisms that result in sales at prices lower than those extant in the United States.

Subsidization is a related phenomenon that can facilitate the penetration of foreign markets. However, price subsidization is deemed to be unfair competition, for which importing countries can impose countervailing duties to offset the subsidy. As in a dumping margin analysis, calculating the amount of the subsidy or determining whether a certain type of program should actually be considered countervailable subsidization can be controversial. Here, also, exporters must be sensitive to the potential.

12.7   Conclusion

Exporters who are aware of the customs aspects of their sales transactions in the anticipated country of importation can plan to minimize the duty impact on their customers and increase sales. Potential duty drawback can also be a windfall to exporters apart from the extent to which drawback may permit the exporter to reduce prices and become more competitive. However, exporters should also be aware of the potential liabilities for submitting inaccurate claims or other documents with Customs, as well as for failing to maintain records to support drawback claims and NAFTA certificates of origin. Potential problems can be reduced through a compliance program that takes into account all these potential customs issues that affect exports. A comprehensive compliance program can be the crucial factor in successful exporting.

CHAPTER 13

Antitrust and Tax Considerations

Robert Feinschreiber

13.1 Introduction

Exporters can obtain antitrust and tax benefits by utilizing an export trading company, that establishes a foreign sales corporation (FSC). With careful structuring, the requirements of both antitrust and tax provisions can be satisfied. Moreover, an export trading company and its shareholders can obtain multiple FSC benefits. The FSC benefits from an export trading company are in addition to the FSC benefits that the shareholder in the export trading company receives separately.

13.2 Export Trading Companies

Export trading companies are antitrust-oriented structures. Nevertheless, export trading companies provide opportunities for international corporations and their tax consultants.

Despite the similarity of their names, an export trading company is not an export trade corporation. Export trade corporations are foreign entities that are controlled foreign corporations that were able to reduce Subpart F income.[1] When DISC was

---

[1] § 971(a)(3).

enacted, Congress partially repealed export trade corporations.[2] Subsequently, export trade corporations were able to elect FSC status.[3]

An export trading company is a specific entity that is authorized by the Export Trading Company Act of 1982. This Act provides antitrust benefits and banking benefits for exporters. An Export Trading Company does not specifically pertain to tax benefits, but export trade company rules do not counteract domestic international sales corporation (DISC) and FSC provisions.[4] In fact, the export trade provisions are largely compatible with DISC and FSC provisions.

Bank provisions are utilized by half of the money center banks and by other banks.[5] Under the Bank Export Services Act, a bank can make investments in export trading companies. These investments are allowable, notwithstanding investment restrictions that would otherwise apply to banks.[6]

Antitrust provisions in the Export Trading Company Act liberalize the Webb-Pomerene provisions[7] that have long encouraged exporting. This antitrust approach was initiated by Senator Stevenson in 1979,[8] and the antitrust incentive was enacted in 1982. Moreover, an exporter can benefit from Webb-Pomerene provisions as well as from Export Trading Company provisions.

(a) Antitrust Benefits

An export trading company receives an antitrust certificate (called a "certificate of review") from the U.S. government. The certificate authorizes export trading company activities that would otherwise be antitrust violations.[9] Antitrust exemptions apply to dealings with competitors of the export trading company, including activities that would otherwise incur treble damages. Civil and criminal actions of the federal government are exempt, as are state government actions.

The FSC or its related supplier can participate in an export trading company and qualify for one or more benefits, allowing it to:

1.   Establish a cartel
2.   Allocate orders among members of the export trading company
3.   Select geographic markets or limit territories

---

[2] Robert Feinschreiber, *Domestic International Sales Corporations* (New York: Practicing Law Institute, 1978).

[3] Reg. § 1.921-1T(c).

[4] 15 USC 4002.

[5] U.S. General Accounting Office, *Export Promotion* (Washington, D.C.: U.S. Government Printing Office, 1986) 38–39.

[6] 12 USC 1843.

[7] 40 Stat. 516 (1918), 15 USC 61–65.

[8] Robert Feinschreiber, "Forming an Export Association for Increased Profile and Tax Savings," International Tax Journal 3 (Winter 1976):161; "Senator Stevenson Proposes Additional Tax Incentive for Exporters," *International Tax Journal* 6 (October 1979):57.

[9] 15 USC 4016.

4. Share information with other participants of the export trading company
5. Utilize industry groups and subgroups
6. Maintain horizontal and vertical antitrust activities
7. Decide on the terms of sale, include credit terms
8. Decide quantities for export, restrict quantities, or use quotas
9. Set prices, or otherwise engage in price fixing
10. Become an exclusive purchasing agent for members
11. Be a foreign purchasing agent
12. Establish price, select customers, and restrict customers
13. Have an exclusive sales representative
14. Have a joint venture
15. Be a sales representative, or have a foreign representative
16. Agree not to sell to others
17. Agree to avoid competitors
18. Have export intermediaries or brokers
19. Have foreign buyers as purchasing agents
20. Represent suppliers, or contact suppliers for bids

(b) Establishing Export Trading Companies

Export trading companies are normally established on an industry-wide basis. Industries that have export trading companies include companies in consumer products, high-tech equipment, basic equipment, and agricultural products. An export trading company can receive antitrust benefits, such as the ability to set prices, select geographic markets, and allocate orders among members.

To qualify as an export trading company, a company must meet certain requirements as to its organization and operation. These two functions must be principally used for the purposes of exporting goods or services, or the facilitation of exports through export trade services.

The range of export services is broader for export trading company purposes than for FSC purposes. FSC services apply only to related and subsidiary services,[10] engineering and architectural services,[11] and certain management services.[12] Export trading company services include legal, financial, communication, and transportation services, as well as informational and any other data-based services, and the facilitation of exports. Accordingly, it may be advantageous to establish an export trading company and its FSC subsidiary. Alternatively, the export trading company can itself be a FSC.

---

[10] § 924(a)(3).

[11] § 924(a)(4).

[12] § 924(a)(5).

(c) Shareholders

A FSC can have as many as 25 shareholders,[13] but no requisites apply to participants in an export trading company. To receive dual FSC benefits, an export trading company must have between 3 and 25 corporate shareholders. If the export trading company establishes its FSC subsidiary, the export trading company is the only shareholder and it meets the 25-or-fewer shareholder requirement for a FSC, regardless of how many shareholders form the export trade company.

Foreign trading gross receipts of a FSC do not include transactions that pertain to a controlled group.[14] For this purpose, the controlled group uses "more than 50 percent," rather than "at least 80 percent."[15] Two fifty percent shareholders can theoretically avoid controlled group status, but this structure is difficult to achieve in practice. Thus, an export trading company that seeks dual tax benefits as well as antitrust benefits must have between 3 and 25 corporate members, and the members must avoid controlled group status.

Preferred stock arrangements can potentially arise because in situations where the participants are not in parity as to size, market share, or profitability, or there are changes in these items. A FSC must not have any preferred stock outstanding at any time during the taxable year.[16] Export trading company provisions do not have any requirements as to share ownership. If an export trading company is a FSC, it is subject to the preferred stock rules.

13.3 Obtaining FSC-ETC-FSC Benefits

In some situations, a carefully structured agreement with members of an export trading company (ETC) can create additional FSC benefits for the export trading company or for some of its members.[17] An example illustrates the FSC income of Companies A, B, and C, which were initially unrelated to each other. Subsequently, each company owns one third of Export Trading Company Y. Companies A and B each have a FSC, but Company C does not utilize a FSC (see Exhibit 13.1).

Before establishing Export Trading Company Y, Company A had combined taxable income (CTI) of 8 percent, Company B had combined taxable income of 6 percent, and Company C would have had combined taxable income of 4 percent if it had utilized a FSC. Company A received FSC income of 1.84 (23 percent of CTI of 8), while Company B received income of 1.83 (1.83 percent of gross receipts of 100).

---

[13] § 922(a)(1)(B).

[14] § 924(f)(1)(C).

[15] § 927(d)(4).

[16] § 922(a)(1)(C).

[17] Robert Feinschreiber, "How to Aggregate DISC Sales to Make Most Effective Use of the Deferral," *J Tax* 36 (1972):300.

Exhibit 13.1

FSC INCOME WITHOUT EXPORT TRADING COMPANY

Company	Sales	CTI	FSC
A	100	8	1.84
B	100	6	1.83
C	100	4	—
Total	300	18	3.67

Each company sells an item for $96 to the export trading company (see Exhibit 13.2). The export trading company then sells the item for $100. If total gross receipts of the export trading company are $300, costs are $288 ($96 × 3) and income is $12. If Export Trading Company Y earns 4 percent of gross receipts for its activities, and this company has a FSC, the FSC income is $5.49 (1.83 percent of $300). In this example, it is not assumed that IRC § 482 transfer pricing is utilized.

Exhibit 13.2

FSC INCOME WITH FOREIGN TRADING COMPANY

Company	Sales	CTI	FSC
A	96	4	1.76
B	96	2	0.92
C	96	0	—
Total	288	6	2.68

In Exhibit 13.3, FSC incomes are $2.68 from the separate companies plus $5.49 for the export trading company, or $8.17 in total. In contrast, the FSC amount would be $3.67 without the export trading company. Thus, the additional FSC income is $4.50.

Exhibit 13.3

EXPORT TRADING COMPANY FSC BENEFITS

Company	FSC Inc. with ETC	FSC Dist. from ETC	Total	Before ETC FSC Income	Difference
A	1.76	1.83	3.59	1.84	1.75
B	.92	1.83	2.75	1.83	.92
C	0	1.83	1.83	0	1.83
Total	2.68	5.49	8.17	3.67	4.50

13.4   Conclusion

Tax issues cannot be viewed as in a vacuum, but must be considered with other factors, such as customs and tax, accounting or tax antitrust, and issues. What makes antitrust and tax unique is that the government provides an additional level of benefits to both.

CHAPTER 14

Exporting and Antidumping Practice

Richard D. Boltuck
Seth T. Kaplan
Stephanie M. Wilshusen

       (j)   Constructed Value
       (k)   Public Interest Factors
       (l)   Injury and Causation
       (m)   Small Import Shares

14.5   Antidumping Regimes of Other Developed Countries
       (a)   Canada: Process Differences
       (b)   Canada: Substantive Differences
       (c)   Australia: Process Differences
       (d)   Australia: Substantive Differences

14.6   Antidumping Regimes of Newly Industrialized Countries
       (a)   Mexico
       (b)   South Korea

14.7   Conclusion

14.1   Introduction

What is dumping? For dumping duties to be imposed, a domestic petitioning industry must show that:

1. The subject imports are being sold at less than fair value; and
2. The subject imports are injuring or threatening to injure the domestic industry.

During the past 15 years, antidumping laws have played an increasingly important role in regulating trade flows around the world. There are a number of reasons for this, some of which are interrelated.

(a)   Reduction in Tariffs

First, successive rounds of General Agreement on Tariffs and Trade (GATT) agreements have substantially reduced tariff levels worldwide. Hence, many countries have resorted to non-tariff measures, such as antidumping laws, to restrict the level of imports—in essence, to take back part of what they surrendered in the GATT negotiations.[1] Quite clearly, antidumping laws throughout the world could have a major negative impact on U.S. exports. Advisors from international organizations such as the World Bank and International Monetary Fund have advised their clients to install dumping safeguard regimes as internationally recognized methods to control injurious surges in imports. Since the establishment of GATT in 1948, average tariff levels have fallen consistently following each of the seven rounds of GATT negotiations. For example, tariff reductions resulting from the Uruguay Round will cut developed countries' tariffs on industrial products by 40

---

[1] *See,* for example, Hufbauer and Shelton Erb, *Subsidies in International Trade* (1984) at 2.

percent (on average, from 6.3 percent to 3.8 percent). Given the current low levels of tariffs and the impermissibility of raising rates under GATT, it is not surprising that the application of antidumping laws has increased.

(b) Developing Countries

Second, a host of developing countries have joined GATT in recent years. The final act of the Uruguay Round negotiations was signed by 117 governments. As suggested earlier, many, if not most, of these countries have adopted antidumping laws as an escape valve for increased imports expected to result from their accession to GATT. Exhibit 14.1 lists the countries that have initiated investigations under their antidumping regulations during the period 1980–1995.

(c) Trade Volume

The volume of international trade exploded during the period from 1980 to 1995. For example, in the case of the United States, from 1980 to 1994 exports more than doubled and imports rose by more than 150 percent.[2] By itself, this increased trade, and the potential friction with domestic industries that comes with it, has led to more frequent resort to antidumping laws.

As newly industrialized countries have been wealthier, they have contributed dramatically to greater trade volume, largely in addition to the growth of trade liberations. The normal displacement of domestic production by imports (and the concomitant expansion of other domestic industries) that occurs naturally over time is accelerated if major segments of the domestic economy were previously insulated from competition. Depending on the political environment in the country, antidumping laws present one channel to afford GATT-permitted protection as the economy becomes more open.

Exhibit 14.1

COUNTRIES INITIATING ANTIDUMPING INVESTIGATIONS

Argentina	Finland	Poland
Australia	India	Singapore
Austria	Japan	South Africa
Brazil	Korea	Sweden
Canada	Mexico	Turkey
Chile	New Zealand	United States
Colombia	Peru	Venezuela
European Community	Spain	Thailand

---

[2] Economic Report of the President 1992, 1995, and *U.S. Department of Commerce News Release* (Feb. 17, 1995).

(d) Recessions

Over that same period of expansion there were two major worldwide recessions—in 1980–1981 and 1990–1991. Almost invariably, such economic downturns cause a "spike" in antidumping cases in the United States and elsewhere.[3] These spikes occur both because domestic industries are more likely to feel the need to seek refuge in antidumping laws during times of economic stress, and because injury tends to be easier to prove during an economic downturn.

All of these factors have combined to make antidumping laws a far more prominent feature of the international landscape than they were previously. Consequently, it has become all the more important for exporters to take antidumping laws into account when planning a business strategy.

The rest of this chapter is organized as follows: Section 14.2 briefly documents the use of antidumping provisions. The review traces the increase in the use of antidumping laws and tracks the countries and products that have historically been associated with the use of these laws. Section 14.3 examines the base concepts of dumping and injury common to all dumping regimes. Section 14.4 compares the United States and European Union regimes. Section 14.5 explores regimes in other developed countries. Section 14.6 briefly examines regimes in developing and newly industrialized countries, and Section 14.7 offers a conclusion.

14.2 Use of Antidumping Provisions

The expansion in the use of antidumping provisions is evident in examining Exhibit 14.2. This exhibit shows that the number of countries in the world making use of antidumping provisions has been increasing over time. In the United States and the European Union alone, the number of existing antidumping orders has risen from 37 cases in 1980 to 85 cases in 1994. Given the long-standing nature of the vast majority of dumping orders, the volume of trade covered has increased steadily over time.

Even more noticeable is the emergence of new antidumping regimes in the last 10 years. Mexico, for example, has now initiated more than 100 investigations, although its antidumping regime was established only in 1986.

(a) Frequency of Respondents

Exhibit 14.3 shows the frequency of countries named as respondents in antidumping investigations. The list includes most developed and many developing countries. While many unfair trade actions are initiated by developed economies against imports from low-labor-cost countries, many of the disputes are among the developed economies themselves. This result should not be surprising, given

---

[3] *See,* for example, Destler, *American Trade Politics,* 3d ed. (1995), 151.

Exhibit 14.2

NUMBER OF ANTIDUMPING CASES INITIATED BY COUNTRY BY YEAR

	1980	1981	1982	1983	1984	1985	1986	1987	1988	1989	1990	1991	1992	1993	1994	Total
Argentina	0	0	0	0	0	0	0	0	0	0	0	0	0	23	7	30
Australia	8	20	79	80	53	61	62	21	16	21	43	64	72	50	15	665
Austria	0	1	0	1	0	0	0	0	0	0	0	0	4	4	0	10
Brazil	0	0	0	0	0	0	0	0	1	1	1	7	9	0	0	19
Canada	25	24	79	26	27	37	16	32	15	13	15	11	45	25	2	392
Chile	0	0	0	0	0	0	0	0	0	0	0	0	0	1	1	2
Colombia	0	0	0	0	0	0	0	0	0	0	0	2	0	1	1	4
EC	16	34	33	30	39	32	12	32	29	14	15	6	15	16	42	365
Finland	2	0	0	0	1	0	0	5	5	2	0	1	0	0	0	16
India	0	0	0	0	0	0	0	0	0	0	0	0	8	0	1	9
Japan	0	0	0	0	0	0	0	0	0	0	0	3	0	0	1	4
Korea	0	0	0	0	0	0	3	1	0	1	5	0	0	4	4	18
Mexico	0	0	0	0	0	0	0	17	10	3	11	12	26	29	5	113
New Zealand	0	0	0	0	0	0	0	0	9	1	0	9	14	0	6	39
Peru	0	0	0	0	0	0	0	0	0	0	0	0	0	0	3	3
Poland	0	0	0	0	0	0	0	0	0	0	0	24	0	0	0	24
Singapore	0	0	0	0	0	0	0	0	0	0	0	0	0	0	2	2
Spain	0	0	0	0	1	0	0	0	0	0	0	0	0	0	0	1
Sweden	2	0	0	0	0	2	0	0	0	6	0	1	0	0	0	11
Turkey	0	0	0	0	0	0	0	0	0	0	0	0	0	0	2	2
Venezuela	0	0	0	0	0	0	0	0	0	0	0	0	0	3	0	3
United States	21	13	58	49	37	76	64	15	39	23	43	47	99	42	43	669
Total	74	92	249	186	158	208	157	123	124	85	133	187	292	198	135	2401

Note: See footnote 109.

Exhibit 14.3

**NEW ANTIDUMPING CASES DIRECTED
AT THE UNITED STATES AND ITS MAJOR
TRADING PARTNERS 1980–1989**

	Number	*Percent*
European Community	344	37.6
Japan	159	17.4
United States	144	15.8
South Korea	91	10.0
Brazil	69	7.6
Canada	41	4.5
Hong Kong	22	2.4
Singapore	18	2.0
Mexico	15	1.6
India	6	0.7
Australia	5	0.6
Total	914	100.0

Source: GAO/NSIAD-90-238FS, July 1990, p. 7.

the extremely high volumes of interindustry trade among the developed economies as well as the fact that trade between developed countries accounts for the lion's share of world trade. Consequently, U.S. exporters should be concerned about potential antidumping actions with both the developed and the developing world.

(b) Products

Historically, the bulk of antidumping actions have been directed against products that are broadly classified as either metals or chemicals. In the United States, for example, cases involving chemicals and metals (especially steel) accounted for more than 64 percent of all antidumping investigations between 1979 and 1989. In Europe, cases involving chemicals and metals accounted for 55 percent.[4] Exhibit 14.4 shows the general classification of products subject to investigations between 1979 and 1989.

While chemicals and metals dominate among products in all investigations, investigations involving more highly manufactured products account for a significant and increasing share. This is likely to continue for several reasons. First, the elimination or lowering of tariffs, coupled with the GATT ban on voluntary re-

---

[4] Patrick A. Messerlin and Geoffrey Reed, "Antidumping Policies in the United States and the European Community, *Economic Journal* (November 1995):1567.

Exhibit 14.4

NUMBER OF CASES INITIATED BY INDUSTRY, 1979–1989

	United States		European Community	
	Number	Share	Number	Share
Chemical industry	69	15.3	155	40.3
Metal industry	224	49.7	57	14.8
Nonelectrical machinery	27	6.0	34	8.8
Electrical equipment	24	5.3	33	8.6
The four industries	344	76.3	279	72.5
All industries	451	100.0	385	100.0

Note: See footnote 109.

straint agreements (VRAs),[5] has forced industries seeking political protection to use legal remedies, including antidumping laws.[6] In the United States, for example, imported flat-rolled steel, automobiles, and machine tools are no longer protected by VRAs. The loss of this protection has led to antidumping investigations of steel and minivans.

(c)   Production Costs

As the trend of multinational firms to spread production capacity among several countries or move production to lower-cost countries continues, dramatic shifts in industry import trends will occur. Such surges in imports are conducive to proving injury in antidumping investigations.

(d)   Executive Attention

Finally, corporate executives in manufacturing enterprises other than chemicals or metals are recognizing the benefits of eliminating so-called unfair competition. This new corporate culture views the trade laws as just another tool to be used aggressively in reshaping the competitive landscape of the domestic market. Enforcement of the antidumping provisions can cause import prices to rise and import quantities to fall. Use of the antidumping laws can be especially beneficial to domestic corporate performance if no alternative third market sources produce the goods under investigation. This is often the case with highly manufactured products. Examples from the United States include products ranging from DRAMs to bearings to color negative photographic paper.

---

[5] Uruguay Round Trade Agreements, Final Draft, GATT 1994, Agreement on Safeguards, Article 11, especially paragraph 1(b).

[6] J.M. Finger, H.K. Hall, and D.R. Nelson, "The Political Economy of Administered Protection," *American Economic Review* 72 (1982): 452–466.

14.3   Concepts of Dumping and Injury Common to All Dumping Regimes

(a)   Historical Background

Article VI, paragraph 1 of the General Agreement on Tariffs and Trade (GATT), dated October 30, 1947 (as amended through 1966), sets out the conceptual basis for the international consensus sanctioning the creation of national antidumping regimes:

> The contracting parties recognize that dumping, by which products of one country are introduced into the commerce of another country at less than the normal value of the products, is to be condemned if it causes or threatens material injury to an established industry in the territory of a contracting party or materially retards the establishment of a domestic industry.

The rest of Article VI establishes in general terms the requirements that a signatory must meet before imposing an antidumping duty, and the limits on the magnitude of the remedial duty. These requirements include, principally, that:

1. A dumping margin must be calculated based on a comparison of the export price to the aggrieved country, to the foreign producer's home market price or, failing that, on a comparison of export price to either the price for sales to a third country or to the cost of production plus selling costs and profit;[7]
2. The remedial duty may not exceed the dumping margin;[8] and
3. No remedial duty shall be levied absent a determination that "the effect of the dumping . . . is such as to cause or threaten material injury to an established domestic industry, or is such as to retard materially the establishment of a domestic industry."[9]

(b)   1994 GATT Rules

The new Uruguay Round GATT Final Act (GATT 1994), completed and signed in 1994 by 117 countries, contains a revised Agreement on Implementation of Article VI of the GATT 1994 (the antidumping code) that replaces the prior such agreement adopted in 1979 following the Tokyo Round. This agreement modifies and interprets Article VI of the GATT. It expands on the basic requirements listed previously and provides for such additional requirements as a five-year sunset review of whether outstanding antidumping duties continue to be justified.

---

[7] Article VI, ¶ 1.
[8] Article VI, ¶ 2.
[9] Article VI, ¶ 6(a).

Specifically, the antidumping code provides:

1. Detailed guidance for the calculation of the dumping margin, with attention to the use of appropriate statistical price comparisons, appropriate additions for selling costs and profit, exclusion of home market prices that do not provide for the recovery of costs within a reasonable period, treatment of start-up costs, adjustments for level of trade or differences in the terms and conditions of sale, and currency conversions, among other items.[10] In general, these restrictions reflect efforts to limit perceived abuses that have, over the years, become part of national practice in one country or another. Several of the provisions in this section were the subject of heated negotiations in Geneva during the Round, as countries that had disproportionately been targets of antidumping action sought greater restrictions, and countries that had active antidumping regulatory regimes sought more lax restrictions. The requirement in this section that the signatory evaluate "the magnitude of the margin of dumping" in the context of the effects of dumping is new in the GATT 1994 Final Act;

2. Detailed guidance regarding the determination of injury, threat, or material retardation, including the various factors that must be assessed to demonstrate that "the dumped imports are, through the effects of dumping, . . . causing injury within the meaning of this agreement";[11] "Injury" is defined to "mean material injury to a domestic industry, threat of material injury to a domestic industry or material retardation of the establishment of such an industry . . ."

3. That "domestic industry," for the purpose of establishing standing to file a written application seeking initiation and for evaluating injury, means "the domestic producers as a whole of the like products or . . . those of them whose collective output of the products constitutes a major proportion of the total domestic production of those products."[12] This provision describes two exceptions to the general industry definition, based on whether particular firms are related to foreign producers and may therefore be excluded, or whether injury is to be assessed on a regional basis (in which case, the industry may be defined on a regional, rather than national, basis as well);

4. The requirements that must be met in a written application by a domestic industry seeking antidumping relief;[13]

5. Procedural and evidentiary standards, and the role and definition of "interested parties" that may participate in the proceedings;[14]

6. Conditions under which provisional or retroactive duties may be imposed;[15]

---

[10] Part I, Article 2.

[11] Part I, Article 3, ¶ 5.

[12] Part I, Article 4, ¶ 1.

[13] Part I, Article 5.

[14] Part I, Article 6.

[15] Part I, Article 7 (provisional duties), and Part I, Article 10 (retroactive duties).

7. Conditions under which antidumping complaints may be settled through a price undertaking.[16]

8. Detailed guidance regarding the imposition and collection of remedial duties.[17]

9. Review of the continuing justification for outstanding antidumping orders where warranted, no later than five years from imposition (or the most recent such review). A review examines "whether the continued imposition of the duty is necessary to offset dumping, whether the injury would be likely to continue or recur if the duty were removed or varied, or both." If the duty is no longer warranted, it must be terminated.[18] The requirement for five-year sunset reviews is new under the Uruguay Round Final Act.

Other sections of the antidumping code establish requirements for judicial review within each signatory country[19] and detailed procedures for dispute settlement within the World Trade Organization.[20]

14.4 Comparison of United States and European Union Antidumping Regimes

Antidumping laws have long played a significant role in the trade regimes of the United States and the European Union (EU). While other countries have increasingly begun to adopt and employ such measures, the United States and the EU have used them far more frequently than other members of the international community. Consequently, their antidumping systems are not only important in their own right; they have also had a substantial influence in shaping the antidumping laws of other nations, both directly through GATT[21] and by serving as a model for others to follow.

(a) Common Characteristics

The common characteristics of the U.S. and EU antidumping regimes far outweigh the characteristics that set them apart. As the foregoing discussion suggests, both regimes share the same definition of dumping and use essentially the same framework in determining whether, and to what extent, dumping has occurred. This common understanding is unsurprising, as the dumping laws of all members of GATT and its successor organization, the World Trade Organization (WTO),

---

[16] Part I, Article 8. In the United States, such a settlement is called a suspension agreement.

[17] Part I, Article 9.

[18] Part I, Article 11.

[19] Part I, Article 13.

[20] Part II, Article 17.

[21] *See* discussion, *infra.*

must conform to the general requirements of the GATT Antidumping Code, which sets out a legal and analytical framework to which the signatories to the Code must adhere. The recent Uruguay Round of GATT negotiations, which produced a revised Antidumping Code,[22] eliminated or significantly narrowed some of the major differences between the two systems. Furthermore, as time has gone by, the United States and the EU have borrowed certain elements from each other's antidumping regimes. Hence, over time, the two systems have tended to converge rather than diverge.

Nevertheless, the two systems are not identical. Indeed, the distinguishing features between the two systems are sufficiently important to lead experts in the field to talk about the "U.S. antidumping model," in contrast to the "European antidumping model."

In the limited space available here, it would be impossible to catalog, let alone describe in detail, all of the features that significantly differentiate the two systems. Many of those differences relate to highly technical matters. However, certain differences between the two systems are so basic that it is important even for nonexperts to be at least generally familiar with them. In broad terms, these differences can be divided into two categories—differences in process and differences in substance. The dividing line between the two categories is not always clear, and differences in process can and do affect substantive outcomes.

(b)   Process Differences

The GATT Antidumping Code requires generally that all antidumping regimes be transparent, rather than hidden, and provide interested persons with due process.[23] Still, these requirements are somewhat vague, and they allow for substantial differences in the basic design of an antidumping regime. Such differences are reflected in various aspects of the processes pursuant to which antidumping laws are applied in the United States and the EU.

(c)   Timing Differences

Until very recently, one major difference between the two systems was that in the United States, by statute, antidumping cases must be completed at the administrative level within a tightly compressed time frame. Generally speaking, this means that once an antidumping petition has been filed with the responsible government authorities, the decision as to whether or not to initiate an investigation must be made quickly, generally within 20 days.[24] Furthermore, the administrative process must also be completed very quickly. The process takes, at most, slightly more than one year.[25]

---

[22] Agreement on Implementation of Article VI of GATT 1994 (GATT Antidumping Code).

[23] *See id.* at Article 6.

[24] 19 USC § 1673a(c)(1).

[25] *See* 19 USC §§ 1673b and 1673d.

In the EU, on the other hand, until recently, the responsible authorities often deliberated for a long time in deciding whether to initiate an investigation. Moreover, once such an investigation was under way, it was often quite protracted.

However, largely as a result of an initiative by France,[26] the EU now provides for a more expeditious process. Under the recently revised EU antidumping regulation (EU Dumping Regulation), a decision on whether to initiate an investigation must be made within 45 days[27] and investigations must be completed within one year if possible; in any event, within no more than 18 months.[28]

(d) Responsibilities

A major difference between the two systems continues to be that in the United States, unlike the practice in the EU, the administrative responsibility is split between two federal government agencies. The U.S. Department of Commerce, which operates under the president as an administrative cabinet department, is responsible for determining whether, and to what extent, dumping has occurred.[29] The U.S. International Trade Commission (ITC), a six-member independent agency, is responsible for determining whether dumped imports have caused, or threaten, material injury to a domestic industry.[30]

In the EU, the EU Commission is responsible for carrying out antidumping investigations, and there is no strict bifurcation of dumping and injury issues. However, unlike that in the United States, the investigating authority does not have ultimate decision-making authority. The Commission instead makes recommendations that must be approved by the EU Council, which is composed of representatives of the EU member states. In practice, however, these recommendations are usually followed.[31]

(e) Payment of Duties

Beyond their differing in administrative responsibility, the two systems have historically differed greatly as to when duties become due and payable. In the United States, the administrative process initially establishes only a contingent duty to pay. The contingent duty rate (if any) is set in a two-stage process. First, a provisional duty is calculated after the Commerce Department completes a preliminary investigation in which it considers, but does not verify, data submitted by the parties. For all subsequent imports from those countries or companies for which an affirmative preliminary determination is made, importers must post a

---

[26] See *Memorandum Politique Commerciale de la Communauté* (24 August 1993).

[27] Article 5.9 of Council Regulation (EC) 3283/94 (22 December 1994).

[28] *Id.* at Article 6.9.

[29] See 19 USC §§ 1673, 1677; Reorg. Plan No. 3 of 1979, § 5(a)(1)(C), 44 Fed. Reg. 1381 (Jan. 2, 1980).

[30] *Id.*

[31] See J. Bellis, "The EEC Antidumping System," in *Antidumping Law and Practice,* ed. J. Jackson and E. Vermulst (1989), 46.

bond with the U.S. Customs Service in an amount sufficient to cover the provisional duties.

After conducting a verification of some or all of the data submitted by foreign producers and importers, the Department then makes a final determination as to whether dumping has occurred. If that determination is affirmative, the Department reports the dumping margin and issues an antidumping order.[32] Thereafter, cash deposits must be made with the U.S. Customs Service in an amount sufficient to cover the potential duties.[33] However, these deposits are subject to refund in whole or in part.

Deposits of the estimated duties become final only after the Commerce Department so determines. The duties become payable at the previously established rate if no party challenges them.[34] However, an interested party (i.e., an importer or foreign producer, or a domestic producer) may request the Department to conduct an "administrative review" of the order annually.[35] If the foreign producer or importer (as the case may be) can satisfy the Department that it has not engaged in dumping during the period covered by the review (or that the magnitude of dumping was less than the dumping margin), it will obtain a full or partial refund of the cash deposit. If the actual margin of dumping is higher than the previously calculated margin, no additional duties are owed, but subsequent cash deposits must be made at the higher rate.[36]

In the EU, the antidumping system has operated differently until recently. It was often said that the EU imposes duties prospectively, while the United States imposes them retroactively. In the EU, provisional duties were established only after a complete investigation—including verification of the relevant data—was completed.[37] Those duties were, as a practical matter, final duties.[38] However, the new EC Antidumping Regulation may bring the EU system more closely in line with the U.S. system.

Now, in the EU, provisional duties may be imposed earlier, before the investigation is completed, and the duties may be kept in place for up to nine months thereafter.[39] Furthermore, the new antidumping regulation creates a procedure that enables importers to apply for a full or partial refund of the duties paid, and the refund application must be processed within 18 months.[40] Previously, refunds were theoretically possible, but the refund process took a long time and was otherwise cumbersome.[41] However, it remains to be seen whether the new process will represent a marked improvement over the old one.

---

[32] *Id.*

[33] 19 USC § 1673g.

[34] *See* 19 USC § 1675.

[35] 19 USC § 1673e(a).

[36] *See* 19 USC § 1675(a)(2)(C).

[37] *See* Bellis, 55.

[38] *Id.*

[39] Articles 7.1 and 7.7 of EC Antidumping Regulation.

[40] *Id.* at Article 11.8.

[41] *See,* for example, *Vinyl Acetate Monomer from the United States,* O.J.L. 80/53 (1991); *Hydraulic Excavators from Japan,* O.J.L. 108/17 (1989).

The revised EU Dumping Regulation also creates a new mechanism under which duties may be imposed retroactively, not only to the time when the provisional duties were established, but to a time well *before* any investigation was initiated. This mechanism, described as a registration process, involves a procedure whereby a domestic industry may petition the EC to monitor imports under certain circumstances.[42] Such monitoring may occur for a period as long as nine months. If an antidumping case is subsequently brought, and results in the imposition of duties, those duties may be applied retroactively to cover the "monitored" imports. Potentially, this is a very far-reaching change, which has no counterpart under U.S. law.

(f) Judicial Review

The right of judicial review of antidumping determinations available under the two systems also differs to some extent. In the United States, although reviewing courts give substantial deference to decisions of the administrative agencies,[43] an agency decision must be overturned if it is not based on "substantial evidence and otherwise in accordance with law."[44] Thus, reviewing courts scrutinize to some degree the agency's fact-finding and, to a greater degree (in theory at least), its interpretation and application of the law. In the EU, however, the role of the reviewing court, the European Court of Justice, is largely confined to correcting "manifest errors," usually of a procedural nature.[45]

Outside the context of judicial review, both systems offer a limited opportunity for the agencies to revisit earlier orders. Prior to the recent Uruguay Round Agreements, which produced a revised GATT Antidumping Code, reconsideration of prior orders occurred more often in the EU than in the United States. The EU has, for some time, provided for a "sunset review" of all outstanding orders, which occurs five years after an order was put in place. In such a review, the order must be revoked unless it is established that revocation would cause or threaten injury to a domestic industry. Until recently, U.S. law did not provide for such a review, instead providing for reconsideration of an order only if it could be demonstrated that "changed circumstances" warranted revocation of the order.[46] In any event, the revised GATT Antidumping Code requires all members of the WTO to conduct five-year "sunset reviews," as well as "changed circumstances" reviews when warranted.[47] Hence, in that sense as well, the U.S. and EU systems have converged.

---

[42] Article 14.5 of EC Antidumping Regulation.

[43] *See* 28 USC § 2639; *Calabrian Corp. v. United States,* 794 F. Supp. 374, 381–82 (Ct. Int'l Trade 1992).

[44] *See,* for example, *Atlantic Sugar, Ltd. v. United States,* 744 F.2d 15565, 1559 n.10 (Fed. Cir. 1984); *American Spring Wire Corp. v. United States,* 596 F. Supp. 1273, 1276 (Ct. Int'l Trade 1984).

[45] *See,* for example, *Ricoh Co. Ltd. v. Council,* Case 174/87 (Mar. 1992); *Fediol v. Commission,* Case 191/82 1983 ECR 2913.

[46] *See* former 19 USC § 1675(b), as added by Pub. L. 96-39, Title I, § 101, 93 Stat. 175 (1979).

[47] Articles 11.3–11.5 of GATT Antidumping Code.

(g)   Settlement

There remains, however, an implicit, albeit very important, "process" difference between the two systems relating to the potential settlement of cases. Historically, the EU has been much more inclined to settlement of cases, usually pursuant to "price undertakings," under which the foreign exporter or importer agrees to control import prices so as to reduce or eliminate damage to the domestic industry.[48]

In contrast, relative to the EU practice, settlement of cases in the United States has been a relatively rare phenomenon. U.S. law contains provisions allowing for the settlement of cases through what is known as a "suspension agreement."[49] However, such measures require a degree of acquiescence from the U.S. industry and the Commerce Department that is often not forthcoming.[50] As a practical matter, the U.S. industry can force the investigation to a conclusion unless it can be demonstrated that the suspension agreement completely eliminates the injurious effects of the dumped imports. Hence, few cases have ended in suspension agreements, although this does occasionally occur.[51]

However, in certain high-profile, politically charged cases involving large volumes of trade (such as those involving steel and semiconductors), exporters have bought legal peace by agreeing informally to quantitative or other import restrictions in the form of a voluntary restraint agreement (VRA). However, even taking the VRAs into account, antidumping cases tend to be settled far less frequently in the United States than in the EU.

(h)   Access to Information

Finally, it is worth noting that the United States and the EU provide significantly different levels of access to information in antidumping cases. In the United States, the Commerce Department and the ITC have given parties access to confidential business information provided by other parties in antidumping investigations pursuant to "administrative protective orders" (APOs).[52] Access to such information is generally limited to counsel for the parties, however, and disclosure of confidential information by counsel to unauthorized persons is subject to heavy sanctions. Although the parties are not in a position to analyze or respond directly to APO information (other than through counsel), the APO process fosters much more meaningful participation by the parties in antidumping cases. As of this writing, the EU has no comparable process.

---

[48] *See,* for example, De Clerca, "Fair Practice, No Protectionism," *Financial Times,* 21 November 1988.

[49] *See generally* 19 USC § 1673c.

[50] *See* 19 USC § 1673c(g)-(h).

[51] *See,* for example, ITC Investigation Nos. 731-TA-661 and 662.

[52] *See* 19 USC § 1677f(c).

(i)   Substantive Differences

The U.S. and EU systems diverge on a number of important points of substance. The methodologies used in the two systems to calculate dumping margins differ in a myriad of ways, most of which are hypertechnical and therefore not readily appropriate for discussion here. However, one major difference is that the EU applies what is known as the "lesser duty rule." The EC Commission attempts to set an "injury margin" that is less than the full amount of the dumping margin if a lower rate will remedy the injury to the domestic industry.[53] This injury margin is established pursuant to language in the GATT Antidumping Code that urges, but does not require, the parties to impose antidumping duties only in the amount to offset injury. In the United States, the full dumping margin is always applied.

On the other hand, in calculating dumping margins, in transactions involving importers who are affiliated with the exporter, the EU has long deducted from the export price any dumping duties absorbed by the exporter or its affiliate. This has often had the effect of substantially increasing dumping margins. The revised GATT Antidumping Code may restrict the EU's ability to continue to do so, however. Article 9.3.3 of the GATT Antidumping Code prohibits the deduction of duties if the exporter or its affiliate provide "conclusive evidence" that the duties have been passed on to unaffiliated purchasers. Article 11(10) of the EU Antidumping Regulation now conforms to this Code provision.

In the United States, the Commerce Department has historically deducted from the export price only those antidumping duties that are directly reimbursed to the importer by the exporter. However, it is likely that reviewing courts will soon be asked to resolve the question of whether a provision of U.S. law that has thus far largely been ignored requires the deduction of *all* antidumping duties absorbed by the exporter, either directly or through an affiliated importer.[54] Although the Commerce Department's refusal to deduct absorbed duties has been unsuccessfully challenged under other provisions of U.S. law, it is an open question whether 19 USC § 1677a(c)(2) requires such a deduction.

(j)   Constructed Value

The two systems also differ in their use of margins based on "constructed value" calculations. U.S. law has always reflected a bias against use of constructed value dumping margins, providing explicitly that these margins are to be used only when price-to-price comparisons are not possible in the home market *or* a third-country market.[55] In the EU, however, constructed value has been the preferred methodology when price-to-price comparisons are not possible in the home market.[56] Most observers believe that the EU's reliance on this methodology has produced inflated

---

[53] Article 7.2 of EC Antidumping Regulation; *see also* Article 9.1 of GATT Antidumping Code.

[54] *See* 19 USC § 1677a(c)(2).

[55] *See* 19 USC § 1677(a)(1)-(4).

[56] *See* Bellis, 72.

dumping margins.[57] However, the revised GATT Antidumping Code may limit the EU's ability to do so in the future.[58] Sales to third-country markets as a basis for normal value should not be rejected unless substantial quantities of such sales have been made below cost for an extended period of time.

(k)   Public Interest Factors

The U.S. system also differs from the EU system, in theory at least, in that U.S. law does not provide for any consideration of "public interest" factors. In other words, under U.S. law, the sole issue is whether dumped imports have caused or threatened injury to the domestic industry. The fact that such imports may benefit consumers is legally irrelevant under U.S. law.

EU law specifically contemplates the possibility that public interest factors may outweigh the domestic industry's interest in a case and allow the EU to refuse to issue an otherwise justified order.[59] However, in practice, this rarely, if ever, happens.[60] This is, no doubt, due in large part to the fact that the EU Council must be satisfied that it "clearly" is not in the Community's interest to apply such measures.[61] Hence, on this point, the difference between the two systems is more apparent than real.

Yet real and major differences between the two systems are evident in the manner in which questions of injury are analyzed under the U.S. and EU systems. In large part, this is simply because there are substantial differences within the United States itself as to the type of injury analysis that is appropriate.

(l)   Injury and Causation

As previously indicated, in the U.S. system the ITC carries out the injury analysis. To a surprising degree, the six individual members of the ITC have been left free to determine what kind of causation analysis is called for under the law. The result has been that widely disparate forms of injury analysis have been carried out by different ITC commissioners. For example, some members of the ITC believe that the statute requires them to determine whether the imports under investigation, as a group, have caused material injury.[62] In this view, the size of the dumping margin is not particularly important.[63] However, consistent with the requirements of

---

[57] Waer, "Constructed Normal Values in EC Dumping Margin Calculations: Fiction or a Realistic Approach," *Journal of World Trade* 27, no. 4 (August 1993): 48–49.

[58] *See* Article 2.2.1. of the GATT Antidumping Code.

[59] Article 21.1 of EU Antidumping Regulation.

[60] *See,* for example *Urea* OJ (1987) L121/11; *Sensitized Paper* OJ (1984) L124/45.

[61] *Id.*

[62] *See,* for example, *Certain Telephone Systems and Subassemblies Thereof from Japan and Taiwan,* Inv. Nos. 731-TA-426 and 428 (Final), USITC Pub. 2237 at 80–84 (Nov. 1989) (Additional Views of Commissioner Eckes).

[63] *Id.* Indeed, until recently, it was considered essentially irrelevant. *See* 19 U.S.C. § 1677(7)(c)(iii)(V).

the revised GATT Antidumping Code, dumping margins are listed among the factors that must now be considered by the ITC under U.S. law. Other members of the ITC believe that their task is to determine whether the effects of dumping have caused material injury to the domestic industry.[64] In this view, the magnitude of the dumping margin is a critically important factor.

There has also been heated debate among the members of the ITC as to what the entire concept of causation means. One group of ITC commissioners has long argued that the proper standard is whether dumped imports have contributed to overall injury to an industry.[65] Another group has taken the view that the law permits an affirmative injury determination only if it is established that the effects of dumping, by themselves, amount to material injury.[66] As of this writing, the debate has reached the level of the U.S. Court of Appeals for the Federal Circuit, and it is not clear which view will prevail or, indeed, whether both views (or neither view) will be upheld.

The EU approach to injury analysis is, in some respects, much clearer than the U.S. system and, in other respects, not clear at all. The EC Commission has traditionally attempted to determine whether the effects of dumping amount to material injury[67] and has considered the dumping margin as a key consideration in that context. However, published EU decisions in antidumping cases generally offer only a very sketchy indication of the exact type of analysis undertaken. In general, they reveal only that injury is likely to be found if imports and import penetration in the EU market are sizable and/or are correlated with poor financial performance and depressed levels of employment within the industry.

(m)   Small Import Shares

Finally, it should be noted that there are technical, but potentially very important, differences between the two systems relating to the circumstances under which countries with small import shares will be excluded. Under U.S. law, such countries will be excluded only if they do not individually account for 3 percent of all imports under investigation, or 7 percent of all such imports when grouped with similarly small countries.[68] This is consistent with Article 5.8 of the revised GATT Antidumping Code and is likely in practice to make it difficult for small players in the U.S. market to escape an order.

In the EU, in contrast, more small players are likely to be treated as negligible, and thereby escape an order. The new EU Antidumping Regulation provides for the exclusion of countries with less than a 1 percent share of the EU market (unless such countries collectively account for 3 percent of the EU market).[69] Under this

---

[64] *Telephone Systems, supra* (Dissenting Views of Vice Chairman Cass) at 150–171.

[65] *See,* for example, *id.* (Additional Views of Commissioner Eckes) at 85–99.

[66] *See,* for example, *Telephone Systems, supra* (Dissenting Views of Vice Chairman Cass) at 171–241.

[67] *See* Article 3.6 of EU Dumping Regulation.

[68] *See* 19 USC § 1677(24).

[69] *See* Article 5.7 of the EU Antidumping Regulation.

standard, it is quite likely that many small exporters will not be subject to an order or, indeed, even to the investigative process itself.

14.5 Antidumping Regimes of Other Developed Countries

Canada and Australia have relied heavily on antidumping laws to resolve trade disputes, although less so in recent years. During the 1980s, Australia actually led the world in the number of antidumping cases filed, while Canada ranked third behind only the United States in the number of cases it filed during that period.[70]

For reasons previously suggested, the framework of the antidumping laws of both countries is, in broad terms, similar to that of the United States and EU; that is, both countries are signatories to the GATT Antidumping Code, and their laws must therefore meet certain basic Code requirements. However, within the confines of the Code guidelines, there are aspects of the respective laws that are unique to Canada and to Australia.

(a) Canada: Process Differences

Like United States and EU law, Canadian law requires completion of an antidumping case within a strict time frame at the administrative level. A decision on whether to initiate an investigation takes place in two phases.

First, a petitioner is required to file a "properly documented complaint."[71] Upon receipt of a complaint, the responsible government authority has 21 days in which to inform the complainant whether or not it has met the criteria by which the adequacy of a complaint is to be judged.[72] If those criteria have not been met, the complainant is informed of the additional information required to remedy the defect(s). Once the additional information is submitted, the authority considers it, along with the material originally submitted, as essentially a "new" complaint, and again has 21 days to determine whether it is adequate. If it is, within 30 days after petitioner has been so notified, the government must decide whether to initiate an investigation formally.[73] Once an investigation has been initiated, a preliminary determination of whether dumping has occurred must be made within 90 days (135 days if an extension is granted).[74] The injury analysis must then be completed within 120 days of that determination. In the interim, Revenue Canada makes its final dumping determination.[75]

---

[70] U.S. General Accounting Office: *International Trade: Use of the GATT Antidumping Code* (Washington, D.C.: U.S. Government Printing Office, 1990), 16.

[71] Special Import Measures Act (SIMA), Subsection 31(1).

[72] *Id.* at Subsection 32(1).

[73] *Id.* at Subsections 34 and 35.

[74] *Id.* at Subsections 38(1) and 39.

[75] *Id.* at Subsection 43(1).

As in the United States, the dumping and injury inquiries in Canada are under-taken by separate administrative authorities. Under the Special Import Measures Act (SIMA), the dumping investigation is conducted by the Department of National Revenue, Customs and Excise, commonly known as "Revenue Canada."[76] The question of material injury (and threat of injury) is investigated by the independent Canadian International Trade Tribunal, commonly known as the CITT or simply as "the Tribunal."[77] The CITT has nine decision-making members and a professional staff.

In Canada, provisional duties are assessed on those imports for which an affirmative preliminary dumping determination has been made. This duty is ordinarily paid in the form of a bond payable to Customs until such time as the CITT has made its injury determination.[78] If a final determination of dumping has been issued by Revenue Canada and the CITT has found evidence of injury, dumping duties are levied on all goods imported from the date of the preliminary dumping determination.[79] All provisional duties collected from the importer may be refunded and/or bonds canceled if either the CITT finds no injury (or threat of injury) or Revenue Canada makes a negative final dumping determination.[80] As in the United States, interested parties may annually request a review of the question as to whether, and to what extent, dumping has continued.

Importers may appeal to Revenue Canada the decision to impose duties.[81] The CITT's decision may also be appealed to the Federal Court and, ultimately, to the Supreme Court of Canada.[82] In addition, the CITT may review, continue, amend, or rescind its own determinations at any time.[83] As is now the case universally under the revised GATT Antidumping Code, antidumping orders are automatically rescinded unless they are reviewed by the CITT within five years of the original determination or latest review.

The Canadian system also has a mechanism that allows for a window of opportunity for the settlement of cases. Foreign exporters may submit written commitments to maintain certain price levels to Revenue Canada prior to its preliminary determination, which are expected to be binding if accepted.[84] Such "undertakings" are acceptable to Revenue Canada only if they eliminate the dumping or injury entirely.[85] Once accepted, the investigation is suspended and collection of duties ends. Undertakings are renewable after their usual duration, i.e., three years.[86]

---

[76] *Id.* at Subsection 78 *et seq.*

[77] *Id.* at Subsections 42 *et seq.*

[78] *See id.* at Subsection 8(1)(d).

[79] *See id.* at Subsection 8.

[80] *See id.* Subsection 8(2).

[81] *Id.* at Subsections 59–61.

[82] *Id.* at Subsection 62.

[83] *Id.* at Subsection 76(2).

[84] *See id.* at Subsections 49–54.

[85] *Id.* at Subsection 49(1)(b).

[86] *Id.* at Subsection 53.

Finally, Canada, like the United States, has a procedure for the disclosure of confidential information under administrative protective order. However, unlike the practice followed in the United States, such access is effectively restricted to Canadian nationals.

(b) Canada: Substantive Differences

Normal value is based on the exporter's home market price, or on the basis of third-country sales or constructed value, if the export home market is not viable or the home market price is otherwise deemed not suitable.[87] Profits have generally been attributed even to those sales made at a loss; Revenue Canada has used a profit margin of 8 percent if actual profit cannot be derived from the information supplied by (or for) the exporter, although by law the applicable measure is "reasonable profit."

The export price is deemed to be the lower of the exporter's sales price or the importer's purchase price.[88] In the case of a related exporter and importer, "the first arm's length sale in Canada is taken as a reference basis."[89] However, Revenue Canada has broad authority to calculate a margin that it deems appropriate if all of the traditional methods are deemed to be inadequate for one reason or another.

In calculating dumping margins, "negative margins" (i.e., sales for which the normal value is lower than the export price) are not included, as they are in the United States and the EU, where they are counted as "zero margins." This invariably tends to produce higher margins.

Canadian law explicitly provides for the consideration of public interest factors in antidumping proceedings. Under SIMA, the Ministry of Finance may decide to reduce or eliminate an antidumping duty upon the recommendation of the CITT, once the CITT has made its injury determination (and has heard public interest arguments against the imposition of duties).[90] In Canada (unlike in the EU) it is generally believed that public interest considerations are taken quite seriously.

(c) Australia: Process Differences

Under the Canadian system, the government authority and industry work together to develop an acceptable complaint; in contrast, within the Australian regime, it is the responsibility of industry alone to compile the necessary information and present an acceptable petition. Nevertheless, experts contend that filing is relatively cheap in Australia as compared to the rest of the world, with the average cost of preparing a petition estimated to be only A\$20,000.[91] Once under way, the

---

[87] *Id.* at Subsection 19.

[88] *Id.* at Subsection 24.

[89] General Agreement on Tariffs and Trade, *Trade Policy Review—Canada* (1992) at 61.

[90] SIMA at Subsection 45.

[91] Senate Standing Committee on Industry, Science and Technology, *Inquiry into Australia Antidumping and Countervailing Legislation* (1991) at 65.

process formally consists of "fact-finding," rather than a judicial or quasi-judicial proceeding.[92] Therefore, parties may not necessarily require—and often do not have—expert assistance in representing their interests before the government.

Within the Australian framework, the investigative responsibilities are split between two agencies, the Australian Customs Service (ACS) and the Antidumping Authority (ADA), but they are not divided in the same way as they are in the U.S. and Canadian systems. In Australia, the decision-making authority is not split between agencies based on the type of issue involved (i.e., dumping vs. injury) but is instead allocated to different agencies at different stages of the investigation.

Within the office of the Minister for Industry, Technology and Regional Development (the Minister), the ACS is responsible for receiving and evaluating the adequacy of complaints, carrying out preliminary investigations, preliminary determining the existence of dumping material injury, and the causal link between the two.[93] As a threshold matter, the ACS may terminate any case by making a prima facie decision that there are no "reasonable grounds" to believe that the imports in question are being dumped and causing (or threatening) injury to an Australian industry.[94] The ACS is allowed 25 days in which to make such a decision; otherwise, the petition is automatically accepted for investigation.

Once a petition has been accepted, the ACS has 100 more days (120 in a very complex case) in which to reach a preliminary determination. If that determination is affirmative, the ACS imposes provisional duties upon the completion of its preliminary investigation.

The Antidumping Authority (ADA), which also reports to the Minister, is responsible for all aspects of the final investigation.[95] Furthermore, even though the ACS investigation is complete in its own right, the ADA carries out a completely de novo inquiry.[96] Following an affirmative preliminary determination by the ACS, the ADA has 120 days in which to conduct the final investigation and present its findings to the Minister. The ADA is allowed 60 days in which to review a negative preliminary ACS determination if it is requested to do so. Upon the recommendation of the ADA, the Minister determines whether to impose an antidumping duty.

The ADA has the authority to review any and all aspects of a case (including a negative ACS prima facie decision) at any stage of a case. The Minister ultimately has the responsibility of setting the final dumping margin and the discretion to impose a lesser duty than the full dumping margin, where appropriate.[97] Once duties

---

[92] D. Feaver and K. Wilson, "An Evaluation of Australia's Antidumping and Countervailing Law and Policy," *Journal of World Trade* (October 1995), at 218–219.

[93] *See* Customs Act 1901, Subsections 269TB and 269TC(4).

[94] Antidumping Authority Act (1988) Subsection 7(1).

[95] *Id.*

[96] Feaver and Wilson, 215.

[97] Customs Act 1901, Subsection 269 TACA; Customs Tariff (Antidumping) Act 1975, Subsections 8(5A) and 10(5A).

are imposed, they are in force for five years, but exporters or importers may ask at any time that the duties be rescinded.

Finally, it should be noted that the Customs Legislation (Tariff Concessions and Antidumping Amendment) Act 1992 (1992 Amendment) contained certain "transparency requirements," which entail the publication of the various normal and export values calculated during the case. Interested parties also have access to certain information contained in the "public file system," which is maintained by the ACS and the ADA. Confidential information is not available, however.

Submissions to the agencies on relevant issues may be made by any interested party to an investigation. The ADA conducts a public discussion of the major issues raised in a case during a "meeting of parties," which interested parties are encouraged to attend.

(d)   Australia: Substantive Differences

In investigating dumping issues, the ACS and ADA first verify the export price by ensuring that the importer and exporter are unrelated, and that the importer has received no compensation designed to inflate the invoice price (which would minimize the magnitude of the dumping margin). If these conditions are satisfied, the export price is deemed to be the invoiced price as provided by the Australian Bureau of Statistics (ABS) (or as seen in the books of the importers and exporters), less transportation and post-export expenses.[98] If the transaction is not at arm's length or it appears that the invoice price was manipulated, a constructed export price will be calculated, if possible, based on the price paid by an independent third-party buyer to the importer.[99] However, if there is no such sale, the ACS and ADA may determine the export price "having regard to all the circumstances of the importation," or by making their "best approximation" of the price an importer would have paid in an arm's-length transaction[100]—formulations that plainly allow ample room for discretion.

In establishing normal value, the preferred measure is to base value on prices in actual arm's-length transactions.[101] Absent arm's-length transactions or third-party purchases, a constructed value methodology is employed to establish normal value if the exporter's costs are verifiable.[102] If they are not, normal value may be based on prices charged by the exporter in a third-country market.[103] Theoretically, best available information is used only as a last resort in determining normal value, but in practice this happens frequently.

It should also be noted that the rules governing the calculation of constructed value as the basis for normal value differ from those of the U.S. regime, in which

---

[98] Customs Act 1901, Subsection 269 TAB(1)(a).

[99] *Id.* at Subsection 269TAB(1)(b).

[100] *Id.* at Subsections 269TAB(1)(c) and 269TAB(3).

[101] *Id.* at Subsections 269TAC(1).

[102] *Id.* at Subsection 269TAC(2)(c).

[103] *Id.* at Subsection 269TAC(2)(d).

foreign exporters who refuse to supply verifiable data are assessed either the normal value alleged in the petition or (if applicable) the highest rate given other respondents in the investigation. Under Australian law, data provided by foreign producers is sometimes used to calculate a constructed normal value even if it cannot be verified.[104]

In analyzing injury, the ACS and ADA essentially use a "trends" approach—that is, injury is more likely to be found if increasing imports are associated with indicators of declining industry performance. The ACS and ADA appear to assign different weights to various factors that contribute to injury, but do not use any definitive quantitative assessment to determine whether the effects of dumping constitute material injury. Pursuant to the 1992 Amendment, an affirmative determination of injury may be deemed warranted if dumping was one of several causes of overall injury to an industry. Prior to the Amendment, the ADA was required to determine whether the effects of dumped imports, by themselves, amounted to material injury.

14.6   Antidumping Regimes of Newly Industrialized Countries

Over the past five years, so many developing countries have instituted antidumping laws that it would be impossible to provide in the limited space available here even a cursory description of those systems. A variety of factors have led to more widespread use of such laws—factors affecting both developed countries that have long had such laws on the books and developing countries that are latecomers to the process. As previously suggested, developments relating to GATT have provided a very strong impetus toward more frequent use of such laws as new countries have joined GATT. Long-standing GATT members have been forced to provide more open access to their markets as a result of successive rounds of GATT negotiations. In addition, to state the obvious, there simply are more countries than there used to be, as a result of the implosion of the former Soviet Union, the breakup of Yugoslavia, and other such occurrences around the world.

It is difficult to offer general observations about the new regimes in all their various permutations. However, an element common to all of them that is potentially most relevant to exporters is that most of the regimes have experienced growing pains, which have been severe at times. This is hardly surprising, given that the laws are new, the government authorities that administer them are inexperienced, and the experts upon whom outsiders might ordinarily rely for guidance (i.e., lawyers, economists, and the like) are by and large themselves not particularly expert.

Consequently, the problems exporters are likely to face in dealing with antidumping laws of developing nations may prove more complex and frustrating than the typical case, and, as the foregoing discussion may suggest, the typical case

---

[104] *See,* for example, ADA Report No. 102: *Canned Tuna from Indonesia and Thailand* (June 1993).

is none-too-pleasant to begin with, from the exporter's perspective. The experience of Mexico and Korea provide two good cases in point.

(a)   Mexico

In Mexico, the laws are administered by a single agency, the Secretaría de Comercio y Fomento Industrial, usually referred to by its acronym, SECOFI. SECOFI has had this responsibility since 1986. Yet, as of this writing, it would be fair to say that the system in Mexico is in chaos.

As a result of a recent decision by a binational panel convened pursuant to the dispute settlement provisions of the North American Free Trade Agreement (NAFTA),[105] virtually every single antidumping order entered by SECOFI through 1994 (and perhaps beyond) is subject to potential legal challenge. The only clear exceptions, relating to standing principles, involve cases where an exporter has participated in annual reviews or other proceedings before SECOFI subsequent to the entry of the antidumping order. That case involved an appeal by certain U.S. steel producers of SECOFI's affirmative determination against imports of certain carbon steel plate products from the United States. In that case, the binational panel held, by a 3 to 2 vote, that the underlying investigation by SECOFI was carried out in violation of the Mexican principle of legality. Among other things, the panel held, in essence, that SECOFI had not been lawfully constituted. Hence, the decision clearly could have implications going far beyond that particular case. Although the final chapter of this story has not yet been written, suffice it to say that this development has created a measure of uncertainty for exporters and a massive uproar within the trade law community in Mexico.

The status of new investigations carried out in Mexico is equally uncertain. For one thing, SECOFI has not yet taken steps that would entirely cure the procedural defects that led the binational panel to rule against SECOFI in the first place. Second, in the wake of the 1994–1995 devaluation of the peso, SECOFI has been processing cases as usual but has refused to impose duties in many cases where this was otherwise deemed warranted, on the grounds that this would unduly harm Mexican consumers in the midst of an economic emergency. It remains to be seen whether, and to what degree, SECOFI will reverse this position when the perceived emergency is over.

Mexico also provides an illustration of a more general problem evident in many developing countries, that is, the relative lack of transparency in the administrative process. Although SECOFI has attempted to provide some semblance of due process to exporters, in several aspects it falls far short of American and Canadian standards. For example, in some cases SECOFI has essentially subcontracted some of its fact-finding and analytical work to outside consultants. SECOFI's policy in such cases has been that it will not disclose the contents of the consultant's report

---

[105] Memorandum Order and Opinion, *Cut-to-Length Plate Imports from the United States* (Mex-94-1904-02, Aug. 30, 1995).

(or, for that matter, even the identity of the consultant itself)—a policy that even the minority in the NAFTA binational panel case, discussed earlier, found to be a violation of due process.[106] Another example can be found in SECOFI's policy as to the disclosure of confidential business information under administrative protective order. SECOFI allows for such access, but only to parties who post a bond in an amount determined by SECOFI.[107] In practice, the amounts demanded have been prohibitively high. And few, if any, exporters with even a minimal amount of common sense would allow themselves to be put in a position where SECOFI could call for payment against the bond if it determines, in its discretion, that there has been a violation of the protective order, however inadvertent or minor.

(b) South Korea

Korea is another country that has faced some difficulties in implementing its antidumping code, but it has made significant progress in recent years. In 1988, Korea revised its antidumping laws to comply with GATT. These changes took effect on January 1, 1989. Its first application of these new regulations came in the 1990 case that Korea filed against the United States and Japan concerning imports of polyacetal resin (PAR). The affirmative Korean determination was appealed to GATT and was eventually overturned. Since the PAR case (1991–1994:II), Korea has initiated eight antidumping investigations involving imports of sodium hydroxide, e-glass fiber, and disintegrated calcium phosphates.[108]

Recently, Korea has amended its antidumping provisions to more closely reflect those in the United States. The continued development of the Korean system, somewhat along American lines, strongly suggests that the early problems with methodology and implementation are being overcome.

14.7 Conclusion

Antidumping regimes have proliferated as new countries have joined GATT and lowered their tariff barriers. The antidumping code allows countries to place duties on imports if they are sold below fair value and cause material injury to a domestic industry. Exporters would be well advised to consider their pricing practices in foreign markets in the context of antidumping laws, especially if they represent a significant and increasing share of the market. A U.S. exporter can retain some control of the process either by "dump-proofing" its export sales through careful self-monitoring of export pricing or by vigorously defending against allegations of unfair trading practices.[109]

---

[106] *See id.*

[107] *See* Articles 159 and 160 of Mexico's Foreign Trade Regulation.

[108] *The Year in Trade, Operations of the Trade Agreements Program, 1994.* USITC Publication 2894, July 1995.

[109] "The Foundations of the World Trading System" are contained in the web site for the World Trading Organization. The final act of the Uruguay Round notification of Acceptances was dated May 3, 1994. Exhibit 14.2 was obtained from "International Trade: Use of the GATT Antidumping Code," p. 16. United States General Accounting Office, July 1990 (GAO/NSIAD-90-238FS). Data has been extended through 1994 by the authors. Exhibit 14.4 has been obtained from Patrick A. Messerlin and Geoffrey Reed, "Antidumping Policies in the United States and the Economic Community, *Economic Journal* (November 1995):1567.

Tables

Table of Cases

Table of Internal Revenue Codes

Table of Treasury Regulations

Table of Temporary Regulations

Table of Revenue Rulings

Table of Revenue Procedures

Table of Technical Advice Memorandums

Table of Private Letter Rulings

7805004	4.3(a)(i)
7815004	3.3(a)(v) n.73, 4.2(f), 4.4(e) n.113
7829038	4.3(a)(i)
7947021	4.2(h)
8112001	4.6(a)
8123112	3.4(b) n.138, 4.5(b) n.133
8126049	2.4(f) n.32
8141016	4.4(a)
8142117	4.2(e) n.27
8147067	2.4(f) n.32
8212043	3.3(b)(i) n.86, 4.3
8251103	2.4(f) n.30
8302070	2.4(f) n.32
8325020	3.2(a)(iii) n.13, 4.6(a)
8436028	3.3(B)(iii) n.98, 4.3(a)(ii)
8530003	4.3(e)
8549003	4.5(b)
8623024	3.3(a)(ii) n.60
8649024	3.3(b)(ii) n.93, 4.3(b)
8649025	4.3(b)
8652001	4.5(b)
8707002	4.5(c)
8729026	2.4(f) n.32, 4.3(b)
8803052	3.2(a)(ii) n.14
8911022	10.3(d) n.30
9029068	2.7 n.50
9051040	2.4(f) n.29, 2.4(f) n.32, 2.7 n.50
9103029	2.4(f) n.31
9210015	3.4(b)(i) n.139, 3.4(b)(i) n.140, 4.5(b)
9325020	2.4(e) n.28
9423011	2.4(e) n.28
9443037	2.4(e) n.27
9450011	2.4(e) n.28
9506026	2.4(e) n.28
9506041	2.4(e) n.28
9506042	2.4(e) n.26
9506043	2.4(e) n.28
9506045	2.4(e) n.28
9537021	2.4(e) n.28
9537022	2.4(e) n.25
9537023	2.4(e) n.24

Index